T0315156

Praise for the Author's Previous Works

The Other Half of Macroeconomics and the Fate of Globalization (2018)

"Richard Koo has had some of the most important economic ideas of the last two decades. This book extends his important perspective to a wider range of long-run issues. Koo's arguments deserve the attention of everyone who cares about achieving strong, sustained economic growth in the industrial world."

—Lawrence H. Summers, Charles W. Eliot
University Professor, Harvard University

"Richard Koo is the most important economist of our time because he alone has devised a revolutionary framework that accurately explains the global economic crisis. His work is revolutionary not because it overthrows all the economic theory that preceded it, but rather because it completes it. Koo's policy prescriptions offer the world the best chance of restoring prosperity before this economic crisis becomes a political crisis and then a geopolitical crisis. The sooner our policymakers understand the implications of this extraordinary book—and act upon them—the safer we all will be."

—Richard Duncan, Author,
The Dollar Crisis; Publisher, Macro Watch

"Richard Koo is one of the most astute analysts of macroeconomic policies, showing that only fiscal policy is effective in balance sheet recessions. He now expands his view to the world economy and the history of advanced countries' economic development, arguing that fiscal expansion is the only effective macroeconomic policy for the foreseeable future. But instead of John Maynard Keynes' suggestion that burying money and digging it up helps, he argues forcibly that socially productive investments are needed for advanced economies to keep up with emerging ones."

—Peter Temin, M.I.T.; Author, *The Vanishing Middle Class:*
Prejudice and Power in a Dual Economy (2017)

"In the wake of the Great Recession, Richard Koo challenges us in his latest book to look at 'the other half of macroeconomics,' one in which the primary concern of the private sector is to 'minimize debt' rather than 'maximize profit.' Koo brings a wealth of knowledge and real-world experience working in both the U.S. and East Asia to his discussion of the stages of economic development. I find his examples from Japan and China especially compelling. I warmly recommend this book."

—**Axel Leijonhufvud**, Professor Emeritus,
UCLA and University of Trento, Italy

"Richard Koo's *The Other Half of Macroeconomics and The Fate of Globalization* will soon rival Piketty's *Capital* as the economics book to-date of our century. Koo's book, as its title suggests, divides in half. The first, like John Maynard Keynes' *The General Theory*, deeply subverts traditional economic theory. The second, like Karl Polanyi's *The Great Transformation*, sets out a new analysis of recent economic history and maps a new fork in the road to humankind's future. Except for dogmatists and anti-humanitarians, it is required reading."

—**Edward Fullbrook**, Founder, World Economics Association;
Editor, *Real-World Economics Review*

"Anyone who has a deep interest in globalization should read this book. It is at one time thoughtful, analytical, original, policy-relevant and highly engaging."

—**Jeffrey E. Garten**, Dean and Professor Emeritus,
Yale University School of Management

"The Great Depression produced Keynes, and the Great Recession produced Koo. With this book, he not only ushers economic analysis into the 21st century but also goes back centuries to show what has been missing in economics all along. This highly accessible book contains new insights worthy of a Nobel Prize."

—**Shousaku Murayama**, CEO, iPS Academia Japan,
Kyoto University; former Research Director, Bank of Japan

The Escape from Balance Sheet Recession and the QE Trap: A Hazardous Road for the World Economy (2014)

"Richard Koo has been a pioneer in recasting macroeconomics for the current era of financial crisis and potential deflation. This book presents his latest thinking in a clear and powerful way. Agree or disagree his work deserves close study if the next decade in the industrial world is going to be better than the last."

—**Lawrence Summers**, President Emeritus and Charles W. Eliot University Professor, Harvard University; former U.S. Secretary of the Treasury

"This is an important, stimulating, exciting and timely book. Guided by the ideas in this book, growing numbers of experts are appreciating the parallels between the current world-wide crisis and the crisis Japan experienced 15 years ago. The basic insight—that in the presence of persistent liabilities, the private sector minimizes debt—is one that needs to be fully appreciated in order for appropriate policies to be devised. This is a must-read for all those seeking to respond to the current economic malaise."

—**Dennis J. Snower**, President, Kiel Institute for the World Economy; Professor of Economics, Christian-Albrechts University, Kiel

"Koo's *The Escape from Balance Sheet Recession and the QE Trap* provides the most insightful guide to current macroeconomic policy available today. Koo's concept of 'balance sheet recessions' adds depth and detail to observations of the 'liquidity trap' and 'zero lower bound' of interest rates. He explains what needs to be done and how long it could take. Everyone concerned with macroeconomic policy needs to read this analysis to learn how the world economy can be revived."

—**Peter Temin**, Elisha Gray II Professor Emeritus of Economics, Massachusetts Institute of Technology

"I have always liked the Richard Koo style – succinct theories, razor-sharp points, self-sustaining logic, and, more importantly, a set of workable solutions. It's definitely a worthy read."

—**Gao Xiqing**, Professor, School of Law, Tsinghua University; former Vice Chairman and President, China Investment Corporation

"In the wake of the financial crisis of 2008, governments and financial institutions have instituted a wide range of changes in such areas as risk management, regulation, market organization, and fiscal and monetary policy. Unfortunately, however, these measures have suffered from lack of a unified recognition of the fundamental problem. In a clear, engaging and penetrating way, Richard Koo has diagnosed the core nature of the challenge and the appropriate response. *The Escape from Balance Sheet Recession* is an essential guide for anyone interested in the future of the global economy."

—**Jeffrey E. Garten**, Juan Trippe Professor of International Trade and Finance and former Dean, Yale School of Management; former Undersecretary of Commerce

"When the history of this depression is written, policymakers who ignore Koo's findings will be judged harshly for imposing unnecessary suffering on their societies."

—**Richard Duncan**, Author, *The Dollar Crisis*; Publisher, Macro Watch

The Holy Grail of Macroeconomics: Lessons from Japan's Great Recession (2008, revised 2009)

". . . the Japanese policymakers who (said) the U.S. was in danger of falling into a prolonged period of economic weakness were right. To understand why . . . you need to read a brilliant book by Richard Koo. . ."

—**Martin Wolf,** Financial Times

"There will probably never be a last word on the Japanese financial catastrophe of the 1990s but Richard Koo's book may be the most significant analysis ever published. Agree or disagree, any analyst of the current United States situation must consider Koo's arguments."

—**Lawrence H. Summers,** Director, National Economic Council; former President, Harvard University and U.S. Secretary of the Treasury

"Richard Koo does it again. By presenting a unique theory regarding the Great Depression and Japan's recession of the last 15 years,

Koo offers a new understanding of current problems in the U.S. and other economies. With many pearls of analytical wisdom, *The Holy Grail of Macroeconomics: Lessons from Japan's Great Recession* is a must-read for economists, policymakers and individual investors alike."

—Nobuyuki Idei, Founder & CEO,
Quantum Leaps Corporation;
former Chairman & CEO, Sony Corporation

"Richard Koo's pioneering work on balance-sheet recession has been invaluable in understanding the difficulty faced by Japan's economy and monetary authorities during the past 15 years. In this book, he has shown that the U.S. Great Depression was also driven by the same balance sheet concerns of the private sector, indicating that this kind of recession can happen to any post-bubble economy. I sincerely hope that the lessons contained in this book are put to good use in fighting similar recessions elsewhere, including the U.S. subprime crisis."

—Yasushi Mieno, former Governor, Bank of Japan

"*The Holy Grail of Macroeconomics* presents a brilliant and original framework for understanding—and overcoming—a post-bubble economic crisis such as the one the world faces today. By discrediting the conventional view that monetary policy is effective in combating a post-bubble recession, Richard Koo has made an invaluable contribution to economic theory and at just the right time."

—Richard Duncan, Author, *The Dollar Crisis: Causes, Consequences, Cures*; Partner, Blackhorse Asset Management

Balance Sheet Recession: Japan's Struggle with Uncharted Economics and its Global Implications (2003)

"*Balance Sheet Recession* offers a breakthrough in understanding recessions, especially the serious and prolonged one that has plagued Japan for so long. Richard Koo presents a unique angle to look at the Japanese economy and many other economies in the world that are in a similar predicament."

—Nobuyuki Idei, Chairman and CEO, Sony Corporation

Pursued Economy

Understanding and Overcoming the Challenging New Realities for Advanced Economies

RICHARD C. KOO

WILEY

To my dearest wife, Chyen-Mei

Contents

Preface

The last few years have been difficult ones for many people, including economists, as the COVID-19 pandemic and the war in Ukraine have ravaged economies around the world. But economists' problems started earlier. The failure of the vast majority of economists in government, academia, and the private sector to predict either the post-2008 Great Recession or the degree and length of its severity has raised serious credibility issues for both the political establishment and the economics profession. After all, the Great Recession started from within—it was not caused by exogenous factors such as a new virus strain or military adventurism by an autocrat.

The widely varying opinions of these "experts" on how this recession should be addressed, together with the repeated failures of central banks and other policy makers to meet inflation or growth targets in spite of astronomical levels of monetary accommodation, have left the public rightfully suspicious of the establishment and its economists.

The concept of the pursued economy, together with the author's earlier concept of balance sheet recessions, is an attempt to explain why an economy that was strong and vibrant loses momentum and stagnates for an extended period of time. While the war in Ukraine and post-pandemic supply constraints have recently pushed inflation rates higher, many people have experienced stagnant real incomes for years, if not for decades, prompting a large part of the population to feel left behind and angry.

The author is old enough to remember how vibrant and hopeful people were in the United States in the 1960s, in Japan in the 1980s, and in Taiwan in the 1990s. In those eras, almost everyone was benefiting from economic growth. The air might not have been as clean as it is today, but everything else was moving forward, and people were confident about the future. That is no longer the case in many advanced countries today.

Being personally familiar with these three economies, the author found it remarkable that all of them went through very similar processes of economic development despite having vastly different cultural backgrounds. The cultural or historical differences among these countries may have added or subtracted a few percentage points of GDP growth here and there, but all of them experienced similar stages of economic development and were facing—at least until the onslaught of the COVID-19 pandemic—extended periods of low interest rates and low inflation rates.

Moreover, this low inflation came in spite of vast amounts of monetary easing by most major central banks starting in 2008. And the low interest rates appeared despite massive increases in budget deficits and public debt, first in Japan after 1990, and then in the West after 2008. Bond yields actually turned negative in Japan and in many parts of the Eurozone.

These phenomena are totally inconsistent with the economics still taught in universities, which holds that massive "money printing" will result in pernicious inflation and that large budget deficits will lead to higher interest rates, if not to higher inflation rates. Simply trying to understand what zero or negative interest rates *mean* in a capitalist system sets the head spinning. One wonders how Karl Marx or Thomas Piketty would explain sub-zero interest rates.

It was twenty-five years ago that the author came up with the concept of balance sheet recessions in Japan to explain why post-bubble economies suffer years of stagnation and why conventional monetary remedies are largely ineffective during such recessions. The key point of departure for this insight was the realization that the private sector is not always maximizing profits, as assumed in textbook economics, but will actually choose to minimize debt when faced with daunting balance sheet challenges, that is, debt overhang.

Once this fundamental assumption of traditional macroeconomics is overturned and the possibility of debt minimization is acknowledged, everything that was built on the original assumption—including many standard policy recommendations—must also be reconsidered. This is because if someone is saving or paying down debt, someone else must borrow and spend those funds to keep the national economy running. If the private sector as a whole is paying down debt even with zero interest rates, the public sector must borrow and spend those funds to keep the economy going.

While the concept of balance sheet recessions was able to explain many of the phenomena observed since 2008 in the West and since 1990 in Japan, it could not explain all of them. This is because some of the changes in these countries predate 2008 or postdate their balance sheet recessions. For example, the slowdown in income growth in the West started long before the balance sheet recession struck in 2008, and sluggish economic growth in Japan continued long after the private sector finished repairing its balance sheet around 2006.

It then occurred to the author that there is another reason for the private sector to be minimizing debt—or simply refraining from borrowing—at a time of very low interest rates. The reason is that businesses cannot find investment opportunities attractive enough to justify borrowing and investing. After all, there is nothing in business or economics that guarantees such opportunities will always be plentiful.

When businesses cannot find investments, they tend to minimize debt—except when tax and return-on-equity considerations argue against it—because the firm's probability of long-term survival increases significantly in the absence of debt. Shortages of investment opportunities, in turn, have two possible causes.

The first is a lack of technological innovation or scientific breakthroughs, which makes it difficult to find viable investment projects. This probably explains the economic stagnation observed for centuries prior to the Industrial Revolution in the 1760s.

The second cause is higher overseas returns on capital, which forces businesses to invest abroad instead of at home. For companies in the advanced countries today, this factor probably plays as big a role as technological breakthroughs in investment decisions. And the rise of Japan in the 1970s and of the emerging economies in the 1990s has changed where Western companies invest. Businesses continue to maximize profits to satisfy shareholder expectations for ever-higher returns on capital, but the bulk of their investment no longer takes place in the home market. This realization that corporate investments are no longer limited to domestic locations led to the concept of pursued economy presented in this book.

The economics profession, however, failed to consider the macroeconomic implications of private-sector balance sheet problems or inferior returns on capital. Even though all the developed countries suffer from both of these issues, economists continue to recommend policies—including monetary easing and balanced budgets—that assume the private sector is still investing at home to maximize profits.

Because the promised economic recoveries took far longer to appear than expected and often did not materialize at all, the public is losing confidence in the competence of established political parties and is starting to vote for outsiders and extremists, a dangerous sign in any society. Although a much improved social safety net means that today's democracies are more resilient to recessions (and policy mistakes) than those in the 1930s, democracy cannot survive if center-left and center-right leaders continue to pursue fundamentally flawed economic policies that lead to suffering for ordinary people.

Once the root cause of stagnation and the failure of conventional economic policies is understood, the remedies turn out to be remarkably straightforward. To get there, however, we must discard conventional notions about monetary and fiscal policy that were developed at a time when the developed economies were not facing balance sheet problems or inferior return on capital problems relative to emerging economies.

Physics and chemistry evolved over the centuries in response to the discovery of new phenomena that defied existing theories. In many of these cases, it was eventually realized that what people thought they knew was not wrong but was in fact a subset of a bigger truth. Similarly, the economics taught in schools is not wrong, but it applies only to situations where the private sector has a clean balance sheet and enjoys an abundance of attractive domestic investment opportunities that are worth borrowing for. When these conditions are not met, we need to look for a new and broader paradigm that can explain what is happening without relying on those two assumptions.

This book was originally intended to be a revised and updated version of my last book, *The Other Half of Macroeconomics and the Fate of Globalization,* with similar structure and chapter headings. But the time freed up by working from home instead of commuting on Tokyo subway trains or commuting to other financial centers by airplanes allowed me to go far beyond the previous book, hence the new title.

It is the author's hope that this book will help explain why policies that worked so well in the past no longer work today, and why nostalgia for the "good old days" is no solution for the future. There are also right ways and wrong ways to respond to these changes. Once the key drivers of change are identified and understood, individuals and policy makers alike should be able to respond correctly to today's new environment without wasting time on remedies that are no longer relevant.

About the Author

Richard C. Koo is the Chief Economist of Nomura Research Institute (NRI), with responsibilities to provide independent economic and market analysis to Nomura Securities, the leading securities house in Japan, and its clients. Before joining Nomura in 1984, Mr. Koo, a US citizen, was an economist with the Federal Reserve Bank of New York (1981–84). Prior to that, he was a Doctoral Fellow of the Board of Governors of the Federal Reserve System (1979–81). In addition to conducting financial market research, he has also advised five Japanese prime ministers on how best to deal with Japan's economic and banking problems. In addition to being one of the first non-Japanese participants in the making of Japan's five-year economic plan, he was also the only non-Japanese member of the Defense Strategy Study Conference of the Japan Ministry of Defense for 1999–2011. Currently he is serving as a Senior Advisor to the Center for Strategic and International Studies (Washington, D.C.). He is also a columnist for the German Handlesblatt newspaper and a frequent contributor to *The International Economy Magazine* published in, Washington, D.C.

Mr. Koo is the author of many books on economics and the Japanese economy, and his *The Holy Grail of Macroeconomics— Lessons from Japan's Great Recession* (John Wiley & Sons, 2008) has become a required read in many university economics classes around the world. It has been translated into and sold in six different languages. Mr. Koo holds BAs in Political Science and Economics from the University of California at Berkeley (1976) and an MA in Economics from the Johns Hopkins University (1979). From 1998 to 2010, he was a visiting professor at Waseda University in Tokyo. In financial circles, Mr. Koo was ranked first among over 100 economists covering Japan in the Nikkei Financial Ranking for 1995, 1996, and 1997, and by the *Institutional Investor* magazine for 1998. He was also ranked first by Nikkei Newsletter on Bond and Money for 1998, 1999, and 2000. He was awarded the Abramson Award by the National Association for Business Economics (Washington, D.C.) for the year 2001. A piano manufacturer before becoming an economist, Mr. Koo, a native of Kobe, Japan, is married and has two children.

CHAPTER 1

Introduction to the Other Half of Macroeconomics

Human progress is said to have started when civilizations sprang up in China, Egypt, and Mesopotamia over 5,000 years ago. The Renaissance, which began in Europe in the 13th century, accelerated the search for both a deeper understanding of the physical world and better forms of government. But for centuries, that progress benefited only the fortunate few with enough to eat and the leisure to ponder worldly affairs. Life for the masses was little better in the 18th century than it was in the 13th century when the Renaissance began. Thomas Piketty noted in his book *Capital in the Twenty-First Century* that economic growth was basically at a standstill during this period, averaging only 0.1 percent per year.[1]

Today, on the other hand, economic growth is largely taken for granted, and most economists only talk about "getting back to trend." People actually become upset when they do not see enough economic growth. Economists arguing that growth will return to the high rates of the past if only inflation reaches the 2-percent target are typical of this group. But what they do not ask is how the growth trend was established in the first place. To understand how centuries of economic stagnation gave way to a period of rapid economic growth that was then followed by where we are today, with decelerating

---

[1] Piketty, Thomas (2014), *Capital in the Twenty-First Century*, translated by Arthur Goldhammer, Cambridge, MA: Belknap Press of Harvard University Press.

economic growth and rising social tensions, we need to review certain basic facts about the economy and how it operates.

Basic Macroeconomics: One Person's Expenditure Is Another's Income

One person's expenditure is another person's income. It is this unalterable linkage between the expenditures and incomes of millions of thinking and reacting households and businesses that makes the study of the economy both interesting and unique. It is interesting because the interactions between these households and businesses create a situation in which one plus one seldom equals two.

Consider a world where there are only two economic entities, A and B, and each is buying $1,000 in goods from the other. If A decides to buy $100 less from B in order to set aside $100, or 10 percent of her income, as savings for an uncertain future, B will have $100 less income to use to buy things from A. If B, whose income has fallen from $1,000 to $900, then reduces his purchases from A by $100, A's income will also fall to $900. If A's original intention was to save 10 percent of her income, she will end up saving $90 instead of her original goal of $100. Thus, the interaction of the two players results in a situation in which one plus one does not equal two.

This feedback loop between A and B is easily recognized if there are only two entities, but not when there are millions. But the principle that one person's expenditure is someone else's income is unchanged.

This interaction between expenditure and income also means that at the national level, if someone is saving money, someone else must be doing the opposite ("dis-saving") for the economy to keep running. If everyone is saving and no one is dis-saving—which usually takes the form of borrowing—those savings will leak out of the economy's income stream, resulting in less income for all.

For example, if a person with an income of $1,000 decides to spend $900 and save $100, the $900 that is spent becomes someone else's income and continues circulating in the economy. The $100 that is saved is typically deposited with a financial institution such as a bank, which then lends it to someone else, most often a business, who can make use of it. When that business borrows and spends the

$100, total expenditures in the economy amount to $900 plus $100, which is equal to the original income of $1,000, and the economy moves forward.

But if there is no borrower for the $100, this amount will remain in the financial sector while total expenditures in the economy shrink to $900 from the original $1,000. If the recipient of the $900 decides to save 10 percent and spend $810, the economy will shrink another 10 percent if there are still no borrowers for the saved $90, and so on. This shows how important it is to have borrowers when there are savers in the country: if someone is saving money, someone else must borrow it in order to keep the economy from contracting. If all saved funds are not borrowed and spent, the economy will shrink.

The Importance of Financial Intermediation

In a normal economy, this critical function of matching savers and borrowers is performed by the financial sector, with interest rates moving higher or lower depending on whether there are too many or too few borrowers. If there are too many, interest rates will be bid up, and some potential borrowers will drop out. If there are too few, interest rates will be bid down, prompting potential borrowers who stayed on the sidelines to step forward. If all saved funds are borrowed and spent in this way, the economy will continue to move forward.

This also means that societies without a functioning financial sector to match savers and borrowers are seriously disadvantaged because some of the saved funds could leak out of the income stream. Ancient societies where money lending was considered a crime stagnated in part because saved funds could not re-enter the income stream until the saver himself chooses to dis-save at some point in the future.

One of the characteristics anthropologists look at when assessing how advanced an ancient society was is the use of money. But the invention of money as a store of value also made it easy for people to save for an uncertain future. That, in turn, increased the risk of leakages from the income stream unless those saved funds were made available to those who could borrow and use them. One of the characteristics economists should look for in determining whether an economy is functioning properly, therefore, is the financial sector's ability to match savers and borrowers.

It must be noted that the borrowings that are relevant here are those for real expenditures—such as for the construction of factories or the purchase of consumer goods—and not for purchases of existing assets such as houses and stocks. The former add to GDP; the latter, which merely involve a change of ownership, do not. Even though a typical lender may not care whether the money is being borrowed to build a new factory or to buy existing real estate as long as the loan is ultimately paid back, the distinction is critical for economists because the former adds to GDP, but the latter does not.

Unfortunately, there are no readily available data that distinguish between the two types of borrowing. Because of this limitation, the data used in this book refer to total borrowings. Readers should therefore keep in mind that the actual borrowing numbers—which are what matters—are smaller than the figures used here.

The Role of Fiscal and Monetary Policy

It would be ideal if the market-driven adjustments in interest rates previously noted were sufficient to match savings and borrowings, and thereby keep the economy from spiraling downward. However, there are many circumstances in which such adjustments are not enough. To address these situations, the government has two types of policy, known as monetary and fiscal policy, that it can use to help stabilize the economy by matching private-sector savings and borrowings.

The more frequently used of the two is monetary policy, whereby the central bank raises or lowers interest rates to assist the matching process. Since an excess of borrowers relative to savers is usually associated with a strong economy, a higher policy rate might be appropriate to prevent overheating of the economy and inflation. In this case, the central bank will reduce the funds available in the banking sector for lending until the desired increase in interest rates is achieved. It can also raise the interest rate paid on deposits commercial banks hold at the central bank so that they will have less incentive to lend to the private sector at rates below the policy rate.

Similarly, a shortage of borrowers relative to savers is usually associated with a weak economy, in which case a lower policy rate might be needed to avert a recession or deflation. In this case, the central bank will increase the funds available in the banking system for lending until the desired decrease in interest rates is attained.

With fiscal policy, the government itself borrows and spends money to build highways, airports, and other social infrastructure. In this case, the government is effectively filling the gap between private-sector savings and borrowings to keep the economy from contracting.

Whereas monetary policy decisions can be made very quickly by the central bank governor and his or her associates, fiscal policy tends to be very cumbersome in a peacetime democracy because elected representatives must come to an agreement on how much money to borrow and where to spend it. Because of the political nature of these decisions and the time it takes to implement them, most recent economic fluctuations have been addressed with central bank monetary policy.

Two Reasons for the Disappearance of Borrowers

Now consider an economy in which the savings generated by the private sector far exceed its borrowings even at near-zero interest rates. There are at least two sets of circumstances in which such a situation might arise.

The first is one in which private-sector businesses cannot find investment opportunities that will pay for themselves. A business will borrow money only if it believes it can pay back the debt with interest. And there is no guarantee that such money-making opportunities will always be available. Indeed, the emergence of such opportunities often depends on scientific discoveries and technological innovations, both of which are highly irregular and difficult to predict (these issues are discussed further in Chapter 5, which covers economic growth).

A more relevant version of the investment opportunity question in today's globalized economies is that businesses may find overseas investment opportunities to be more attractive than those available at home. If lower wages and other factors result in higher returns on capital in emerging markets, for example, pressure from shareholders will force businesses to invest more abroad while reducing borrowings and investments at home. If a business finds that its competitors are investing abroad because of cheaper labor, it may also be forced to do the same in order to remain competitive.

Since expanding operations abroad requires funds denominated in foreign currency, these firms will increase borrowings abroad, but not at home. In this case, the businesses are still maximizing profits, but because they are investing abroad, domestic operations and their macroeconomic impact resemble those of companies that are not borrowing at all. In globalized modern economies, this pressure from shareholders to invest where the return on capital is highest may play a bigger role than any technological breakthroughs, or lack thereof, in deciding whether to borrow and invest at home. And this return on capital issue is the key defining element of the concept of "pursued economy" that is explained starting in Chapter 3.

In the second set of circumstances, private-sector borrowers have sustained huge losses and are forced to restore their financial health by paying down debt or rebuilding their savings. For example, businesses that borrowed heavily to develop a new product may end up in such a predicament if the product they brought to market turned out to be a flop. And there will always be businesses that experience financial difficulties or go bankrupt because they lost out to competitors, even when the economy is doing well. But as long as these companies with financial difficulties are a small minority and the corporate sector as a whole is forward-looking, the economy itself will continue to move forward.

When a nationwide debt-financed asset bubble collapses, however, the number of businesses and households experiencing financial difficulties explodes. This is because the debt incurred to buy assets remains at its original value, but the assets purchased with those borrowed funds have collapsed in value. Balance sheets that were balanced before the bubble burst are now underwater, with liabilities far exceeding assets. Facing a huge debt overhang, these borrowers have no choice but to pay down debt or increase their savings—regardless of the level of interest rates—in order to restore solvency.

For businesses, negative equity or insolvency implies the potential loss of access to all forms of financing, including trade credit. In the worst case, all transactions will have to be settled in cash because no supplier or creditor wants to extend credit to an entity that may seek bankruptcy protection at any time. Many banks and other depository institutions are also prohibited by government regulations from extending or rolling over loans to insolvent borrowers in order to safeguard depositors' money.

For households, negative equity means savings they thought they had set aside for retirement or a rainy day are no longer there. Many families are likely to find such a situation extremely stressful and will do whatever they can to replenish their savings.

Both businesses and households will respond to these life-threatening conditions by placing highest priority on restoring their financial health—*regardless of the level of interest rates*—until their survival is no longer at stake. This means they will not only stop borrowing money but may also start repaying debt or increasing savings despite zero interest rates. After a nationwide asset bubble bursts, therefore, the entire private sector may become a large net saver. And that is exactly what happened after asset bubbles burst in Japan in 1990 and in the West in 2008.

A similar rush to replenish savings by businesses and households may take place after the COVID-19 recession that started in early 2020. This is because those who had to withdraw savings to make up for the loss of income during the lockdowns may want to rebuild their savings once incomes return to normal. And they are likely to continue replenishing savings, regardless of the level of interest rates, until a level deemed safe is reached.

Mechanism of Deflationary Spirals

What happens when borrowers disappear for the two reasons previously noted? As indicated in the preceding example, if there are no borrowers for the $100 in savings despite zero interest rates, total expenditures in the economy will drop to $900, while the saved $100 remains in the financial sector. The economy has effectively shrunk by 10 percent, from $1,000 to $900. That $900 now becomes someone else's income. If that person decides to save 10 percent and there are still no borrowers, only $810 will be spent, causing the economy to contract to $810. This cycle will repeat, and the economy will shrink to $730 if borrowers remain on the sidelines.

This $1,000–$900–$810–$730 process of contraction is driven by people who are all doing the right and honorable thing, which in this case is to restore their financial health by paying down debt and increasing savings. But because they are all doing it at the same time, the economy falls into what is called a deflationary spiral. Depending on the size of the bubble and the amount of savings that has to be replenished, this process can go on for many years, and sometimes even for decades.

The $100 that remains in the financial sector will still be invested in various asset classes. Financial institutions entrusted with this money will try their best to find borrowers or promising assets to invest in. But if there are no borrowers in the real economy, institutions can only lend to those who want to buy or invest in existing assets, such as stocks or real estate. Their asset purchases may even foster mini-bubbles from time to time. But without borrowers in the real economy, those savings will never be able to leave the financial sector and support transactions that add to GDP or lift inflation. In other words, the deflationary spiral will continue as long as there are no borrowers in the real economy.

The $1,000–$900–$810–$730 deflationary process previously described does not continue forever since the savings-driven leakages from the income stream end once people become too poor to save. If a person cannot save any money on an income of $500, the entire $500 will naturally be spent. If the person who receives that $500 as income is in the same situation, she will also spend the entire amount. The result is that the economy finally stabilizes at $500 in what is typically known as a depression. And that is exactly what happened during the Great Depression in the 1930s, when the United States lost 46 percent of its nominal gross national product (GNP).

The Paradox of Thrift as Fallacy-of-Composition Problem

John Maynard Keynes, the father of macroeconomics, had a name for a situation in which everyone wants to save, but is unable to do so because no one is borrowing. He called it the paradox of thrift. It is a paradox because if everyone tries to save, the net result is that no one can save because they all end up in the $500 world.

The phenomenon of good behavior at the individual level leading to bad collective outcomes is known as the "fallacy of composition." An example would be a farmer who strives to increase his income by planting more crops. If all farmers do the same, and their combined efforts result in a bumper crop, crop prices will fall, and farmers will end up with less income than they had originally expected.

The paradox of thrift is one such fallacy-of-composition problem, but macroeconomics is full of such problems. Indeed, the *real* reason to study macroeconomics—as opposed to microeconomics or business administration—is to learn to identify these often counterintuitive fallacy-of-composition problems and thereby avoid their pitfalls.

Put differently, if one plus one always equaled two, one would only need to add up the actions of individual households and businesses to obtain an aggregate result. In that sort of world, if A and B in the previous example both wanted to save $100, total savings in the economy would be $200. There would then be no reason to separate the disciplines of macro- and microeconomics. But when interactions and feedback loops among the various actors cause fallacy-of-composition problems, one plus one seldom equals two, and that is where macroeconomics (as opposed to the simple aggregation of microeconomic results) has a role to play. In that sense, macroeconomics is a science of feedback loops, whereas microeconomics and business administration take the external environment as a given.

Until Keynes realized the prevalence of fallacy-of-composition problems in an economy and developed the concept of aggregate demand, most people thought that one plus one always equals two, and the discipline of macroeconomics did not exist. It is for this reason that his *General Theory*, first published in 1936 in the midst of the Great Depression (the $500 economy), is considered the starting point of macroeconomics. These fallacy-of-composition problems become particularly troublesome when borrowers disappear.

The Importance of Borrowing for Economic Growth

The same fallacy of composition operates in reverse when the economy is growing. For an economy to expand, someone must spend more than he earns, usually by borrowing money. If everyone spends only as much as she earns, the economy will be stable, but it will not grow. For it to expand, some entities must *over-stretch* themselves—either by borrowing money or drawing down savings.

A business will do so if it finds an attractive investment opportunity that seems to offer returns that exceed the borrowing costs.

A household might borrow money or reduce its savings if it finds an item that it feels it cannot live without. In other words, economic growth requires the continued emergence of attractive investment opportunities for businesses and must-have products for consumers that are worth borrowing for.

When a large part of the private sector is over-stretching, incomes will also be rising. That makes the initial decision to over-stretch less onerous than feared and may encourage even more people to over-stretch. This (positive) fallacy of composition accelerates economic growth. The conditions needed to prompt businesses to borrow money are discussed in detail in Chapter 5.

No Follow-Through on Keynes's Insights after World War II

Until 2008, the economics profession considered the contraction-ary equilibrium of a $500 economy to be an exceptionally rare occurrence—the only recent example was the Great Depression, which was triggered by the stock market crash in October 1929 and resulted in the loss of 46 percent of nominal GNP in the United States. Although Keynes recognized the paradox of thrift problem in macroeconomics, he failed to apprehend the $1,000–$900–$810–$730 deflationary mechanism driven by people trying to repair their balance sheets. Ben Bernanke, an expert on the Great Depression, even wrote in 1995 that anyone who can explain how the United States lost so much GNP in the Depression will have found the holy grail of macroeconomics.[2] Although Japan fell into a similar predica-ment when its asset bubble burst in 1990, its lessons were almost completely ignored by the economics profession[3] until the West was hit by the collapse of Lehman Brothers in 2008 and the Great Reces-sion that followed.

---

[2] Bernanke, Ben S. (1995), "The Macroeconomics of the Great Depression: A Comparative Approach," *Journal of Money, Credit, and Banking*, 27(1).

[3] One exception was the National Association of Business Economists in Washington, D.C., which awarded its Abramson Award to a paper by the author titled "The Japanese Economy in Balance Sheet Recession," pub-lished in its journal *Business Economics* in April 2001.

Economists failed to consider the scenario of a shortfall of borrowers because when macroeconomics was emerging as a separate academic discipline after World War II, all the damage private-sector balance sheets incurred in the Great Crash of 1929 had been repaired by massive government procurement during the war. When the government started placing orders with companies for thousands of fighter planes and tanks, even businesses with less-than-stellar balance sheets could obtain loans from the banks to expand production. The banks became willing lenders because they knew the borrowers had orders from a highly credible buyer, the government. That started a positive feedback loop in which everyone was over-stretching to build more fighter planes and tanks. The resulting rapid increases in income, in turn, allowed everyone to repair their balance sheets.

Technological advances during the war also resulted in plentiful postwar investment opportunities for businesses as new "must-have" products ranging from washing machines to television sets were brought to market. With businesses eager to start or expand production of these new products, there was an abundance of private-sector borrowers, and interest rates were quite high.

It was indeed a great irony in the history of macroeconomics that when Keynes was writing about the importance of aggregate demand in the midst of the Great Depression, the United States was suffering from a \$1,000–\$900–\$810–\$730 deflationary spiral caused by a lack of borrowers. When the war ended 10 years later and the importance of aggregate demand was finally recognized, the borrower shortfall had already disappeared because massive government procurement during the war had repaired private-sector balance sheets. Keynes's death in 1946 also added to the irony. How the world changed before and after the war is touched on again in Chapters 7 and 10.

With borrowers no longer in short supply, economists' emphasis after the war shifted to the availability of savings and the correct use of monetary policy to ensure that businesses obtained the funds they needed at interest rates low enough to enable them to continue investing. Economists also disparaged fiscal policy—that is, government borrowing and spending—when inflation became a problem in the 1970s because of concerns that the public sector would squander precious private-sector savings on inefficient pork-barrel projects.

The phenomenon of government borrowing preventing the country's private sector from borrowing the limited amount of savings to finance supposedly more productive private-sector investment is known in economics as "crowding out." It is one reason why economists view such borrowing with disdain.

Before 2008, economists also assumed the financial sector would ensure that all saved funds were automatically borrowed and spent, with interest rates moving higher when there were too many borrowers relative to savers and lower when there were too few. This assumed automaticity is why most macroeconomic theories and models developed prior to 2008 contained no financial sector.

However, the advent of major recessions starting in 1990 in Japan and in 2008 in the West demonstrated that private-sector borrowers can disappear altogether—even at a time of zero or negative interest rates—when they face daunting balance sheet problems following the collapse of a debt-financed bubble. In both post-1990 Japan and the post-2008 Western economies, borrowers vanished due to the sequence of events described in the following section.

Borrowers Disappeared When Faced with Solvency Constraint

It all starts with people leveraging up in an asset price bubble in the hope of getting rich quickly. If the value of a house rises from $1 million to $1.2 million in a year, a person who paid cash for the home enjoys a 20 percent return. But if the same person makes a 10 percent down payment and borrows the rest, she will have increased her initial investment of a $100,000 down payment to $300,000, for a return of 200 percent.

If the interest rate on the $900,000 loan is 5 percent, she will have made $200,000 less the interest cost of $45,000, or $155,000, representing an annual return of 155 percent. The prospect of easily earning 155 percent instead of 20 percent leads many people to leverage up during bubbles by borrowing and investing more.

When the bubble bursts and asset prices collapse, however, these people are left with huge debts and no assets to show for them. In the preceding example, if the value of the house falls by 30 percent to $700,000 but the buyer is still carrying a mortgage worth $900,000, the mortgage will be $200,000 underwater. If the owner has little in the way of other assets, she will be effectively bankrupt. People with underwater balance sheets have no choice but to try to restore their financial health by paying down debt or rebuilding savings. With their financial survival at stake, they are in no position to borrow even if interest rates drop to zero. Regulatory constraints also prevent banks from lending to bankrupt borrowers.

Nor will there be many willing lenders—especially when the lenders themselves have balance sheet problems, which is frequently the case after a bubble bursts. This happens because banks lent vast amounts of money to bubble participants who are now effectively bankrupt and unable to service their debts. With nonperforming loans (NPLs) increasing rapidly, banks are forced to cut lending to preserve their capital. These banking issues are discussed further in Chapter 8.

Households and businesses therefore shift their priority from profit maximization to *debt minimization* once they confront the solvency constraint posed by a debt overhang. Since asset bubbles can collapse abruptly, the private sector's shift to debt minimization can also happen quite suddenly.

Economists Never Considered Recession Driven by Debt Minimization

Although it may come as a shock to non-economist readers, the economics profession did not envision a recession driven by private-sector debt minimization until quite recently. In other words, the $1,000–$900–$810–$730 deflationary process resulting from over-leveraged borrowers desperately trying to repair their balance sheets was never discussed. The recessions considered by economists were limited to those caused by inventory swings during the course of the business cycle and by central bank tightening of monetary policy to rein in inflation. As previously noted, even Keynes failed to recognize the mechanism of a deflationary spiral driven by a private sector that is minimizing debt.

Economists failed to consider recessions caused by private-sector debt minimization when building their theories because they assumed the private sector would always be trying to maximize profits. But two conditions must be satisfied for the private sector to maximize profits: it must have a clean balance sheet, and it must have attractive investment opportunities.

By taking it as a given that the private sector is always maximizing profits, economists assumed, mostly unconsciously, that both conditions are always fulfilled. And that was indeed the case for most of the postwar era—at least until Japan's asset bubble burst in 1990 and the West's own bubble collapsed in 2008. Those collapses resulted in the impairment of millions of private-sector balance sheets, which not only led to the disappearance of borrowers but also prompted many borrowers to begin paying down debt despite record-low interest rates. And the amounts involved were enormous.

The Scale of the Deleveraging Problem

Flow-of-funds data for the advanced economies indeed show a massive shift in the private sector's behavior before and after 2008 (Figure 1.1). Flow-of-funds data show whether a sector is a net supplier (= saver) or borrower of funds in the economy by examining changes in its financial assets and financial liabilities. The data divide the economy into five sectors: household, nonfinancial corporate, financial, government, and foreign sectors.

If a sector's financial assets increased more than its financial liabilities, it is considered to be running a financial surplus—in other words, it is a net saver or a net supplier of funds to the economy. If the sector's financial assets increased less than its financial liabilities, it is considered to be running a financial deficit, which means it is a net borrower of funds. The data therefore show who saved and who borrowed within the economy. These five sectors should add up to zero because the financial liability of one group is always the financial asset of another.[4]

It should be noted that the concept of a financial surplus in the flow of funds data is not the same as the frequently used "savings

---

[4] Note that in U.S. data the five sectors do not sum to zero. This is because the Federal Reserve, which compiles them, believes it is better to publicly share the raw data it collects rather than go through the additional iteration of adjustments and estimations needed to ensure the numbers add up to zero.

Average annual private-sector[1] financial surplus(+) or deficit(-)

	5 years to 2008 Q3	From 2008 Q4 to present[4]	Latest 4 quarters		5 years to 2008 Q3	From 2008 Q4 to present[4]	Latest 4 quarters
			(% of GDP)				(% of GDP)
UK	−0.18	**2.65**	7.39	Germany	8.03[3]	**6.41**	6.17
US	3.31	**7.01**	9.52	France	2.83	**4.14**	9.19
Canada	−0.03	**−0.82[5]**	5.92	Italy	1.35	**4.55**	10.69
Japan	7.38[2]	**8.08**	10.22	Spain	−7.93	**7.64**	10.10
Korea	−1.80	**3.48**	3.61	Greece	0.33	**1.68**	6.68
Australia	−7.37	**2.14**	9.37	Ireland	−4.94	**0.62**	16.16
Eurozone	1.29	**5.11**	9.54	Portugal	−3.79	**4.29**	4.47

[1] Private sector = household + corporate + financial sectors.

[2] Entered balance sheet recession in 1990.

[3] Entered balance sheet recession in 2000.

[4] Until 2021 Q3.

[5] Except Canada.

FIGURE 1.1 Private-Sector Borrowers Disappeared after 2008

Source: Nomura Research Institute, based on flow of funds and national accounts data

rate" because the latter is adjusted for depreciation and other factors that affect net additions to the saver's wealth.

These data, like many macroeconomic statistics, are frequently revised as more complete information becomes available. And as noted in the author's previous work,[5] these revisions can be quite large. Anyone who uses these data must therefore view each statistic with a certain amount of latitude given the possibility of subsequent

---

[5] Koo, Richard C. (2015), *The Escape from Balance Sheet Recession and the QE Trap*, Singapore: John Wiley & Sons, pp. 143–146.

revisions. The numbers used in this book reflect the information that was available online as of March 7, 2022. In this book, the term *private sector* is used to mean the sum of the household, nonfinancial corporate, and financial sectors.

According to these data, which are shown in Figure 1.1, the entire U.S. private sector was saving an average of 7.01 percent of gross domestic product (GDP) per year from the third quarter of 2008 through the third quarter of 2021 (and 6.16 percent of GDP through the last quarter of 2019, just before the onslaught of COVID-19), a period in which Lehman Brothers' collapse led to mostly zero interest rates. Under ordinary circumstances, zero interest rates should have prompted the private sector to borrow more, but that was not what happened: in fact, the opposite did. The U.S. private sector increased its savings from an average of 3.31 percent of GDP during the five years prior to the Lehman shock—when interest rates were much higher—to 6.16 percent of GDP after interest rates fell to zero. In other words, sharply lower interest rates were accompanied by an 86 percent increase in savings as a percentage of GDP, from 3.31 percent to 6.16 percent.

Similar shifts in private-sector behavior were also observed in Europe. Savings by Spain's private sector moved from –7.93 percent of GDP to +7.64 percent of GDP post-Lehman. The corresponding figures for Ireland were –4.94 percent before and +0.62 percent after, while for Portugal it was –3.79 percent before and +4.29 percent after. The fact that these massive changes took place at a time of zero or negative interest rates suggests that Europe's private sector also sustained heavy balance sheet damage when the housing bubble burst in 2008.

In Japan, whose bubble burst in 1990 and where interest rates have been essentially zero or negative since 1997, the private sector was saving an average of 7.38 percent of GDP in the five years prior to Lehman's failure in 2008 and an average of 8.08 percent in the 13 years that followed. In Germany, which experienced no housing bubble because the dot-com bubble in the Neuer Markt, the local equivalent of the tech-heavy NASDAQ index, burst in 2000 and threw the economy into serious recession, the private sector was saving a full 8.03 percent of GDP *before* Lehman failed and 6.41 percent thereafter.

The Economics Profession Failed to Consider Deleveraging Economies

These large and positive savings numbers at a time of zero interest rates are very disturbing statistics. Businesses and households should be massive *borrowers* at such low interest rates, but instead they have been huge savers because they are trying to repair damaged balance sheets. In effect, the private sectors in all the advanced countries except Canada are operating outside the realm of textbook economics. And Canada is an exception only because it is the one country whose housing bubble has yet to burst.

The abrupt shift from the pre-Lehman to the post-Lehman world was nothing short of spectacular. In Spain, for example, the private-sector swing from borrowing to saving amounted to well over 10 percent of GDP—and that is comparing the five-year average before Lehman with the 13-year average after Lehman.

The shift in private-sector behavior immediately before and after the Lehman failure was even bigger, reaching well over 20 percent of GDP in many countries. Such a huge and abrupt swing from net borrowing to net saving will throw any economy into a recession. And households and businesses will not resume borrowing until they feel comfortable with their financial health, a process that can take years.

For each borrower who went bankrupt after a bubble burst, there were probably dozens of honest and responsible borrowers who sought to avoid that ignominious fate by paying down debt to restore their financial health and respectability. And it was the collective actions of these honorable borrowers that pushed the economy into the $1,000–$900–$810–$730 deflationary spiral.

When there is enough of this sort of deleveraging to tip the entire private sector into a financial surplus, even entities with clean balance sheets, who may still constitute a majority, are hurt as their income shrinks along with the economy. The contraction also hurts the banking system because borrowers, in general, have less income, even if those bankers and borrowers had no hand in the bubble.

Yet economists continue to assume implicitly and often unconsciously that borrowers are always plentiful because their models and theories all assume the private sector is maximizing profits.

Their forecasts for growth and inflation, which are based on those models and theories, have consistently and repeatedly missed the mark since 2008 because the assumption of a profit-maximizing private sector is no longer valid in the post-bubble world.

When Bank of Japan (BOJ) Governor Haruhiko Kuroda and Deputy Governor Kikuo Iwata stated confidently at the start of their terms in 2013 that they would achieve the 2-percent inflation target within two years, they were assuming that Japan's economy was still in the textbook world. Iwata was so confident of reaching the 2-percent objective that he pledged to resign if the BOJ failed to hit the target within two years. Their utter failure to come anywhere near the target despite negative interest rates and astronomical amounts of monetary easing demonstrated that the Japanese economy is nowhere near the textbook world.

All the Western economists—in both the public and private sectors—who have continued to miss their inflation and growth targets since 2008 are making the same mistake. The problem is that because the assumption of a profit-maximizing private sector is so fundamental to their models and theories, most economists are still unaware that their models have foundered because this critical assumption is no longer valid. Most of them, together with the average public, are not even aware of the disturbing numbers shown in Figure 1.1.

No Name for Recession Driven by Debt Minimization

Mikhail Gorbachev famously said, "You cannot solve the problem until you call it by its right name." When the economic crisis hit in 2008, the economics profession had not only neglected to consider the possibility of a recession caused by a debt-minimizing private sector, but it did not even have a name for the phenomenon. Indeed, the author had to coin the term *balance sheet recession* in the late 1990s to describe this economic disease in a Japanese context.[6] This term finally entered the lexicon of economics in the West following the housing bubble collapse in 2008.

---

[6] The author acknowledges the inspiration given to him by Mr. Edward Frydl, his former boss at the Federal Reserve Bank of New York, who used the term *balance sheet–driven recession* when we were discussing the U.S. economy of the early 1990s.

Economists' inability to envision a world in which borrowers stop borrowing or even start paying down debt has already led to some terrible historical outcomes, including the Great Depression in the United States and the rise of Adolf Hitler and the National Socialists in Germany during the 1930s. European policy makers' continued failure to understand balance sheet recessions has also enabled the emergence of similar far-right political groups in the Eurozone since 2008. These economic and political issues in Europe are addressed in Chapter 7.

The Paradox of Thrift Was the Norm before the Industrial Revolution

Economic stagnation due to a lack of borrowers, however, was actually the norm for thousands of years before the Industrial Revolution in 1760. As shown in Figure 1.2, economic growth had been negligible for centuries before 1760. Even then, there were probably

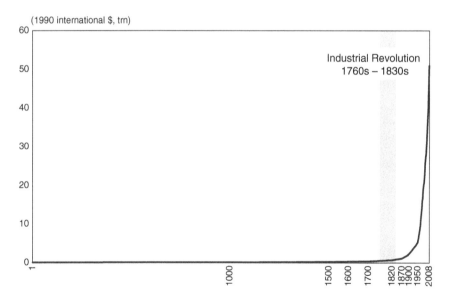

FIGURE 1.2 Economic Growth Became the Norm Only after the Industrial Revolution

Source: Angus Maddison, "Historical Statistics of the World Economy: 1-2008 AD." http://www.ggdc.net/maddison/Historical_Statistics/vertical-file_02-2010.xls

millions who tried to save—after all, human beings have always worried about an uncertain future. Preparing for old age and the proverbial rainy day is an ingrained aspect of human nature. But if it is only human to save, the centuries-long economic stagnation prior to the Industrial Revolution must have been due to a lack of borrowers.

Private-sector borrowing requires a promising investment opportunity. After all, businesses will not borrow unless they feel sure the debt can be paid back with interest. In other words, the risk-adjusted return of the project must be substantially higher than the borrowing cost. But before the Industrial Revolution, which was essentially a technological revolution, there was little or no technological innovation, and therefore few investment projects capable of paying for themselves.

Businesses also tend to minimize debt when they see no investment opportunities because the probability of bankruptcy can be reduced drastically by eliminating debt. Japan is home to many firms dating back several centuries, many of which are located in and around Kyoto and Nagoya. These firms typically do not borrow money for this reason. And if they do, they pay it back at the earliest opportunity in order to minimize the risk of bankruptcy. Except for tax and return-on-equity (ROE) considerations, therefore, it is reasonable for businesses to minimize debt until attractive investment opportunities present themselves. Given the dearth of such opportunities prior to the Industrial Revolution, it is not hard to understand why there were so few willing borrowers.

Amid this absence of investment opportunities and borrowers in the pre-1760 world, efforts to save only caused the economy to shrink. The result was a permanent paradox of thrift in which people tried to save but their very actions and intentions kept the national economy in a depressed state. These conditions lasted for centuries in both the East and the West.

Powerful rulers sometimes borrowed private savings and used them to build monuments or undertake social infrastructure projects. The vicious cycle of the paradox of thrift was then suspended as the government borrowed the private sector's savings (the initial savings of $100 in the previous example) and injected those funds back into the income stream, fueling rapid economic growth. But unless the project paid for itself—and politicians are seldom good at selecting investments that pay for themselves—the government, facing a mounting debt load, would at some point get cold feet and discontinue its investment. The broader economy would then fall back into the stagnation that characterizes the paradox of thrift. Consequently, these regimes were often outlived by the monuments they created. The challenging task of selecting viable public works projects is discussed in Chapter 4.

Countries also tried to achieve economic growth by expanding their territories, that is, by acquiring more land, which was the key factor of production in pre-industrial agricultural societies. Indeed, for centuries before 1945, people believed that territorial expansion was desirable if not essential for economic growth (the significance of this date is explained in Chapter 3). This territorial drive for prosperity provided an economic rationale for colonialism and imperialism. But both were basically a zero-sum proposition for the global economy and also resulted in countless wars and deaths.

Ironically, the wars and resulting destruction produced investment opportunities in the form of postwar reconstruction activity. And wars were frequent occurrences in those days. But without a continuous flow of innovation, investment opportunities soon exhausted themselves and economic growth petered out.

Four Possible States of Borrowers and Lenders

The preceding discussion suggests an economy is always in one of four possible states depending on the presence or absence of lenders (savers) and borrowers (investors in the real economy). Either (1) lenders and borrowers are both present in sufficient numbers, (2) there are more borrowers than lenders, even at high interest rates, (3) there are more lenders than borrowers, even at low interest rates, or (4) lenders and borrowers are both absent. These four cases are illustrated in Figure 1.3.

Of the four, traditional economics only looks at Cases 1 and 2. This is because the presence of borrowers already assumes there are entities with acceptable balance sheets who see attractive investment opportunities and are maximizing profits. And they will indeed borrow as long as real interest rates are low enough. Put differently, those arguing that the central bank should ease monetary policy to stimulate the economy are making the unspoken assumption that the economy is in Case 1 or 2.

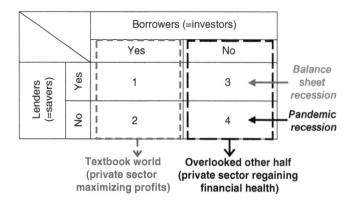

FIGURE 1.3 Borrowers and Lenders: Four Possible States

Of the two, only Case 1 requires a minimum of policy intervention—such as slight adjustments to interest rates—to match savers and borrowers and keep the economy from shrinking. This state of affairs is therefore associated with ordinary interest rates and can be considered the ideal textbook case.

A Shortage of Lenders Has Well-Known Remedies

Case 2 (insufficient lenders) can be caused by macro, financial, or cultural factors. The most common macro factor is when the central bank tightens monetary policy to rein in inflation. The tighter credit conditions that result certainly leave lenders less willing to lend. But once inflation is brought under control, usually within a year or two, the central bank typically eases monetary policy, and the economy returns to Case 1.

Financial factors weighing on lenders may also push the economy into Case 2. One such factor is a banking crisis brought about by an excess of NPLs on banks' books. When loans go bad, banks' capital is eroded. And when a bank's capital-to-assets ratio falls below the legally required minimum, it must desist from lending. When many banks find themselves in this situation and are unable to lend, the economy suffers from what is known as a credit crunch. Overzealous supervision of financial institutions by the authorities can also trigger a credit crunch, something that actually happened after the disastrous late-1980s savings and loan debacle in the United States. When many banks encounter NPL problems at the same time, mutual distrust among the banks may lead not only to a credit crunch but also to a dysfunctional interbank market, a state of affairs typically referred to as a financial crisis. This type of crisis is discussed further in Chapter 8.

When lenders have NPL problems, the central bank's policy rate can diverge significantly from actual lending rates set by the banks. This happens because NPL problems in the banking system weaken the economy and prompt the central bank to lower interest rates. But because bank lending is constrained by insufficient bank capital, competition among borrowers for available funds pushes actual lending rates far higher than what is suggested by the central bank's policy rate. The resulting "fat spreads" mean only those willing to pay the high market rates will be able to borrow. Monetary authorities may also deliberately allow such fat spreads in certain circumstances to allow banks to earn more so that they can use those profits to recapitalize themselves.

Certain cultural and religious factors, such as prohibitions on lending, as well as income levels that are too low to allow people to save, may also result in an underdeveloped financial system and a shortage of lenders. These developmental issues are typically found in pre-industrialized societies and can take many years to address. The recent development of so-called Islamic finance is an attempt to overcome some of these religious constraints to lending in Muslim countries.

A country may also be too poor or underdeveloped to save. But if a country is too poor to save because of the paradox of thrift, it would be classified as being in Case 3 or 4 because the problems are actually attributable to a lack of borrowers.

Noncultural or religious causes of a shortage of lenders have well-known remedies. For example, the government can inject capital into the banks to restore their ability to lend, or it can relax regulations preventing financial institutions from serving as financial intermediaries. In the case of a dysfunctional interbank market, the central bank can act as lender of last resort to ensure the clearing system continues to operate. It can also relax monetary policy. Lender-side problems in Case 2, such as credit crunches and financial crises, are discussed in more detail in Chapter 8.

The conventional emphasis on monetary policy and concerns over the crowding-out effect of fiscal policy are justified in Cases 1 and 2, where there are ample private-sector borrowers but (for a variety of reasons in Case 2) not enough lenders.

The Absence of Borrowers and the "Other Half" of Macroeconomics

The problem is with Cases 3 and 4, where the bottleneck is a shortage of *borrowers*. When borrowers disappear for either of the two reasons previously noted, monetary policy loses its effectiveness because lower interest rates do not lead to an increase in borrowing. And without an increase in borrowing or private-sector overstretching, there is no reason for the economy to expand.

Fiscal policy—that is, government borrowing—then becomes indispensable in filling the gap between private-sector savings and borrowings. There is no reason for the economy to contract if the government borrows and spends the excess savings of the private sector (the $100 in the example previously given). Nor will such government actions cause crowding-out problems when there are no private-sector borrowers. This is the *other half of macroeconomics* that has been overlooked by traditional economists.

Fixation with Profit-Maximization Assumption Prevented Full Breakthrough

Keynes, writing during the Great Depression, realized that the macroeconomy is full of fallacy-of-composition problems and came up with the concept of aggregate demand as distinct from just a summing-up of individual wish lists. Although that was a revolutionary insight, he was still constrained by the traditional notion that the private sector is always maximizing profits. That fixation forced him to fashion a variety of convoluted explanations for why aggregate demand had suddenly shrunk in the early 1930s, when everyone was supposedly still maximizing profit. For example, he argued that there must have been a decline in what he called the marginal efficiency of capital that undermined the reasons to invest. He also argued that a sudden increase in "preference for liquidity" made people less willing to spend money. But these theoretical concoctions could not explain why such changes had occurred so suddenly in the first place.

Since the post-1990 Japanese experience, it has become clear that what Keynes mistook for a fall in the marginal efficiency of capital and an increase in liquidity preference was simply the result of a private sector that was minimizing debt. And people were minimizing debt so as to restore their financial health after the collapse of a debt-financed bubble pushed them up against solvency constraints.

It was also said that "liquidity trap," where low interest rates failed to stimulate the economy, was due to lenders refusing to lend at such low interest rates. But post-1990 Japan and the post-2008 West proved that the trap is due to borrowers not borrowing money because of balance sheet problems. This also implies that "money demand functions" and "liquidity preference–money supply (LM) curves," the two pillars of Keynesian economics that all students of economics had to learn decades ago, are largely irrelevant concepts.

Keynes also coined the term *animal spirits* to account for shifts in people's behavior that he could not explain. But people will suddenly and understandably swing from profit maximization to debt minimization when they hit the solvency constraint. And they will continue to deleverage until their balance sheets are repaired, a process that can take years. A necessary condition for animal spirits to kick in and increase investments, therefore, is that the private sector has clean balance sheets.

As previously noted, there are two main reasons why private-sector borrowers might disappear. The first is that they cannot find attractive investment opportunities at home, and the second is that their financial health has deteriorated to the point where they cannot borrow until they repair their balance sheets. Examples of the first case include the world that existed prior to the Industrial Revolution and in advanced countries today, where the return on capital is lower than that in emerging economies. Examples of the second case are typically found following the collapse of debt-financed asset bubbles. The private sector's move to replenish savings depleted during the COVID-19 pandemic, if it happens, can be considered a variation of the second case.

Most advanced countries since 2008 have suffered from both of these factors, which served to reduce the number of borrowers

(Figure 1.1). In other words, these economies are all in Case 3 or 4, that is, they are in the "other half" of macroeconomics. Unfortunately, most policy makers and economists are still operating on the assumption that their economies are in Case 1 or 2. But policies designed for Case 1 or 2 are often counterproductive when the economy is in Case 3 or 4, something that is discussed in the rest of this book. The resultant failure of governments and central banks to meet their own growth and inflation targets is one of the key reasons why the public has grown so impatient with the establishment.

Because balance sheet problems can depress the economy very quickly and are therefore more urgent, they are discussed first, in Chapter 2. However, this book focuses on the second case and explores it in Chapters 3, 4, and 5. Readers who are already familiar with the concept of balance sheet recessions and are aware of the current status of the world's major economies may wish to proceed directly to Chapter 3.

Balance Sheet Problems Create a Shortage of Borrowers

As is noted in Chapter 1, entities that have stopped borrowing because of negative equity will not resume borrowing until their balance sheets have been repaired. Depending on the size of the bubble, this can take many years. For example, if the borrower in Chapter 1 who was $200,000 underwater has an after-tax income of $150,000 and a savings rate of 20 percent, she is saving $30,000 per year. If she can earmark two-thirds of that amount, or $20,000, for addressing her debt overhang, it will still take her ten years to clean up her balance sheet.

And with so many people trying to restore their financial health at the same time, the economy will be in constant danger of entering the sort of deflationary scenario that is described in Chapter 1. If the resulting recession reduces the income of the person in the example, she will have even less money to pay down debt and will therefore need more time to fix her balance sheet. The recession may also push house prices lower, which would make the process even more difficult. Both factors—reduced income and falling asset prices—can easily extend the time needed for balance sheet repairs.

One nasty characteristic of balance sheet recessions is that they are largely invisible and inaudible. After all, businesses will not want to admit that their balance sheets are underwater if they think they can patch up their balance sheets within a reasonable time frame. And that is not an unreasonable expectation for many because there are actually two types of firms with underwater balance sheets: those with cash flow and those without. The latter will have to go bankrupt and that is bad for the economy. But the former is also bad for the economy because their effort to avoid bankruptcy by paying down debt using cash flow from their main line of business means there is that much less borrowings and that much more savings (debt repayment counts as savings) in the economy.

Lenders to those businesses may also want to keep quiet if they believe their borrowers will eventually be able to pay back their debts. Individuals who have incurred heavy losses speculating with borrowed funds during the bubble will also want to stay silent because they will be too ashamed to admit their mistakes (and greed). With everyone with cash flow pretending that everything is fine, it takes some effort on the part of economists to find out what is really happening in the economy.

Fortunately, there are flow-of-funds statistics that indicate what businesses and households have been doing with their financial assets and liabilities. Even though these data are far from perfect and are subject to frequent revisions, they enable us to see whether businesses are looking forward (i.e., maximizing profits) or backward (i.e., minimizing debt) by showing what they are doing with their financial liabilities relative to the current level of interest rates. If businesses are reducing financial liabilities—that is, paying down debt—at near-zero interest rates, we can be reasonably sure they are facing balance sheet problems and are minimizing debt. In other words, these data make it possible to visualize a balance sheet recession.

Japan in Balance Sheet Recession

Japan was the first advanced country to experience a private-sector shift to debt minimization for balance sheet reasons since the Great Depression. The Japanese bubble was massive. At the peak, it was said that the gardens of the Imperial Palace in central Tokyo, with a circumference of about 5 kilometers, were worth as much as the entire state of California. After the bubble burst in 1990, nationwide commercial real estate prices fell 87 percent to levels last seen in 1973 (Figure 2.1), devastating the balance sheets of businesses and financial institutions across the country. The amount of wealth lost as a percentage of gross domestic product (GDP) in post-1990 Japan was three times the loss incurred by the United States during the Great Depression.

Figure 2.2 shows interest rates and the funds procured by Japanese nonfinancial businesses from both the banking system and

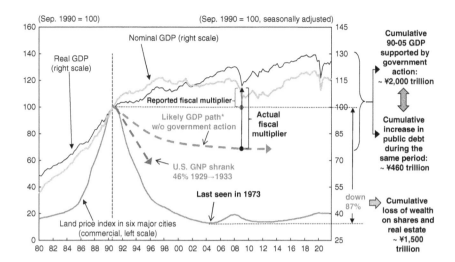

FIGURE 2.1 Japan's GDP Grew Despite a Major Loss of Wealth and Private-Sector Deleveraging

*GDP returning to pre-bubble level of 1985.

Sources: Cabinet Office, Japan and Japan Real Estate Institute

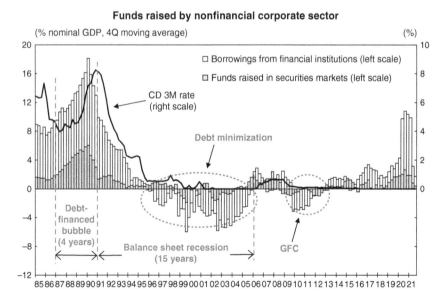

FIGURE 2.2 Japanese Companies Deleveraged under Zero Interest Rates for Over 10 Years, until 2005

Sources: Bank of Japan and Cabinet Office, Japan

the capital markets. From 1985 to 1990, when the Japanese bubble was rapidly expanding, these businesses leveraged up by borrowing massive amounts to invest in a wide variety of assets. The Bank of Japan (BOJ), realizing that there was a bubble and that the economy was overheating, steadily raised short-term interest rates (see three-month CD rate in Figure 2.2) to as high as 8 percent in an attempt to contain the boom (the inflation rate at the time was only about 3 percent).

When the bubble finally burst in 1990, demand for borrowings shrank rapidly. Noting that the economy was also slowing sharply, the BOJ lowered interest rates from 8 percent to almost zero by 1995. But loan demand not only failed to recover, it actually turned negative that year. In other words, Japan's entire corporate sector was paying down debt at a time of zero interest rates (see circled areas in Figure 2.2).

This is a world that no university economics department or business school had ever envisioned. Conventional theory says that businesses should be aggressively borrowing at such low interest rates, but Japanese companies not only stopped borrowing but actually began to pay down debt and continued to do so for well over ten years.

Figure 2.3 uses flow-of-funds data to provide a more general view of the Japanese economy during this period. These data, as explained in Chapter 1, divide the economy into five sectors—household, nonfinancial corporate, financial, government, and the rest of the world—and indicate whether a given sector is a net supplier or net borrower of funds. Sectors above the horizontal line at zero are net suppliers of funds (financial surplus = savers), while those below the line are net borrowers (financial deficit = investors). The data are compiled in such a way that the five sectors sum to zero and show which sectors in the economy saved money and which borrowed money in each period.

To simplify the presentation for the national economy, the original five sectors are reduced to four in this book by combining nonfinancial and financial companies into a single "corporate sector." In addition, all national flow-of-funds data in this book (the exhibits with four lines) are presented as four-quarter moving averages to smooth out seasonal fluctuations, a fairly common practice when using these data.

It should also be noted that shifts within a sector's financial assets or liabilities are netted out in these charts. For example, businesses

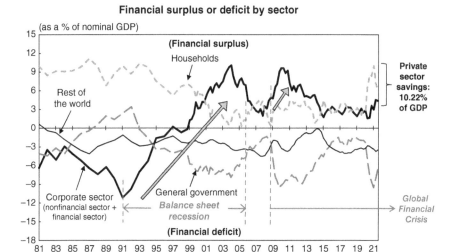

FIGURE 2.3 Japan's Challenge: Persuade Traumatized Businesses to Borrow Again

Note: All entries are four-quarter moving averages. For the latest figures, four-quarter averages ending in 2021 Q3 are used.

Sources: Bank of Japan, *Flow of Funds Accounts* and Government of Japan, Cabinet Office, *National Accounts*

issuing debt to buy back shares will have zero net impact on the national flow-of-funds data because both debt and equity represent financial liabilities of the same corporate sector. This means corporate leverage may still be growing even if there is no change in the corporate sector's financial deficit if companies are engaged in share buybacks using borrowed funds. To capture this type of risk, one must look at the composition of gross financial liabilities in the flow-of-funds data and not just the net numbers.

In an ideal textbook world, the household sector should be above zero, or in financial surplus (saving), the corporate sector should be below zero, or in financial deficit (borrowing), and government and the rest of the world should be around zero, which implies that both the government's budget and the nation's current account are in balance.

In contrast to this ideal world, Figure 2.3 clearly indicates that Japan's post-bubble difficulties were driven by massive corporate deleveraging (see the large arrow). As a result of the asset bubble, which started around 1985, Japanese corporate borrowings increased to 11.2 percent of GDP by 1991. But once the bubble burst, businesses abruptly began deleveraging, and their financial surplus grew to 10 percent of GDP by 2004. The deflationary impact of businesses' swing from borrowing to saving was over 20 percent of GDP—from a financial deficit of 11.2 percent of GDP in 1991 to a financial surplus of 10 percent of GDP in 2004. This massive corporate shift from profit maximization to debt minimization is the cause of the prolonged economic stagnation in Japan that continues to this day.

In an ideal textbook economy, the household sector saves while the corporate sector borrows. But in Japan, both sectors became net savers after 1999, and the corporate sector has been the nation's largest saver since 2002 in spite of zero interest rates. Fully 30 years after the bubble burst, Japan's corporate sector is still saving over 4.3 percent of GDP at a time of negative interest rates. It is this disappearance of corporate borrowers that caused the Japanese economy to stagnate over the last three decades. The real culprit in the phenomenon of "Japanization" was corporate debt minimization.

Visualizing Balance Sheet Recessions in the West

Western economies also experienced massive housing bubbles in the run-up to 2008 (Figure 2.4). When those bubbles collapsed on both sides of the Atlantic in 2008, the balance sheets of millions of households and many financial institutions were devastated. The resulting loss of wealth reached well into the tens of trillions of dollars and euros, while the liabilities incurred during the bubble remained on the books at their original values. As a result, the private sectors in nearly all the major advanced economies have been increasing savings or paying down debt since 2008 in spite of record-low interest rates (Figure 1.1).

In the United States, it was the household sector that led the deleveraging because the bubble was in housing. This can be seen from Figure 2.5, which separately shows the financial assets and liabilities of the U.S. household sector. In this chart, a white bar above zero means the household sector is increasing its financial assets, that is, increasing its savings. A white bar below zero means the household sector is reducing its financial assets, that is, withdrawing its savings. Similarly, a shaded bar below zero means the sector is increasing its financial liabilities, that is, increasing its borrowings. A shaded bar above zero means the sector is reducing its financial liabilities, that

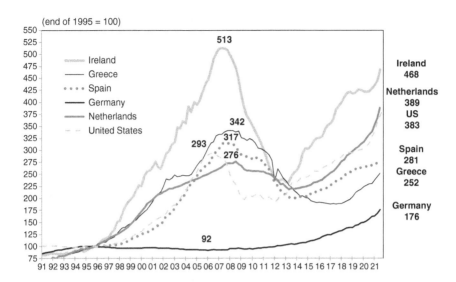

FIGURE 2.4 West (ex Germany) also Experienced a Housing Bubble Collapse

Notes: 1. Figures for Ireland before 2005 are existing house prices only.

2. Figures for Greece are prices of flats in Athens and Thessaloniki.

Sources: Nomura Research Institute, calculated from Bank for International Settlements, Federal Reserve Economic Data (FRED) and S&P Dow Jones data

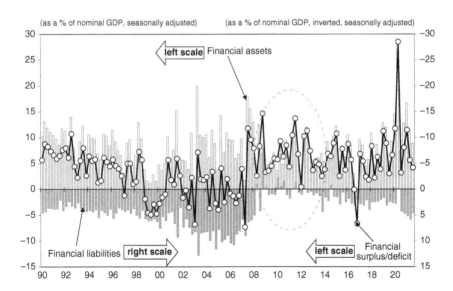

FIGURE 2.5 U.S. Households Were Net Borrowers during Bubble

Notes: Latest figures are for 2021 Q3.

Sources: Nomura Research Institute, based on flow of funds data from Federal Reserve Board (FRB) and U.S. Department of Commerce

is, paying down debt. The net number is shown by the broken line with little circles.

Economics textbooks say the household sector should save while the corporate sector borrows. But the U.S. household sector was a huge net borrower during the housing bubble, as shown in Figure 2.5, indicating just how wild conditions became.

Once the bubble burst, the household sector not only became a massive net saver, but also stopped borrowing altogether for about four years despite zero interest rates (circled area in Figure 2.5). The household sector's abrupt shift to a financial surplus torpedoed the U.S. economy after 2008.

Even though households resumed borrowing around 2012, they remained a huge net saver—in spite of zero interest rates—even before the COVID-19 lockdowns. That suggests U.S. households are still not comfortable with their balance sheets. If they were, they would be borrowing more at these historically low interest rates.

In Europe, the housing bubbles were particularly large in Spain, Ireland, and Greece (Figure 2.4). Figure 2.6 illustrates the flow of

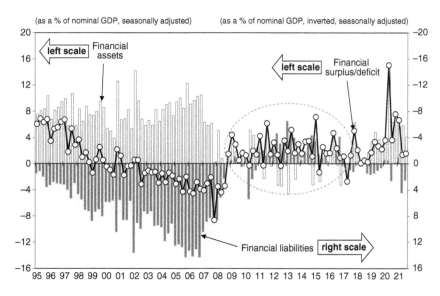

FIGURE 2.6 Spanish Households Deleveraged for Eight Years after Housing Bubble

Notes: Seasonal adjustments by Nomura Research Institute. Latest figures are for 2021 Q3.

Sources: Nomura Research Institute, based on flow of funds data from Banco de España and National Statistics Institute, Spain

funds in the Spanish household sector. The sector behaved quite conservatively until the bubble hit, then began borrowing massively. When the bubble burst in 2007, the sector not only ceased borrowing altogether in spite of zero (and now negative) interest rates, but also started paying down debt (indicated by the shaded bars above zero) in a trend that continued for over eight years.

Although the Spanish economy started to recover in the second half of 2016 and continued to improve until the pandemic recession in 2020, it seems unlikely that the recovery was driven by domestic demand. After all, both the household sector and the corporate sector (shown in Figure 7.2) remained net savers in spite of negative interest rates.

The Irish household sector, shown in Figure 2.7, went through even more dramatic changes. Starting from a very conservative position around 2000, the sector went deeply into debt during the bubble. But after the bubble burst, borrowing stopped completely and debt repayment (see shaded bars above zero) continued almost every quarter for more than 10 years. This indicates that the supposedly

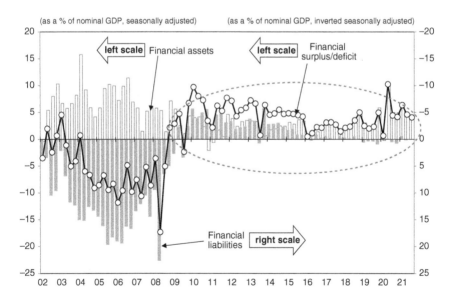

FIGURE 2.7 Irish Households Deleveraged for 10 Years after Housing Bubble

Notes: Seasonal adjustments by Nomura Research Institute. Latest figures are for 2021 Q3.

Sources: Nomura Research Institute, based on flow of funds data from the European Central Bank (ECB) and Central Statistics Office, Ireland

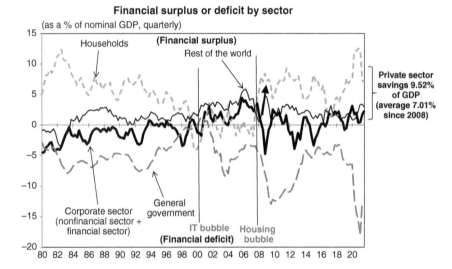

FIGURE 2.8 U.S. Private Sector Has Been Saving 7.01 Percent of the GDP since 2008 Despite Zero Interest Rates

Note: All entries are four-quarter moving averages. For the latest figures, four-quarter averages ending in 2021 Q3 are used.

Sources: FRB and U.S. Department of Commerce

strong performance of the Irish economy observed from 2016 until the onslaught of COVID-19 in 2020 had little to do with the country's household sector, which remained a net saver despite negative interest rates.

The preceding charts for Japan, the United States, and Europe indicate that there were dramatic shifts from profit maximization to debt minimization in the post-bubble economies and that the latter can last for many years.

The reversal since 2008 has been nothing short of spectacular. The U.S. private sector went from saving a net 0.49 percent of GDP in 2007 Q2 to saving a net 10.88 percent of GDP in 2011 Q3 in spite of the lowest interest rates in history. The United States not only suffered an exodus of borrowers, but also lost private-sector demand equal to 10.39 percent of GDP over the same period, plunging the economy into a serious recession. In the United Kingdom, private-sector demand equal to 7.65 percent of GDP disappeared between 2007 Q4 and 2009 Q4. Spain lost 19.6 percent of GDP from the turnabout in private-sector behavior between 2007 Q3 and 2010 Q1, also

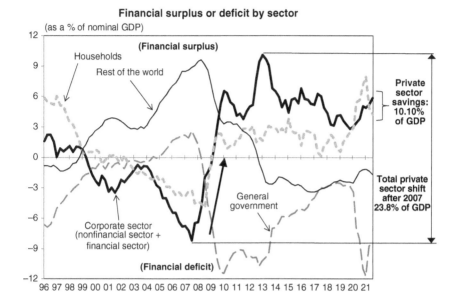

FIGURE 2.9 Spanish Household and Corporate Sectors Remained Huge Net Savers after Housing Bubble

Note: All entries are four-quarter moving averages. For the latest figures, four-quarter averages ending with 2021 Q3 are used.

Sources: Banco de España and National Statistics Institute, Spain

at a time of record low interest rates. These private sectors' scramble to repair damaged balance sheets tipped the global economy into the Great Recession.

In 2019, just before the pandemic struck, the U.S. private sector was still saving 9.50 percent of GDP. The private sector in the Eurozone saved an average of 4.74 percent of GDP from 2009 to 2018 in spite of negative interest rates, although that number dropped to 2.67 percent in 2019 when the corporate sector became a net borrower for the first time in twelve years (Figure 2.11).

In many of these countries, not only the household sector, but also the corporate sector has been increasing savings or paying down debt at these record-low interest rates (Figures 2.8 to 2.11).[1]

_____

[1] Unfortunately, Irish data on the corporate and overseas sectors are compromised by the country's status as a tax haven for many global corporations, which makes it difficult to interpret these two entries.

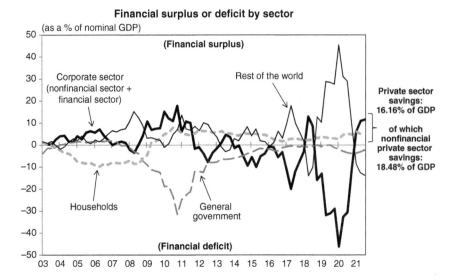

Financial surplus or deficit by sector

FIGURE 2.10 Irish Household Sector Remained Huge Net Saver after Housing Bubble

Note: All entries are four-quarter moving averages. For the latest figures, four-quarter averages ending in 2021 Q3 are used.

Sources: Central Bank of Ireland and Central Statistics Office, Ireland

Such corporate behavior entirely contradicts the textbook notion that profit-maximizing firms should be taking advantage of record-low interest rates by borrowing more. In other words, the developed world is experiencing private-sector behavior that falls totally outside the conventional framework of neoclassical economics. It is now in Case 3 of the lender/borrower quadrant that is described in Figure 1.3.

The private sectors in all of these countries are increasing savings or paying down debt because their balance sheets were damaged badly when debt-financed asset bubbles burst. With a huge debt overhang and no assets to show for that debt, affected businesses and households had no choice but to put their financial houses in order. A failure to do so would mean a loss of access to credit if not bankruptcy. They therefore had to increase savings or pay down debt until they safely emerged from a state of negative equity, leaving the economy in Case 3—the "other half" of macroeconomics—for years.

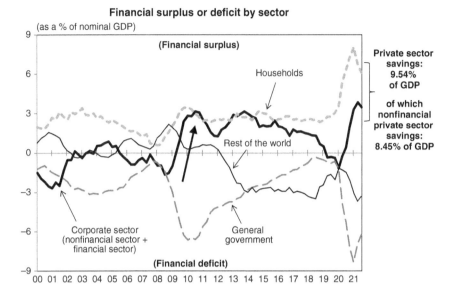

FIGURE 2.11 Eurozone's Private Sector Remained Large Net Saver after Housing Bubble

Note: All entries are four-quarter moving averages. For the latest figures, four-quarter averages ending in 2021 Q3 are used.

Sources: European Central Bank (ECB) and Eurostat

The First Casualty of Disappearing Borrowers: Monetary Policy

When borrowers disappear and the private sector as a whole becomes a net saver despite zero interest rates, the economy faces a deflationary gap (the $100 in the initial example in Chapter 1). The problem is that monetary policy, economists' preferred policy tool, can do very little to support the economy when borrowers absent themselves. For monetary policy to stimulate GDP, someone must be willing to respond to the easier monetary conditions by increasing borrowings and spending those funds in the real economy. When borrowers absent themselves because of an urgent need to restore financial health, however, monetary easing by the central bank can produce no increase in borrowing and over-stretching.

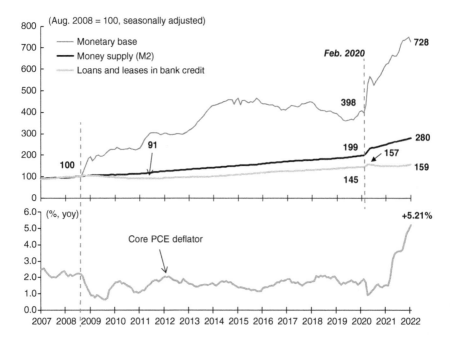

FIGURE 2.12 Massive Liquidity Injections Produced Minimal Increases in Money Supply and Credit (1): United States

Note: Commercial bank loans and leases, adjustments for discontinuities made by Nomura Research Institute.

Sources: FRB and U.S. Department of Commerce

Figures 2.12 to 2.14 and 2.17 show that the close relationship observed prior to 2008 between central-bank-supplied liquidity, known as the monetary base, and growth in the money supply and private-sector credit broke down completely after the bubbles burst and the private sector began minimizing debt. Here, money supply refers to the sum of all bank accounts plus bills and coins circulating in the economy, and credit means the amount of money lent by financial institutions.

These exhibits underscore the fact that the monetary base, money supply, and credit were closely correlated prior to 2008, just as economics teaches. In this textbook world, a 10-percent increase in liquidity supplied by the central bank increases both the money supply and credit by 10 percent. That is because liquidity supplied by the central bank is the primary constraint on money supply growth and credit creation (this point is explained in Chapter 8). In other words, there are enough private-sector borrowers to borrow all the funds supplied by the central bank, and that the economy is in Case 1 or 2.

But after the bubble burst, forcing the private sector to minimize debt in order to repair its damaged balance sheet, no amount of liquidity injection by the central bank was able to increase private-sector borrowings. The U.S. Federal Reserve, for example, expanded the monetary base by 298 percent from the time Lehman Brothers went under to just before the COVID-19 pandemic struck in February 2020. But the money supply grew by only 99 percent and credit by only 45 percent. A 45-percent increase in private-sector credit over a period of 11½ years represents a minuscule average annual increase of only 3.4 percent.

Of the three monetary aggregates, the most noteworthy is bank credit. This is because a central bank can always add liquidity to the banking system by purchasing assets from financial institutions. But for that liquidity to enter the real economy, banks must lend out those funds: they cannot give them away because the funds are ultimately owned by depositors. A 45-percent increase in lending since 2008 means new money entering the real economy from the financial sector has grown by only 45 percent. In other words, most of the liquidity supplied by the central bank (the 298 percent) remains stuck in the financial sector due to a lack of borrowers.

Moreover, the private-sector deleveraging in the United States actually shrank credit outstanding by 9 percent, from 100 at the time of Lehman's collapse to 91 in 2011 (Figure 2.12). This occurred even though the Fed injected massive amounts of liquidity and took interest rates down to zero. It shows the impotence of monetary policy when borrowers disappear in a balance sheet recession: even the Fed's tremendous monetary easing failed to stop credit from contracting in the United States.

Similar decoupling has been observed in all post-bubble economies, including the Eurozone (Figure 2.13) and the United Kingdom (Figure 2.14). In the Eurozone, bank lending had shrunk 3 percent by 2015, and at the time of this writing is only 16 percent higher than it was in 2008. In the United Kingdom, bank lending plunged 20 percent by 2014 and is currently up only 5 percent over 2008.

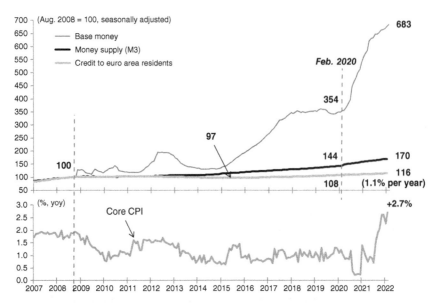

FIGURE 2.13 Massive Liquidity Injections Produced Minimal Increases in Money Supply and Credit (2): Eurozone

Note: Base money figures seasonally adjusted by Nomura Research Institute.

Sources: ECB and Eurostat

This absence of borrowers explains why inflation and growth rates in the advanced economies have failed to respond to zero interest rates and astronomical injections of central bank liquidity since 2008. Central banks consistently failed to meet their inflation targets because the disappearance of borrowers kept the actual money circulating in the economy from growing. Milton Friedman and his disciples have argued that inflation is always and everywhere a monetary phenomenon, and that a central bank in charge of monetary policy can therefore create inflation at will. If that were the case, the 298 percent growth in the monetary base should have led to similar increases in the money supply and credit, driving a corresponding surge in inflation. But nothing of the sort happened after 2008.

The Great Depression as Balance Sheet Recession

Not surprisingly, the same decoupling of monetary aggregates was observed in the United States after the collapse of the asset price bubble in 1929, which led to the Great Depression, the greatest of all

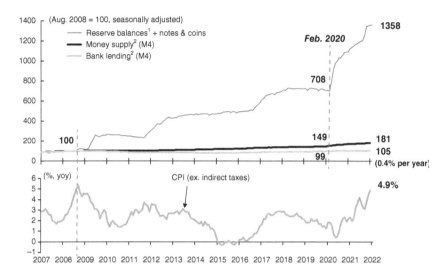

FIGURE 2.14 Massive Liquidity Injections Produced Minimal Increases in Money Supply and Credit (3): United Kingdom

Notes: 1. Reserve balances data are seasonally unadjusted.

2. Money supply and bank lending data exclude intermediate financial institutions.

Sources: Bank of England and Office for National Statistics, U.K.

balance sheet recessions. The same decoupling was also observed in Japan after its bubble burst in 1990.

Figure 2.15 illustrates the monetary base, the money supply, and credit supplied to the private sector before and after the October 1929 stock market crash. It shows that the three were moving in tandem until the crash, just as textbooks teach, but then decoupled in exactly the same way as they did in the post-2008 economies. Loans to the private sector, shown at the bottom of the upper graph, were down 54.7 percent from their 1929 peak in 1935 as the U.S. private sector sought to pay down debt and repair its battered balance sheet. The money supply, which was also down 33 percent in 1933, is just above loans in the graph, and the monetary base is shown at the top.

The Depression was noteworthy for the drastic declines observed in *both* the money supply and credit. The money supply contracted by as much as 33 percent during this period because people withdrew money from their bank accounts to pay down debt, which declined by 54.7 percent. Under ordinary circumstances—that is, when the economy is in Case 1 or 2 with a plentiful supply of private-sector

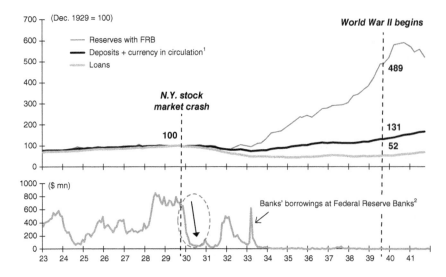

FIGURE 2.15 Same Decoupling of Monetary Aggregates Observed in 1930s

Notes: 1. Deposits = demand deposits adjusted + other time deposits.

2. Only this data series is based on member banks in 101 leading cities. All other series are for all member banks.

Source: Nomura Research Institute, based on data from Board of Governors of the Federal Reserve System (1976), *Banking and Monetary Statistics 1914–1941*, pp. 72–75, pp. 138–163, and pp. 409–413

borrowers—any funds received by banks in the form of debt repayments will quickly be lent out to some other borrower, leaving total deposits in the banking system unchanged. But when the entire private sector becomes a net saver or re-payer of debt, both credit and the money supply end up contracting.

Milton Friedman and other believers in monetary policy argued that the Great Depression of the 1930s got as bad as it did because the Fed did not expand the monetary base quickly enough following the New York stock market crash (in contrast to its post-Lehman behavior, shown in Figure 2.9). The implication is that the depression would not have been as severe as it was if only the Fed had increased the monetary base immediately after the crash.

But the monetary base consists largely of funds commercial banks hold in their accounts with the central bank. This amount, known as bank reserves, consists of funds obtained from depositors and bond holders along with funds borrowed from the central bank.[2]

A closer look at the borrowed reserve data at the bottom of Figure 2.15 indicates that American banks were *paying back* borrowed reserves to the Fed in huge amounts immediately after the stock market crash. The graph indicates that prior to the crash, commercial banks were borrowing heavily from the Fed because the reserves collected from depositors were not sufficient to meet strong demand for borrowings from the (speculating) private sector.

But after the stock market crash, banks *reduced* their borrowings from the Fed by 95 percent between July 1929 and August 1930, from $801 million to just $43 million (see circled area in lower graph of Figure 2.15). This was most likely in response to the post-crash collapse in loan demand, where borrowers were either paying down debt or increasing savings to shore up their balance sheets. That left banks with no reason to hold borrowed reserves. With banks so eager to return those reserves, there was no reason for the Fed to supply more of the same. Friedman's argument that the Fed should have increased reserves in the banking system therefore makes no sense. Ben Bernanke, who remembered Friedman's argument, doubled the monetary base immediately after the collapse of Lehman Brothers, but was still unable to stem the contraction of credit, as shown in Figure 2.12. Bernanke's quick action, in effect, proved that Friedman's earlier argument had no merit.

Monetary policy believers also argued that the post-1933 U.S. recovery was made possible not by President Roosevelt's New Deal policies, which involved government borrowing and spending, but rather by the Fed's monetary easing. They pointed out that while the fiscal-deficit-to-GDP ratio did not grow substantially after 1933, the money supply did (Figure 2.15). But as the author noted in his 2008 book, *The Holy Grail of Macroeconomics*, the money supply, which consists mostly of bank deposits, is a liability of the banking system and can grow only if the asset side of the banking system also increases (this point is also explained in Chapter 8).

Bank deposits (i.e., the money supply) did increase from $23.36 billion in June 1933 to $34.10 billion in June 1936 (Figure 2.16).

---

[2]This point is explained further in Chapter 8, which discusses banking.

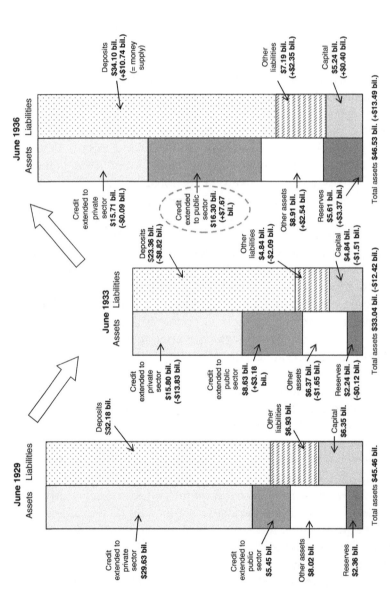

FIGURE 2.16 Reflationists Overlooked Role of Government Borrowing in Enabling Post-1933 Growth in U.S. Money Supply

Source: Richard C. Koo (2008), *The Holy Grail of Macroeconomics: Lessons from Japan's Balance Sheet Recession*, John Wiley & Sons, p. 112, based on data from The Board of Governors of the Federal Reserve System (1976), *Banking and Monetary Statistics 1914–1941*, pp. 72–78

But a look at the asset side of U.S. banks' post-1933 balance sheets clearly indicates that it was only lending to the *public* sector that expanded during this period, from $8.63 billion to $16.30 billion (see circled area in Figure 2.16). And that was a direct result of President Roosevelt's New Deal fiscal policies.

Lending to the private sector actually continued to shrink until 1936 and remained sluggish well beyond that date. In 1939, when World War II began, bank lending in the United States was still 48 percent below its 1929 level (Figure 2.15). The gap between money supply growth and private-sector credit growth was due to government borrowing.

The correct interpretation of the post-1933 U.S. recovery, therefore, is that New Deal–driven government borrowing and spending boosted *both* GDP and the money supply. When the government is the only borrower standing, the effectiveness of monetary policy depends on the size of government's fiscal stimulus. And because GDP increased rapidly, the deficit-to-GDP ratio did not increase as much as the scale of the fiscal stimulus initially suggested.

The U.S. money supply grew after 1933 because the government served as borrower of last resort. With the government now willing to borrow the $100 and possibly more of the savings in the earlier example, the economy was finally able to emerge from its $1,000–$900–$810–$730 deflationary spiral.

Same Decoupling of Monetary Aggregates Seen in Post-1990 Japan

The same decoupling of monetary aggregates was also observed in Japan after its bubble burst in 1990, as shown in Figure 2.17. Here, too, the Bank of Japan's massive injections of reserves to the banking system, especially after 2013, failed to increase lending to the private sector or boost inflation (shown at the bottom of Figure 2.17) because there were simply not enough borrowers. Instead, it was government borrowing that kept the Japanese money supply from shrinking after 1990 amid a rapid contraction in private-sector borrowing.

Bank lending in Japan fell from a bubble peak of 100 to a low of 96 in 2005 as businesses paid down debt to repair their balance sheets (Figure 2.17). But because the government became a huge net borrower during the same period (government line below zero in

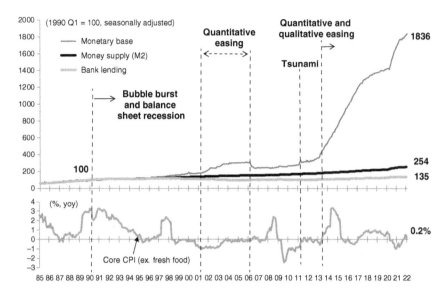

FIGURE 2.17 Massive Liquidity Injections Produced Minimal Increases in Money Supply and Credit (4): Japan

Note: Figures for bank lending are seasonally adjusted by Nomura Research Institute.

Source: Bank of Japan

Figure 2.3), the economy was able to keep both GDP (Figure 2.1) and the money supply (Figure 2.17) above the highs of the bubble years.

The previous examples from the Great Depression, post-1990 Japan, and post-2008 United States and Europe all indicate that monetary policy loses its effectiveness when the private sector is minimizing debt and the traditional relationship between monetary aggregates breaks down. In other words, monetary policy becomes largely impotent when an economy is in Case 3.

Central banks have continuously failed to meet their inflation targets since 2008 because their private sectors are all minimizing debt in response to impaired balance sheets. Continued insistences by a number of central bank governors that further monetary easing will enable them to meet their inflation targets suggests they still do not understand why their models and forecasts have failed. They have failed because their models assume the private sector is maximizing profits and the economies are in Case 1 or 2.

Lender of Last Resort Needed in Case 4

In the immediate aftermath of a bubble collapse, the economy usually finds itself in Case 4, characterized by a disappearance of *both* lenders and borrowers. Lenders stop lending because they provided money to borrowers who participated in the bubble and are now unable to service the debt or are facing insolvency. Banks themselves may be experiencing severe solvency problems if many borrowers are unable to service their debts. Because bank lending is capped at 12.5 times capital, most will not have sufficient capital to continue lending if more than 8 percent of their loans go bad. That could lead to a highly debilitating credit crunch in which banks refuse to lend or roll over loans.

When many banks find themselves confronting nonperforming loan (NPL) problems at the same time, mutual distrust among the banks can also lead to a dysfunctional interbank market, often referred to as a *financial crisis*. In such cases, the central bank must act as lender of last resort to ensure the continued functioning of the settlement system. These issues are more fully explained in Chapter 8, which discusses banking crises.

In the immediate aftermath of the global financial crisis (GFC), when most advanced economies were in Case 4, all of the major central banks correctly served as lenders of last resort to keep settlement systems functioning. Governments also injected capital into the banks and took other measures that succeeded in restoring the normal workings of the financial system within about two years of the Lehman collapse. In other words, monetary policy is both effective and essential when the problem lies with the lenders. But when the problem is on the borrower side, monetary policy is largely ineffective in stimulating the economy, as previously described.

Government Must Act as Borrower of Last Resort in Cases 3 and 4

Once the bubble bursts and households and businesses find themselves facing a debt overhang, no amount of monetary easing by the central bank will persuade them to resume borrowing until their balance sheets are fully repaired. The economy then falls into the

$1,000–$900–$810–$730 deflationary spiral that is described in Chapter 1 because an absence of borrowers prevents saved and deleveraged funds from re-entering the economy's income stream.

When private-sector borrowers disappear and monetary policy stops working, the correct way to prevent a deflationary spiral is for the government to borrow and spend the excess savings of the private sector ($100 in the preceding example). In other words, the government should mobilize fiscal policy and serve as *borrower of last resort* when the economy is in Case 3 or 4.

If the government borrows and spends the $100 left in the financial sector in the earlier example, total expenditures will amount to $900 plus $100, or $1,000, and the economy will move on. Since private-sector income is largely unchanged at $1,000, households and businesses can use current income to service debt or rebuild savings. Government borrowing will also keep the money supply from shrinking because it allows deleveraged funds to re-enter the economy via government borrowing and spending. In other words, it prevents the asset side of bank balance sheets from shrinking, as exemplified by government borrowings between 1933 and 1936 (Figure 2.16). This policy should continue until the private sector is ready to borrow again.

Any attempt by the government to reduce budget deficits when the economy is in Case 3 or 4 risks restarting the deflationary spiral. Such risks actually materialized in Japan in 1997 (this is discussed later in the context of Figure 2.21) and in the Eurozone in 2010 (see Chapter 7).

In Case 3, Bond Market Invites Government to Borrow

More government borrowing means a larger public debt and higher deficits. That makes many people uncomfortable, since they believe that increasing the public debt is a bad thing. But the bond market in Case 3 economies will *encourage* the government to act as borrower of last resort by pushing government bond yields down to exceptionally low levels. This happens because in a balance sheet recession (1) the government is the only remaining borrower and (2) the financial sector is awash with funds from private-sector deleveraging, newly generated household savings, and central bank monetary accommodation.

Fund managers at institutional investors such as life insurers and pension funds who must earn a return but are not allowed to take on excessive foreign exchange risk or principal risk (i.e., they cannot invest all their money in stocks or foreign-currency assets) have little choice but to buy government bonds once they have exhausted their risk limits on stocks and foreign assets. This is because the government is the only borrower issuing high-quality fixed income assets denominated in the domestic currency. Fund managers' rush into government debt then pushes government bond yields down to unusually low levels, as observed in Japan after 1990 and in the West after 2008.[3]

Exceptionally low government bond yields were first observed in post-1990 Japan at a time when the country's budget deficit and public debt were skyrocketing. By 1997, Japan's public debt surpassed 100 percent of GDP, yet its 10-year bond yield had fallen to 1.7 percent. By 2009, the public debt had reached 200 percent of GDP, but the 10-year bond yield had declined to 1.34 percent. Just before the Bank of Japan unveiled the policy of quantitative and qualitative easing (QQE) in April 2013, the 10-year yield had slid to 0.735 percent even as the public debt rose to 230 percent of GDP. The same drastic decline in bond yields has also been observed in Western economies since 2008.

The Self-Corrective Mechanism of Economies in Balance Sheet Recessions

These exceptionally low bond yields, which encourage the government to act as borrower of last resort, are the manifestation of the *self-corrective mechanism* of economies in balance sheet recessions (and in Cases 3 and 4 in general). This mechanism is self-corrective in two senses.

First, when the private sector is generating excess savings in spite of zero or negative interest rates, the funds required to finance fiscal stimulus to stabilize the economy (the $100) are already sitting in the

---

[3] Unfortunately, this yield-lowering mechanism does not always function in the Eurozone because the 19 government bond markets use the same currency. The nature of this Eurozone-specific problem and its solution are discussed in Chapter 7.

financial sector waiting for a borrower. Since those funds will flow into bonds issued by the last borrower standing—the government—there is no need for the central bank or any other entity to worry about financing government deficits. In other words, the financing of government deficits should not be a problem when the economy is in Case 3.

Second, this mechanism is self-corrective in the sense that the bond market will encourage the government to borrow by lowering the cost of borrowing to unusually low levels. These ultra-low yields are a message to the government that, if there is any social infrastructure needed for the future, *now* is the time to build it because the cost of financing will never be lower. It may even be that some social infrastructure projects will have a social rate of return that is higher than the super-low yields on government bonds (this point is pursued further in Chapter 4).

If the government heeds the bond market's message and acts as borrower of last resort, not only will it prop up the economy and money supply, but it will also minimize the burden on future taxpayers by locking in low financing costs for necessary infrastructure projects.

This scenario of drastic declines in government bond yields when budget deficits are skyrocketing is unthinkable in textbook economics, which assumes the private sector is always maximizing profits and the economy is in Case 1 or 2. The assumption that the private sector is maximizing profits is crucial because for that to be true, the private sector must (1) have a clean balance sheet and (2) enjoy an abundance of attractive domestic investment opportunities. If those two conditions are met, private-sector borrowers will have to compete with public-sector borrowers for a limited pool of savings, and interest rates will be much higher.

But neither of these conditions is satisfied in most advanced countries today. Instead, the private sector is often minimizing debt because of post-bubble balance sheet problems, and many businesses are investing in emerging economies because they offer higher returns on capital. Low government bond yields are natural when an economy is in Case 3 because fund managers are unable to find any private-sector borrowers.

Unfortunately, most macroeconomic models developed up to now did not contain a financial sector. These models also assumed that the private sector was always maximizing profits. As a result, they failed to capture the difficulty fund managers face in find-ing borrowers when the economy is in Case 3 or 4. That, in turn, exaggerated economists' fears that large government deficits would *always* result in soaring bond yields and a fiscal crisis.

With the bond market making it possible for governments to bor-row at exceptionally low rates in Cases 3 and 4, the real challenge for policy makers is to ensure that (1) all saved funds are borrowed and spent and that (2) this policy is maintained until the private sector is ready to borrow again. In other words, the fiscal stimulus must be both substantial and sustained.

The stimulus must be continued for an extended period of time because even after businesses and households have finished repair-ing their balance sheets, some may be so traumatized by years of painful deleveraging that they may never borrow again. Indeed, most Americans who lived through the Great Depression never borrowed again because of this kind of trauma. This shows how serious and long-lasting the problem of deleveraging can be, and how strong the government's commitment must be to sustain the economy in Case 3.

G20 Reverses Course at 2010 Toronto Summit

In November 2008, just two months after Lehman Brothers went under, the G20 countries agreed at an emergency meeting held in Washington, D.C., to implement coordinated fiscal stimulus, effec-tively agreeing to act as borrowers and spenders of last resort. That decision kept the world economy from falling immediately into a deflationary spiral.

However, the fiscal orthodoxy of national authorities who lacked an understanding of balance sheet recessions reasserted itself at the June 2010 Toronto G20 meeting, where members agreed to reduce deficits by one-half over the next three years even though the private sector was still in the midst of massive deleveraging and its balance sheet was nowhere near healthy. This may have happened because the host, Canada, was the only country whose housing bubble had not burst yet and whose economy was in Case 1. As can be seen in Figure 1.1, Canada is the only nation where the private sector has been running a financial deficit since 2008. In other words, reducing the fis-cal deficit was the right thing to do for Canada and for Canada alone.

The summit caused a sudden loss of global economic momentum that unnecessarily prolonged the recession in most parts of the world. After 2010, countries that understood the danger of balance sheet recessions did well, while those that did not suffered badly.

Four Central Banks' Track Records

This disparity of awareness became very clear as the United States, the United Kingdom, Japan, and Europe all implemented an unconventional monetary easing policy known as quantitative easing (QE). In QE, the central bank continually injects reserves into the banking system by purchasing assets held by the private sector. The actions of the central banks in these economies produced a massive expansion of the monetary base, as shown in Figures 2.12 to 2.14. But the authorities in these countries seem to have a very different understanding of how these policies work, leading to very different outcomes. In particular, there has been much discussion in Europe as to why the United States is doing so much better than the Eurozone.[4]

When most people hear the term *quantitative easing*, they think of Professor Milton Friedman's aforementioned assertion that inflation is "everywhere and always a monetary phenomenon," the implication being that the central bank—which is responsible for monetary policy—should be able to control the inflation rate by increasing or decreasing the monetary base.

According to this view, inflation can always be generated if the central bank simply runs the printing presses and creates enough money. Professor Paul Krugman emphasized this point repeatedly in a two-hour debate with the author that was published in the November 1999 issue of *Bungeishunjū*, a leading monthly magazine in Japan.[5] Central bank heads in post-2008 Japan, the United Kingdom, and Europe also declared that QE would increase lending

---

[4] Greenwood, John (2016), "Successful Central Banks Focus on Greater Purchasing," *Financial Times*, May 31, 2016.
[5] Koo, Richard and Krugman, Paul (1999), "Gekitotsu Taidan: Nihon Keizai Endaka wa Akuka" ("Big Debate on Japan's Economy: Is Strong Yen a Bad Thing?"), *Bungeishunjū*, November 1999, edited by Yasuhara Ishizawa, pp. 130–143.

and expand the money supply, thereby making it possible to reach their inflation targets.

Paul Fisher, an official at the Bank of England (BOE) when it launched its version of QE on March 6, 2009, stated explicitly that the policy was intended to produce an economic recovery by boosting bank lending and enlarging the money supply.[6] Bank of Japan Governor Haruhiko Kuroda declared in his first speech as governor on April 12, 2013, that QE would stimulate lending and allow the Bank to reach its two-percent inflation target in two years.[7] Deputy Governor Kikuo Iwata was so confident in his belief that inflation is a monetary phenomenon[8] that he declared he would resign if the bank failed to achieve its inflation target within two years. Similarly, ECB President Mario Draghi, who unveiled a QE policy for the Eurozone on January 22, 2015, argued that this policy would "support money supply and credit growth, and thereby contribute to a return of inflation rates toward 2%."[9]

QE Did Not Accelerate Money Supply Growth in Japan, the United Kingdom, or Europe

All of these countries, however, have been in severe balance sheet recessions since their asset bubbles burst in 2008 (1990 in the case of Japan). Even though a central bank can always inject as much liquidity into the banking sector as it wants via QE, banks must lend that money for it to enter the real economy. They cannot give it away since it belongs to depositors. But if the private sector as a group is deleveraging, an absence of borrowers will prevent that

---

[6] Oakley, David (2009), "A Bold Bid to Revive Lending," *Financial Times*, March 7, 2009. https://next.ft.com/content/9b3fd930-0a90-11de-95ed-0000 779fd2ac.

[7] Kuroda, Haruhiko (2013), "Quantitative and Qualitative Monetary Easing," speech at a meeting held by Yomiuri International Economic Society in Tokyo, April 12, 2013.

[8] Iwata, Kikuo (2001), *Defure no Keizaigaku* (*The Economics of Deflation*), Tokyo: Toyokeizai.

[9] Draghi, Mario (2015), "Introductory Statement to the Press Conference (with Q&A)," ECB press conference in Frankfurt am Main, January 22, 2015.

liquidity from entering the real economy. As a result, the liquidity remains trapped within the financial system, leaving the central bank with no way to expand the amount of money circulating in the real economy.[10] Growth in both the money supply and bank lending in all of these countries has therefore been modest at best, as indicated in Figures 2.12 to 2.14 and 2.17.

In the United Kingdom, which Paul Fisher boldly declared would not repeat "Japan's mistakes," the BOE expanded the monetary base by an enormous 608 percent from September 2008 to February 2020. But lending remained 1 percent below the pre-Lehman period, and the nation's economy continued to seesaw between periods of no inflation and outright deflation (Figure 2.14), much like Japan. The U.K. inflation rate did pick up after the 2016 Brexit vote, but that was due largely to the sharp fall in the value of the pound following the vote. In the Eurozone, Mario Draghi expanded the monetary base by 154 percent from the time he introduced QE in January 2015 to just before the pandemic hit in February 2020, but bank lending grew only 11.1 percent, or about 2.1 percent per year, and the inflation rate remained close to zero (Figure 2.13).

In Japan, Haruhiko Kuroda has increased the monetary base by 277 percent since introducing QQE in April 2013, but bank lending had grown by just 21 percent as of February 2020, which represents zero acceleration from the era of his predecessor, Masaaki Shirakawa. This can be seen in Figure 2.18 as a continuous straight line for both credit and the money supply before and after the change in governorship. Zero acceleration means the massive expansion of

---

[10] Technically, a central bank can increase the money supply by buying financial assets directly from nonbank private entities. However, such actions will only increase the savings component of the money supply since the nonbank entity selling the assets to the central bank was presumably holding those assets as a form of savings. Changing the form of that savings from, say, government bonds to bank deposits is unlikely to prompt that entity to increase consumption. Accordingly, even if the money supply increases due to such purchases by the central bank, the growth will not add to GDP or stoke inflationary pressures. In contrast, if the central bank buys cars and cameras from the nonbank private sector, such purchases will increase the transaction component of the money supply and thereby boost GDP. But the public purchase of goods and services is usually considered to lie within the realm of fiscal policy, not monetary policy.

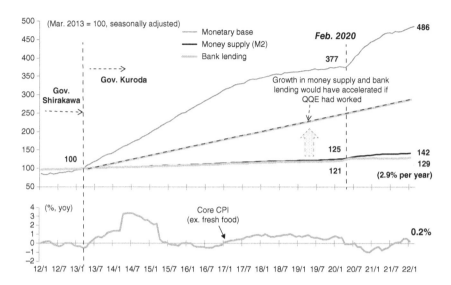

FIGURE 2.18 No Acceleration of Private-Sector Credit or Money Supply Growth after BOJ's QQE

Note: Figures for bank lending are seasonally adjusted by Nomura Research Institute.

Sources: Bank of Japan and Ministry of Internal Affairs and Communications

the monetary base under Kuroda has had no impact on the real economy, and the inflation rate remains anchored around zero.

These three examples should help to demonstrate that the argument that inflation is everywhere and always a monetary phenomenon may be valid when there is strong private-sector demand for funds (Cases 1 and 2), but is basically irrelevant when the private sector refuses to borrow despite zero or even negative interest rates (Cases 3 and 4). While it can be argued that *realized* inflation is often a monetary phenomenon, it is simply not the case that the central bank can always create inflation by expanding the money supply.

Fed Officials Did Not Pledge to Raise Inflation by Expanding Money Supply

In contrast to the three central banks previously noted, Fed officials, including former chairs Ben Bernanke and Janet Yellen, said something very different when they introduced QE. While they, too, were among the pioneers of quantitative easing, they have never—to the author's knowledge, at least—claimed they would stimulate inflation by enlarging the money supply. On the contrary, Bernanke made the opposite point in an article in the November 4, 2010, *Washington Post* titled, "What the Fed Did and Why: Supporting the Recovery and Sustaining Price Stability."[11] The article sought to explain QE2, which was intended to stimulate the economy, as opposed to QE1, which was originally framed as a "lender of last resort" injection of reserves in response to the financial crisis triggered by the Lehman bankruptcy. The liquidity provided by QE1, however, was deliberately left in the market even after the crisis subsided in the hope that it would help fuel a recovery.

Unlike his counterparts at the other three central banks, Bernanke did not mention increasing the money supply even once in this article. Instead he said, "Our earlier use of this policy approach had little effect on the amount of currency in circulation or on other broad measures of the money supply, such as bank deposits. Nor did it result in higher inflation." In effect, he is saying that all the liquidity supplied under QE1 had *not* increased the money supply, which is why QE2 would *not* lead to inflation. And in the event, neither QE2 nor the QE3 that followed generated inflation.

Bernanke Rescued the U.S. Economy with Policy that Clashed with His Teacher's Views

Bernanke understood that the United States was in a balance sheet recession by the time QE2 was introduced in 2011. Flow-of-funds data compiled by the Fed when QE2 was introduced showed the U.S. private sector was saving close to 8 percent of GDP in spite of zero interest rates. Furthermore, a significant portion of that savings was taking the form of debt repayment, as indicated by the 9 percent drop in lending from 2008 to 2011 shown in Figure 2.12. This means that funds returning to the banking system as debt was paid down

---

[11]Bernanke, Ben S. (2010), "What the Fed Did and Why: Supporting the Recovery and Sustaining Price Stability," *Washington Post*, November 4, 2010. http://www.washingtonpost.com/wp-dyn/content/article/2010/11/03/AR2010110307372.html.

were unable to leave it because of a lack of borrowers. Because U.S. businesses and households were saving so much, the money multiplier[12] for the private sector was negative at the margin. In other words, the U.S. money supply would have contracted if no other borrower had emerged to take up the slack.

The U.S. money supply actually shrank by 33 percent during the Great Depression (1929–1933) after the New York stock market crashed (Figure 2.15) as the private sector collectively paid down debt and no one else was borrowing. Under such circumstances, the only way to prevent a contraction in GDP and the money supply is for the government to borrow and spend.

Bernanke and Yellen both understood this, and they used the expression "fiscal cliff" to warn Congress about the danger posed by fiscal consolidation, which had the support of the Republicans and many orthodox economists. The extent of Bernanke's concerns about fiscal consolidation can be gleaned from a press conference on April 25, 2012, when he was asked what the Fed would do if Congress pushed the U.S. economy off the fiscal cliff. He responded, "There is . . . absolutely no chance that the Federal Reserve could or would have any ability whatsoever to offset that effect on the economy."[13] Bernanke clearly understood that the Fed's monetary policy not only could not offset the negative impact of fiscal consolidation, but would also lose its effectiveness if the government refused to act as borrower of last resort.

Even though the United States came frighteningly close to falling off the fiscal cliff on a number of occasions that included government shutdowns, sequesters, and debt-ceiling debates (all initiated by fiscal hawks in the Republican Party), it ultimately managed to avoid that outcome thanks to the efforts of officials at the Fed and the Obama administration. That is why the post-2008 U.S. economy has done so much better than that of Europe, where nearly every country fell off the fiscal cliff.

Bernanke had previously stated that he was a direct disciple of Milton Friedman, who was stridently opposed to fiscal stimulus. And

---

[12] This term is explained in Chapter 8.

[13] Board of Governors of the Federal Reserve System (2012), "Transcript of Chairman Bernanke's Press Conference," Washington, D.C., April 25, 2012.

he was still issuing warnings on the size of fiscal deficit in mid-2009.[14] But in the end, he rescued the U.S. economy from its worst-ever postwar economic crisis by supporting a policy that ran contrary to the views of his teacher. In short, he understood that an economy in a balance sheet recession is doomed unless the government acts as borrower of last resort. He knew that the impact of QE is limited to the so-called portfolio rebalancing effect,[15] which is far from sufficient to offset the headwinds from both private- and public-sector deleveraging. He recognized that when the private sector is not borrowing money, the effectiveness of monetary policy is dependent on the last borrower standing, that is, the government. And he had the courage to change his stance. The U.S. economy had done better precisely because Bernanke and Yellen prevented the government from abdicating its responsibility to serve as borrower of last resort.

Other Central Banks Supported Fiscal Austerity

The warnings about the fiscal cliff set the Fed apart from its counterparts in Japan, the United Kingdom, and Europe. In the United Kingdom, then-BOE Governor Mervyn King publicly supported David Cameron's draconian fiscal austerity measures, arguing that the central bank's QE policy would provide the necessary support for the British economy. At the time, the U.K. private sector was saving a full 6 percent of GDP[16] (Figure 2.19) when interest rates were at their lowest levels in 300 years. That judgment by the BOE led to the disastrous performance of the U.K. economy during the first two years of the Cameron administration and prompted George Osborne,

---

[14] Guha, Krishna (2009), "Bernanke Warns on Deficits," *The Financial Times*, Asian edition, June 4, 2009.

[15] This effect refers to the support the economy receives from higher asset prices brought about by central bank purchases of assets under quantitative easing.

[16] This number was originally reported as 9 percent, but a major revision was made to U.K. flow-of-funds data nine years later in 2017. Because pre-2017 policy makers and market participants made decisions based on the original data series, one has to be careful when using the revised data to understand the rationale behind their decisions.

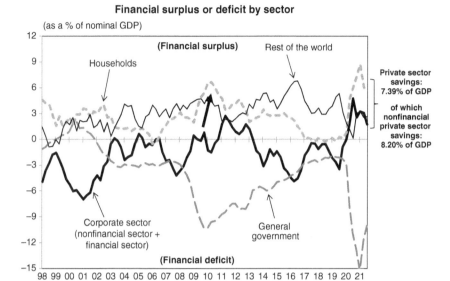

FIGURE 2.19 U.K. Private Savings Surged after 2008

Notes: All entries are four-quarter moving averages. For the latest figures, four-quarter averages ending with 2021 Q3 are used.

Source: Office for National Statistics, U.K.

Cameron's Chancellor of the Exchequer, to ask a Canadian to head the British central bank.

BOJ Governor Haruhiko Kuroda also argued strongly in favor of hiking the consumption tax rate in 2014, believing a Japanese economy supported by his quantitative easing regime would be strong enough to withstand the shock of fiscal consolidation. This was in spite of the fact that the Japanese private sector was saving 6.11 percent of GDP at a time of zero interest rates (Figure 2.3). The tax hike, carried out in April 2014, threw the Japanese economy back into recession, and global enthusiasm for Abenomics, a three-pronged policy to pull the Japanese economy out of its doldrums, evaporated completely thereafter. Another, somewhat smaller, tax hike in October 2019 also helped push the economy back into recession.

European Central Bank (ECB) President Mario Draghi earnestly advised member governments to meet the fiscal austerity target imposed by the Growth and Stability Pact at each of his press conferences, even though his own inflation forecasts were revised downward nearly every time they were updated. He seemed completely oblivious to the danger posed by fiscal austerity while the Eurozone private sector continued to save an average of 5 percent of GDP after 2008 despite zero or even negative interest rates (Figure 2.11).

These repeated failures suggest that these central bankers lacked a correct model of their economies. Not only did they not realize the extent to which the private sector was saving (or minimizing debt), but they also encouraged their governments to abdicate their role as borrower of last resort. The United States did better than the rest not because it had a better version of QE, but because it was the only country with a central bank that openly opposed fiscal austerity.

People in Real Economy Understand that QE Is Meaningless

How do people outside the rarefied world of central banking view QE? Households and businesses in the real economies of Japan, the United States, the United Kingdom, and Europe are either in the process of repairing their balance sheets or are still suffering from the aftereffects of debt trauma. Consequently, QE has not prompted a significant change in their behavior. If it had, they would have resumed borrowing at these historically low interest rates, producing a measurable pickup in both bank lending and money supply growth.

This means households and businesses facing balance sheet problems remain unimpressed by the argument made by many economists and the three central bankers previously mentioned—namely, that there will always be willing borrowers as long as real interest rates are lowered far enough. They know that such arguments do not apply to them or to anyone else facing similar balance sheet problems. And those people tend to represent a large portion of society following the collapse of a nationwide asset bubble.

Market Participants Still Assume Economy Is in Case 1 or 2

Participants in the foreign exchange and equity markets, however, hold a different view. Indeed, many of them continue to act based on the assumption that the global economy is still in the textbook world of Cases 1 and 2. Evidence of this is offered by the fact that every time a central bank announces another round of QE, it sells that country's currency and buys its equities. The market participants do so on the assumption that the money supply will grow far faster in QE countries than in non-QE countries, and that the currency of a country with a rapidly expanding money supply and a corresponding pickup in inflation will decline in value against that of a country where the money supply and inflation rate are not growing so quickly.

When the United States and United Kingdom implemented QE policies after the GFC, for example, the dollar fell 30 percent against the Japanese yen and the pound plunged 40 percent, both reaching historical lows (Figure 2.20, left graph). In effect, foreign exchange market participants assumed that money supply growth in the United States and United Kingdom would massively outpace money supply growth in Japan, and that the vastly increased supply of dollars and pounds would weaken their exchange rates versus the yen.

When Japan implemented its own version of QE four years later, the yen dropped 35 percent against the dollar and the pound (Figure 2.20, right graph), also on the assumption that money supply

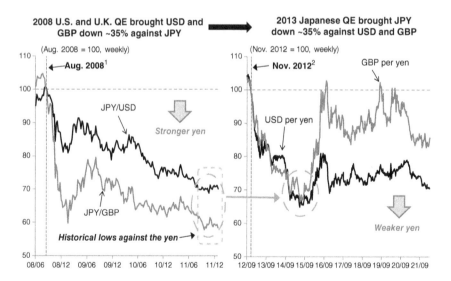

FIGURE 2.20 Currency Market Participants Still Believe in Textbook World

Notes: 1. One month before Lehman failed.

2. One month before Abenomics was launched.

Source: Nomura Research Institute, based on Nikkei data

growth would diverge significantly as a result of Japanese QE. The euro fell sharply due to the same logic when Draghi announced that the ECB was ready to introduce QE.

In reality, however, money supply and credit growth did not accelerate meaningfully in *any* of the nations implementing QE, as demonstrated by Figures 2.12, 2.13, 2.14, and 2.17. Although interest rate differentials did widen somewhat following QE, they were nowhere near large enough to justify 30- to 40-percent movements in exchange rates.

Equity prices and exchange rates moved so dramatically each time another round of QE was announced because many market participants continued to act based on mistaken textbook views. The resulting movements in stock prices and exchange rates, in turn, affected the behavior of households and businesses in these countries and enabled QE proponents to claim that their policies had worked.

Bernanke reportedly said that QE does not work in theory, but it does work in practice. He was probably referring to the behavior of market participants who continue to hold a textbook view of the world.

More recently, however, markets—and especially the foreign exchange market—have become much less sensitive to monetary policy actions by central banks. For example, the Fed raised its policy rate nine times from 2015 to 2018 while the BOJ and ECB left their rates unchanged. In spite of such large, dollar-favoring increases in the interest rate differential, the yen-dollar rate hardly moved, at least until the spike in energy prices starting in late 2021. Although this lack of response was attributable in large part to the arrival of the Trump administration, as is described in Chapter 9, market participants' realization that monetary policy was losing its effectiveness also played a role. And they probably came to that conclusion by observing that credit growth had not picked up in any of the countries that implemented QE.

The CFA Institute, which grants the Chartered Financial Analyst credential and is the most influential certification body for investment professionals around the world, also recognized the importance of the concept of balance sheet recessions early on, and it has featured the author in many of its key educational events around the world since 2010. As more investment professionals become aware of the economic malady called a balance sheet recession, QE's influence on the market is likely to diminish further.

Fiscal Policy's Track Record

If the track record of monetary policy in balance sheet recessions is clear, so is that of fiscal policy. As previously noted, the first country to experience a balance sheet recession after the Great Depression was post-1990 Japan. When the asset bubble burst, commercial real estate prices fell 87 percent nationwide, touching levels last seen in 1973. And since real estate was always used as collateral for borrowing money in Japan, the collapse of land prices devastated private-sector balance sheets, causing the economy to implode.

The Liberal Democratic Party (LDP) government was quick to administer fiscal stimulus in an attempt to stop the collapse. But this was not because officials understood the horrors and mechanics of balance sheet recessions, but rather because they thought that government spending would "prime the pump" and get the economy moving again.

The economy responded positively each time fiscal stimulus was implemented, but then lost momentum as soon as it was removed. The stimulus failed to "prime the pump" because, after an 87-percent decline in real estate values, the private sector required a decade or more of deleveraging to restore its financial health, and businesses and households were using every yen that could be spared to pay down debt. Because the concept of balance sheet recessions had yet to be discovered by the economics profession, policy makers did not realize that they were faced with a 10-year problem instead of a typical business-cycle downturn lasting at most a year or two.

The orthodox fiscal hawks who dominated the press and academia in Japan also tried to stop fiscal stimulus at every step of the way, arguing that large deficits would soon lead to skyrocketing interest rates and a fiscal crisis. These hawks forced politicians to cut stimulus as soon as the economy showed signs of life, prompting another downturn. The resulting on-again, off-again fiscal stimulus did not imbue the public with confidence in the government's handling of the economy. Fortunately, the LDP had enough pork-barrel politicians to keep a minimum level of stimulus in place, and as a result Japanese GDP never once fell below its bubble-era highs (Figure 2.1). Nor did the Japanese unemployment rate ever exceed 5.5 percent.

That was a monumental achievement in view of the fact that the Japanese private sector was saving an average of 8 percent of GDP from 1995 to 2005, and the Japanese lost three times as much wealth when the bubble burst (as a share of GDP) as the United States did during the Great Depression, when nominal gross national product (GNP) plunged 46 percent.

But in 1997, seven years into the recession, the International Monetary Fund (IMF) and Organization of Economic Co-operation and Development (OECD)—organizations that understood nothing about balance sheet recessions—started pressuring Japan to cut its fiscal deficit by arguing that the population was aging and that all those well-publicized roads and bridges "to nowhere" would have dire economic consequences. These institutions completely failed to understand that without government spending on those roads and bridges, the Japanese economy would have followed the trajectory of the U.S. economy after 1929.

Unfortunately, the Hashimoto administration listened to them and embarked on a fiscal austerity program amounting to 3 percent of GDP, or ¥15 trillion, in April 1997. The resultant tax hikes and spending cuts were an utter disaster for both the economy and the banking system. Japan's GDP contracted for five consecutive quarters and Japanese banks, which successfully endured the first seven years of the recession, finally threw in the towel in late 1997, resulting in a full-blown banking crisis (this topic is covered in Chapter 8).

The deficit, instead of shrinking by ¥15 trillion, actually *increased* by ¥16 trillion, or 72 percent, as shown by the first set of arrows in Figure 2.21. It took the country 10 years to bring the deficit back to where it had been in 1996, and during that time the public debt increased by nearly ¥100 trillion.

Hashimoto realized his mistake by December 1997 and started to reverse the direction of fiscal policy while injecting capital into the banking system to address the nationwide credit crunch. The Obuchi and Mori administrations that followed also implemented enough fiscal stimulus to keep the economy from contracting, but fiscal orthodoxy made a comeback with the Koizumi administration and the first Abe cabinet, and the economy stagnated again.

In particular, it was Koizumi's insistence that the deficit should be capped at ¥30 trillion, or 6 percent of Japan's GDP, when the private sector was saving more than that amount that led to economic stagnation. Tax receipts fell and the deficit actually increased, as indicated by the second set of arrows in Figure 2.21. That is why his administration was never able to deliver on its pledge to keep the deficit below ¥30 trillion.

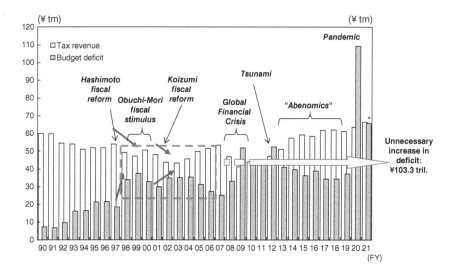

FIGURE 2.21 Japan's Fall from Fiscal Cliff in 1997 and 2001 Weakened the Economy, Reduced Tax Revenues, and *Increased* Deficit

Notes: Latest figures (*) are estimated by Ministry of Finance (MOF). From FY2012, figures include reconstruction taxes and bonds.

Source: Ministry of Finance, Japan

Following the short-lived Abe and Fukuda governments, Prime Minister Taro Aso, who understood the importance of deficit spending during a balance sheet recession, administered four rounds of fiscal stimulus to combat the GFC. While that was extremely helpful, he had the misfortune to be in power when the Lehman crisis erupted, and the ruling Liberal Democratic Party (LDP) was voted out of office in 2009. The Democratic Party of Japan (DPJ) administrations that followed had learned nothing from the 1997 Hashimoto disaster or the 2001 Koizumi failure, and the economy languished again under fiscal orthodoxy.

When the LDP returned to power in 2012, Taro Aso, now serving as finance minister, inserted fiscal stimulus as the second of the three "arrows" of Abenomics to get the economy moving again. However, even this effort was torpedoed by the return of fiscal orthodoxy as many pushed for a consumption tax hike in 2014 and again in 2019, both of which led to a significant loss of forward economic momentum.

In the United States, Lawrence Summers, the Obama administration's first National Economic Council (NEC) chairman, initially thought a large jolt of fiscal stimulus would be enough to prime the economy's pump, much like Japanese officials 18 years earlier. He talked about the "three Ts" of fiscal stimulus, saying it should be timely, targeted, and temporary. But he soon had a change of heart and began pushing for the "three Ss," saying fiscal stimulus actually needed to be speedy, sustained, and substantial.[17] He also indicated that the problem facing the United States was the same problem Japan had confronted 18 years earlier.

At the Fed, Chair Bernanke also realized within the first two years of the Lehman crisis that the economy was suffering from a balance sheet recession and that fiscal stimulus was absolutely essential, as noted earlier. He and his Vice Chair Yellen then went on to warn Congress about the dangers of falling off the fiscal cliff.

Although the Fed and the Obama administration had to fight Congressional fiscal orthodoxy in the form of government shutdowns, debt ceiling debates, and the sequester, they managed to keep the U.S. economy away from the fiscal cliff, which is why it has done better than the rest of the developed world. In fact, the United States is the only advanced country that managed to avoid the fiscal cliff by putting into practice the lessons of Japan's disastrous experiment in premature fiscal consolidation in 1997. It should be noted that Lawrence Summers, as U.S. Treasury Secretary, was one of the very few who, together with the author, publicly argued against the fiscal austerity demanded of Japan by the IMF and OECD in 1997.

In the United Kingdom, Prime Minister Gordon Brown was aware of the dangers of a balance sheet recession and administered a large fiscal stimulus as soon as the Lehman crisis erupted. That kept the U.K. economy going, but he still lost the next election to David Cameron in a series of events reminiscent of what happened to Taro Aso in Japan. As noted earlier, Cameron received BOE Governor Mervyn King's blessing to implement austerity policies, believing the bank's monetary easing would be enough to keep the economy from

---

[17] Summers, Lawrence, H. (2009), "Rescuing and Rebuilding the U.S. Economy: A Progress Report," remarks at the Peterson Institute for International Economics on July 17, 2009. https://piie.com/commentary/speeches-papers/rescuing-and-rebuilding-us-economy-progress-report.

contracting. The resulting recession helped trigger nationwide riots in August 2011 and prompted Cameron to jettison austerity in favor of a more moderate fiscal policy.

The United Kingdom, however, was helped by the crisis in the Eurozone because it prompted many on the Continent to shift funds to the United Kingdom. As a result, London and other parts of the United Kingdom capable of attracting foreign capital have done well, while the rest of the country continues to struggle. This can be seen from the fact that, in spite of massive numbers of foreign shoppers and the continued appreciation of London real estate prices—at least before COVID-19—the general inflation rate in the United Kingdom fell to zero by 2015 (Figure 2.14, bottom graph), echoing the situation in Japan, until the Brexit vote sent the pound sharply lower.

Chapter 7 is devoted entirely to the Eurozone economies' continuing problems. For now, suffice it to say that the Stability and Growth Pact, which created the euro, prohibited member governments from running fiscal deficits in excess of 3 percent of GDP *regardless* of the amount of savings generated in the private sector. That constraint prevented the region from properly addressing balance sheet recessions at a time when its private sector has been saving an average of 5 percent of GDP, as noted in Figure 1.1.

For example, Spain's private sector has been saving an average of 7.6 percent of GDP since the Lehman crisis (Figure 1.1), but its government was allowed to borrow only 3 percent out of the 7.6 percent, leaving a deflationary gap equivalent to 4.6 percent of GDP. That gap led to the collapse of the Spanish economy and sent unemployment soaring to 26 percent in 2012. Many other Eurozone countries have suffered for the same reason. The long stagnation experienced by Eurozone economies is testimony to that fact.

The preceding discussion indicates that when private-sector borrowers disappear and the economy is in Case 3, fiscal stimulus is absolutely essential to keep the economy from spiraling downward. Every time fiscal stimulus was implemented, the economy improved, and every time it was removed, the economy collapsed. The experiences of the United States, the United Kingdom, Japan, and Europe also underline the political difficulty of maintaining fiscal stimulus in a democracy during peacetime, a topic that is discussed further in Chapter 10.

The Difficulty of Measuring Fiscal Multiplier during Balance Sheet Recessions

It has long been said in the economics profession that fiscal policy has a low multiplier effect. Elasticities and multipliers refer to the amount of impact a given policy is likely to have on the economy. For example, if a dollar of government spending increases GDP by 1.4 dollars over a given time period, the fiscal multiplier would be 1.4.

The post-2008 experiences previously discussed indicate that, unlike in Cases 1 and 2, where fiscal stimulus can crowd out private-sector investments and end up having a low multiplier effect, the fiscal multiplier in Cases 3 and 4 tends to be very large. The fact that economies in Cases 3 and 4 responded so strongly to fiscal stimulus—or the lack thereof—is testimony to a high multiplier. This also means that the fiscal multiplier is not a constant: it varies greatly depending on whether the economy is in Cases 1 and 2 or Cases 3 and 4.

However, there are two difficulties in accurately measuring the fiscal multiplier in Cases 3 and 4. The first is that the measurement must be made from where the economy would have been *in the absence* of fiscal stimulus. But it is difficult to estimate the counterfactual path for GDP along the $1,000–$900–$810–$730 deflationary spiral. This is because, except for the first three years of the Great Depression, there are no statistical examples of past balance sheet recessions *without* fiscal stimulus that would allow economists to simulate a counterfactual path for GDP.

In other words, it might be possible to come up with a reasonable estimate of a counterfactual GDP if there were numerous historical examples of balance sheet recessions without fiscal stimulus to establish how much GDP was likely to be lost over a certain number of years after a given amount of wealth was destroyed in a bubble collapse. Once that counterfactual GDP is obtained, it is subtracted from the actual GDP. The difference is then divided by the actual amount of fiscal stimulus to derive the correct fiscal multiplier. Unfortunately, there are no data with which to estimate counterfactual GDP.

But without a good estimate of counterfactual GDP, the policy debate will be fundamentally flawed. For example, most economists both inside and outside Japan have argued that the nation's fiscal multiplier is low because GDP went nowhere despite ¥460 trillion in fiscal stimulus between 1990 and 2005. They then argued that the money must have been spent on useless projects such as roads and bridges "to nowhere." Indeed, these were the arguments the IMF and OECD used to push Japan into its disastrous 1997 experiment with fiscal austerity, as noted earlier.

Their argument that the fiscal multiplier is low necessarily implies that fiscal austerity, the opposite of fiscal stimulus, will *also* have minimal adverse impact on the economy. But the Japanese economy collapsed when the stimulus was cut in 1997. This indicates that fiscal stimulus was actually providing tremendous support to the economy and that the counterfactual GDP in the absence of fiscal stimulus was far less than observed GDP.

A related problem is that too many economists unconsciously assume that the worst-case scenario for an economy without fiscal or monetary policy support is zero percent GDP growth. The argument that Japan's fiscal multiplier is low is based on this assumption, that is, economists presume that even if the construction of roads to nowhere is stopped, economic growth will simply fall to zero. But when the economy is in Cases 3 and 4, the worst-case scenario is not zero growth but a $1,000–$900–$810–$730 deflationary collapse.

The second difficulty is that the measurement must start the moment the private sector shifts its focus from profit maximization to debt minimization. Any measurement that includes data from before that shift, when the economy was still in Case 1 or 2, should not be used because it will underestimate the actual size of the fiscal multiplier in Cases 3 and 4. But there will not be many data points to measure fiscal multiplier when the balance sheet recession is just starting. These two statistical limitations make it almost impossible to quantify the size of the fiscal multiplier at the beginning of a balance sheet recession, when fiscal stimulus is most urgently needed.

Because of these statistical limitations, a rather simplistic counterfactual scenario for Japan is presented in Figure 2.1, where counterfactual GDP in the absence of fiscal stimulus is assumed to return to pre-bubble (1985) levels. This is an optimistic scenario because after 1929 the United States lost 46 percent of its GNP along with wealth equivalent to a full year of (1929) GNP. In contrast, Japan lost wealth equivalent to three years of (1989) GDP after 1990. This suggests Japan could have suffered a drop in GDP of far more than 46 percent if it had followed the path of the Hoover administration in the United States and refused to implement fiscal stimulus.

In this simplistic scenario, the cumulative difference between actual and counterfactual GDP from 1990 to 2005 (i.e., before the GFC) is over ¥2,000 trillion, whereas the cumulative increase in public debt during the same period was ¥460 trillion. This means the Japanese government spent ¥460 trillion to buy the GDP equivalent of ¥2,000 trillion, which suggests the fiscal multiplier was actually in the range of 4 to 5 instead of the figure of around 1 commonly suggested by orthodox fiscal hawks.

The point is that, even though it is difficult to quantify the actual size of the fiscal multiplier at the beginning of a balance sheet recession, the multiplier in Case 3 or 4 is likely to be much larger than one. This means the government must act as borrower of last resort when the private sector is not borrowing or, even worse, is minimizing debt.

The tendency of the fiscal multiplier to change depending on whether the economy is in Cases 1 and 2 or in Cases 3 and 4 also applies to the effectiveness of monetary policy, but in reverse. Monetary policy will be most effective during Cases 1 and 2 when there is a surfeit of borrowers and least effective during Cases 3 and 4 when there is a shortage of borrowers.

Tax Cuts or Government Spending?

The preceding discussion suggests that fiscal stimulus is essential when the economy is in Case 3 or 4. But there are two kinds of fiscal stimulus: government spending and tax cuts. The correct form of fiscal stimulus when the economy is in a balance sheet recession is government spending, not tax cuts. If the economy is suffering from a lack of domestic investment opportunities, a topic that is discussed over the next three chapters, the proper response is government spending augmented by tax cuts and deregulation to increase returns on capital.

Government spending is essential because when the private sector is minimizing debt for balance sheet reasons, any tax cut will simply be used to pay down debt. Although that will enable the private sector to regain its financial health sooner than it would have otherwise, it will not help eliminate the economy's deflationary gap. And if the economy is allowed to fall into a deflationary spiral, both incomes and asset prices will decline further, making the task of repairing private-sector balance sheets that much harder. The government's highest priority should therefore be to stop the deflationary spiral. If it succeeds in preventing a contraction in GDP, the private sector will have the income it needs to pay down debt and eventually repair its balance sheet.

Oil Price Declines during Balance Sheet Recessions

The importance of not using tax cuts during balance sheet recessions was demonstrated in 2014 in a most unexpected quarter. When oil prices started falling late that year, most economists predicted it would lift economic growth in developed countries reliant on imported oil. They argued that a fall in the price of oil was equivalent to a tax cut for importing nations and should increase disposable income and boost consumption.

In spite of such expectations, these economies remained weak despite a fall in oil prices that was nothing short of spectacular. Oil plunged from a high of $107.73 a barrel in June 2014 to a low of $26.05 a barrel in February 2016. But economies remained weak because they were in balance sheet recessions, and private sectors were busy minimizing debt. The ongoing deleveraging at a time of zero or negative interest rates shows just how urgently people felt the need to repair their balance sheets. For many businesses it was indeed a matter of life or death.

In response to the "tax cut" that came in the form of lower oil prices, most people used the extra cash to repair or strengthen their balance sheets. In other words, most of the bounty from lower oil prices was used for stock adjustments—repairing balance sheets—leaving very little for flow items such as increasing consumption. This example demonstrates that tax cuts are not particularly useful in supporting the economy during a balance sheet recession.

The Size of Balance Sheet Problems Matters

It should be noted that if the debt overhang at borrowers is small enough for the rest of society to absorb, tools such as debt forgiveness, debt-for-equity swaps, and straightforward liquidations can be used to address the problem. In other words, if the balance sheet problems are small enough, market-based solutions can be used because the economy is large enough to absorb the negative shock.

But if the problems are large, that is, if a large portion of society is simultaneously facing a debt overhang—which is usually the case when a nationwide asset bubble bursts—such measures merely transfer the problem from one part of society to another without resolving it. Moreover, a reliance on market solutions when the problem is large can easily push the economy into the \$1,000–\$900–\$810–\$730 deflationary spiral, as demonstrated by the U.S. experience during the Great Depression.

When the problems are broad-based, therefore, measures to help *all* borrowers rebuild their balance sheets are needed. Such a process necessarily takes time for both political and economic reasons. That is why a democratic country in a peacetime can find itself stuck in Case 3 for many years even under the best of circumstances.

Debt Trauma May Last a Long Time

Borrowers may also remain traumatized by the long and painful experience of deleveraging even after they have finished repairing their balance sheets. This phenomenon was observed in the United States for decades after the Great Depression, and also in Japan more recently. In the United States, most private-sector balance sheets were repaired by 1945 thanks to a flood of orders from the government for fighter planes and tanks to fight the war. But those who had suffered the horrible pain of deleveraging before the war refused to borrow money even after their balance sheets had been cleaned up. Many never borrowed money again for the rest of their lives. As a result, short- and long-term U.S. interest rates did not recover to pre-Depression levels until 1959, fully 30 years after the Great Depression (Figure 2.22) and 14 years after the war's end, when private-sector balance sheets had been completely cleaned up.

In post-1990 Japan, the same trauma manifested itself in the form of so-called "cash flow management," an approach under which all expenditures, including capital investment, must be financed by ongoing cash flows. In other words, companies refused to borrow money for any reason. And this happened at a time when lending rates were the lowest in history, bankers were very willing to lend, and borrowers had the cleanest balance sheets in over half a century.

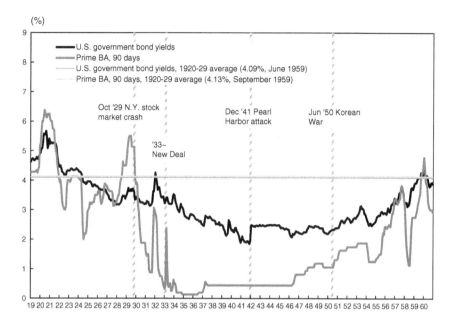

FIGURE 2.22 30 Years Needed for U.S. Interest Rates to Normalize after 1929
Source: FRB, *Banking and Monetary Statistics 1914–1970 Vol.1*, pp. 450–451 and pp. 468–471, Vol. 2, pp. 674–676 and pp. 720–727

This sort of trauma is also likely to be observed in the post-2008 West, which means the deflationary gap will remain long after the private sector finishes repairing its balance sheet.

To overcome this trauma, the authorities may want to implement accelerated depreciation allowances or other incentives for businesses to borrow and invest. Since a trauma is no longer a trauma once it is overcome, such incentives should be as generous and conspicuous as possible to attract the maximum number of participants.

Such tax breaks, however, are not useful until balance sheets have been fully cleaned up, leaving only the psychological issue of debt trauma. Any tax cuts implemented before balance sheets have been nursed back to health will only be used to speed up the repair process, as noted earlier.

Since the political capital needed to continue deficit spending in a peacetime democracy is limited, the government should direct all its energy toward infrastructure spending instead of tax cuts to ensure the maximum boost to GDP from each dollar of deficit spending. Accelerated depreciation allowances and similar tax incentives to overcome the debt trauma should be introduced only after balance sheets themselves have been repaired.

Fiscal Stimulus Must Be Maintained Despite Large Public Debt

In contrast to lender-side problems, there are no quick fixes for borrower-side problems, whether they are due to balance sheet difficulties or to a lack of domestic investment opportunities. An economy in Case 3 can therefore remain there for years, if not decades, until the private sector regains both its financial health and the self-confidence needed to borrow and invest again.[18] This means fiscal support may have to be administered for years.

With the level of public debt already so high in many countries, the prospect of the government running large and prolonged deficits is likely to elicit strong opposition not only from fiscal hawks but also from the general public, who may argue that the country cannot continue spending money it does not have. Even those who agree that government should act as borrower of last resort during a balance sheet recession might worry about it taking on excessive debt. Since the issue of debt sustainability is even more acute when the absence of borrowers is due to a lack of investment opportunities—the problem that plagued the human race for *centuries* before the Industrial Revolution—this challenge is discussed in conjunction with the issue of domestic investment opportunities in Chapter 4.

---

[18] This phase of the economy corresponds to what the author called the Yin phase of Yin-Yang economic cycles, discussed in his *Holy Grail of Macroeconomics: Lessons from Japan's Great Recession,* Singapore: John Wiley & Sons, 2008, p. 160.

CHAPTER 3

Introduction to the Concept of Pursued Economy

When borrowers disappear because of an absence of attractive investment opportunities, which was also the cause of the centuries of economic stagnation that preceded the Industrial Revolution, a very different mindset is needed to address the problem. This is because the reasons for this problem vary depending on the stage of economic development, and each requires a different policy response.

Today's developed economies all started out as agrarian societies, and the centuries-long paradox of thrift only ended with the arrival of the Industrial Revolution. The invention of new products and the machines needed to manufacture them produced a huge number of investment opportunities for the first time in history. Private-sector businesses that would not borrow money unless they were certain they could pay it back found numerous promising projects and started borrowing. The financial sector also developed to meet the newfound demand for funds. This process continued as long as there were debt-financed projects sound enough to pay for themselves.

Thus began a virtuous cycle in which investment created more jobs and income, which, in turn, created more savings to finance additional investment. Unlike the government investments in earlier centuries that eventually ran into financing difficulties, private-sector investments could sustain themselves as long as attractive new products were continuously brought to market. With new household appliances, cars, airplanes, and many other products invented and developed in rapid succession, a lack of investment opportunities was seldom a constraint to growth. The end result has been the rapid economic growth observed since the Industrial Revolution.

At the beginning of this revolution, constraints to growth included insufficient social infrastructure (e.g., transportation networks), inadequate savings to fund investments, an illiterate work force, and the slow pace of technological innovation. But some of these constraints were soon transformed into investment opportunities in the form of railways and other utilities. The urbanization of the population alone created massive investment opportunities as rural workers needed accommodation when they migrated to the cities to work in factories.

The growth of investment opportunities also increased corporate demand for borrowings, and from a macroeconomic perspective, savings became a virtue instead of a vice for the first time in history. Economies where people felt responsible for their own futures and saved more began to grow more rapidly than economies where people saved less.

Borrower Availability and the Three Stages of Economic Development

The availability of investment opportunities, however, is never guaranteed. It depends on myriad factors, including the pace of technological innovation and scientific breakthroughs, the ability of businesspeople to identify such opportunities and their willingness to borrow, the cost of labor and other inputs, the availability of reasonably priced financing, the protection of intellectual property rights, and the state of the economy and world trade.

The importance of each factor also depends on a nation's stage of economic development. The pace of innovation and breakthroughs is probably more important for countries already at the forefront of technology, while in emerging economies the availability of financing and the protection of intellectual property rights may be equally important.

When Germany was emerging as an industrial power, for instance, the United Kingdom accused it of copying its products and demanded the use of "Made in Germany" labels to distinguish its products from the British originals. Japan faced similar accusations from Western countries. Today, "Made in Germany" and "Made in

Japan" are both highly valued labels because of the effort invested by the Germans and the Japanese in producing quality products.

China was also accused of copying products by both the West and Japan. Yet today, many Chinese businesses are demanding that Beijing implement stronger intellectual property rules because they worry that any product they develop will be quickly imitated by domestic competitors, rendering their research and development efforts worthless. In this way, the ability to copy goes from being a huge positive at one stage of economic development to a major negative later.

To understand how these factors change over time, the concept of pursued economy divides economies into three categories based on the stage of industrialization: urbanizing economies, which have yet to reach the Lewis Turning Point (LTP), maturing economies, which have already passed the LTP, and pursued economies, where the return on capital is lower than in emerging economies. The LTP refers to the point at which urban factories have finally absorbed all surplus rural labor. (In this book, the term *LTP* is used only because it is a well-known expression for a specific point in a nation's economic development; it is not used to refer to the model of economic growth proposed by Sir Arthur Lewis.)

Stage I of Industrialization: The Urbanization Phase

At the advent of industrialization, most people are living in rural areas. Only the educated elite, who are few in number, have the technical know-how needed to produce and market goods. Families whose ancestors have lived on farms for centuries have no such knowledge. When they migrate to the cities in search of jobs, all they can offer is their labor. Most of the gains during the urbanization phase of industrialization therefore go to the educated few, while the rest of the population simply provides labor for the urban industrialists. And with so many surplus workers in the countryside, worker wages remain depressed for decades until the LTP is reached.

Figure 3.1 illustrates this from the perspective of labor supply and demand. The labor supply curve is almost horizontal (from D to K) until the Lewis turning point (K) is reached because there is an essentially unlimited supply of rural laborers seeking to work in the

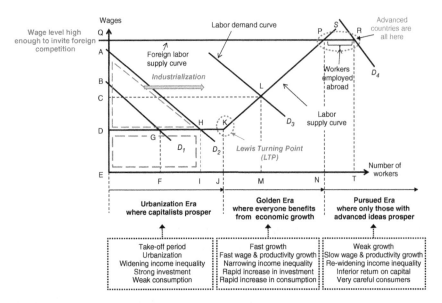

FIGURE 3.1 Three Phases of Industrialization/Globalization

Source: Nomura Research Institute

cities. A business owner in the urbanization phase can attract any number of such laborers simply by paying the going wage (D).

In this graph, capital's share is represented by the area of the triangle formed by the vertical axis on the left, the labor demand curve, and the labor supply curve, while labor's share is represented by the rectangle below the labor supply curve. At labor demand curve D_1, capital's share is the triangle BDG, and labor's share (i.e., total wage income) is the rectangle DEFG. Strictly speaking, BGD is not the profits that accrue to capitalists, as there are other non-labor costs involved in the production and marketing of goods and services. But except for imported inputs and payments to government, this triangle should approximate the share of capitalists as a group since all wage-related expenditures are accounted for by the rectangle DEFG. In terms of income distribution and inequality, what is important is the change in the relative size of the triangle to the rectangle over time, not the exact content of the triangle and the rectangle as long as that remains unchanged. During this phase of industrialization, the capital share BDG may be shared by only a few persons or families, whereas the labor share DEFG may be shared by millions of workers.

Successful businesses continue investing in an attempt to make even more money. That raises the demand for labor, causing the labor demand curve to shift steadily to the right (from D_1 to D_2) even as the labor supply curve remains flat. As the labor demand curve shifts to the right, total wages received by labor increase from the area of the rectangle DEFG at time D_1 to the area of the rectangle DEIH at time D_2 as the length of the rectangle below the labor supply curve grows. However, the growth is linear. The share of capital, meanwhile, is likely to increase at more than a linear rate as the labor demand curve shifts to the right, expanding from the area of the triangle BDG at D_1 to the area of the triangle ADH at D_2.

Growth Exacerbates Income Inequality in Pre-LTP Urbanization Stage

During this phase, income inequality, symbolized by the gap between rich and poor, widens sharply as capitalists' share of income (the triangle) often increases faster than labor's share (the rectangle). One reason why a handful of families and business groups in Europe a century ago and the *zaibatsu* in Japan prior to World War II were able to accumulate such massive wealth is that they faced an essentially flat labor supply curve (wealth accumulation in North America and Oceania was not quite as extreme because these economies were characterized by a shortage of labor). Some in post-1978 China became extremely rich for the same reason.

Because capitalists during this period are profiting handsomely, they continue to reinvest profits in a bid to make even more money. With depressed wages leaving workers unable to save much, most investment must be self-financed by the capitalist class—in other words, capitalists' investments are limited by their savings. Sustained high investment rates mean domestic capital accumulation and urbanization also proceed rapidly. This is the take-off period for a nation's economic growth.

Until the economy reaches the LTP, however, low wages mean most people still lead hard lives, even though the move from the depressed countryside to the cities may improve their situations modestly. For many workers this was no easy transition, with 14-hour factory workdays not at all uncommon until the end of the

19th century. According to the Organisation for Economic Co-operation and Development (OECD), the annual working time in Western countries averaged around 2,950 hours in 1870, or double the current level of 1,450 hours.[1] Business owners, however, were able to accumulate tremendous wealth during this period.

Stage II of Industrialization: The Post-LTP Maturing Economy

As business owners continue to generate profits and expand investment, the economy eventually reaches the LTP. Once that happens, urbanization is largely finished and the total wages of labor—which had grown only linearly until then—start to increase much faster because any additional demand for labor pushes wages higher along the upward-sloping labor supply curve (from K to P in Figure 3.1).

Even if labor demand increases only modestly, from J to M in Figure 3.1, total wages accruing to labor will rise dramatically, from the area of rectangle DEJK to the area of rectangle CEML. This means labor's share of output is likely to expand relative to capital's share. It is at this point that the income inequality problem begins to correct itself. But businesses will continue to invest as long as they are achieving good returns, leading to further tightness in the labor market.

A significant portion of the U.S. and European populations still lived in rural areas until World War I, as shown in Figure 3.2. Even in the United States, where—unlike in Europe—workers were always in short supply, nearly half the population was living on farms as late as the 1930s. Continued industrialization as well as the mobilizations for two world wars then pushed these economies beyond the LTP, and the standard of living for the average worker began to improve dramatically.

Once the economy reaches the LTP and wages start growing rapidly along the upward-sloping labor supply curve, workers begin to utilize their newfound bargaining power. The numerous strikes experienced by many Western countries from the 1950s to the 1970s reflect this development.

---

[1] Maddison, Angus (2006), *The World Economy: A Millennial Perspective (Vol. 1), Historical Statistics (Vol. 2)*. Paris: OECD, p. 347.

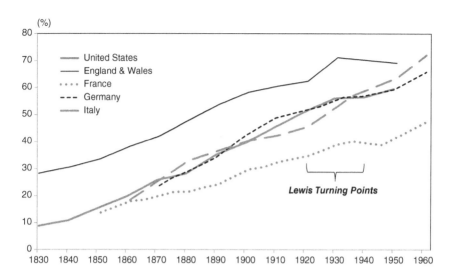

FIGURE 3.2 Western Urbanization* Continued until the 1960s

*Percentage of population living in urban areas with 20,000 people or more in England and Wales, 10,000 or more in Italy and France, 5,000 or more in Germany, and 2,500 or more in the United States.

Sources: U.S. Census Bureau (2012) *2010 Census*, and Peter Flora, Franz Kraus and Winfried Pfenning, ed. (1987), *State, Economy and Society in Western Europe 1815–1975*

Capitalists initially respond to labor movements by hiring union busters and strike busters. But as workers grow increasingly scarce and expensive, the capitalists must back down and begin accepting some of labor's demands if they want to keep their factories running. After 20 years or so of such struggles, both employers and employees begin to understand what can be reasonably expected from the other side, and that leads to a new political order. The current arrangement in the West and Japan, which is dominated by center-left and center-right political parties, is largely an outgrowth of this learning process.

Put differently, countries where center-left and center-right political parties dominate are characterized by an understanding among politicians and voters that they are in an interdependent system—which is what a macroeconomy is. Meanwhile, countries where this learning process is fading or never existed may swing from one political extreme to the other, which is detrimental to both society and the economy.

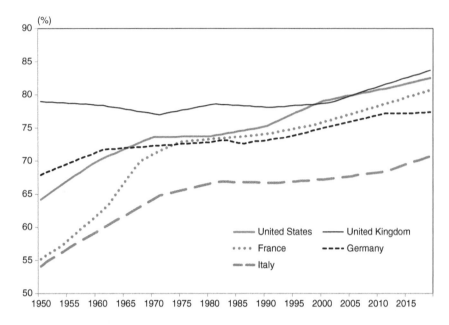

FIGURE 3.3 Western Urbanization Slowed in the 1970s

Note: The definitions on data of urban populations in these countries are below. France: communes with 2,000 inhabitants or more in dwellings separated by at most 200 meters. Germany: communes with at least 150 inhabitants per square kilometer. Italy: communes with 10,000 inhabitants or more. United Kingdom: settlements with 10,000 inhabitants or more. Unites States: meets minimum population density requirements and with 2,500 inhabitants or more.

Source: United Nations, Department of Economic and Social Affairs, Population Division (2019). World Urbanization Prospects: The 2018 Revision (ST/ESA/SER.A/420). New York: United Nations, and its custom data acquired via website

Explosion of Borrowing for Capacity- and Productivity-Enhancing Investments

As labor's share increases, consumption's share of GDP will increase at the expense of investment. At the same time, the explosive growth in the purchasing power of ordinary citizens means most businesses are able to boost profits simply by expanding existing productive capacity. Both consumption and investment increase rapidly as a result.

From that point onward, the economy begins to "normalize" in the sense in which the term is used today. Inequality also diminishes as workers' share of output increases relative to that of capital. In the United States, that led to the so-called Golden Sixties where everyone benefited from economic growth. With incomes rising and inequality falling, this post-LTP maturing phase is referred to as the "golden era" of economic growth in this book.

This trend toward reduced inequality receives further impetus from the fact that the economy in this phase is typically driven by the manufacturing sector. Manufacturing jobs do not require high levels of (expensive) education, so when this sector is leading job creation, wages are bid up from the lowest level of society. Wage increases starting at the bottom will naturally lift wages at higher levels as well, benefiting everyone in society.

Higher wages and the resulting explosive growth in the purchasing power of ordinary workers prompts businesses to invest for two reasons. First, they seek to enhance worker productivity so they can pay those steadily rising wages. Second, they want to expand capacity to address workers' growing purchasing power. Both productivity- and capacity-enhancing investments increase demand for borrowings that add to economic growth. That keeps the economy squarely in Case 1 and 2, with demand for borrowings often outstripping savings and resulting in higher interest rates.

With rapid improvements in the living standards of most workers, the post-LTP golden era is characterized by broadly distributed benefits from economic growth. In this phase, business investment often increases worker productivity without any improvement in worker skills. Even those with limited skills are able to make a good living, especially if they belong to a strong union. Rapid growth in tax receipts during this period also allows the government to offer a continuously expanding range of public services. That, in turn, further reduces the sense of inequality among the population. This golden era lasted into the 1970s in the West.

When Western manufacturers were leading the world, the West was also in an export-led globalization phase as it exported consumer and capital goods to the rest of the world. American cars and German cameras were the global standard to which other countries aspired.

Stage III of Industrialization: The Pursued Economy

But the golden era does not last forever. At some point, wages reach the level Q in Figure 3.1, where it becomes profitable for domestic manufacturers to shift production overseas. As businesses must add in the cost of all risk factors when considering whether to relocate production overseas, Q is that "high enough" domestic wage level at which it makes sense for businesses to relocate after taking into account all the risk factors. This means the actual wage foreign workers receive will be far less than Q.

The first signs of a serious threat to Western economic growth appeared when businesses in the United States and Europe encountered Japanese competition in the 1970s. Initially this was blamed on the wage gap between Japan and the Western economies. But the wage gap had always existed. The real reason was that Japanese businesses were approaching and, in some cases, surpassing the technological and marketing sophistication of the West while at the same time benefiting from lower wage costs.

Many in the West were shocked to find that Japanese cars required so little maintenance and so few repairs. The Germans may have invented the automobile, and the Americans may have established the process by which it could be manufactured cheaply, but it was the Japanese who developed cars that did not break down. The arrival of the Nikon F camera in the 1960s also came as a huge shock to the German camera industry because it was so much more rugged, adaptable, easy to use and serviceable than German Leicas and Exaktas, and professional photographers around the world quickly switched to the Japanese brand. For the first time since the Industrial Revolution, the West found itself being pursued by a formidable competitor from the East.

Once a country is being chased by a technologically savvy competitor, often with a younger and less expensive labor force, it has entered the third or "pursued" stage of economic development. In this phase, it becomes far more challenging for businesses to find attractive investment opportunities at home—it often makes more sense to buy directly from the "chaser" or to invest in that country themselves. In other words, the return on capital is higher abroad than at home. Businesses in pursued economies are still investing to meet shareholder demands to maximize profits, but not necessarily in their home countries. Many businesses are also forced to invest overseas when their competitors start producing abroad.

Many U.S. and European companies in the 1970s happily added Japanese products to their product lines or sold them through their dealerships. These products carried proud American or European brand names but were actually made in Japan. General Motors was buying cars from Toyota; Ford, from Mazda; and Chrysler, from Mitsubishi. Ford acquired a large ownership stake in Mazda, and Chrysler did the same with Mitsubishi. In the "German" camera industry, Leicas were increasingly made with Minolta components—if not produced entirely by the Japanese company—and cameras with such venerable names such as Exakta and Contax were made entirely in Japan.

Once this phase of development is reached, businesses no longer have the same incentive to invest in productivity- or capacity-enhancing equipment at home because there is now a viable alternative—investing in or buying directly from lower-cost production facilities abroad. With constant pressure from shareholders to improve the return on capital, firms are forced to shift investments to locations offering higher returns on capital.

Once this stage is reached, investment in productivity-enhancing equipment at home slows significantly, resulting in lower productivity gains. According to U.S. Bureau of Labor Statistics data compiled by Stanley Fischer at the Fed,[2] productivity growth in the nonfarm business sector averaged 3.0 percent from 1952 to 1973 before falling to 2.1 percent between 1974 and 2007 and dropping further to 1.2 percent between 2008 and 2015. These numbers not only confirm the trend previously noted, but also suggest that worker productivity in the future will depend increasingly on the efforts of individual workers to improve their skills instead of on corporate investment in productivity-enhancing equipment.

In a pursued economy, where outsourcing to foreign production sites becomes a viable alternative, the labor supply curve as perceived by businesses becomes largely horizontal at wage level Q in Figure 3.1. Any increase in labor demand from this point onward will be satisfied with foreign labor. For example, if the labor demand curve is at D_4, total workers employed will be ET in Figure 3.1, of which NT workers will be employed abroad. Real wage growth will therefore be minimal from this point onward, except for workers with abilities that are not easily replicated abroad.

[2] Fischer, Stanley (2016), "Reflections on Macroeconomics Then and Now," remarks at Policy Challenges in an Interconnected World, 32nd Annual National Association for Business Economics Economic Policy Conference, Washington D.C., March 7, 2016. https://www.federalreserve.gov/newsevents/speech/fischer20160307a.htm.

It should be noted that Q depends not just on domestic wage inflation but also on foreign productivity gains. For example, if Japanese products in the 1970s had not been so competitive, Q for the West would have been much higher. Q also depends on changes in the global labor supply. When China joined the world economy after opening up to the world in 1978, the Q for many countries probably declined. When Mexico joined North American Free Trade Agreement (NAFTA) in 1992 and when China became a member of the World Trade Organization (WTO) in 2001, the Q for many advanced countries probably fell again.

With domestic investment opportunities shrinking, economic growth also slows in the pursued countries, which are now in an import-led globalization phase as capital seeks higher returns abroad and inexpensive imports flood the domestic market. With an ever-increasing number of emerging countries joining the ranks of the chasers, constant downward pressure on Q helps keep the price level from rising.

In addition, the loss of investment opportunities at home means a fall in business demand for borrowings. The household sector, however, will continue to save for an uncertain future as it has always done.

That combination of continued household savings and sharply reduced corporate borrowings pushes the economy toward Case 3, where the private sector begins running a financial surplus. The surge in inexpensive imports and slower growth of wages at home ease the upward pressure on prices, while lower inflation rates and reduced demand for borrowings weigh on interest rates.

In the phenomenon known as the Great Moderation of the 1990s, both inflation rates and interest rates came down significantly. Although this is often attributed to central banks' success in taming inflation, the dominant cause was more likely advanced countries' entry into the pursued phase of development.

Japan's Ascent Forced Changes in the West

Japan's emergence in the 1970s shook the U.S. and European industrial establishments. As manufacturing workers lost their jobs, ugly trade frictions ensued between Japan and the West. This marked the first time that Western countries that had already passed their LTPs had been chased by a country with much lower wages.

Zenith, Magnavox, and many other well-known U.S. companies folded under the onslaught of Japanese competition, and household names such as General Electric (GE) and Radio Corporation of America (RCA) stopped producing most household products. The West German camera industry, the world's undisputed leader until around 1965, had all but disappeared by 1975. While Western companies at the forefront of technology continued to do well, the disappearance of many well-paying manufacturing jobs led to worsening income inequality in these countries.

Initially there was tremendous confusion in the West over what to do about the Japanese threat. As the Japanese took over one industry after another, industry and labor leaders sought protection via higher tariffs and nontariff barriers. France, for example, ruled that all Japanese videocassette recorders (VCRs) must clear customs in the remote countryside village of Poitiers, which not surprisingly had few customs officers, to discourage their entry into the country. This was done even though there were no French manufacturers of VCRs. Others argued for exchange rate realignments that were realized in the Plaza Accord of September 1985, which halved the dollar's value against the yen (from 240 to 120 yen to the dollar) by the end of 1987.

Still others said the West should study Japan's success and learn from it, which led to a Western infatuation with so-called "Japanese management" techniques. Many well-known business schools in the United States actively recruited Japanese students so they could discuss Japanese management practices in the classroom. Some even argued that eating fish—and sushi in particular—would help to make Western managers as smart as the Japanese. All in all, Western nations' confidence that they were the world's most technically advanced economies was shattered.

Some of the pain felt by Western workers was offset by the fact that, as consumers, they benefited from cheaper imports from Asia, which is one characteristic of import-led globalization. During the golden era, rising wages and rising prices were the norm. During the pursued era, stagnant wages and stagnant prices become the norm.

Businesses with advanced technology and individuals with advanced degrees continued to do well, but it was no longer the case that everyone in society was benefiting from economic growth.

Those whose jobs could be transferred to lower-cost locations abroad saw their living standards stagnate or even fall.

Inequality Worsens in the Pursued Era

Figure 3.4 shows the real income of the lowest quintile of U.S. families from 1947 to 2020. Even in this group, incomes grew rapidly in the post-LTP golden era that lasted until around 1970. But income growth subsequently stagnated as the country entered the post-LTP pursued phase. Figure 3.5, which illustrates the income growth of other quintiles relative to the lowest 20 percent, demonstrates that the ratios remain remarkably stable until 1970 but diverge thereafter.

Figure 3.6 shows annualized income growth by income quintile in the post-LTP golden era from 1947 to 1970 and the post-LTP pursued phase from 1970 to 2020. It shows that the bottom 60 percent actually enjoyed slightly faster income growth than those at the top before

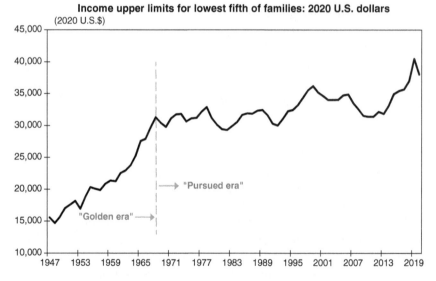

Income upper limits for lowest fifth of families: 2020 U.S. dollars

FIGURE 3.4 Incomes of Lowest 20 Percent of U.S. Families Shot Up until 1970 but then Stagnated

Source: Nomura Research Institute, based on the data from U.S. Census Bureau, Current Population Survey, Annual Social and Economic Supplements (CPS ASEC), "Income Limits for Each Fifth and Top 5 Percent of All Families: 1947 to 2020"

1970, indicating a reduction in income inequality. This was indeed a golden era for the U.S. economy, with everyone growing richer and enjoying the fruits of economic growth.

But the situation changed drastically once Japan started chasing the United States. Figure 3.4 shows that income growth for the lowest quintile has been stagnant ever since. Figures 3.5 and 3.6 illustrate that income growth for other groups was only slightly better—except for the top 5 percent, which continued to experience significant income gains even after 1970. This group probably includes those who were at the forefront of innovation and those who were able to take advantage of Japan's emergence.

Figure 3.6 demonstrates that income growth for different income quintiles was quite similar during the golden era, but began to diverge significantly once the United States became a pursued economy. Income growth for the top 5 percent dropped from 2.50 percent per year during the golden era to just 1.48 percent during the

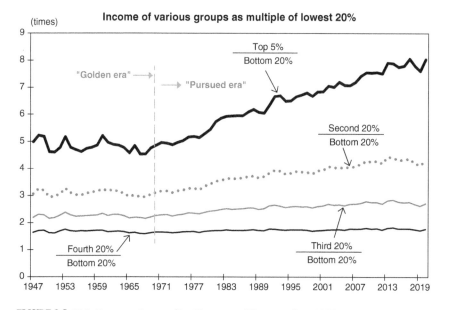

FIGURE 3.5 U.S. Income Inequality Began to Worsen after 1970

Source: Nomura Research Institute, based on data from U.S. Census Bureau, Current Population Survey, Annual Social and Economic Supplements (CPS ASEC), "Income Limits for Each Fifth and Top 5 Percent of All Families: 1947 to 2020"

					(annualized, %)
	Lowest 20%	Second 20%	Third 20%	Fourth 20%	Top 5%
Post-LTP golden phase 1947–1970	2.805	2.854	2.861	2.719	2.496
Pursued phase 1970–2020	0.440	0.605	0.841	1.126	1.479

FIGURE 3.6 Annualized Growth Rates of U.S. Family Income by Income Quintile

Source: Nomura Research Institute, based on data from U.S. Census Bureau, Current Population Survey, Annual Social and Economic Supplements (CPS ASEC), "Income Limits for Each Fifth and Top 5 Percent of All Families: 1947 to 2020"

pursued phase, but that was still 3.36 times the rate of growth for the lowest 20 percent.

Similar developments were observed in Europe. Figure 3.7 illustrates real wages in six European countries. With the possible exception of the United Kingdom, all of these countries experienced rapid wage growth until the 1970s followed by significantly slower growth thereafter.

Three Stages of Japanese Industrialization

Japan reached the LTP in the mid-1960s, when the mass migration of rural graduates to urban factories and offices, known in Japanese as *shudan shushoku*, finally came to an end. Investment opportunities in Japan were plentiful during this period because the hard work needed to develop new products and processes had already been done in the West. All Japan had to do was make those products better and less expensive, a task the Japanese system was well suited for. Rapid urbanization and the need to rebuild cities devastated by U.S. bombing during World War II also offered an abundance of low-hanging investment opportunities.

Indeed, the main constraint on Japanese growth at the time was savings—there was simply not enough savings to meet the investment demand from Japanese businesses. Japan found itself in an

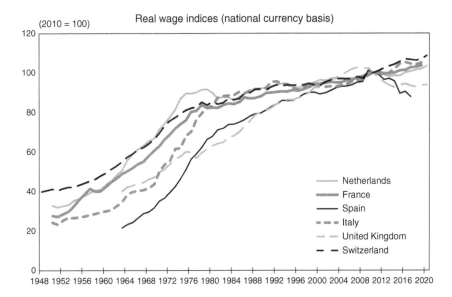

FIGURE 3.7 Real Postwar Wages in Six European Countries

Source: Nomura Research Institute, based on data from the International Monetary Fund (IMF), *International Financial Statistics*; French National Institute of Statistics and Economic Studies (INSEE), *Annual wages*; Office for National Statistics, U.K., *Average weekly earnings time series, Retail Prices Index: Long run series*; and Swiss Federal Statistical Office, *Swiss Wage Index*

extreme variant of Case 1 where the number of borrowers completely overwhelmed the number of lenders. As a result, inflation and interest rates in those years were quite high, leading the government to ration savings to high-priority industries. The government and the Bank of Japan (BOJ) also implemented numerous measures to encourage Japanese households to save.

Once Japan reached the LTP in the mid-1960s, the number of labor disputes skyrocketed, as shown in Figure 3.8, and Japanese wages started to increase sharply (Figure 3.9). In other words, Japan was entering the post-LTP golden era that the West had experienced 40 years earlier.

Japan was fortunate in that it was not being pursued at the time, enabling it to focus on catching up with the West. No one was chasing it because most emerging countries at the time had embraced the so-called import-substitution model of economic development. Why this model was eventually scuttled in favor of the export-led model pioneered by Japan is explained in Chapter 5.

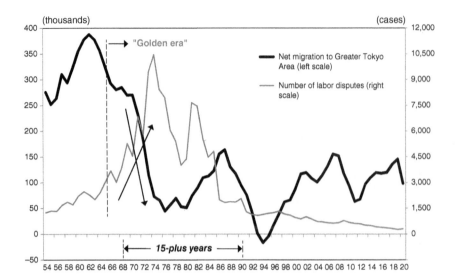

FIGURE 3.8 Labor Disputes Surge Once Lewis Turning Point Is Passed (1): Japan

Note: Greater Tokyo Area consists of Metropolitan Tokyo, Kanagawa prefecture, Saitama prefecture and Chiba prefecture.

Sources: Ministry of Internal Affairs and Communications, *Report on Internal Migration in Japan* and Ministry of Health, Labour and Welfare, *Survey on Labour Disputes*

Japanese wages were rising rapidly, but Japanese companies invested heavily at home to boost workforce productivity. The nation's golden era of strong growth and prosperity could continue as long as productivity rose faster than wages. With the quality of its exports appreciated by consumers around the world, Japan was very much in an export-led globalization phase.

Labor's share of output rose along with wages, and Japan came to be known as the country of the middle class, with more than 90 percent of the population identifying itself as such. The Japanese were proud of the fact that their country had almost no inequality. Some even quipped in those days that Japan was how Communism was supposed to work.

The happy days for Japan lasted until the mid-1990s, when Taiwan, South Korea, and China emerged as serious competitors. By then, Japanese wages were high enough to attract pursuers, and the country entered its pursued phase. Japanese wages stopped growing in 1997 and then stagnated or fell, as shown in Figure 3.9.

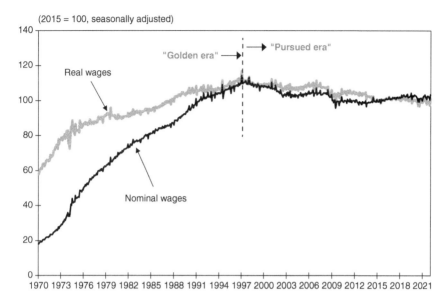

FIGURE 3.9 Japanese Wages Peaked in 1997 upon Entering Post-LTP Pursued Phase

Source: Ministry of Health, Labour and Welfare, Japan, *Monthly Labour Survey*

Although the three Asian countries were also chasing the West, the shock to Japan was greater because this was the first time the country had been pursued since it opened itself up to the world in the 1868 Meiji Restoration. All of Japan's institutions, from education to employment, had been optimized for catching up with the West, not fending off competitors from the East. Meanwhile, the Europeans and Americans who had experienced the Japanese onslaught 25 years earlier had already recalibrated their economies and were therefore less affected by China's emergence.

Today, the Japanese are worried about income inequality as highly paid manufacturing jobs have migrated to lower-cost countries. They are also concerned about the emergence of the so-called working poor, people who were once employed in manufacturing but have now been forced to take low-end service jobs. Some estimate that as many as 20 million out of a total population of 130 million are now living in poverty.[3] Their suffering, however, has been

---

[3] *Nikkei Business* (2015), "Tokushu: Nisen Mannin-no Hinkon" ("20 million Japanese in Poverty"), in Japanese, Tokyo: Nikkei BP, March 23, 2016, pp. 24–43.

eased somewhat by a flood of inexpensive imports that has substantially reduced the cost of living. This means Japan has entered an import-led globalization phase and is reliving the West's experience when it was being chased by Japan.

Similar concerns are being voiced in post-2005 Taiwan and South Korea as they experience the same migration of factories to China and other even lower-cost locations in Southeast Asia. These two countries passed their LTPs around 1985 and entered a golden era that lasted perhaps until 2005. The frequency of Korean labor disputes also shot up during this period (Figure 3.10) as workers gained bargaining power for the first time and won large wage concessions. In Taiwan, wages climbed sharply during the post-LTP golden era but peaked around 2005 and stagnated thereafter (Figure 3.11). Except in the area of semiconductor manufacturing, both countries are now feeling the pinch as China steadily takes over the industries that were responsible for so much of their past growth.

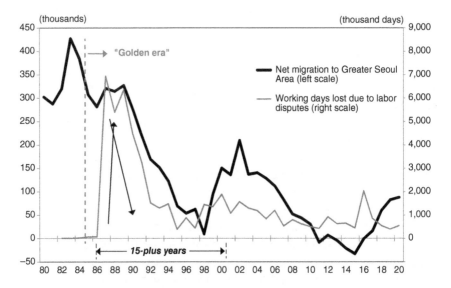

FIGURE 3.10 Labor Disputes Surge Once Lewis Turning Point Is Passed (2): South Korea

Note: Greater Seoul Area consists of Seoul, Incheon, and Gyeonggi-do

Sources: Ministry of Employment and Labor, *Strikes Statistics*, Statistics Korea, *Internal Migration Statistics* and *Korea Statistical Year Book*

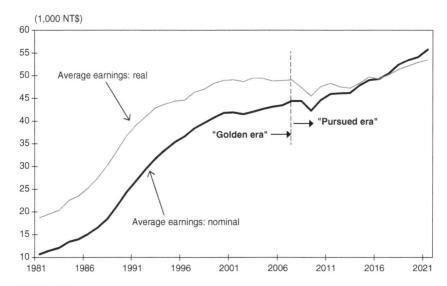

FIGURE 3.11 Taiwanese Wages Peaked around 2005 When Country Entered Pursued Phase

Source: Nomura Research Institute, based on data from Directorate General of Budget, Accounting and Statistics (DGBAS), the Executive Yuan, Taiwan, *Consumer Price Indices* and *Average Monthly Earnings*

Free Trade Accelerated Globalization while Rendering War Obsolete

This process of chasing and being chased, otherwise known as globalization, can trace its beginnings to the U.S. introduction of a free-trade regime after World War II. Before then, a variety of barriers to trade hindered economic growth. Most countries in those days imposed high tariffs on imported products both to raise revenues and to protect domestic industries. But if workers constituted the main source of consumption demand in the pre-LTP urbanizing world, they could not have provided enough demand for all the goods produced because their share of income was so low, while capitalists typically had a higher marginal propensity to save. As a result, aggregate supply often exceeded aggregate demand.

To overcome this constraint, European powers turned to colonialism and imperialism in a bid to acquire both sources of raw materials and captive markets where they could sell the goods they

produced. Indeed, it was believed for centuries that national economies could not grow without territorial expansion. That belief led
to centuries of wars and killings.

When World War II ended, the victorious Americans introduced
a free-trade regime known as the General Agreement on Tariffs and
Trade (GATT) that essentially allowed any country with competitive
products to sell to any other country. As a reluctant participant in
two world wars, the Americans wanted to build a system in which
countries sharing democratic values could prosper without the need
to expand their territories. The United States was also motivated by
the need to fend off the Soviet threat by rapidly rebuilding Western
Europe and Japan.

Although the concept and practice of free trade were not
new, the U.S. decision to open its vast domestic market, which
accounted for nearly 30 percent of global GDP at the end of World
War II, to the (free) world was a game-changer. The resultant free-
trade regime allowed not only Japan and West Germany but also
many other countries to prosper without the need to expand their
territories. Indeed, it is difficult to find a country that grew rapidly
in the post-1945 world that did not benefit from the U.S. market.

The advent of a U.S.-led free trade framework rendered obsolete
the whole notion that territorial expansion was a necessary condition
for economic growth and prosperity. After World War II, the victorious allies found themselves busy fighting indigenous independence
movements in their colonies at enormous expense. Meanwhile, Japan
and West Germany—which had lost all of their overseas and some
of their domestic territories—quickly grew to become the world's
second- and third-largest economies. In other words, postwar Japan
and West Germany proved that economic growth requires markets
and investment opportunities, not territories. Economic growth will
accelerate if markets can be accessed without the expense of acquiring and managing overseas territories.

The relative infrequency of wars after 1945 is often attributed
to the Cold War and the deterrence doctrine of mutually assured
destruction ("MAD"), but the drastic reduction in conflict between
countries that had been fighting since history began is also due to
the fact that territorial expansion was no longer viewed as a necessary condition for economic prosperity. Colonies actually became
more of a liability than an asset for economic growth under the free-
trade regime.

Today, thanks to the fabulous track record of the U.S.-led adoption of free trade, almost no one in the (advanced) world sees territorial expansion as a prerequisite for economic prosperity. This monumental change in mindset, at least in the advanced countries, should qualify as one of the greatest chapters in the history of human progress. It is unfortunate that this new mindset is not yet shared by the leaders of both China and Russia.

In Asia, it was the Japanese who discovered in the 1950s that their economy could still grow and prosper by producing high-quality products for the U.S. market. They then put their best and brightest to the task while leaving complicated diplomatic and national security issues to be decided by the Americans. Indeed, many high-end products made in Japan during the 1950s and 1960s, such as TEAC audio gear, were sold only in the United States because Japanese consumers were still too poor to afford them.

Japan's spectacular success then prompted Taiwan, South Korea, and eventually the rest of Asia to follow the same export-oriented growth formula in a process dubbed the "flying geese" pattern of industrialization. These countries' golden eras became synonymous with export-led globalization. In the 1990s, even Mexico, one of the emerging countries that had pursued the import-substitution model of economic growth, decided to join the globalization bandwagon by signing NAFTA.

China Now in Post-LTP Golden Era of Industrialization

The biggest beneficiary of the U.S.-led free-trade regime was China, which succeeded in transforming a dirt-poor agrarian society of over a billion people into the world's second-largest economy in just 30 years. The three decades after Deng Xiaoping opened the Chinese economy in 1978 probably qualify as the fastest, greatest economic growth story ever, as per capita GDP for over a billion people increased from a little over $300 to more than $10,000 in 2019. China wasted no time integrating itself with the global economy and attracted huge quantities of foreign direct investment, first from Hong Kong and Taiwan, but soon from all the advanced countries.

Those investments came because the U.S.-led free-trade system allowed businesses—both Chinese and foreign—to sell their products anywhere in the world. Even though China was nowhere near democracy when it opened itself to the outside world, many in the United States believed that the nation would become a freer and more open society before long. And that hope was not without justification: millions of bright Chinese students were studying in Western universities, and millions more tourists were traveling around the world as the country became more prosperous. This stood in sharp contrast to the totally closed systems of the Soviet Union and Eastern Europe, where contact with foreigners was strictly controlled. That contrast convinced many Americans that China would soon open up its political system as well. The fact that many Americans held this idealistic hope was what allowed China to enter the WTO in 2001.

The entrance to WTO and the resulting access to global markets prompted businesses from around the world to build factories in China. Chinese economic growth skyrocketed, with exports accounting for as much as 35 percent of GDP at the peak. Were it not for the markets provided under the U.S.-led free-trade regime, it probably would have taken China many more decades to achieve the growth it did.

Businesses in the West and elsewhere that were able to take advantage of China's low-cost, hard-working labor force found almost unlimited investment opportunities and operated like the capitalists in their own countries' pre-LTP urbanization eras. Those investments added massively to China's economic growth and transformed the country into "the world's factory."

But those investments also exacerbated inequality in the advanced countries in the same way that inequality had increased during their own pre-LTP urbanizing eras. This happened in part because foreign businesses expanding rapidly in China were likely to invest less at home, which served to depress domestic economic and productivity growth. Indeed, slow productivity growth in the advanced economies is the flipside of the rapid productivity and income growth in China and other emerging markets that was made possible by investment from developed nation businesses. Workers in Asia and the West who had to compete with Chinese workers have therefore seen their wages stagnate or even fall.

Those in the advanced economies who still wonder where the golden era enthusiasm for fixed capital investment has gone need only get a window seat on a flight from Hong Kong to Beijing (or vice versa) on a nice day. They will see below them an endless landscape of factories stretching out in all directions. Many of those plants were first started with foreign capital because when Deng Xiaoping opened up the economy in 1978, there were no capitalists left in China: they had all been killed or driven into exile by the Communist revolution in 1949.

In the beginning, only foreign capital, mainly from Taiwan and Hong Kong, was available to jump-start China's industrialization. Indeed, it was these businessmen in the 1980s who taught the Communist Chinese how to run a market-based economy. And capitalists from Taiwan and Hong Kong came in only because they realized they could sell whatever they produced in China to the rest of the world. After their pioneering efforts, they were joined by others from the West and Japan who realized that the return on capital in China was far higher than what was available at home—*if the goods produced there could be sold around the world.*

China is also subject to the same laws of urbanization, industrialization, and globalization as other countries. It actually passed the LTP around 2012 and is now experiencing sharp growth in wages. That means the country is now in its post-LTP golden era. However, because the Chinese government is wary of strikes, labor disputes, or other public disturbances of any kind, it is trying to preempt such conflict by administering significant wage increases each year, with local governments issuing directives forcing businesses to raise wages. In some regions, wages were rising at double-digit annual rates as the authorities sought to prevent labor disputes. It remains to be seen whether such top-down actions can substitute for a process in which employers and employees learn through confrontation what can reasonably be expected from the other party.

The higher wages that have resulted in China are now leading both Chinese and foreign businesses to move factories to lower-wage countries such as Vietnam and Bangladesh. In effect, the laws of globalization and free trade that benefited China when it was the lowest-cost producer are now posing challenges.

That means the easy part of China's economic growth story is now over. If the country hopes to maintain economic growth in the face of rising wages, it needs to improve the domestic business environment so that businesses will continue to invest at home at a time when they are discovering that the return on capital is higher abroad, at least for certain industries. The challenges facing Chinese policy makers, including the nation's shrinking workforce and its confrontation with the United States, is addressed further in Chapter 5, which discusses growth.

The Happiness of Nations

The preceding discussion regarding the stages of economic development is summarized in Figure 3.12. Here, the bold arrows indicate the direction of pursuit.

Countries appear to be reaching their "golden eras" sooner owing to accelerated globalization, which has been made possible by free trade and rapid advances in information technology. However, the length of the golden era appears to be shortening as more countries join the globalization bandwagon. For example, the golden era for the United States and Western Europe probably lasted for about 40 years until the mid-1970s, while Japan's ended after around 30 years in the mid-1990s. The golden era for Asian Tigers like Taiwan and Korea was about 20 years long, coming to an end around 2005. It will be interesting to see how long China's golden era lasts, with policy makers already worried about poor demographics and the middle-income trap, which are discussed in Chapter 5.

If a nation's happiness can be measured by (1) how quickly inequality is receding and (2) how fast the economy is growing, then the post-LTP golden era would qualify as the period when a nation is at its happiest. During this period, strong demand for workers from a rapidly expanding manufacturing sector forces all other sectors to offer comparable wages to retain workers. Because manufacturing jobs do not require advanced education, when manufacturing is driving job creation, it raises the wages of even the least skilled, thereby positively affecting wages in all other sectors. In this sense, manufacturing is a great social equalizer: when manufacturing industries are prospering, people without advanced (and expensive) education can still earn a decent living. With everyone benefiting from economic growth, people are hopeful for the future, and inequality shrinks rapidly.

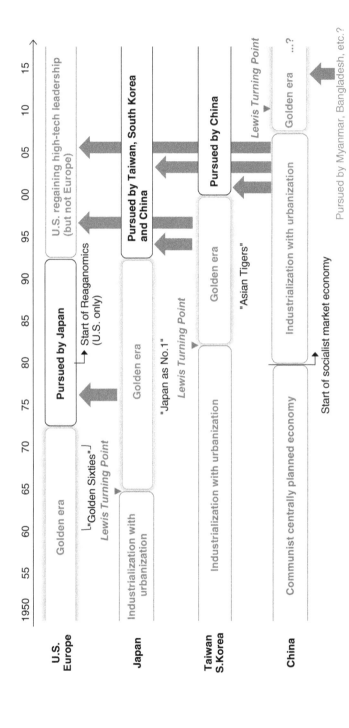

FIGURE 3.12 Growth, Happiness, and Maturity of Nations

Note: A ⇒ B = A pursuing B

Source: Nomura Research Institute

U.S. manufacturing employment peaked in 1979 at 19.6 million, with the bulk of the growth taking place from 1946 (12.7 million) to 1969 (18.8 million). This timeframe coincides with the period of shrinking income inequality in the United States, as noted earlier. Manufacturing employment has now fallen to 12.6 million, or just 8.4 percent of total nonfarm employment. The corresponding figure in 1946 was 32 percent.

Insufficient Attention to Trade Deficits and Loss of Manufacturing Jobs

Many economists continue to argue that those manufacturing jobs disappeared not because of outsourcing to foreign countries but because of automation. And it is true that more goods—such as automobiles—are now produced with fewer workers in advanced countries. But that is often the case because many intermediate products are now made abroad. This reliance on suppliers from abroad was amply demonstrated during the pandemic when supply-chain disruptions reduced production everywhere. If automated factories in the United States are so efficient, stores in the country should be carrying more goods made in the United States, and the United States should not be running such large trade deficits for the last four decades. The U.S. trade deficit reached more than $900 billion for the first time in 2021 (Figure 9.1).

Nor is the automation argument consistent with allegations, made by Japanese visiting the factories of U.S. companies, that it was a lack of investment in automation due to the short-sightedness of U.S. management that led to the manufacturing decline. The decline was so severe that the country had next to zero ability to manufacture the ventilators, masks, and various other items needed to fight the COVID-19 pandemic.

These problems emerged in part because the free trade regime lost its rebalancing mechanism when the free movement of capital was introduced on top of free trade in 1980 without careful consideration. How that led to the loss of U.S. manufacturing and the anti-globalization backlash of Donald Trump's "America First" movement and even Joe Biden's "Buy American" program is discussed in Chapter 9.

Income inequality begins to worsen once manufacturers start migrating to lower-cost countries because only those with advanced education and skills can keep up with the changes and continue to do well. The increase in their incomes, however, seldom trickles down to boost the wages of those without advanced education on the lower rungs of society.

Manufacturers also have a far greater need to borrow for capital expenditures than companies in most other industries, which is crucial in keeping the macroeconomy in Case 1 and 2. The loss of manufacturing, therefore, is one of the key drivers of advanced countries' shift to Case 3. Manufacturing is also where the greatest productivity gains can be expected. The shrinkage of the U.S. manufacturing sector is therefore consistent with the productivity growth numbers from Stanley Fischer previously noted.

The West was at its happiest before Japan started chasing it in the 1970s because its manufacturing industry led the rest of the world. It was a French person who said before the Berlin Wall came down that the world would be a much nicer place if there were no Soviet Union and no Japan.

The Japanese were at their happiest when their manufacturing sector was chasing the West, but nobody was chasing them. Those happy days ended when the Asian Tigers and China began pursuing Japan in the mid-1990s. The Tigers then enjoyed their own golden era for about 20 years until China started chasing them.

Conceptual Origins of "Post-Industrial Society" and Pursued Phase

The concept of the pursued phase introduced here and the concept of the "post-industrial society," popularized by authors such as Daniel Bell, both refer to the same period in history. When the latter concept was unveiled in the 1970s, people were excited about the prospect of societies becoming cleaner and more humane as knowledge-based industries became increasingly dominant in the economy. This was in contrast to the age of industrialization, which forced people to work long hours in oily, dirty factories.

Today, most advanced countries enjoy cleaner air with fewer factories operating inside their borders. But for a large part of the population, the rosy, humane scenario promised by the proponents of post-industrial society never materialized. Instead, many feel far less secure and hopeful today than in the earlier era. Some have become angry and desperate enough to vote for populists and extremists.

The overly optimistic post-industrialization scenarios never came to pass because those scenarios require a world in which knowledge-based industries are expanding so fast and paying so well that they draw workers away from the manufacturing sector. Manufacturers will then be forced to leave the country because they cannot compete for workers when knowledge-based businesses are offering such high wages.

What actually happened, however, was that advanced countries were forced into de-industrialization because emerging economies started offering higher returns on capital than those that are available at home. Although knowledge-based businesses have been expanding in most societies, they need workers who are highly educated, unlike the workers who manufacturers employed. More importantly, loan demand from knowledge-based industries has clearly been insufficient to offset the loss of borrowings from manufacturers that are needed to absorb private savings and keep the economy in Case 1 or 2. This issue is discussed further in the next chapter with Figure 4.1.

Society has suffered from slower growth and widening income inequality because corporate borrowings have fallen relative to savings, and only those with special abilities or advanced degrees have done well in knowledge-based, de-industrializing economies. Since slower growth and rising inequality are not positive developments, the author coined the term "pursued economies" to convey the sense of urgency with which the problem of inferior domestic returns on capital must be addressed. How to deal with the challenges faced by pursued economies is discussed in Chapters 4 and 5.

The Rise and Fall of Communism

The preceding description of how inequality increases and decreases before and after the LTP also explains why so many people have found Communism appealing at certain points in history. Karl Marx and Friedrich Engels, who lived in pre-LTP urbanizing Europe, were appalled by the horrendous inequality around them and the miserable working and living conditions of ordinary people. As previously noted, it was not uncommon for people to work 16 hours a day in dark, dirty, and dangerous industrial environments while capitalists rapidly grew rich. Any intellectual with a heart would have found it difficult to turn a blind eye to the social and economic inequality of the time.

Marx responded by proposing the concept of Communism, which called for capital to be owned and shared by the laborers. He argued that if capital were owned by the workers, the exploitation of labor would end, and workers would enjoy a greater share of the output. Many "exploited" workers who had been working long hours in dreadful conditions embraced the new theory enthusiastically because it appeared to offer the hope of a better life with little to lose. In that sense, the birth of Communism may itself have been a historical imperative of sorts.

Marx and Engels' greatest mistake, however, was to assume the extreme inequality they witnessed (points G and H in Figure 3.1) would continue forever without a Communist revolution. In reality, it marked just one inevitable step on the path toward industrialization. If capitalists are earning large profits in the pre-LTP urbanizing period, they are likely to continue investing in the business in the hope of making even more money. It is that drive for more profits that eventually pushes the economy to reach and pass the LTP, when a totally different labor-market dynamic kicks in.

As soon as the economy reaches the LTP and wages start rising along the positively sloped labor supply curve (from K to P in Figure 3.1), the appeal of Communism wanes as workers begin to realize they can get what they want within the existing framework. The early years of the golden era, however, are typically characterized by frequent strikes and labor disputes as workers start to utilize their newfound bargaining power for the first time. The scenes of workers marching under Red Communist banners in the 1960s and 1970s in many countries gave the impression that a Communist takeover was imminent. But their success in winning higher wages ended up undermining the movement's appeal.

After 15 or 20 years of such struggles, employers and employees alike begin to understand what can be reasonably expected from the other side, and a new political order is established based on that understanding. The result is the prevalence of center-right and center-left political parties seen in advanced countries today.

Although this political arrangement served advanced countries well in their post-LTP golden eras, it remains to be seen whether it is the most appropriate arrangement under the very different labor market dynamic of the pursued phase. The rise of far-right and populist political parties in the West that are opposed to free trade and globalization is already presenting a major challenge to the established political order. These political issues are discussed further in Chapters 5 and 9.

Ironically, countries that adopted Communism before reaching their LTPs, such as pre-1978 China and pre-1986 Vietnam, ended up stagnating at very low income levels because the profit motive needed to promote investment and push the economy beyond the LTP was lost. Even in countries where industrialization was forced through, many of the resulting industries turned out to be less than viable because they did not have to face the discipline imposed by the need to earn profits in a competitive marketplace. Most of these enterprises therefore folded, with no buyers for their products, when their Communist governments collapsed.

Interestingly, the economy also ends up stagnating when labor becomes too powerful and expensive before the country reaches the LTP, for both economic and political reasons. First, the economy stops growing and becomes stuck in the pre-LTP urbanizing phase because the protected workers are too expensive for businesses to expand production. Second, unionized and privileged workers end up creating a two-tier labor market with a permanent underclass that is denied meaningful employment because the economy is not growing fast enough. This leads to political alienation and divisions that slow the economy even further, as has been seen in some Latin American countries since the 1950s.

LTP and Inclusive Social Order

The preceding discussion suggests that many inclusive social and political reforms are possible only after a country passes the LTP. Even in the advanced countries, the majority of inclusive reforms, such as the U.S. civil rights movement, took place in the post-LTP era. That means sequencing matters, and those in emerging countries seeking more inclusive social and political order might want to push their economies beyond the LTP first if they want to avoid the pitfalls previously noted.

Although the preceding discussion suggests that all countries pass through the same development process, there has also been general progress toward more agreeable working conditions in all countries. For instance, European workers were working as long as 16 hours a day in the pre-LTP urbanizing phase, whereas post-1978 Chinese workers were working only a little more than 8 hours a day even before the country reached its LTP. That suggests the progress made elsewhere in the world is reflected in working conditions in at least some of the emerging economies today.

The Real Source of Thomas Piketty's Inequality

Income inequality has become one of the hottest, most controversial issues in economics, not only in the developed world but also in China and elsewhere. Many are growing increasingly uncomfortable with the divide between the haves and the have-nots, especially after Thomas Piketty's book, *Capital in the 21st Century*, sparked a fresh debate on the optimal distribution of wealth, an issue that had been largely overlooked by the economics profession.

The author cannot claim to have understood the full implications of Piketty's enormous contributions, but the analysis presented here, which is based on how economies develop over time, contradicts one of the key historical points he makes. Namely, he claims that the extreme inequality that existed prior to World War I was corrected by the wealth destruction of two world wars and the Great Depression. He then goes on to argue that the retreat of progressive taxation in the developed world starting in the late 1970s ended up creating a level of inequality that approaches that seen prior to World War I.

Although he has ample data to back his assertions, his pre–World War I results might also be due to the fact that those countries were all in the pre-LTP urbanization phase, which is characterized by a rapid increase in inequality. Similarly, his post–World War I findings might be attributable to the West's entering the post-LTP golden era, where everyone enjoys the fruits of economic growth and inequality shrinks. Piketty attributes this to the destruction of wealth brought about by two world wars and the introduction of progressive income taxes, but this period was also characterized by an end to rapid urbanization in most of these countries. Furthermore, the four decades through 1970 marked a golden era for Western economies as their manufacturing sectors led the world and were being chased by no one.

Finally, Piketty's post-1970 results may be due to the fact that Western economies entered their pursued phase when Japan and other countries began chasing them. For Western capitalists able to utilize Asian resources, this was a golden money-making opportunity quite similar to what they had enjoyed during the pre-LTP urbanization era. But it was not a welcome development for Western factory workers, who found themselves competing with cheaper imports from Asia.

This also suggests that the favorable income distributions observed by Piketty in the West before 1970 and in Japan until 1990 were *transitory* phenomena. These countries enjoyed growing incomes and shrinking inequality not because they had the right kind of tax regime but because they were in the golden era, when manufacturing prospered. And it prospered because the global economic environment was such that these countries either were ahead of everyone else or were chasing others but were not themselves being pursued. In other words, the return on capital was highest at home.

Just because such a desirable state of affairs was observed once does not mean it can be maintained or replicated. Any attempt to preserve that equality in the face of fierce international competition would have required massive and continuous investment in both human and physical capital, something that most countries are not ready to implement.

It is not even certain whether such investment constitutes the best use of resources since businesses may still find that the return on capital is higher elsewhere. To the extent that businesses are under pressure from shareholders to invest in countries offering the highest returns, forcing them to invest at home is no easy task. That means a more extreme form of protectionism than what was proposed by Donald Trump may be needed to keep cheaper foreign goods out and force businesses to invest at home. What is certain, however, is that a completely different mindset is required to secure economic growth in the pursued countries.

Now that most advanced countries are in the pursued phase, the key question for policy makers should be how to increase investment and borrowings, both public and private, to absorb all the savings generated by the private sector and allow the economy to grow again. Unfortunately, very little of the policy debate in advanced countries is couched in these terms. And there have been almost no macroeconomic studies on the policy implications of capital earning higher returns abroad than at home. Instead, almost all macroeconomic theory and policy debate is based on the golden era assumption that attractive domestic investment opportunities are always available.

For example, central banks in the advanced countries had been trying to increase the rate of inflation to 2 percent during the post-2008 balance sheet recession because that was the optimal rate for attaining maximum long-term growth during the golden era. But at the time, most businesses had factories only at home.

In today's pursued era, companies have production facilities all over the world. When domestic inflation rates outstrip those abroad because the central bank is aggressively easing monetary policy, many companies will shift production to their foreign plants to remain competitive, resulting in less employment and investment at home. This is the opposite of what the 2-percent inflation target is supposed to achieve. Unfortunately, economics has failed to reflect these and many other fundamental changes that have taken place over the last three decades.

Economic policy debate in advanced countries is still conducted as though they are still in the golden era because the foundations of macroeconomics were laid in the 1950s when the West was in the golden era. And because it was a beautiful era (apart from air quality), politicians and economists alike long for its return. But they will not be able to improve people's lives until they fully appreciate the current economic reality in a global context. These points are discussed in greater detail in the next two chapters.

CHAPTER 4

Macroeconomic Policy during the Three Stages of Economic Development

Labor's Progression during the Three Stages of Economic Development

In order to understand the unique policy challenge faced by pursued economies, it is useful to see how various sectors of the economy change as they pass through the different stages of economic development. It was already noted that when an economy is in the pre–Lewis Turning Point (LTP) urbanizing phase, capitalists can take advantage of workers because there are so many of them in rural areas who are willing to work for the going wage D in Figure 3.1 in urban factories. Workers also have no bargaining power prior to reaching the LTP. During this phase, the limited opportunities for education and vocational training in rural areas mean most workers are neither well educated nor highly skilled when they migrate to the cities. And with so many of them competing for a limited number of urban jobs, there is little job security.

Once the economy passes the LTP and enters the golden era, however, the tables are turned completely in favor of the workers. The supply of surplus workers in rural areas is exhausted, and the labor supply curve slopes upward from points K to P in Figure 3.1. As long as some businesses seek to increase their workforce, all businesses will be forced to pay ever-higher wages. At this stage, businesses also have many reasons to expand because workers' purchasing power is growing rapidly. Expansion here means *domestic* expansion: firms have little of the experience or know-how needed for overseas production, and domestic wages, although rising, are still likely to be competitive.

To satisfy growing demand while paying steadily rising wages, businesses invest in both productivity- and capacity-enhancing equipment. Strong domestic demand for both types of machinery during this phase manifests itself in the form of robust demand for borrowings to finance capital investments. In other words, the economy is firmly in Case 1. Investments in additional equipment effectively raise the productivity of employees even if the workers themselves are no more skilled or educated than before the country reached its LTP.

With wages rising rapidly, job security for workers also improves significantly as businesses try to hold on to their employees. Lifetime employment and seniority-based remuneration systems become more common. Working conditions improve as businesses offer safer, cleaner working environments to attract and retain workers. The emerging power of unions also forces employers to enhance job security. In contrast to the pre-LTP period, when businesses were effectively exploiting workers because there were so many of them, businesses in the post-LTP golden era "pamper" their employees with productivity-enhancing equipment so they can afford to pay them more. As a result, everyone is able to enjoy the fruits of economic growth.

At some point, however, wages reach level Q in Figure 3.1, and businesses are forced to look for alternative production sites abroad because domestic manufacturing is no longer competitive. It is at this point that firms realize that capital invested abroad earns higher returns than capital invested at home. This also means that the effective labor supply curve for businesses flattens at Q because at that point they have access to an almost unlimited supply of foreign labor. In other words, the economy starts moving along the "global labor supply curve," which is horizontal (from P to R in Figure 3.1).

Producing abroad, however, requires that management possess foreign language competency and other specialized skills, and that takes time. If the process appears too daunting, which is often the case for small and medium-sized firms, they may simply abandon the business altogether or outsource all production to foreign firms.

The transition from golden era to pursued era may therefore take many years. But once the know-how to produce abroad is acquired, the firm will consider the entire emerging world when looking for possible locations for new factories. The overseas investment process therefore becomes increasingly irreversible. Although different industries may reach this point at different times, a country can be said to have entered its pursued phase when a meaningful number of industries have reached the point where they perceive foreign labor as a good substitute for domestic labor.

Workers Are on Their Own in the Pursued Phase

The way businesses perceive workers changes once again in the new pursued phase because they now have the option of tapping overseas labor resources. With capital going much further abroad than when invested at home in labor-saving equipment, businesses have fewer incentives to undertake domestic investment. Fixed-capital investment, which was such a large driver of economic growth during the post-LTP golden era, begins to slow. As investment slows, growth in labor productivity, which shot up during the golden era, also starts to decelerate, a trend that has been observed for some time now in most advanced countries. In pursued economies, therefore, both productivity growth and wages begin to stagnate.

It is at this point that the ability of *individual* workers begins to matter for the first time because only those able to do things that overseas workers cannot will continue to prosper. This stands in sharp contrast to the previous two stages, where wages were determined largely by macro factors such as labor supply/demand and institutional factors such as union membership, both of which had little to do with individual skills. Once the supply constraint is removed by the option of producing abroad or engaging in outright outsourcing, the only reason a company will pay a higher wage at home is because a particular employee can do something that cannot be easily replicated by a cheaper foreign worker.

If workers were exploited during the pre-LTP urbanization era and pampered during the post-LTP golden era, they are entirely *on their own* in the pursued era because businesses are much less willing to invest in labor-saving equipment to increase the productivity of the domestic workforce. Workers must invest in themselves to enhance their productivity and marketability.

In this pursued phase, job security and seniority-based wages become increasingly rare in industries that must become more agile and flexible to fend off pursuers. It is no accident that lifetime employment and seniority-based wages, which were common in the United States until the 1970s, disappeared once Japanese competition appeared. The same thing happened to the Japanese labor market with the increased use of "non-regular" workers after the Asian Tigers and China emerged as competitors in the mid-1990s. Achieving a more flexible labor market has also been a major issue for Europe.

Workers who take the time and effort to acquire skills that are in demand will continue to do well, while those without such skills will end up earning close to minimum wage. Those who benefited from union membership during the post-LTP golden era will find that the benefits of membership in the new pursued era are not what they used to be. As a result, the share of unionized workers in the United States has fallen from a high of over 30 percent of the labor force[1] to just around 10 percent now.[2] Income inequality will increase again, even though *when adjusted for skill levels* it may not change all that much.

Workers who want to maintain or improve their living standards in a pursued economy must therefore think hard about their individual prospects and the skills they should acquire in the new environment. To the extent that the answer to this question differs for each individual, workers are truly on their own. The "good old days," when businesses invested to increase worker productivity so they could pay employees more, are gone for good. In some sense this is only fair since it means workers who put in the time and effort

---

[1] According to data from Harvard Business School's website, the U.S. trade union membership rate in 1960 was 30.9 percent. https://www.hbs.edu/businesshistory/courses/resources/historical-data-visualization/Pages/details.aspx?data_id=37.

[2] Union density in the United States, indicated by union membership rates, was 10.8 percent in 2020. U.S. Bureau of Labor Statistics, "Union Members – 2020," U.S. Bureau of Labor Statistics Economic News Release, January 22, 2021. https://www.bls.gov/news.release/union2.nr0.htm.

to improve their productivity will be rewarded more generously than those who do not.

Consumers' Progression during the Three Stages of Economic Development

Workers are also consumers, and their consumption behavior changes along with the stage of economic development. During the pre-LTP urbanization phase, most workers are paid very little. Their limited share of output serves as a constraint on consumption, and their low incomes prevent them from saving much. Most of the saving and investing is therefore done by the capitalist class, which typically has a higher marginal propensity to save. Because capitalists in this era have a high share of output but also a high propensity to save, domestic supply often exceeds domestic demand. That, together with depressed wages, tends to keep prices low. In other words, inflation is seldom a problem in the urbanization era.

Once the economy passes the LTP and wages began to rise rapidly along the upward-sloping labor supply curve (from K to P in Figure 3.1), the consumer mindset changes. With bright prospects for ever higher wages, they begin demanding higher quality products and luxury goods that they could only dream of acquiring during the pre-LTP period. Many begin to compete with each other on the basis of their possessions, a phenomenon dubbed "keeping up with the Joneses" in the United States. Businesses strive to offer a full lineup of products capable of attracting these upwardly mobile consumers.

In the automobile industry, for example, General Motors had the Chevrolet marque at the entry level, Pontiac as an upgrade, Buick and Oldsmobile further up the ladder, and Cadillac at the top. For Ford, the order was Ford, Mercury, and Lincoln, while Chrysler had Plymouth, Dodge, and Chrysler. And within each marque, different grades of cars were offered to fuel the customer's desire to upgrade.

Consumers in those days were willing to buy a new car every two years not only to feel good but also to keep up with their neighbors and friends. Automakers' effort to capture these upwardly mobile consumers for the rest of their lives was called "full-line marketing."

In Japan, similar behavior was observed once the economy entered the post-LTP golden era and households began to compete on the basis of their possessions. When one family bought a piano so that its children could take piano lessons, others in the neighborhood felt pressured to buy some sort of musical instrument so that their children could also have music lessons. This sort of peer pressure became so intense in the early 1990s that women of high school age and older felt they had to have at least one Louis Vuitton bag, resulting in a huge proportion of the nation's female population carrying such bags to school and work every day. Such competition to own better things or to keep up with the Joneses constituted a huge positive feedback loop for the economy, and both consumption and gross domestic product (GDP) grew rapidly.

But once an economy enters the pursued phase and the prospect of unlimited income growth disappears, consumers have to reorient their priorities. With incomes growing slowly or not at all, they are forced to ask whether they are receiving value for their money. At the same time, a huge inflow of inexpensive foreign goods, a key feature of pursued economies, creates shopping options that did not exist before.

During this reorientation, the keeping-up-with-the-Joneses mentality is thrown out the window, and most consumers stop buying a new car every other year. Instead, they begin checking consumer websites like Consumer Reports to ensure they are getting good value for money regardless of what brand name the product carries, where it is sold, or where it is made.

In the United States, this resulted in the growth of large discount retailers such as Walmart and Costco. The reduced importance of brand hierarchies also prompted the disappearance of venerable brands such as Oldsmobile and Plymouth.

In Japan, this reorientation led to the explosive growth of so-called 100-yen shops, where everything from electronic calculators to kitchenware can be purchased for 100 yen. Indeed, most new households in Japan now start with a shopping spree at a 100-yen shop because of the impressive quality and selection of goods offered. They then go to other stores to acquire those items that cannot be found at the 100-yen shops.

When Poundland, which sells everything from scientific calculators to snacks for one British pound, first opened its doors in the United Kingdom, many consumers said they did not want to be seen in one. Apparently they were not yet ready to shed the "keeping up with the Joneses" mentality. But more recently, such resistance is said to have diminished as British consumers begin demanding more value for money.

In retrospect, this evolution of consumer behavior is perfectly reasonable: it was ridiculous for people to buy a new car every other year when the cars themselves were made to last much longer, or for a large percentage of the female population to be walking around with a Louis Vuitton bag. Just as workers are "on their own" in the pursued phase, consumers must become smarter, more independent, and not as easily swayed by silly fads and fashions. Many simply cannot afford that sort of behavior anymore.

Different Inflationary Trends during the Three Stages of Economic Development

These changes in the behavior of businesses, workers, and consumers during the various stages of economic development have profound implications for monetary and fiscal policy via their impact on economic growth and inflation.

In terms of inflation and monetary policy, workers are paid very low wages during the pre-LTP urbanization period, meaning that wage- or consumption-led price growth is severely constrained. Low wages also mean workers are unlikely to be great contributors to the nation's savings pool. The financial markets, as intermediators of savings and investment, are therefore relevant only for the top echelon of society. Although those at the top are likely to have a higher propensity to save, the availability of those savings effectively limits the investment that can take place during this period.

When many workers cannot afford to buy the products they are making, over-supply and deflation are likely to result unless there is demand for those products abroad. If domestic demand is insufficient to absorb domestic production, the authorities may be forced to keep exchange rates low in order to promote exports. In other words, inflation is not likely to be a major problem during this period.

When the economy enters the post-LTP golden era, however, wage inflation becomes so common as to become ingrained in the system. This leads to rapid increases in both the total wage bill and final demand from consumers. Consumers with ever-rising incomes are also more willing to accept higher prices during this phase if those prices give them higher quality goods or greater prestige in their social circles. A prime example of this would be the ownership of Louis Vuitton bags in Japan, as previously noted.

Businesses facing rising wages and increasing domestic demand must undertake substantial investment in productivity- and capacity-enhancing equipment. Indeed, one of the key characteristics of the post-LTP golden era is a high level of capital expenditures and correspondingly strong demand for borrowings to finance those investments. This means the economy is squarely in Case 1.

Strong consumption demand from the household sector and strong investment demand from the corporate sector, together with ever-rising wages, are likely to push prices steadily higher, and inflation becomes a real threat to economic growth. Strong demand for borrowings from businesses also means there is no leakage to the income stream and the money multiplier is pushed to its maximum value[3] and stays there. Economic conditions are fundamentally inflationary, but monetary policy is also at its most effective.

Indeed, private-sector demand for funds can increase dramatically during this period unless the central bank makes sustained efforts to keep it in check by adjusting interest rates and the supply of reserves. In other words, the central bank must ensure that higher interest rates and the availability of reserves are the binding constraint on money supply and credit growth during this era. Such actions may occasionally push the economy into Case 2, but that allows the central bank to control the inflation rate.

The golden era also marks the first time in history that the central bank is tasked with fighting inflation. As explained later in Chapter 8, the original purpose of creating a central bank is not to fight inflation but to avert financial crises by serving as lender of last resort. In the pre-LTP urbanization era, wages are depressed, as shown in Figure 3.1, meaning that the threat of inflation is minimal. On the contrary, the depressed purchasing power of workers, along with capitalists' high marginal propensity to save, mean *deflation* is often the problem.

During the golden era, however, central banks have their hands full fighting inflationary pressures. It is no coincidence that central

---

[3] This point is explained further in Chapter 8.

banks are given ever-greater powers and independence during this phase of economic development. Those powers are indispensable in the golden era because the central bank would find it hard to combat inflation without them. Milton Friedman's argument that inflation is everywhere and always a monetary phenomenon is actually valid during the golden era, when private-sector demand for borrowings is strong and the money multiplier is stable at its maximum value.

As domestic inflationary pressures grow, a stronger exchange rate also becomes more desirable. The fact that inflation is a problem means demand is outstripping supply, and a stronger exchange rate would help to contain demand by decreasing exports and help increase supply by increasing imports. This also means a country's exchange rate policy should change with the stage of economic development.

When the economy enters the pursued phase, however, both incomes and wages are growing slowly, resulting in more moderate growth in consumption. Businesses' demand for capacity- and productivity-enhancing equipment also slows during this phase as they find higher returns on capital abroad. The resultant reduction in borrowings is also deflationary because it pushes the economy into Case 3 and increases the chance of leakage to the income stream. Weak or nonexistent income growth leads to the emergence of more fastidious, value-conscious consumers, making it more difficult for businesses to raise prices. Rapid growth in inexpensive imports also has a depressing effect on domestic prices. All in all, inflation becomes much less of a problem than in the post-LTP golden era.

The Fall in Corporate Borrowings and Loss of Monetary Policy Effectiveness

Figure 4.1 shows that U.S. companies were still making domestic investments through the 1980s and were therefore running a financial deficit—that is, they were net borrowers. In other words, they were borrowing and investing household savings as described in economic textbooks. But with the arrival of the Japanese, the hollowing-out of U.S. industry accelerated in the 1990s. In addition, the North American Free Trade Agreement (NAFTA) helped Mexico emerge as a leading production base, and China's economic reforms opened

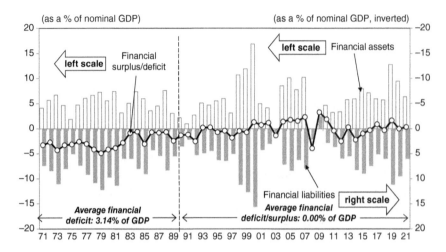

FIGURE 4.1 U.S. Businesses Stopped Borrowing Money after 1990

Note: Figures for CY2021 are four-quarter moving averages through July–September 2021.

Sources: Nomura Research Institute, based on data from Federal Reserve Board (FRB) and U.S. Department of Commerce

up the country to direct investment from around the world. The net financial deficit of nonfinancial companies in the United States shrank precipitously as a result.

Those companies ran a financial deficit averaging 3.14 percent of GDP during the 20 years from 1970 Q1 to 1990 Q4, but that dropped to just 0.00 percent of GDP in the 30 years from 1991 Q1 to 2021 Q3. In other words, they effectively ceased to be net borrowers. Interest rates were much higher in the earlier period because those years were characterized by strong corporate demand for borrowings, and were much lower in the later period because corporate demand for borrowings contracted by a full 3 percent of GDP to average just 0.00 percent of GDP. Instead of asking why more companies are not borrowing despite such low interest rates, economists need to understand that interest rates are so low *because* more companies have stopped borrowing.

This decline in interest rates, which became more pronounced as time went on, was referred to as a "savings glut" by then–Fed governor

Ben Bernanke.[4] He attributed it to the fact that China was running large trade surpluses with the United States and was using most of those dollars earned to buy U.S. Treasury securities. While that may have been one reason for the drop in U.S. interest rates, the plunge in U.S. corporate demand for funds from 3.14 percent of GDP to just 0.00 percent of GDP probably played a far greater role.

When the collapse of the U.S. housing bubble triggered a balance sheet recession in 2008, the household sector, which had been a net borrower during the bubble as is noted in Chapter 2 (Figure 2.5), suddenly became a large net saver as households rushed to repair their damaged balance sheets. The financial surplus of the entire U.S. private sector thus doubled from an average of 3.31 percent of GDP in the five years leading up to 2008 Q3, just before Lehman Brothers failed, to an average of 7.01 percent from 2008 Q4 to the present (Figure 1.1).

In other words, the U.S. private sector did not increase its borrowings when post-2008 interest rates fell almost to zero; in fact, it began saving more by running larger financial surpluses. Businesses and households started minimizing debt and increasing their savings in a bid to repair damaged balance sheets, and it was their actions that led to further reduction in interest rates.

Ultra-Low Interest Rates Became Entrenched in Japan for the Same Reason

Japan experienced the same phenomenon starting in 1990, although it underwent a balance sheet recession *before* it became a pursued economy. Before the asset bubble collapsed in the 1990s, Japan's nonfinancial companies were borrowing savings from the household sector to expand their operations in classic textbook fashion. The corporate sector ran a financial deficit averaging 5.96 percent of GDP throughout the 1980s (Figure 4.2).

---

[4] Bernanke, Ben S. (2005), "The Global Saving Glut and the U.S. Current Account Deficit," at the Sandridge Lecture, Virginia Association of Economists, Richmond, Virginia, March 10, 2005. https://www.federalreserve.gov/boarddocs/speeches/2005/200503102/.

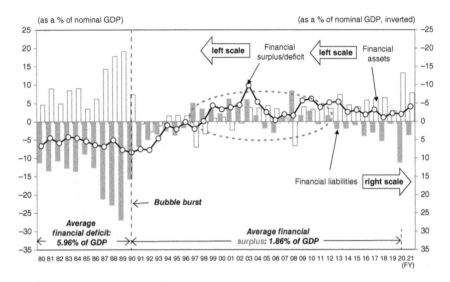

FIGURE 4.2 Japanese Nonfinancial Companies Have Finally Resumed Borrowing, but Are Still Net Savers

Note: Figures adjusted for assumption of debt related to Japan National Railways Settlement Corp. and National Forest and Field Service Special Accounts (FY1998) and privatization of postal services (FY2007). Figures for FY2021 are four-quarter moving averages through July–September 2021. Average financial surplus/deficit figures are calculated through FY2020.

Sources: Bank of Japan, *Flow of Funds Accounts*, and Government of Japan, Cabinet Office, *National Accounts*

But the bubble burst in 1990, forcing companies to rush to plug the holes in their balance sheets. The corporate sector then ran a financial *surplus* averaging 1.86 percent of GDP from FY1991 through FY2020. From around 1998 onward, not only the household sector but also the corporate sector began running a large financial surplus, causing the entire private sector to become a massive net saver. In 2003, the worst year of corporate deleveraging, the corporate sector alone was running a financial surplus equivalent to 10 percent of GDP.

This state of affairs has continued to the present day in spite of near-zero interest rates. The biggest reason why Japan's economy has stagnated over the last 30 years is that businesses went from borrowing (and spending) 5.96 percent of GDP in the 1980s to saving

1.86 percent of GDP in the 1990s and beyond, causing a reduction in demand equal to 7.82 percent of GDP.

As Figure 4.2 shows, the financial surplus due to balance sheet problems ended around 2010, when companies stopped paying down debt (i.e., when the shaded bars in the graph moved back below the center line). But the corporate sector has continued to run a financial surplus since then because Japan is now a pursued economy, and many of its companies prefer to invest abroad instead of at home.

In Japan, the balance sheet recession came first because the country was still chasing the West when the bubble burst in 1990. Only later, toward the end of the 1990s, did it become a pursued economy. In contrast, Western countries first found themselves being pursued by Japan in the late 1970s and did not experience a balance sheet recession until 2008. Both of these factors led to a decline in borrowing and pushed the economies into Case 3, which is why all of the developed nations had been experiencing ultra-low interest rates until COVID-19–driven supply problems pushed inflation rates higher starting in 2021.

As the United States entered its pursued phase and domestic demand for borrowings to finance real investment fell, monetary policy also became less effective. This can be seen from the weakened correlation between the Fed's monetary policy actions and the Federal Reserve Bank of Chicago's financial conditions index starting in the 1990s.

As Figure 4.3 indicates, this index—a measure of the difficulty borrowers face in procuring funds—moved in line with Fed policy actions through the end of the 1980s, when corporate borrowers were plentiful. In other words, when the Fed raised interest rates to make it more costly to borrow, this index also moved higher, indicating that financial conditions had tightened.

But this linkage broke down in the 1990s. There have been four major monetary tightening cycles since then (see the circled areas in Figure 4.3), but in each case the financial conditions index failed to respond to Fed actions and stayed at very favorable levels for borrowers. From 2015 to 2019, the financial conditions index actually fell at times even though the Fed raised interest rates nine times.

It is also likely that a larger share of the borrowing that took place after 1990 went to finance purchases of existing assets, such as real

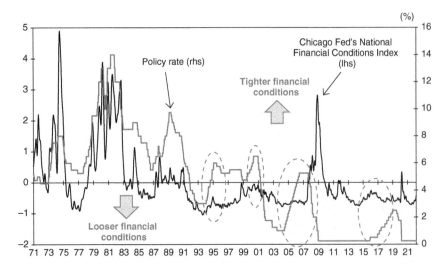

FIGURE 4.3 U.S. Monetary Policy Grew Less Effective Starting in the 1990s

Notes: In the Chicago Fed's National Financial Conditions Index (NFCI), 0 represents average from 1971 to present. Prior to 1987, when Fed began targeting fed funds rate, policy rate in graph refers to official discount rate. Since Fed began targeting corridor of values for fed funds, graph shows top end of Fed's target range.

Sources: Board of Governors of the Federal Reserve System, The Federal Reserve Bank of Chicago "National Financial Conditions Index"

estate, mergers, acquisitions, and share buybacks, which do not add to GDP. Even though those borrowings do add to the money supply and lending statistics in Figures 2.9 to 2.14, they have little impact on inflation and real growth. They also have little effect on financial conditions because funds borrowed to finance purchases of existing assets stay within the financial sector. This is because sellers must find another asset in which to invest the proceeds of those sales. It is probably no coincidence that both the level of interest rates and the effectiveness of monetary policy declined as nonfinancial corporations, the traditional borrowers of funds, began borrowing less to finance real investment.

The emphasis here is on nonfinancial corporations because their borrowings are more likely to be spent on capital investment, at least during the golden era, which allows the borrowed funds to enter the real economy. In contrast, a large portion of the funds borrowed by the household sector is used to purchase existing houses. Such purchases result only in a change of ownership of existing assets, and the funds themselves remain in the financial market.

The point here is that funds borrowed for investment in factories and equipment will leave the financial sector and enter the real economy. That, in turn, puts upward pressure on interest rates, the inflation rate, and the financial conditions index. In contrast, funds borrowed for the purchase of existing assets will stay in the financial sector because the seller must invest the proceeds of the sale in some other asset. As a result, such funds do little to boost interest rates, the inflation rate, or the financial conditions index. The fact that interest rates have fallen not just in the United States but in all advanced countries, with a corresponding loss of monetary policy effectiveness, suggests that the savings glut is a fundamental feature of economies in the pursued era.

The implication here is that both the importance and effectiveness of monetary policy change as the economy develops. Inflation is not a big problem for the monetary authorities during the pre-LTP urbanization phase, when wages are depressed. But it becomes a major issue during the post-LTP golden age, and the central bank must be extremely vigilant, employing monetary restraint to keep higher wages and stronger domestic consumption and investment demand from pushing prices higher. Monetary policy is also effective during this period because strong demand for borrowings keeps the money multiplier at its maximum value.

Once the economy enters the pursued phase, inflation becomes less of a problem amid slower wage growth, a surge of inexpensive imports, weaker consumption, and reduced demand for fixed capital investment. Hence there is less need for the central bank to exercise monetary restraint.

Monetary policy also becomes much less effective during this phase because of the reduced demand for borrowed funds: fewer borrowers mean fewer people able to respond to the central bank's policy actions. That also reduces the money multiplier. With more jobs flowing overseas and reduced inflationary pressures at home, the monetary authorities may also be pressured to lower the exchange rate.

The Neutral Rate of Interest Also Depends on the Stage of Economic Development

This also means that the neutral rate of interest—the rate of interest that does not add to or subtract from economic activity—also varies with the stage of economic development. It stays low during the pre-LTP phase, which is characterized by subdued inflation due to depressed wages. It then rises substantially during the golden era, which features stronger demand for borrowings and higher inflation. If the central bank appears insufficiently vigilant toward inflation, the neutral rate may increase even further as depositors and bondholders demand higher returns to compensate for the possibility of a spike in inflation and a corresponding erosion in the value of their financial holdings.

The neutral rate comes down again when the economy enters the pursued phase, which is characterized by both reduced demand for borrowings and lower inflationary pressures. The economy's sensitivity to interest rate changes also declines in this phase along with the lower and less stable money multiplier. As a result, monetary authorities may have to move rates much further than during the golden era to achieve the same economic impact. For example, if the neutral rate is 3 percent, the central bank might have to raise rates to 5 percent to produce any tightening impact or lower them to 1 percent to see any loosening effect. This reduced sensitivity may also be responsible for the decline in the effectiveness of monetary policy in the 1990s as illustrated in Figure 4.3.

If it is balance sheet problems that drove the abrupt changes in private sector behavior as happened after 2008 in the West and after 1990 in Japan, then it is much more accurate to say that the neutral rate of interest *disappeared*, not declined, after the bubble burst. The Fed took the policy rate to zero after Lehman Brothers collapsed and kept it there until December 2015, but the U.S. private sector continued to run a highly deflationary financial surplus equal to 7 percent of GDP, as shown in Figure 1.1.

It is quite natural for the private sector to post large financial surpluses at higher interest rates. After all, that is the desired outcome when the central bank tightens monetary policy to rein in inflation. But for the private sector to continue running a highly deflationary financial surplus at zero interest rates means the neutral rate must be deeply negative, if it exists at all.

Since technically insolvent businesses and individuals struggling to return to solvency will not alter their deleveraging behavior no matter how low the central bank takes the policy rate, and private-sector financial institutions will not lend money at negative interest rates, it is more accurate to say that there is no neutral rate during balance sheet recessions because there is no interest rate that can keep the economy from shrinking. The whole concept of neutral rate, therefore, is basically useless as a policy guidepost when the economy is in balance sheet recession.

This also means that some other sector outside the private sector—that is, the government—must borrow and spend the financial surplus of the private sector to keep the economy from shrinking. That is why Fed Chairs Ben Bernanke and Janet Yellen, who understood this point, dissuaded the U.S. Congress from engaging in premature fiscal consolidation after 2008 by warning about the danger of falling off the "fiscal cliff."

Fiscal Policy Challenges in the Three Stages of Economic Development

The importance and effectiveness of fiscal policy, or government borrowing and spending, also change over the course of economic development. In the pre-LTP urbanization phase, fiscal policy not only is effective but is often crucial in providing essential infrastructure so that private-sector investments can flourish. The social rate of return on infrastructure investments during this phase is therefore very high. Financing infrastructure spending during this period may require help from abroad—often there are limited domestic savings that can be mobilized in the pre-LTV urbanization phase with an underdeveloped financial sector.

But when the economy is in the golden era, fiscal policy has limited ability to stimulate the economy except during balance sheet recessions because of its tendency to "crowd out" private-sector investment. The ability of fiscal policy is limited because its final stimulative effect is the amount the government borrowed and spent *minus* the amount the private sector would have borrowed and spent if it were able to borrow the savings the government borrowed.

During the golden era, the competition among private-sector borrowers alone may push interest rates to high levels, and the addition of public-sector borrowers will send them even higher. Higher interest rates, in turn, will prompt some private-sector borrowers to drop out, resulting in the crowding-out of private-sector investments. Because private-sector borrowings for productivity- and capacity-enhancing investments are usually more efficient than public-sector projects, the crowding-out of the former by the latter weighs on growth. It is for this reason that economists tend to disparage fiscal stimulus.

But once the economy enters the pursued phase, fiscal policy is less likely to cause crowding-out since private-sector demand for borrowings is weaker. As noted in Figure 4.1, U.S. nonfinancial corporate net borrowings decreased from 3.14 percent of GDP on average during the final years of the golden era to just 0.00 percent of GDP during the pursued era. Fiscal policy therefore becomes far more effective than it was in the golden era.

Indeed, if private-sector demand for borrowings falls below the level of private savings (i.e., if the private sector is running a financial surplus) even at very low interest rates, the economy is effectively in Case 3 and fiscal policy becomes absolutely essential to keep the economy out of the $1,000–$900–$810–$730 deflationary spiral. This is when fiscal policy is most effective.

At the same time, the absence of private-sector borrowers translates to extremely low borrowing costs for the government, which is sometimes the only borrower left. Many public works projects, if carefully chosen, become wholly or nearly self-financing at such low borrowing costs.

The 2008 collapse of asset price bubbles in the West exacerbated this trend of shrinking private-sector borrowings in the pursued economies by throwing these economies into balance sheet recessions. As indicated in Figure 1.1, the private sectors of nearly all the pursued economies have been running large financial surpluses despite zero interest rates. These private-sector balance sheet problems have further reinforced the tendency for monetary policy to grow less effective and fiscal policy more effective. Even if these countries were not in balance sheet recessions, fiscal policy would most likely have become more effective than during the golden era, with the reverse being true for monetary policy.

These changes in the impact of fiscal and monetary policy are illustrated in Figure 4.4. During the pre-LTP urbanization era, fiscal spending on infrastructure delivers a large stimulus to the economy because it induces private-sector investment. Meanwhile, monetary policy has a limited role because depressed wages lead to subdued inflationary pressures. Many countries at this stage of economic development also adopt fixed exchange rates, which further limits the effectiveness and flexibility of monetary policy.

During the golden era, monetary policy is king and is extremely effective while fiscal policy is much less potent and should be mobilized only when there are natural disasters or other negative external shocks or when the economy falls into a balance sheet recession.

The effectiveness of fiscal and monetary policy reverses again when the economy enters the pursued era as corporate demand for borrowings to finance capacity- and productivity-enhancing investment declines. The effectiveness of fiscal policy then increases while monetary policy loses its potency.

Figure 4.4 shows two lines each for monetary and fiscal policy in the pursued phase because most economies in this phase since 2008 have also been suffering from balance sheet recessions or their

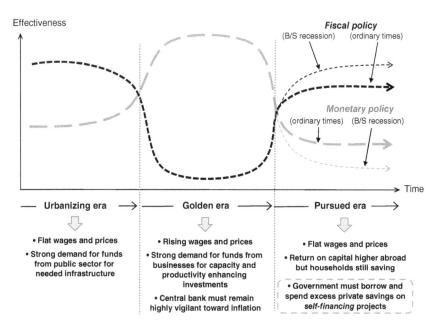

FIGURE 4.4 The Effectiveness of Monetary and Fiscal Policy in the Three Stages of Economic Development

aftermath. Since the pursued economy problems and the balance sheet problems both reduce the number of borrowers, the presence of the latter makes fiscal policy even more effective than usual and monetary policy even less so. It also means that monetary policy in advanced countries will *not* regain its golden-era effectiveness even after balance sheet problems are resolved unless domestic demand for capacity- and productivity-enhancing investment returns to the level of the earlier golden era.

The golden era is the era of monetary policy, with limited opportunities for fiscal policy to serve a useful role. But in the pursued era these roles are essentially reversed. Textbook economics almost always assumes that the economy is in a golden era, but most advanced economies today are already in the pursued era. That is why textbook economic policies have produced so many unexpected and undesirable outcomes recently.

The Danger of Using Multipliers and Elasticities from the Wrong Era

The preceding discussion also suggests that one must be careful when using elasticities and multipliers for various policy tools estimated in an earlier era because they may no longer be relevant in the current period. As mentioned in Chapter 2, these elasticities can also change abruptly even in the same era if the economy falls into a balance sheet recession.

For example, the belief in a low fiscal multiplier has become "common sense" for many economists. But this is something that is observed almost exclusively during the golden era or periods including the golden era, that is, when the economy is in Case 1 or 2. At such times, the low fiscal multiplier argument is valid because governments running budget deficits are in fact competing with private-sector borrowers for a limited amount of savings. That leads to higher interest rates, the crowding-out of private-sector investments, and the frequent misallocation of resources, all of which result in a low fiscal multiplier.

But the assumption of a low fiscal multiplier is totally inappropriate for economies in Case 3 or 4. As noted in Figure 2.1, the fiscal multiplier in post-1990 Japan has been 4 to 5 if measured correctly, based on the counterfactual GDP that would have resulted in the absence of fiscal stimulus. That number is easily double or triple the typical multiplier observed during the golden era, which is usually estimated to be not much bigger than one. In other words, fiscal multipliers measured during the golden era should *not* be used in the policy debate when an economy is in the pursued era or suffering from a balance sheet recession.

Unfortunately, those who (like the author) studied economics during the golden era or used textbooks written during that period have had it hammered into their heads that fiscal policy has a low multiplier effect. Some cite fiscal and monetary multipliers obtained using data exclusively from the golden era because those are the data they are familiar with. Hence there is always a danger that they will subconsciously base policy recommendations on those outdated multipliers and elasticities. Even though a low fiscal multiplier was "common sense" three decades ago, the global environment surrounding the advanced economies has changed dramatically since then.

Fundamental Macro Policy Challenges Facing Pursued Countries

The most fundamental macroeconomic challenge for all pursued countries is that households are still saving for an uncertain future, much as they always have, but businesses are unable to absorb those savings because they cannot find enough domestic investment opportunities, even at very low interest rates. This marks a huge change from the golden era, when businesses were eagerly borrowing all the savings generated by the household sector. It is also an existential challenge for all pursued economies because if someone is saving money, someone else must borrow and spend that money to keep the economy from contracting.

Under such circumstances, either foreigners or the government must borrow and spend the private sector's savings. Some countries, including Japan and Germany, have relied on the former by running trade surpluses, but this is not a universal solution because all countries cannot run trade surpluses at the same time. That means the correct remedy is for the government to administer fiscal stimulus without sacrificing its fiscal future.

This a truly monumental challenge, for at least two reasons. First, the public debt has already reached very high levels in most advanced countries. Second, the pursued phase can go on for decades in today's globalized economy.

This challenge is similar to the problem that economies in balance sheet recessions confront, as discussed in Chapter 2. In a balance sheet recession, it is the millions of underwater balance sheets that lead to the disappearance of private-sector borrowers, whereas in pursued economies, it is the lack of attractive domestic investment opportunities that produces the same outcome.

In the former case, the lack of private-sector demand for borrowings will persist until balance sheets are repaired, while in the latter case, the lack of demand for borrowings will continue until sufficient domestic investment opportunities present themselves. In both cases, the problem could last for years. In the meantime, both economies will face deflationary pressures from excess private-sector savings unless someone outside the private sector (i.e., government) borrows and returns those savings to the income stream.

Fundamental Solution to Fundamental Problem

The key to addressing this seemingly impossible challenge for pursued economies can be found in the ultra-low government bond yields that all these economies are experiencing. These low bond yields, dubbed a "self-corrective" mechanism for Case 3 economies in Chapter 2, are an invitation to the government to identify and implement public works projects capable of producing a social rate of return in excess of those yields. If such projects can be found, fiscal stimulus centered on them will enable the government to act as borrower of last resort without placing an added burden on future taxpayers. As long as the projects are self-financing, the government can implement them without worrying about the size of the deficit or hitting some hypothetical "upper limit" for public debt because the projects do not constitute a burden on future taxpayers.

The most important macroeconomic challenge for policy makers in pursued countries, therefore, is to find infrastructure and other projects capable of earning social rates of return in excess of these ultra-low government bond yields. As long as such projects can be identified and implemented, the economy will continue to do well even though it is being pursued (or is experiencing a balance sheet recession). Economies in Cases 3 and 4 should therefore mobilize their best and brightest to find and implement such projects instead of wasting time worrying about the size of the public debt.

For example, thoroughly modernizing the ancient rail link connecting Washington, D.C., and Boston in the Northeast Corridor of the United States would almost certainly have a social rate of return that is many times higher than the present 10-year Treasury bond yield, which is around 3 percent. Upgrades to internet connectivity are also likely to have a very high social rate of return in many parts of the world. These are the kinds of projects that fiscal authorities in pursued economies desperately need to consider to keep their economies going.

In contrast, few public works projects are "self-financing" in the golden era, when the economy is in Case 1 or 2 and strong private-sector demand for borrowings keeps interest rates high. That means the policy option of undertaking self-financing public works projects is largely unavailable during the golden era. That also means there *is* an upper limit on the amount of debt a government can accumulate in Cases 1 and 2 because the borrowing cost that is too high can result in fiscal crisis.

That also explains why it has been difficult for economists to specify an upper limit on public debt. The correct answer depends on the amount of such debt that is self-financing, which, in turn, depends on the quality of the public works projects selected and the prevailing level of government bond yields. Government bond yields, in turn, will vary depending on whether the economy is in Cases 1 and 2 or Cases 3 and 4.

Not a Job for the Private Sector

Some may argue that if such self-financing projects exist, they should be undertaken by the private sector instead of by the government. There are two reasons why that may not work. First, private-sector businesses are under pressure from shareholders to maximize their return on capital. That means that even if there are self-financing projects at home, businesses must invest abroad if higher returns are available. Since the government has no mandate to maximize its return on capital but is expected to keep the economy out of a deflationary spiral, it can and should implement public works projects to keep the economy from contracting.

Second, the rate of return that is relevant here is the *social* rate of return. This rate captures all externalities, which private-sector operators may not be able to do. In other words, there may be projects that do not offer sufficiently high returns as private ventures but that make sense as public projects because of their positive externalities for society as a whole.

Independent Commission Needed to Select and Oversee Projects

To achieve this shift of emphasis from monetary to fiscal policy, the country will need an independent commission consisting of highly trained experts who can judge whether projects are likely to produce a social rate of return in excess of government bond yields. These calculations are not at all easy or straightforward, since a typical public works project involves many externalities that are hard to quantify but will have to be considered before making a final judgment.

Some techniques have been developed to this end by institutions such as the World Bank, but because the quality of the decisions made has huge implications for a country's future when the government is the only entity borrowing and investing for the future, existing methodologies may have to be reviewed and refined. If the selected projects turn out not to be self-financing, they can literally extinguish a country's economic future by burdening taxpayers with costly white elephants and a massive debt load.

In theory, at least, these projects need not be limited to brick and mortar. In tourism-dependent economies such as Spain, a targeted English-language training program might generate a social rate of return that is higher than the government bond yield.

To ensure that the proposed projects are actually self-financing, a politically independent commission staffed with the nation's best and brightest is essential. It has to be independent because politicians will naturally try to win projects for their constituencies, and governments in general have a poor track record in selecting good projects.

The importance of this commission's independence cannot be overemphasized: its independence is no less important in a pursued-era economy than the central bank's is in a golden-era economy. Much like independent central banks, the commission will require a robust legal status because it must have the authority to reject projects proposed by democratically elected representatives of the people.

There are historical examples of such commissions. When the United States was closing military bases after the end of the Cold War, an independent commission was set up to decide which bases to shut down. Although there were some complaints from politicians in affected districts, the process went reasonably smoothly. A similar commission is needed for countries in Cases 3 and 4 so that while projects may be proposed by elected representatives, the commission itself will have responsibility for ranking them and ensuring that those that are self-financing receive the highest priority. Even if the commission is not given the final say on which project gets implemented, just having a credible independent commission vetting projects and ranking them should go a long way in influencing the debate on which project should be funded.

The commission must also ensure that the selected projects are designed and implemented correctly. Such continued scrutiny is essential to prevent cost overruns and the inclusion of unnecessary features, and the construction contracts should be given to reliable contractors offering the lowest price. This watchdog function is crucial to ensure that projects remain self-financing as approved.

It may also take years to develop and refine proper techniques and guidelines for assessing projects and to train people to use them. If the government serves as borrower of last resort in an increasing number of projects, the commission will have to hire more trained staff. Inasmuch as pursued economies are likely to remain in that state for an extended period, there is no time to waste in developing the human capital needed for these independent fiscal commissions.

Problems with the Debt Limit Argument

Traditional fiscal hawks with a golden-era mindset may still argue that government borrowing and spending is out of the question because public debt in the advanced countries has already reached alarmingly high levels. They might also add that, while government borrowing to finance fiscal stimulus may be acceptable during balance sheet recessions (since the need for stimulus will end once private-sector balance sheets are repaired), there is no obvious end to the need for fiscal stimulus in a pursued economy. With public debt already at very high levels, they would argue that unleashing fiscal stimulus with no end in sight is nothing short of madness.

As the population in most advanced countries continues to age, many have also argued that the public and private sectors should *both* be working to cap the growth of debt, if not to reduce it. Such views are particularly strong in Germany. Indeed, the amount of debt has become a much-discussed topic among economists not only in the advanced countries, but also in places like China. They argue that, instead of relying on government spending, economies need structural reforms to enhance their competitiveness.

There are at least four problems with this debt limit argument. First, there is no question that pursued economies need many reforms if they are to fend off pursuing economies, and those issues are discussed in Chapter 5. But the problem is that such reforms require a decade or more to produce results, even under the best of circumstances. In the meantime, the government must continue to serve as borrower of last resort to keep the economy afloat, especially when the nation is also suffering from a balance sheet recession.

The Debt Limit Argument Ignores the Fact that Debt Is the Flipside of Savings

The second problem is that their obsession with the amount of debt ignores what is behind those numbers. Debt is simply the flipside of savings. Someone must be saving for debt to grow.[5] If no one is saving, debt cannot grow because there is no money to lend. But if someone is saving, someone else *must* borrow and spend those savings to keep the economy from shrinking, as is noted in Chapter 1.

Many economists appear to have forgotten this when they argue that the private and public sectors should both save more

---

[5] Those who have been led to believe that debt and the money supply are created by bankers with the stroke of a pen are referred to Chapter 8, which deals with banking.

and borrow less to prepare for an aging population. If both sectors followed their advice, there would be no borrowers for the saved funds and the economy would immediately enter the $1,000–$900–$810–$730 deflationary spiral described in Chapter 1. The paradox of thrift means that such an economy will eventually shrink down to the $500 level at which no one is able to save. In other words, if someone is saving but debt levels fail to grow (i.e., if no one borrows and spends the saved funds), the economy will contract. That means debt must increase as long as someone in the economy is still saving.

If debt appears to be growing faster than actual savings, it simply means there is *double counting* of the debt somewhere. In other words, someone has borrowed money but instead of spending it lent it to someone else, possibly with a different credit rating, maturity structure (maturity transfer), or interest rate (fixed to floating or vice versa). In this case, the debt statistics include the debts of both initial and final borrowers, but only the final borrower is actually borrowing and spending the money.

For example, if a bank sees an opportunity to expand lending to a rapidly growing industry, but its exposure to the sector is already at the regulatory limit, it may use another vehicle to make the loan possible. For instance, it may set up a nonbank entity and lend money to it. That entity, in turn, lends the money to the final borrower in the targeted industry. In this case, debt grows for both the nonbank entity and the final borrower, but the latter is the only actual borrower.

Similarly, a company with a high credit rating may procure funds at a low interest rate and lend them to a subsidiary with a lower credit rating. In this case, the debt of both firms grows, but the only real borrower is the subsidiary. An interest rate swap between the holders of fixed-rate and floating-rate notes will also produce additional liabilities (and assets) on the holders' balance sheets without actually increasing "borrowings." With an explosive increase in so-called structured products, which combine participants in the option, futures, and swap markets to produce financial products with desired risk characteristics, the liability numbers can grow rapidly. If all of the liabilities previously discussed are added together, they might become a huge number, but the actual debt is only a fraction of the total because it can never be larger than actual savings.

This can also be seen from the flow of funds data that shows both gross and net liabilities. Figures 4.1 and 4.2, for example, show both the gross and net financial assets and liabilities. If the gross liabilities are added together, it would become a huge number, but what matters for the macroeconomy is the net number, which is a fraction of the gross number.

This is not to suggest that the big debt numbers are totally meaningless. For those concerned about financial stability, the big number is important because it shows how many financial institutions and financial assets will be affected when the final borrower defaults on a loan. In other words, the domino effect of a default could be that much bigger when more parties are involved in the creation of a final financial product. But this is a financial stability issue and not a macroeconomic issue.

Unfortunately, many economists in both the public and private sectors are mindlessly quoting huge debt numbers and issuing warnings about the size of the debt. But if their numbers are correct, the savings in those economies must be growing by an equal amount. Not surprisingly, the economists calling attention to these huge debt numbers to impress their audiences seldom bring up savings data.

The Lack of Public Awareness of Excess Savings

In fact, one of the biggest problems with the policy debate in most countries today is that few are aware that the private sector has become such a large net saver despite zero interest rates. Most have never seen the numbers shown in Figure 1.1. And that is because most economists and journalists focus exclusively on the size of the debt, while only a handful talk about the size of the savings. But if debt is excessive relative to savings, interest rates should be higher, not lower. The fact that interest rates are at historical lows means that, in fact, it is savings—which no one talks about—that are too large relative to debt.

If the fiscal hawks in the United States realized (1) that the private sector has been saving an average of 7 percent of GDP at a time of zero interest rates and (2) that if someone is saving, someone else must borrow and spend those funds to keep the economy running, they would likely soften their opposition to government borrowing and spending to support the economy. This lack of public awareness is also testimony to the fact that the author's efforts over the last quarter century have been largely in vain, and he has only himself to blame for that failure. But without understanding the fundamental driver of a pursued economy—the generation of massive excess savings by the private sector—the policy debate is unlikely to produce appropriate actions to help the economy. The point is that one should not be influenced by a large debt number that has nothing to do with the reality of borrowings and savings.

The Quality of Projects and Their Macroeconomic Context Are Important

The third problem with those preaching austerity is that they are ignoring the macroeconomic and financial context in which the debt is issued. The level of debt anyone can carry depends on the level of interest rates and the quality of the projects being financed with the debt. If the projects earn enough to pay back both borrowing costs and principal, then no one should care about the debt load, no matter how large, because it does not represent a future burden on anyone.

All private-sector debt, if taken on correctly and with due diligence, should satisfy these criteria. As is noted in Chapter 1, no business or household in its right mind would want to borrow money if there is no prospect of paying it back, nor would anyone in the private sector want to *lend* money to someone who has no prospect of paying it back. The point is that it is nonsense to talk about the amount of debt without discussing the quality of the projects financed with that debt.

About the only time this rule is violated is when there is a bubble that causes both lenders and borrowers to be blinded by greed. A similar violation may occur when those in power force financial institutions to lend to unviable projects, but that is a political and not an economic issue.

The same is true with public debt. No matter how large the public debt, if the funds are invested in public works projects capable of generating returns high enough to pay back both interest and principal, the projects will be self-financing and will not increase the burden on future taxpayers.

Even if the projects are not self-sustaining, the ratio of public debt to GDP will not increase if the fiscal stimulus increases GDP more than debt and interest payments. In other words, the debt sustainability issue will not worsen even if the public debt itself increases. This is particularly important during balance sheet recessions where (1) fiscal stimulus has a high multiplier and (2) without fiscal stimulus, GDP may actually *shrink* along the $1,000–$900–$810–$730 path.

This was clearly demonstrated in the United States after 1933. Although fiscal deficits increased with New Deal policies, GDP also recovered quickly, resulting in minimal growth in the deficit-to-GDP ratio. That led Christina Romer and others to conclude mistakenly that it was not the government's fiscal stimulus but the Fed's monetary easing, which also commenced in 1933, that expanded the money supply and brought about the U.S. recovery.

But as the author showed with Figure 2.15 in Chapter 2, lending to the private sector did not increase at all from 1933 to 1939 because businesses and households were still repairing their balance sheets. It was lending to the *public* sector that increased during this period as the New Deal enabled government to serve as borrower and spender of last resort. And it was this lending that increased the money supply (Figure 2.16). The post-1933 New Deal, therefore, is a perfect example of fiscal stimulus increasing GDP more than it raised debt and interest payments, resulting in minimal growth in the deficit-to-GDP ratio. This is also consistent with the notion that the fiscal multiplier is very high when the economy is in Case 3 or 4.

Repeating the Mistake of Communist Central Planners

A fourth problem with the debt-limit argument is that it looks only at the quantity of debt and ignores the price, which is the same mistake Communist central planners made and which invariably ended in tears. By looking only at debt levels, these people are ignoring messages from the bond market, that is, the price of government bonds, in deciding whether fiscal stimulus is good or bad for the economy. Whether government borrowing is welcomed by the economy or not should be decided by the bond market, that is, those who are actually lending money to the government, and not by some economist using arbitrarily chosen criteria.

During the golden era, when the economy is in Case 1 or 2 and the private sector is eager to borrow funds to finance productivity- and capacity-enhancing investments, fiscal stimulus will have a mini- mal and possibly negative impact on the economy because of the crowding-out effect. The bond market during this era correctly sets low prices (high yields) to government bonds, indicating that such stimulus is not welcome.

But during the pursued era or during balance sheet recessions when the economy is in Case 3 or 4, private-sector demand for funds is minimal if not negative. At such times, fiscal stimulus is not only essential but has maximum positive impact on the economy because there is no danger of crowding-out. During this period, the bond market correctly sets high prices (low yields) for government bonds, indicating that they are welcome.

They are welcome because for economies in Cases 3 and 4, the only destination for surplus private-sector savings that cannot assume excessive foreign exchange risk or principal risk is debt issued by the sole remaining domestic borrower—the government. Fund managers entrusted with the private sector's surplus savings therefore rush to buy government bonds, pushing the prices of those bonds higher and the yields lower. Consequently, yields fall to levels that would have been unthinkable when the economies were in Cases 1 and 2.

Low bond yields, in turn, provide the government with the fiscal space it needs to offset deflationary pressures originating from excess private-sector savings. This self-corrective mechanism of economies in Cases 3 and 4, represented by ultra-low government bond yields, has already been observed in most pursued economies in recent years (Figure 4.5), including those not suffering from balance sheet recessions.

The fact that Japan's economy collapsed when the government ignored signals from the bond market and tried to reduce its bor- rowings in 1997, and that European economies did the same when governments there tried to reduce their borrowings in 2011, under- scores the danger of ignoring the bond market's warnings (Chapter 7 explains in detail why government bond yields in some Eurozone peripheral countries rocketed higher in 2011). In Japan's case, the fis- cal deficit actually *increased* 72 percent (Figure 2.21) when the econ- omy collapsed due to fiscal austerity, as is noted in Chapter 2. The bond market has been using ultra-low yields to tell policy makers in

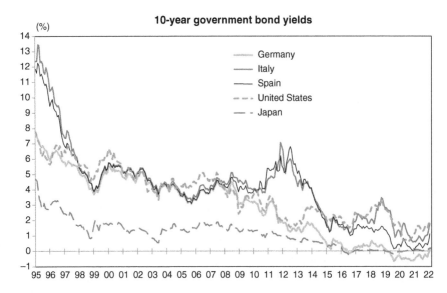

FIGURE 4.5 Limited Private-Sector Borrowings Lowered Interest Rates in
Pursued Economies

Source: Nomura Research Institute, based on data from European Central Bank
(ECB), FRB, and Ministry of Finance, Japan

Japan (since 1995) and the West (since 2008) that this is no time to
cut deficits.

Pursued Economies Are Susceptible to Bubbles

Not taking the kind of fiscal action previously described also entails
huge costs for pursued countries. Fed Chair Jerome Powell said in
a June 20, 2018, speech that the last two recessions in the United
States were caused by financial imbalances and not by central bank
tightening aimed at stamping out inflation. The emergence of these
imbalances has much to do with the fact that the United States and
all other developed economies are now in the pursued era, but the
policy responses in these economies continue to center on golden-
era monetary policy. In other words, those financial imbalances are
the result of relying too heavily on monetary policy when the economy is already in Case 3.

Once businesses start investing overseas and the economy enters the pursued phase, their need to borrow household savings drops sharply. That creates a difficult situation for the financial institutions that used to lend household savings to businesses. With businesses no longer borrowing for capacity- or productivity-boosting investments, fund managers must invest household savings in *existing* assets, which is conducive to the formation of asset bubbles, the worst manifestation of financial imbalances.

Not only do interest rates fall sharply once demand for real investment-related borrowings shrinks significantly, but central banks also cut interest rates when a lack of borrowers weakens the economy. The problem is that fund managers are still expected to produce the kind of high returns seen during the golden era, even though such returns are no longer realistically possible in a pursued economy.

That puts pressure on fund managers to participate in emerging asset bubbles, which offer high returns as long as they last. Even managers who are cognizant of the fact that they are in a bubble may join the party if they believe they can leave before the music stops playing. Of course, if everyone thinks that way, no one will be able to leave when the crash comes because everyone will be a seller and there will be no buyers. The resultant collapse in asset prices is another example of a fallacy-of-composition problem.

In the old pre-LTP era, when only the rich were involved in the financial markets, a shortage of borrowers would probably have prompted the (rich) lenders to stop lending altogether instead of accepting interest rates too low to be justified on a risk-adjusted basis. This is what Keynes called the liquidity preference, and it is probably why historical records do not show excessively low interest rates—lending generally ceased long before such extremes could be reached.

In the modern world, however, salaried fund managers do not have the option of sitting on cash: they are under pressure from their employers to produce a return. That was not a problem during the golden era because businesses had strong demand for funds to expand capacity and enhance productivity. Interest rates were quite high as a result, and most saved funds were borrowed and spent by expanding businesses in textbook fashion. In other words, the golden era was a lender's market.

In the pursued phase, however, traditional demand for funds from corporate borrowers shrinks while households continue to save for an uncertain future. The resultant savings surplus pushes interest rates to very low levels, as noted earlier. But unlike those wealthy lenders in the pre-LTP era who could simply sit on cash and cease lending, many of today's fund managers working for financial institutions are under pressure to produce returns at all times.

Furthermore, many are now competing against market indexes. This means that even if a fund manager's absolute return is low, praise will still be forthcoming as long as he or she generates a higher return than the index. As a result, the notion of risk-adjusted return is often pushed aside as fund managers strive to beat the index in an environment of extremely low interest rates.

Central Banks Are Part of the Problem, Not Part of the Solution

Some central banks' willingness to embrace negative interest rates erodes even further the notion of risk-adjusted-return. Indeed, one wonders how a central bank that supervises commercial banks is able to demand that the latter charge appropriate risk-adjusted interest rates on loans when the central bank itself is espousing negative interest rates that simply cannot be justified on a risk-adjusted basis.

Central banks in pursued economies also contribute to this problem by responding to economic weakness with interest rate cuts and liquidity injections known as quantitative easing (QE). These monetary easing policies have a similar effect to increasing the number of lenders in the economy. But when the economy is suffering from a lack of *borrowers* in spite of extremely low interest rates, those newly added funds have no place to go except into existing assets.

The situation is made worse by the efforts of central banks in pursued economies, which are fundamentally disinflationary, to achieve a 2-percent inflation target. Without borrowers in the real economy, liquidity provided by the central bank cannot leave the financial sector, as is described in Chapter 2. That means neither inflation nor GDP growth will accelerate. But low rates of inflation and economic growth push the central bank to do even more QE in an attempt to lift inflation to the 2-percent target. That increases the pool of funds that fund managers must invest in existing assets, thereby contributing to the growth of bubbles. In other words, QE in a pursued economy will do little to create inflation, but it *will* exacerbate existing financial imbalances. These factors suggest that bubbles are more likely to form in a pursued economy, which is a borrower's market, than in the two previous stages of development.

Money Invested in Existing Assets Stays in Financial Markets

Moreover, when those funds are used to acquire existing assets, the only change that takes place is a transfer of ownership: the funds themselves remain in the financial markets because the seller must invest the proceeds of the sale in some other asset. For example, if one investor purchases equities from another, the seller must then invest the proceeds in stocks or other assets. The fact that the money stays in the financial sector contributes to the practice of "flipping" assets often observed during bubbles.

In contrast, funds lent to businesses for productivity- or capacity-enhancing investments are typically applied to the purchase of machinery, and so on, causing money to flow from the financial sector to the real economy. In other words, the funds are no longer available for investment in existing assets. Such outflows of funds to the real economy will add to upward pressure on inflation in the real sector and interest rates in the financial sector.

Pursued Economies Prone to Cycles of Bubbles and Balance Sheet Recessions

Once an asset price bubble becomes a problem for society, the central bank typically raises interest rates in a bid to take some of the air out of it. As the bubble starts to collapse, participants all try to sell their assets at the same time, only to find that there are no longer any buyers. Asset prices collapse, and those who had purchased assets with borrowed money are left holding only the associated debt. This loss of wealth pushes the economy into a balance sheet recession.

The central bank responds to the recession by quickly taking interest rates down to zero, or even lower, in an attempt to prop up the economy. But monetary accommodation has limited impact when there are no borrowers, and the recession can continue for years until the private sector finally completes its balance sheet repairs.

The economy will begin to move forward when the private sector finally regains confidence in its balance sheet. But as long as the economy is in a pursued phase where corporate borrowing is not sufficient to absorb household savings, the cycle may repeat, creating another asset bubble—most likely in a different asset class—that will ultimately collapse.

Fund managers burned by the bubble's collapse naturally grow more cautious, at least temporarily. But the tragedy is bound to repeat itself several years later as long as excess savings persist at the macro level. The central bank's impatience with the slow recovery and subdued inflation may also prompt it to inject more funds into the financial system, providing the seed for the next bubble.

The last two recessions noted by Chair Powell followed this pattern. As shown in Figure 4.6, then–Fed Chairman Alan Greenspan responded to the collapse of the dot-com bubble in 2000 by taking

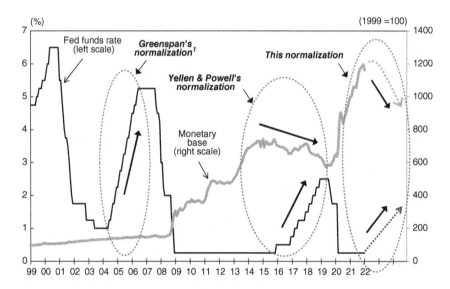

FIGURE 4.6 Overreliance on Monetary Policy Leads to Cycle of Bubbles and Balance Sheet Recessions

Notes: 1. Last two rate hikes were made under Bernanke.

Sources: Nomura Research Institute and Board of Governors of the Federal Reserve System.

FIGURE 4.7 New Bubble Forming Due to Overreliance on Monetary Policy

* *Note:* "Policy Statement on Prudent Commercial Real Estate Loan Workouts" (October 30, 2009).

Sources: Nomura Research Institute, based on Real Capital Analytics, RCA CPPI; S&P Dow Jones Indices, S&P CoreLogic Case-Shiller Home Price Indices; and Federal Reserve Bank of St. Louis, Federal Reserve Economic Data

the federal funds rate down to a postwar low of 1 percent and sparking a housing bubble before raising rates 17 times (the last two under Ben Bernanke) in an attempt to cool down the boom. When the housing bubble burst in 2008, Bernanke quickly took fed funds down to zero and implemented QE.

As a consequence, U.S. house prices have already recovered and surpassed the 2006 bubble peak by 50.9 percent. At the time of this writing, home prices in San Francisco were 58.2 percent above their bubble peak. U.S. commercial real estate prices had exceeded their previous peak in 2007 by 68.3 percent (Figure 4.7). In other words, the United States is entering another cycle of bubbles and balance sheet recessions because of its overreliance on monetary policy in the pursued era. Although bubbles have formed in all sorts of economic conditions throughout history, pursued economies should be especially careful because the factors previously noted make them especially susceptible to bubbles.

Violent Swings Do Not Help Anyone

The preceding discussion suggests that a pursued economy that is excessively dependent on monetary policy can oscillate between bubbles and balance sheet recessions. These violent swings do nothing to improve the lives of ordinary people because the frenzied buying and selling that take place merely involve a transfer of ownership of existing assets and do not add to GDP. A bubble also misallocates resources like no government can. And when it invariably bursts, trillions of dollars in private-sector savings (i.e., wealth) is squandered, leaving millions of impaired private-sector balance sheets in its wake.

That, in turn, pushes the economy into a balance sheet recession, which only government borrowing and spending can stop. Even with such government support policies, it will take years for households and businesses to make the balance sheet repairs that are required before borrowing can resume. In the meantime, both fiscal deficits and public debt levels increase sharply. In other words, an overreliance on monetary policy in an attempt to avoid fiscal deficits in a pursued economy in Case 3 ends up *increasing* fiscal deficits and the public debt when the economy eventually falls into a balance sheet recession.

All of this could have been avoided if the government, using an independent fiscal commission, had borrowed the excess private-sector savings in the first place and used them to fund self-financing public works projects. That way, the economy will still be moving forward and there will be plenty of quality infrastructure instead of millions of underwater balance sheets at the end of the day.

The economy also oscillates in the golden era, but for a different reason. In the golden era, inflation is constantly a problem because workers' wages and purchasing power are increasing while businesses are eagerly borrowing and investing household savings to finance productivity- and capacity-enhancing investments. In other words, the economy is in Case 1.

A central bank in such a setting typically responds to inflationary pressures by tightening monetary policy, thereby inducing a recession and pushing the economy into Case 2. Once the recession brings inflation under control, usually within two to three quarters, the central bank will normalize monetary policy, and the economy returns to Case 1 and resumes its growth until another bout of inflation forces the central bank's hand. Indeed, most recessions in the golden era are brought about by central banks tightening monetary policy to rein in inflation.

Despite those swings, however, no wealth is destroyed, and people continue to grow more affluent. This is because the private sector's capital stock steadily increases during the process, leading to higher productivity and GDP. Economists have also devised preemptive policies, such as inflation targeting, for central banks to follow in order to minimize the magnitude of the oscillations.

Governments Should Invest Actively until Structural Reforms Start to Bear Fruit

The long-term solution to the lack of investment opportunities in the pursued economies is to raise the domestic return on capital with structural reforms, as explained in Chapter 5. However, these microeconomic reforms typically take a decade or two to produce macroeconomic results even under the best of circumstances. Until then, it is essential that the government continue borrowing and spending excess private-sector savings on self-financing public works projects.

By borrowing and spending the private sector's surplus savings, which might otherwise be squandered on an asset bubble, the government helps prevent bubbles from forming and thereby averts the subsequent balance sheet recession. When the economy is in Case 3 or 4, therefore, government fiscal stimulus stabilizes both the real economy *and* financial markets. It also prevents a huge loss of wealth as long as the money is spent on self-financing projects. The bond market also encourages the government to act as borrower of last resort by pushing government bond yields down to very low levels.

Just as an overreliance on fiscal policy is undesirable in the golden era, an overreliance on monetary policy is undesirable in the pursued era. There is a correct policy mix for a pursued economy just as there is a correct policy mix for a golden-era economy. Instead of the monetary policy–centric approach (symbolized by inflation targets) that is appropriate for the golden era, pursued economies need to focus on fiscal policy, and particularly on finding and implementing self-financing infrastructure projects. The cost of not shifting the emphasis from monetary to fiscal policy should be obvious from the series of bubbles and balance sheet recessions advanced countries have experienced in the last three decades.

After all, there have been at least three global bubbles during the last three decades—starting with the Asian bubble in the mid-1990s—financed mostly by Western money looking for attractive returns. The bursting of the Asian bubble, triggered by the collapse of the Thai baht in the summer of 1997, was quickly followed by the global dot-com boom. When that bubble burst at the turn of the century, it was soon followed by massive housing bubbles on both sides of the Atlantic. When those bubbles collapsed, they were followed by a series of mini-bubbles in emerging market debt, commodities, oil, cryptocurrencies and, more recently, equities and commercial real estate. All of these were financed by excess private-sector savings along with excess liquidity supplied by central banks in the advanced economies.

"Financial Capitalism" and Pursued Economies

Some have called the swings originating in the financial sector affecting the rest of the society "financial capitalism." The phenomenon of the tail (in this case, the financial sector) wagging the dog (the real economy) becomes especially conspicuous when advanced countries enter the pursued phase with reduced borrowings for productivity- or capacity-enhancing investments.

If the part of capitalism that strives to increase productivity and productive capacity is called "operating capitalism" and the part that seeks to facilitate transactions in existing assets is called "financial capitalism," then the golden era was dominated by the former while the pursued era appears to be driven by the latter.

Things ended up this way, in part, because policy responses in the pursued economies continue to center on monetary policy when what is needed is fiscal policy. Once fiscal policy, together with the kind of independent fiscal commission previously noted, enables the government to begin playing a bigger role as borrower of last resort, it should be possible to tame the worst excesses of financial capitalism and bring back some stability to the lives of ordinary citizens, not only in advanced countries but also in emerging economies.

After 2008, U.S. banking regulators introduced so-called macro-prudential regulations that would allow monetary authorities to limit banks' ability to lend to certain sectors or borrowers that might foster bubbles and other financial imbalances. Although such regulations are far better than nothing at all, they are unlikely to be sufficient without the kinds of fiscal measures previously discussed. This is because funds seeking higher returns will eventually find their way into bubbles via unregulated nonbank institutions or shadow banks even if such regulation keeps the licensed commercial banks out of trouble.

When Waiting for Good Projects Is a Bad Idea

The creation of an independent commission to identify self-financing public works projects is the fundamental solution for all economies in Cases 3 and 4. However, countries currently in balance sheet recessions may be unable to wait for such a commission. Some may need immediate fiscal stimulus to stave off the $1,000–$900–$810–$730 deflationary spiral.

Since the cost of recovering from an unattended deflationary spiral (i.e., the $500 economy) is so high, these countries should implement whatever projects that are "shovel-ready" now, without waiting for ideal self-financing projects. The GDP and jobs saved by *not* waiting for perfect projects will greatly exceed any savings the latter might have yielded.

This can be seen by comparing the United States after 1929 with Japan after 1990. In the United States, President Herbert Hoover and Treasury Secretary Andrew Mellon allowed the U.S. economy to find its own bottom even though it was squarely in a $1,000–$900–$810–$730 deflationary spiral after the New York stock market crash. By taking no fiscal action until 1932, the United States lost 46 percent of its nominal GNP (Figure 2.1), and the unemployment rate exceeded 50 percent in many cities. In other words, the United States ended up in the $500 economy. The unemployment rate was still 19 percent in 1938 or fully nine years after the stock market crash.

The U.S. economy then required astronomical wartime fiscal stimulus to achieve a recovery. In 1944, at the height of the war, the unemployment rate finally fell to 1.2 percent, but that required a budget deficit of more than 30 percent of the nation's GDP.

In contrast, post-1990 Japan was able to keep its GDP from falling below the bubble peak (Figure 2.1) by implementing fiscal stimulus from the outset without waiting for ideal projects. Although some of the projects did attract criticism, the post-bubble Japanese unemployment rate never exceeded 5.5 percent even though the nation suffered balance sheet damage (i.e., a loss of wealth) three times larger as a percentage of GDP than what the United States incurred after 1929.

Some commentators have also argued that using fiscal policy to keep GDP at bubble-era levels is wrong and unsustainable. But the comparison between the post-1929 United States and post-1990 Japan demonstrates that the option of letting the economy find its "contractionary equilibrium" at a depression-level GDP is far too expensive in terms of lost output. It also means that, if the economy is already in the $1,000–$900–$810–$730 deflationary spiral, waiting for good public works projects is not an option: even bad projects are better than nothing at all if they can pull the economy out of the spiral.

Once macroeconomic stability is achieved, governments should shift fiscal stimulus to carefully vetted self-financing (or nearly self-financing) projects as they become available. When the patient is in the intensive care unit and every second counts, doctors should not be wandering around for hours in search of the most cost-effective treatment. That should come only after the patient is out of intensive care and in stable condition.

A List of Selected Projects Should Be Prepared for Future Crises

One way to shorten the time it takes to implement good public works projects is to have the independent commission constantly vetting and ranking proposed projects. That way, the government will always have fully vetted projects ready when the need arises. Given the level of today's asset prices, governments may want to produce such a list as a crisis management measure in case the bubble bursts and fiscal stimulus becomes necessary.

When the bubbles in Japan and the United States burst in 1990 and 2008, respectively, neither government had any shovel-ready projects. That delayed the fiscal stimulus needed to offset deflation-ary pressures coming from private-sector deleveraging. The resulting delay pushed the economy deeper into the $1,000–$900–$810–$730 deflationary spiral and raised the cost of recovery.

In post-1990 Japan, the government implemented whatever pub-lic works projects it could find to stop the economy's slide. While that succeeded in keeping GDP from falling below bubble-era highs (see Figure 2.1), which is no mean achievement, it exposed the government to political criticism for building bridges and roads "to nowhere" from those who could only see the micro and not the macro picture.

Those attacks, joined by hundreds of foreign pundits and even the IMF, made it *politically* difficult for the government to sustain the fiscal stimulus needed to overcome the balance sheet recession. That led to Japan's disastrous attempt at austerity in 1997, which length-ened the recession by at least a decade and added ¥100 trillion to Japan's public debt before the economy had recovered sufficiently to bring the deficit back to the pre-austerity level of 1996 (Figure 2.21). This ¥100 trillion and the loss of output and income Japanese people suffered as a result of the protracted recession were a million times greater than the loss they suffered as a result of a few poorly con-ceived pre-1997 roads and bridges.

In the post-2008 United States, the Obama administration exer-cised extra caution in selecting projects so as to avoid what hap-pened to the Japanese government 18 years earlier. That delayed the implementation of needed fiscal stimulus, leading to the loss of 8 million jobs and deepening the balance sheet recession. The extra costs incurred by the two countries could have been avoided if their governments had prepared a list of properly vetted public works projects before the bubble burst as part of their crisis manage-ment efforts.

Fiscal stimulus should continue until the private sector is ready to borrow again. When it is, the public sector should reduce its borrow-ings by the amount of new private-sector demand for borrowings. At that time, the bond market will be issuing warnings—in the form of higher bond yields—to indicate that the private sector has resumed borrowing. If no private-sector borrowing is forthcoming, the inde-pendent commission will have to continue finding self-financing pro-jects to keep the economy from contracting.

Policy Makers Unable to Shake Off Memories of Golden Age

Despite the fact that all advanced economies are now in the pursued phase, neither economics textbooks nor policy makers in these countries have been able to shake off the cobwebs of the golden era, a period that ended more than 30 years ago. The mentality of the golden era is still very much with us, for at least two reasons.

First, it was a great time when all incomes were growing and everyone was hopeful for the future. People want to return to that era because it defined what is possible for an economy. For many, in fact, this era determined the economy's "trend growth."

Second, it was the period when the discipline of macroeconomics was founded. Big names such as Paul Samuelson and Milton Friedman all wrote against the backdrop of the golden era. Most theories and models taught in economics assume that the private sector is maximizing profits because that was largely true during this era. When the private sector has a clean balance sheet, a host of attractive domestic investment opportunities, and an upward-sloping labor supply curve (from K to P in Figure 3.1), the close relationship between the monetary base and the money supply, the tight linkage between the money supply and inflation/growth, and the Phillips curve relationship between the unemployment rate and inflation rate are all basically valid.

But once the golden era ends and the economy starts to be pursued by foreign competitors, private-sector capital investment and demand for borrowings both fall markedly. Inflation slows as wages stop rising, imports increase sharply, and consumers grow more cautious. The implication is that monetary policy has a much smaller role to play (as inflation fighter) and is much less effective than during the golden era, while the reverse is true for fiscal policy.

The problem is that the policy debate in most countries has yet to acknowledge that these inevitable and fundamental changes attributable to changes in the stage of economic development have taken place. In the advanced countries, for example, most economists continue to claim that monetary policy is the right tool for addressing economic fluctuations and that fiscal policy should be discouraged because the public debt is already "too large." This is in spite of the fact that the private sector is now a huge net saver and government borrowing costs have dropped to record lows in most advanced economies. Both the media and market participants are also intensely focused on changes in central bank monetary policy, as is noted in Chapter 2, even though such policies lost a significant part of their effectiveness once these countries entered the pursued phase.

Defiance Helped Keep Japanese Pensioners from Losing Everything

In spite of strong and consistent messages from the bond market for the last 30 years, Japanese Ministry of Finance (MOF) officials with a golden era mindset have continued to warn that the huge public debt and massive fiscal deficits will soon push yields on Japanese government bonds (JGBs) sky-high and trigger a fiscal crisis. Fiscal hawks in the United States, including the Tea Party faction of the Republican Party, have also warned that the large public debt will eventually cripple the U.S. economy. The German government has been making a similar case in Europe by arguing for *Schwarz Nul* or Black Zero, meaning that governments should aim for a budget surplus or at least a balanced budget.

All the investors who listened to the warnings of imminent fiscal crisis in Japan, including some U.S. hedge funds that shorted JGBs, lost their shirts as government bond prices steadily rose over the last 30 years. The yield on 10-year Japanese government bonds fell below 2 percent in 1998, long before the Bank of Japan (BOJ) embarked on QE. By then the public debt had already reached 116 percent of GDP, the highest among the G7 countries, and the Japanese government was running a budget deficit amounting to 10.1 percent of GDP. The 10-year bond yield then fell to 0.7 percent on the eve of Governor Kuroda's QE announcement even though the public debt had by then climbed to 230 percent of GDP,[6] all because of the self-corrective mechanism of economies in balance sheet recessions.

It was fortunate that Japanese pension fund managers did not act on the warnings from the MOF. If they had followed its advice and

---

[6] These budget figures are from the International Monetary Fund (IMF) dated October 2021. https://www.imf.org/en/Publications/WEO/Issues/2021/10/12/world-economic-outlook-october-2021.

shorted JGBs over the last 30 years like certain U.S. hedge funds, they would have lost every yen of their retirees' money by now.

The 10-year U.S. Treasury bond yield also slipped below 3 percent in 2009 even as the federal deficit skyrocketed from 2.4 percent of GDP in 2007 to 10.7 percent in 2009. The yield then sank as low as 1.5 percent in 2016 *after* the Fed had stopped buying bonds with its QE program. By then, the U.S. public debt had increased to 100.1 percent of GDP, up from 35.2 percent in FY2007.[7] Government bond yields in pursued countries that are not in balance sheet recessions, including Canada, Taiwan, and South Korea, have also fallen to unusually low levels.

Such developments, where a massive expansion of the public debt is associated with sharply lower government bond yields, are unthinkable for textbook economies in Cases 1 or 2, but are perfectly understandable when an economy is in Case 3 or 4 when the government is often the last borrower standing. Those who were taught economics based on the assumption that the economy is always in Case 1 or 2, however, are still unable to grasp the huge changes in private-sector borrowing behavior that have taken place since then.

Is a 2-Percent Inflation Target Appropriate for Pursued Economies?

Much like the golden-era aversion to fiscal policy because of its supposed "low fiscal multiplier," the golden-era obsession with monetary policy is dying hard. As previously noted, the 2-percent inflation target adopted by many advanced countries today has the potential to push such economies into a cycle of bubbles and balance sheet recessions.

The 2-percent target was proposed by economists who studied the inflationary experiences of many countries over an extended period. The problem is that this period mainly covers a time when the economies were in their post-LTP golden era. The Reserve Bank of Australia (RBA) in 1992 became one of the first central banks to adopt a 2-percent inflation target. According to Glenn

---

[7] These figures are from historical budget data provided by the U.S. Congressional Budget Office in February 2021. https://www.cbo.gov/data/budget-economic-data.

Stevens, then–Deputy Governor of the RBA, it did so in order to emulate the success of the German Bundesbank in the *1970s* when it was fighting rapid increases in German wages.[8] But sharply rising wages, while typical of the golden era, are not an issue in the pursued era.

In the golden era, continuous growth in wages and domestic demand creates a fundamental tendency toward higher inflation. Businesses invest heavily at home to achieve the capacity and productivity improvements needed to meet that demand. Nor are consumers particularly fastidious about value when wages are rising year after year.

Indeed, except for OPEC-led oil shocks, most recessions during the golden era are caused by central banks tightening monetary policy to bring inflation back to a more acceptable level. And frequent tightening is necessary because golden-era economies are fundamentally inflationary. It is therefore understandable that economists sought an inflation target that the central bank should try to maintain *preemptively* so it would not be forced into belated and abrupt tightening that was so costly in terms of both uncertainty and lost output.

When the economy entered the pursued phase, however, most of the factors fueling inflation during the previous era disappeared. Instead, huge inflows of cheap imports, stagnant wages, and price-conscious consumers made it difficult for businesses to raise prices. At the same time, corporate demand for borrowings decreased as attractive investment opportunities at home disappeared while the household sector continued to save, producing a fundamentally deflationary environment. Even without a balance sheet recession, which adds another layer of deflationary pressures not seen during normal times, economies in the pursued phase are far less inflationary than those in the golden era. As noted earlier, the so-called Great Moderation was a result of economies entering the pursued era.

The question then becomes whether it is advisable for central banks to stick with a 2-percent inflation target that was designed to keep inflation rates from *accelerating* during the golden era. If the

---

[8] Stevens, Glenn (2003), "Inflation Targeting: A Decade of Australian Experience," address to South Australian Centre for Economic Studies April 2003 Economic Briefing, April 10, 2003. http://www.rba.gov.au/speeches/2003/sp-dg-100403.html.

same target is used to keep inflation rates from *decelerating* below 2 percent in the pursued era, the expectation must be that this level of inflation will prompt businesses and consumers to behave as if they were in the golden era.

But far too many things have changed during the last 30 years to expect businesses and consumers to return to the old and, in retrospect, rather inexplicable ways. For example, it is hard to expect consumers to resume buying a new car every other year or to choose their purchases based on social pressure just because inflation is running at 2 percent. Stores like Costco in the United States, 100-yen shops in Japan, and Poundland in the United Kingdom will not disappear just because the inflation rate has risen to 2 percent: consumers are much wiser now. Indeed, the fact that consumers have become much wiser should be viewed as an important indicator of human progress.

Instead of shooting for the 2-percent target, which will require continued infusions of liquidity and thereby exacerbate the already extreme overvaluation of asset prices, central banks should accept the naturally low inflation rates of pursued economies and let governments fill in the remaining deflationary gap with carefully chosen public works projects.

The Phillips Curve Is for the Golden Era

During the golden era, it was popular for economists and policy makers to talk about the Phillips curve. This curve plotted the unemployment rate against the inflation rate and suggested that there was a statistically significant negative correlation between the two. The central bank then picked the most desirable trade-off between the two, which differed depending on the country. Central banks in countries that considered inflation the greater evil were willing to accept a somewhat higher unemployment rate, while those that wanted to avoid unemployment at all costs allowed inflation to run somewhat higher. It was also within this statistical framework that economists concluded that a 2-percent inflation rate and the corresponding unemployment rate would result in the most satisfactory economic growth over time.

Once a country enters the pursued era and begins moving along the global labor supply curve, which is horizontal (from P to R in Figure 3.1), most of the factors that contributed to higher inflation rates in the golden era are no longer present. Consequently, the trade-off observed between the inflation and unemployment rates during the golden era is either greatly weakened or gone altogether. That makes the whole concept of the Phillips curve largely irrelevant as a policy guide in pursued economies.

Businesses in pursued countries are also under pressure from shareholders to be constantly watching for overseas opportunities to ensure that their capital is invested where returns are highest. By then, many of them also have ample experience producing abroad, which was not the case during the golden era, when their focus was largely domestic. This is in sharp contrast to textbook economics, which is based on the golden-era assumption that businesses have factories *only* at home.

During the golden era, rising wages due to labor market tightness force businesses to invest in productivity-enhancing equipment to stay competitive. In the pursued era, with businesses operating factories around the world, higher inflation rates—and especially rising wages at home—are likely to *discourage* them from investing more at home for competitive reasons, as is noted in Chapter 2. Thus, higher inflation rates in the pursued economies could be associated with higher unemployment rates, especially if the former are created artificially by the central bank instead of originating from tightness in the labor market. This is the opposite of the Phillips curve relationship observed during the golden era.

Spain and other Eurozone peripheral economies actually recovered starting around 2016 because internal *deflation* brought down unit labor costs and made them competitive again. This point is discussed further with Figure 7.9 in Chapter 7, which covers the Eurozone.

In spite of these huge changes, 2 percent has become *the* inflation target for many central banks around the world, and they have injected huge amounts of liquidity in an attempt to achieve it. Those pushing for this target argue that it is necessary to realign the public's inflationary expectations in order to lower expected real interest rates.

But borrowers have absented themselves not because (expected) real interest rates are too high, but because either (1) they cannot find attractive investment opportunities at home or (2) they are not comfortable with their balance sheets. Few businesses in this state will be impressed by central bankers' 2-percent inflation targets.

More importantly, the general level of prices is irrelevant for most businesses: it is the prices of their products that matter. And they know from their own daily struggle in the fiercely competitive pursued era that it is not easy to raise prices. They understand as well as anyone that they are competing every day with competitors from all over the world and that today's consumers are different from those of the golden era.

Furthermore, companies invest when they run up against capacity constraints or when they find opportunities to enhance productivity or move into new sectors. No business will start investing more just because the inflation rate has recovered to 2 percent.

The excess liquidity injected by central banks in pursuit of the 2-percent target has created bubbles in various asset classes via the portfolio rebalancing effect. Although these bubbles do have a positive wealth effect on the real economy in the short run, the effect is usually reversed when those bubbles invariably burst, pushing the economy into a destructive cycle of bubbles and balance sheet recessions. Furthermore, there are significant costs to removing the excess liquidity in the system if and when inflation or borrowers return. This difficulty, which is becoming increasingly real with post-pandemic inflationary pressures, is discussed in detail in Chapter 6.

In view of the preceding discussion, it is hoped that monetary authorities will reexamine the relevance of the 2-percent inflation target in pursued economies that are also suffering from balance sheet recessions. Mindlessly adding excess reserves in pursuit of the target not only creates a destructive cycle of bubbles and balance sheet recessions when the economy is in Cases 3 and 4, but also causes huge problems when the economy subsequently returns to Cases 1 and 2. Instead, central banks should be pushing governments to borrow the private sector's excess savings and invest the funds in self-financing public works projects because that is the correct way to support both the money supply and GDP when the economy is in Cases 3 and 4.

Recovery in Private Investment Would Not Bring Back the Golden Era

Although scientific discoveries and technological innovations are notoriously difficult to predict, there is always the possibility that such developments will lead to substantial growth in private-sector investment and demand for borrowings. The need to shift from fossil fuels to renewable energy to mitigate climate change will also require massive domestic investments that could completely alter the industrial landscape.[9]

If that were to happen, central bank monetary policy would once again have a bigger role to play—just as it did during the golden era—while fiscal policy would have to be reined in to prevent the crowding-out of private investment. In that sense, one cannot rule out the return of a world resembling the golden era given enough investment demand.

However, the chances of pursued economies returning to a *real* golden era, in which all members of society are able to benefit from economic growth, do not seem very high. During the golden era, it was the manufacturing sector that provided an ever-expanding number of well-paying jobs, thereby forcing service-sector firms to offer comparable wages to keep their workers. Because manufacturing jobs did not require advanced education, the entire population was able to benefit from economic growth. In other words, manufacturing enriched the economy from the bottom up.

It is difficult to envision future innovations that will create a large number of well-paying jobs for those without higher education. If anything, the current trend is for *reducing* headcount via automation, robotics, and artificial intelligence. In other words, technological innovation may bring back investment opportunities, but it is unlikely to restore lost jobs.

The Proper Way to Run a Pursued Economy versus a Golden Era Economy

It has become popular to decry the size of the private- or public-sector debt. But when correctly measured, debt is increasing only because savings continue to grow. Since it is difficult to tell people *not* to save, policy makers need to ensure those savings are borrowed and invested wisely in projects that will earn returns in excess of the borrowing costs. That is where the policy debate should be focused. Simply discussing the size of the debt is a meaningless waste of time.

---

[9] This point is discussed further in Chapter 6, which covers monetary policy.

In the textbook world of Cases 1 and 2, when domestic investment opportunities are plentiful, economists rightfully focus on strengthening monetary policy's ability to rein in inflation while disparaging profligate fiscal policy. Interest rates are also relatively high, which makes it difficult to find self-financing public works projects.

Now most advanced countries find themselves in Cases 3 and 4, where the private sector becomes a large net saver. Economists and policy makers must therefore reorient their focus from monetary policy to finding viable infrastructure projects so that the government can, in good conscience, continue to play the crucial role of borrower of last resort. And that task of finding viable projects has become much easier now that government bond yields are near record lows.

In summary, just as there are proper ways to run an economy in the golden era, there are proper ways to run an economy in the pursued era. The most fundamental macroeconomic challenge in the pursued era is that the household sector is still saving money as it has done for the last 5,000 years, but the corporate sector that eagerly borrowed those savings during the golden era is no longer doing so, despite extremely low interest rates.

To sustainably offset the deflationary pressures originating from the private-sector savings surplus, governments must create an independent fiscal commission to identify and undertake public works projects that promise a social rate of return in excess of ultra-low government bond yields. This is an entirely new challenge for fiscal authorities in the pursued era, just as fighting inflation was an entirely new challenge for central banks in the golden era.

The best and the brightest, many of whom headed for independent central banks during the golden era, are now needed in an as-yet-to-be-created independent fiscal commission to identify and implement public works projects that are self-financing or close to it. It is hoped that the economics profession has the courage to jettison inflation targets, its aversion to fiscal stimulus, and other legacies of the golden era and take up the task of identifying the self-financing public works projects that are so desperately needed in all pursued economies.

CHAPTER 5

Economic Growth and Challenges of Remaining an Advanced Country

Over-Stretching Is Required for Economic Growth

The preceding four chapters are all about how an economy could stagnate, sometimes for an extended period, when it is in Cases 3 and 4. This chapter discusses the opposite case, the *drivers* of economic growth. Not surprisingly, economic growth is highly relevant to an economy in Case 1 or 2.

Much has been written about economic growth since the days of Thomas Malthus. However, the recent emphasis on productivity and demographics by economists seeking to explain growth has placed the growth debate on the misleading path.

At the most fundamental level, someone must spend more than they earn for an economy to grow. If businesses and households behave prudently and spend only what they earn in each period, the economy may be stable, but it will not grow. For it to expand, some entities must over-stretch themselves—either by borrowing money or drawing down savings.

A business will do so if it finds an attractive investment opportunity that seems to offer returns that are higher than the borrowing costs. Similarly, a household might borrow money or reduce its savings if it finds an item that it feels it cannot live without. It should be noted that business and household borrowings to purchase existing assets do not count here—these transactions only result in a change of ownership and do not add to GDP.

Economic growth, therefore, requires either (1) a continuous supply of attractive investment opportunities capable of persuading companies to borrow money or (2) a continuous flow of new and exciting products that consumers want to buy, even if that means reducing savings or going into debt. Many factors influence the availability of investment opportunities and "must have" products, and demographics and productivity considerations are just two of them.

A government can also over-stretch by borrowing and spending money to increase economic growth. So-called pump-priming via fiscal stimulus is an attempt by the government to over-stretch itself in order to put a weak economy back on a growth path. Government investment in social infrastructure may also give businesses more reasons to over-stretch and thereby spur growth.

But unless the economy is in Case 3 or 4, government over-stretching cannot be relied on for too long because it can crowd out private-sector investments and increase the burden on future taxpayers. As government investments tend to be less efficient than the private-sector equivalent, economic growth often slows when the former start to crowd out the latter.

If attractive investment opportunities and "must-have" products are plentiful, there will be no shortage of private-sector borrowers, and the economy is in Case 1 or 2. When that is the case, policy makers should rely more on monetary policy because it will be highly effective in steering the economy. An overreliance on fiscal policy under such circumstances will only result in the crowding-out of private-sector investments and a general misallocation of resources. In other words, when the economy is in either of those two cases, standard textbook theory regarding the undesirability of fiscal policy and the desirability of monetary policy applies.

Consumer- and Business-Driven Economic Growth

For the economy to continue growing, there must be good reasons for businesses and households to over-stretch themselves on a sustained basis. For consumer-driven growth to continue, the recurrent emergence of new "must-have" products is necessary.

The problem is that it is difficult to forecast when such blockbuster products might emerge, because predicting the inventions and innovations that lead to such products has proved to be notoriously difficult. It is also hard to foresee what will appeal to consumers' rapidly changing tastes. This uncertainty is particularly acute in the developed world, where households already own most of life's necessities.

In contrast, business-driven growth is more robust because companies are always under pressure from shareholders to expand their operations and generate more profits. It is also businesses that create the products that consumers find irresistible. While there is no guarantee that businesses will hit upon such products or find other investment opportunities, they tend to be more dependable drivers of economic growth than fickle consumers.

Positive Fallacy-of-Composition during Golden Era

During the golden era, when businesses are faced with a surfeit of domestic investment opportunities and the purchasing power of consumers is growing rapidly, as is explained in Figure 3.1 in Chapter 3, corporate decisions to over-stretch by investing in capacity- and productivity-enhancing equipment are not difficult to make. That, in turn, often creates a *positive* fallacy of composition that serves to accelerate economic growth.

Because one person's expenditures are another's income, if all households and businesses "live beyond their means" and begin consuming and investing more, their incomes will increase by an amount equal to the growth in expenditures. For example, if everyone decides to over-stretch by spending 10 percent more than they earn, either by dis-saving or by borrowing money, their incomes will also increase by 10 percent because everyone else will be spending 10 percent more than before.

With incomes up by 10 percent, the initial decision to over-stretch no longer appears especially reckless relative to current incomes—this is what might be called the "paradox of *dis*-saving." This positive fallacy of composition with rapidly increasing incomes may lead to an even greater willingness to consume and invest on the part of consumers and businesses. This virtuous growth cycle is observed frequently during the golden era and is another example of one plus one not equaling two in macroeconomics. The growth momentum created by this positive feedback loop is also one reason why economic growth is taken for granted during the golden era.

A vast number of Japanese households in the late 1950s sought to acquire *sanshu-no-jingi,* or the "three sacred items"—a black-and-white television set, a refrigerator, and a washing machine—even if they had to borrow money to do so. Those purchases added significantly to the Japanese economy's rapid growth during that period. This is the opposite of Keynes's "paradox of thrift"; by collectively living beyond their means, consumers can drive the economy into a virtuous growth cycle. The rapid growth experienced by an economy in a bubble—for example, the surge in Japanese gross domestic product (GDP) before the bubble burst in 1990 (Figure 2.1)—is probably due to this paradox. As long as the paradox is producing positive outcomes, however, most people are happy to go along with it.

For this positive fallacy of composition to continue, there must be sufficient and concurrent growth in savings to draw upon. That is why economies that favor savings will grow faster than those that do not when there are plenty of good reasons for businesses and households to over-stretch themselves. When the economy is in Case 1 or 2, therefore, saving is a virtue, as is noted in Chapter 3.

Two Strategies for Businesses to Follow

While there is no guarantee that there will always be attractive investment opportunities worth borrowing money for, there are basically two growth paths for businesses to follow amid that uncertainty. They can try to develop either new products and services capable of wowing customers (Strategy A) or new ways to supply existing products and services at lower cost (Strategy B).

Strategy A, when successful, will lead to rapid growth not only for the company but also for the economy as a whole by spurring consumer-driven economic growth. If the new product displaces old products, total expenditures in the economy may not increase significantly, apart from the investment required to develop the new product. But chances are high that companies that lost market share to the new entrant will try to regain it by investing in the development and production of near-substitutes. Those investments will add to GDP growth.

On the other hand, this strategy is also risky because predicting profitable inventions and innovations is notoriously difficult, as noted earlier. This strategy may also require access to leading-edge technologies that only a few companies have access to. This strategy is therefore pursued mostly by businesses in the developed world with both the financial strength to take risks and access to the intellectual property rights framework needed to protect newly developed products.

Strategy B, which involves making existing products more cheaply, also provides a powerful motive to borrow and invest for entrepreneurs who believe they have devised a better way to produce existing services and products. Because consumers do not have to over-stretch as much to buy these cheaper products, a company pursuing Strategy B may earn a healthy return on capital by capturing market share quickly.

The emergence of companies offering competitively priced products may also force existing producers to invest more in productivity-enhancing equipment to stay competitive. The resultant over-stretching by rival firms adds to both economic and productivity growth.

Most businesses follow a mixture of Strategy A and Strategy B depending on their product lines. But the main source of growth is likely to be Strategy A in the advanced economies and Strategy B in the emerging economies.

Profit Motive and Productivity

Whether following Strategy A or B, most businesses are constantly on the lookout for ways to increase profitability by enhancing productivity, and they are likely to borrow and invest in machinery and innovations that lead to lower costs and higher profits. Many businesses may also be forced into investing in new equipment to raise productivity just to remain competitive. Those investment expenditures will add to economic growth.

It should be noted, however, that the economy in this case did not grow because of increased productivity. It grew because firms over-stretched themselves in the hope of raising profits when cost-cutting innovations presented themselves. If they did not over-stretch in acquiring the new equipment, their productivity might improve, but the economy would not expand because total expenditures would remain the same. This means the concept of "cash flow management" in post-bubble Japan that is noted in Chapter 2, where companies refuse to borrow money and invest only as much as cash flow will allow, has not been helpful to the country's economic growth.

The preceding discussion also suggests that the profit motive and technological progress in cost-reducing equipment are important drivers of productivity-enhancing investments. Of the two, the importance of the profit motive was amply demonstrated by the persistence of slow economic growth in communist economies where such a motive was absent. Technological progress in cost-cutting equipment, on the other hand, often depends on scientific discoveries and technological innovations that are difficult to forecast, as noted earlier.

Problems with the Concept and Measurement of Productivity

The concept of productivity is also not so straightforward. It has been said for decades that Japan's manufacturing sector is highly productive, but its service sector is not. There is no question that the former is true, but if the latter were also true, Japan should have been flooded with foreign retailers and other service providers that are more productive than their Japanese rivals.

U.S. and European retailers have made numerous attempts over the decades to enter the Japanese market. After all, Japan was the world's second largest consumer market until 2010, when China took away that title. But almost all of these attempts failed, and there is still no meaningful foreign penetration of the Japanese retail market.

The reason for this failure is simple. There is a big difference in the relative factor prices of real estate, energy, and labor between Japan and the West. In Japan, real estate and energy prices are high relative to the cost of labor, whereas the opposite is true in the West. As a result, a typical Japanese retailer will try to use as little real estate and energy as possible relative to workers to maximize profits, whereas a Western retailer will take the opposite tack. Japanese stores therefore tend to be smaller establishments staffed by many employees, while Western stores are generally huge, well-lit establishments staffed by only a few people.

When revenues are divided by the number of workers, Japanese stores are naturally outperformed by Western establishments. But this so-called "labor productivity" figure is meaningless without considering the productivity figures for the floor space and energy used, where Japan comes out looking significantly better than the West.

Western retailers who did not understand this point and operated stores in Japan the same way they did at home lost a great deal of money before eventually having to leave. Any attempt to raise so-called "labor productivity" in Japan is futile unless relative factor prices in the country are the same as in the West.

This also implies that actual labor productivity should be measured per unit of capital—including land. But measuring the amount of capital available to each worker is extremely difficult, if not impossible. There are, however, some anecdotal cross-country comparisons.

A traveling Australian entertainment group has been performing "Thomas the Tank Engine" for children around the world with the same stage props for years. The props are set up in theaters in each country by the same number of young part-time workers. The Australian manager of the group told the author's son, who was one of the part-time workers in Japan, that in any other country, setting up the props takes a minimum of four hours, and often six hours or more. But in Japan, he said, it never takes more than two hours even though different workers are involved each year. This anecdote suggests young Japanese part-time workers may be more productive than their peers elsewhere.

It could be argued that cross-country productivity comparisons should be made based on total factor productivity instead of labor productivity. This is easier said than done, since it may require adding apples and oranges when different factors of production are involved.

One way to get around this problem in comparing retail sector productivity is to examine final selling prices across countries, since retailers with higher total factor productivity should be able to sell products at lower prices.

The Big Mac index compiled by the *Economist* magazine is useful in this regard because the quality of Big Macs is the same everywhere in the world (see Figure 9.3 in Chapter 9). Although the original objective of the index was to determine the over- and under-valuation of currencies on a purchasing power parity basis, it is interesting to note that in Japan, which has the same per capita GDP as Europe, Big Macs are sold at a much lower price than in Europe, even though Japan imports almost all of its ingredients from abroad.

This suggests either that the yen is undervalued, or that the Japanese operation has a much higher total factor productivity than the European operations.

It was not always this way. Prices in Japan used to be much higher than the international norm, and Tokyo was consistently voted the world's most expensive city well into the 1990s. The gap in prices was so bad that there was even a Japanese word, *naigai-kakakusa*, to describe the huge disparity between domestic and international prices. The gulf was so wide that the author used to buy everything from daily necessities to motor oil in the United States and bring them back to Tokyo in suitcases.

But this all changed when the shock of an incredibly strong yen—the Japanese currency climbed to 79.75 yen/dollar in April 1995[1]—finally kicked open the domestic market to imports. The relentless competition among domestic retail establishments that followed made Japan one of the cheapest places to dine and shop in the developed world.

Japan now has over 4,000 so-called 100-yen shops offering everything from quality household wares to stationary items from around the world for 100 yen (about $.80) each. Many of these stores are selling goods at the lowest prices seen anywhere in the world. The fact that they are often sitting on some of the most expensive real estate in the world suggests that total factor productivity is high. Since these shops have appeared, no one in Japan talks about *naigai-kakakusa* anymore.

Profitability and Physical Productivity

Another problem with productivity is that it is often confused with profitability. In the mid-1980s, many Japanese companies borrowed and invested heavily in the latest equipment and factories to make themselves even more competitive. The exchange rate at the time was 240 yen to the dollar. But when those factories came on line in the late 1980s, the exchange rate had fallen to 120 yen to the dollar, reflecting a stronger yen. The companies that had made these investments were badly hurt, and economic growth slowed.

---

[1] Why the yen moved so dramatically then is explained in Chapter 9.

Japanese companies enjoyed higher physical productivity with their newer equipment and factories, but capacity utilization and profitability were far lower. When the exchange rate went to 80 yen to the dollar in the mid-1990s, many of these companies were referred to as "zombies" because of their earlier over-stretching, even though their physical productivity was still second to none.

Many observers who argue that Japanese GDP growth declined because of reduced productivity growth are mistaking profitability for productivity. It is the decline in profitable investment opportunities due to the strong yen that has weighed on investment (i.e., over-stretching) and GDP growth. Investment also declined after the bubble burst in 1990 because so many companies faced balance sheet problems, and productivity growth slowed because there was less investment.

As is noted in Chapter 4, productivity growth has recently slowed in almost all advanced countries because they have become pursued economies, with lower returns on capital than are available in emerging markets. With shareholders clamoring for higher returns on capital, it has become difficult for companies in these countries to justify investing in less profitable projects at home. That, in turn, has lowered both economic and productivity growth in the advanced nations.

Higher Productivity Does Not Necessarily Lead to Higher Wages in Pursued Economies

Even if businesses invest in productivity-enhancing equipment at home in a pursued era, such investments do not increase the wages or purchasing power of workers the way they did during the golden era. U.S. President Joe Biden noted during his 2020 election campaign that U.S. productivity had risen 70 percent between 1979 and 2018 while wages had grown only 12 percent in real terms. This decoupling of wages and productivity growth has much to do with the fact that the United States and other advanced economies are now in the pursued era.

The Western economies until the 1980s, and Japan until the 1990s, were in a golden era where attractive domestic investment opportunities were plentiful but the supply of labor was limited. That led to annual increases in wages as the expanding economy moved along the upward-sloping labor supply curve from K to P in Figure 3.1. This wage growth was also the key driver of domestic demand because it increased workers' purchasing power.

Businesses facing rising wages as well as greater demand for their products expanded investment both to boost productivity (to remain competitive) and to expand capacity (to meet additional demand). Wage growth and productivity growth therefore moved together, with the former driving the latter.

For the last 30 years, however, businesses in advanced countries have realized that the return on capital is higher in low-wage emerging markets than in their high-wage home markets, and they have shifted their investment destinations accordingly. Instead of paying higher wages at home, they simply moved production abroad. That has resulted in the loss of millions of manufacturing jobs at home and slower economic growth. The loose domestic labor market conditions that resulted removed the key reason for wages to rise. Consequently, companies are no longer forced to enhance productivity to pay ever-increasing wages.

If businesses invest at home in the pursued era, they do so to improve profitability. Even if wages are not rising, there is no reason not to invest in equipment that lowers costs and boosts profitability. The resultant improvements in productivity do not translate into higher wages because wages themselves are determined by the labor market, where conditions are much looser than during the golden era.

During the golden era, labor productivity and wages moved in tandem because it was the rising wages that forced companies to enhance worker productivity. During the pursued era, the benefits of improved productivity brought about by corporate investments go to those who made the investments, not to the workers.

Will Higher Minimum Wage Boost Productivity?

Some have argued that the government should then raise the minimum wage to boost labor productivity. Although rising wages will force some companies to make more productivity-enhancing investments, higher unemployment could also result if the wages are rising because of government decree and not because of tighter labor market conditions.

An attempt to raise the minimum wage in a pursued economy also risks shifting even more investment to emerging economies by further depressing the domestic return on capital. Unlike their predecessors in the golden era, many businesses in the pursued era have production facilities located around the world. That means proposals to raise the minimum wage should be approached carefully inasmuch as they have the potential to further reduce already low domestic returns on capital and create more unemployment.

The point is that businesses do not engage in productivity- or capacity-enhancing investments if they see no money in it. Productivity growth is the result of businesses responding to the emergence of cost-cutting investment opportunities that increase their return on capital. When such opportunities present themselves in the form of technological progress and are acted on by businesses that over-stretch themselves, both economic and productivity growth will accelerate.

Whether that growth benefits labor depends on the tightness of the labor market. That, in turn, is often determined by whether the economy is in the golden era or the pursued era. In the golden era, the macroeconomic tide originating from a surfeit of domestic investment opportunities prompts businesses to expand, increasing demand for labor in a tight labor market, thereby raising all wages. In the pursued era, when returns on capital are higher abroad than at home, there is unlikely to be a macroeconomic tide that lifts all wages. Instead, individual workers must enhance their own productivity by learning new skills if they want to increase their income. Businesses will continue to invest more to boost productivity, but the resultant increase in productivity does not often lead to higher wages in a much looser labor market of the pursued era.

Export-Driven Economic Growth Faces Fewer Hurdles

For many industries in the developed world, significantly cheaper labor costs in the emerging economies eliminate the option of pursuing Strategy B at home. Barring revolutionary discoveries or innovations that drastically improve domestic productivity, it simply does not make sense for them to continue with Strategy B. That is why they became pursued economies in the first place, and why so many companies in these countries are forced to pursue the more difficult Strategy A.

For businesses located in the emerging world, on the other hand, wage levels often make the pursuit of Strategy B highly attractive. For instance, wages in Japan and China were far lower than those in the West when the two countries first entered the global market in the 1950s and 1980s, respectively. All manufacturers had to do was to produce quality products cheaply (which, of course, is not easy), and the products would basically *sell themselves* in overseas markets.

These less-expensive products sold themselves because there was no need for consumers in importing nations to over-stretch when buying them. On the contrary, consumers in the importing nations were *saving* money by switching to lower-priced imports, which is the opposite of over-stretching. From the perspective of exporting countries, foreign consumers were doing the over-stretching that helped their exports and economies to grow, but individual consumers in importing countries saw themselves as *under*-stretching by shifting their purchases to cheaper imports. (The inherent contradiction here is discussed further in Chapter 9, which looks at global trade.)

That means that even if the products themselves are not new and do not "wow" consumers, exporting companies and countries can grow rapidly as long as their products can be priced competitively in overseas markets. Japan and all the other countries that successfully achieved export-led economic growth in the postwar period started out with Strategy B.

Even though most businesses pursue a combination of Strategy A and B depending on the product line, most companies in pursued countries are forced into the riskier and more difficult Strategy A, resulting in slower growth for the economy. Businesses in emerging markets, on the other hand, are either in the pre–Lewis Turning Point (LTP) urbanization era or the post-LTP golden era and tend to pursue the easier, less risky Strategy B, which leads to faster economic growth.

Import-Substitution Model Seldom Sustainable

The emphasis on over-stretching to explain economic growth also helps to explain why the export-driven model of economic growth has been more successful than the import-substitution model pursued by some countries. In the latter case, the captive market provided by protectionist government policies initially boosts the profitability of businesses benefiting from the protection. That prompts them to increase investment at home, accelerating economic growth. But someone in the economy must continuously over-stretch themselves for this growth model to remain viable.

For that to happen, businesses must continuously come up with new and exciting products to wow domestic consumers, something that has proved difficult for underdeveloped local industries requiring government protection. The limited size of the domestic market also leads to correspondingly high production costs, making these products less attractive to consumers. In addition, their high cost limits their appeal to foreign consumers, making it difficult for businesses to pursue Strategy B. In other words, this growth model effectively asks businesses in developing countries to pursue the more difficult Strategy A.

That is why after a promising initial boost to growth, this model has never remained viable for long in any country—although it has been tried by many countries in Latin America and elsewhere in the 1950s and 1960s.

Transparency Is the Greatest Attraction of U.S. Market

The export-driven model of growth does have one requirement that the import-substitution model never had to worry about: access to foreign markets. Before 1945, access to foreign markets was limited for most countries because all nations had erected numerous barriers to trade. Indeed, revenue from tariffs had been a major source of government income for centuries. With many foreign markets effectively closed, most countries had no choice but to pursue the import-substitution model of growth. That, in turn, placed substantial constraints on global economic growth.

All that changed after World War II when the United States introduced a free-trade regime under General Agreement on Tariffs and Trade (GATT), as is noted in Chapter 4. Even though the concept and practice of free trade had been observed from time to time in the past, the U.S. decision to open its vast domestic market—which accounted for nearly 30 percent of global GDP at the time—was a game-changer.

Japan, realizing the far-reaching implications of the U.S. policy change, placed its best and brightest in exporting industries and started growing rapidly. The Japanese success was soon followed by Taiwan, South Korea, and others. Wartime technological break-throughs helped, of course, but without free trade it would be difficult to explain the rapid economic growth of countries such as West Germany and Japan, which depended heavily on the U.S. market.

The end of the Cold War in 1990 then allowed Communist and former Communist countries to join the free trade bandwagon. China, with its low labor costs, benefited most. Capitalizing on the U.S.-built free trade regime, China raised its per capita GDP from a paltry $300 in 1978 to over $10,000 in 2019 for 1.4 billion people, representing the greatest burst of economic growth in history. Indeed, all countries that have relied on exports to achieve economic growth after 1945 have done so by tapping into the U.S. market.

The Importance of Recognizing the Source of Over-Stretching

The importance placed on the U.S. market by the Japanese came as a cultural shock to the author when he moved from the Federal Reserve Bank of New York to Nomura Research Institute (NRI) in Tokyo in 1984. When forecasting GDP growth, it was typical in the United States to start the exercise by estimating personal consumption, which is the biggest component of U.S. GDP. From there, projections of other, smaller components of GDP such as fixed capital investment and net exports were added to come up with a final figure.

In Japan, which was already the second largest economy in the world, the forecasting exercise at NRI, the oldest, largest, and most influential private think-tank in the country at the time, started with an elaborate forecast of the U.S. economy. Projections for Western Europe were then added to come up with a forecast of Japan's exports. Exports were followed by fixed capital investment, and forecasts of personal consumption and other items came after that. This was in spite of the fact that personal consumption was the biggest single component of Japan's GDP and was far larger than exports.

The Japanese knew that exports were the key driver of growth, and that it was foreigners who were doing the crucial over-stretching. They knew from experience that if exports slumped, other components of GDP would also stagnate. They understood that as far as growth is concerned, *where* the over-stretching is happening is more important than the size of the sector itself. Even if exports are not the biggest sector, if that is where most of the over-stretching is taking place, then that is where the focus should lie when forecasting overall economic growth.

Even today, the United States remains a crucial market for both developed and developing countries, including Japan, Europe, and China. This is due not only to the size of the U.S. market, but also to its great transparency and the absence of nontariff trade barriers. From a business standpoint, transparency is often as important as—if not more important than—the size of the market itself.

For instance, the nominal GDP of the 27 European Union nations was equal to 73.1 percent of U.S. GDP in 2020, and in the mid-1990s Japanese GDP approached 70 percent of U.S. output. In 2020, China's nominal GDP was 71.2 percent of the U.S. figure.[2] However, the companies and countries that would suffer from being shut out of U.S. market far outnumber those that would be hurt by being kept out of the other three markets.

The reason is that the other three markets are less transparent than the United States and therefore require much greater efforts by foreign exporters. The return on capital for marketing efforts in these three markets is therefore lower than in the United States. As a result, many companies do not even try to penetrate the other three markets.

The difficulty of breaking into the Japanese market, for example, was amply demonstrated until quite recently by the existence of many so-called export-only manufacturers in Japan. These companies existed because they could earn a much higher return on capital by concentrating their marketing efforts in more transparent overseas markets—and particularly the U.S. market—instead of trying to crack the more difficult domestic market. This transparency is also why many governments—including those of Japan, China, and Europe—were so eager to conclude a "deal" with former President Donald Trump when he was pushing a protectionist "America First" agenda.

---

[2] These figures are based on data from International Monetary Fund (IMF) World Economic Outlook in October 2021.

The Middle-Income Trap and Difficulty of Transitioning from Strategy B to Strategy A

Advanced countries at the receiving end of emerging economies' export drive have largely exhausted low-hanging investment (i.e., over-stretching) opportunities at home, and their economic growth has slowed, even though business executives are paid a great deal to identify profitable investment opportunities. The West was shocked when Japan emerged as a fierce competitor in the 1970s, pushing many well-known manufacturers out of business and forcing remaining companies to focus on the more difficult Strategy A.

Japan then experienced a similar shock when the Asian Tigers began chasing it in the 1990s, as did the Asian Tigers themselves when Chinese competition appeared in the 2000s. Today, the Chinese are worried that many of their industries and jobs will migrate to Vietnam and other lower-wage countries, even though China's per capita GDP is still significantly lower than that of the advanced economies.

Wages in successful emerging economies will eventually approach the levels of the developed world. However, only countries that leveraged know-how and capital acquired during the pursuit of Strategy B to develop superior products that are necessary for Strategy A have succeeded in breaking into the ranks of developed nations. Those that fail to accumulate the necessary know-how and capital might initially achieve a certain amount of export-driven economic growth, but investment slows once domestic wages rise to a level that makes Strategy B unprofitable. Growth in these countries then stagnates as they find themselves in the so-called middle-income trap.

The middle-income trap refers to the slowdown in economic growth that occurs when rising domestic wages cause a country to lose its status as a low-cost producer. When that point is reached, domestic and foreign companies start moving factories to emerging economies with even lower wage costs. That causes investment and growth to decline unless explicit reforms are undertaken to increase the return on capital, thereby prompting both domestic and foreign companies to continue expanding their investment in the country.

Indeed, only a handful of countries outside the West have managed to escape this trap and achieve advanced-economy status. This short list contains Japan, Taiwan, South Korea, and Singapore, while the number of countries struggling to escape from the trap continues to increase with globalization. As more and more developing countries adopt the export-led growth model and enter the global supply chain, many middle-income countries are facing challenges—in the form of this "trap"—that are similar to those faced by pursued countries.

Demographics and Corporate Investment Decisions

Where do demographics, a favorite subject of economists, fit in this framework? In today's globalized market, domestic demographics should have increasingly less influence on corporate investment decisions—except when a firm has difficulty finding workers or its business is closely tied to the fortunes of a certain geographic region. In all other cases, it should be global demographics that matter for businesses operating in a globalized market.

Amid this diminished influence, an increase in the population will certainly be viewed by businesses as a good reason to expect consumer-led growth *if* those new additions to the population are able to find jobs and earn income. For those jobs to materialize, however, businesses themselves must feel that demand for their products will increase in the future.

A growing population is certainly one reason for businesses to believe that demand for their products and services will increase. However, few businesses are likely to rely solely on this factor when making investment decisions unless they are a monopoly, or something close to it. Instead, they will probably pay more attention to what their research and development departments are doing relative to competitors at home and abroad. They will also be watching factors that drive short- and medium-term fluctuations in demand, such as the COVID-19 pandemic. In other words, demographic trends are one factor in businesses' investment decisions, but usually not the dominant one.

Demographics may, however, have an outsized psychological influence on investment decisions if growth turns negative. If businesses are unable to find enough employees for their factories, that is a legitimate reason to move the plants overseas. But too often, businesses—even those that are globally active—may use a shrinking population as an excuse to do nothing. The author has encountered many global portfolio investors who skipped Japan altogether because "soon there won't be any Japanese left." This is in spite of the fact that Japan remains the third largest economy in the world, and its companies still dominate many fields requiring cutting-edge technologies.

Even in those countries where the population is growing rapidly, if new entrants to the labor market are unable to find gainful employment—perhaps because of insufficient education or opportunity—the expanding population will only worsen poverty without adding much to economic growth. If poverty undermines social stability, businesses may be even less inclined to invest, and the country's economic growth will stagnate further. Many developing countries today are suffering from this kind of population explosion and the resulting social unrest.

When war-torn Japan faced this problem of too many people chasing too few jobs and social services in the 1950s, the government actively encouraged emigration of its people to destinations in South America so that those who remained had a chance to advance themselves economically. Many governments in the emerging economies of South and Southeast Asia today are also encouraging their workers to go abroad to reduce overcrowding at home. Some of these governments are even counting on those workers' overseas remittances to bolster their foreign currency reserves.

The fact that such *de*-population policies have had a positive impact on economic growth in certain developing countries suggests there may be an optimal rate of population growth that varies with the stage of economic development. In other words, both excessively high and excessively low population growth (relative to the optimal rate) can be detrimental to economic growth. Ultimately, the economic growth that relies on population growth is neither desirable nor sustainable because the planet simply cannot take unlimited expansion in human population.

Demographics as Endogenous to Economic Development

Demographic trends are also dependent on the stage of economic development. Before the Industrial Revolution, when most people lived on farms, families tended to have more children because the infant mortality rate was high, and children were expected to work on the family farm. There were also religious pressures in many parts of the world not to limit the number of children.

Once the economy enters the urbanizing industrial age, families tend to have fewer children, but rapidly increasing incomes—especially during the post-LTP golden era—and a fall in the infant mortality rate due to better public health often cause the population to expand, sometimes dramatically. Some of the emerging economies currently exporting workers are facing just this sort of population explosion.

Once the economy enters the pursued phase and becomes a post-industrial "knowledge-based society," the birth rate falls even further. This happens not only because more women join the workforce, but also because parents realize that only children who receive a good education are likely to do well in such a society. This last point is most prominent in the education-obsessed East Asia, where birth rates have dropped sharply as families decided to have fewer children so that the children they do have can receive a quality education.

This trend has been amply demonstrated by the sustained decline in China's birth rate to the second lowest in the world after South Korea even after the government ended its one-child policy. It suggests that demographic trends are to a large degree endogenous to the stage of economic growth.

The Three-Pronged Reforms Needed for a Pursued Economy to Stay Ahead

In the pursued economies, where there are no more low-hanging investment opportunities and populations are aging, policy makers pushing for growth should concentrate their structural reform efforts on at least three areas. First, they should seek supply-side reforms such as deregulation and tax cuts that are designed to increase the return on capital at home. Second, they should encourage labor market flexibility so that businesses can take evasive action to fend off pursuers. Third, they should revamp the educational system to address both the increased human-capital requirements and the greater inequality that are specific to pursued economies.

These three challenges are unique to countries in the pursued phase, and these three policies are necessary for pursued countries to remain advanced economies. Policy makers must also pay more attention to trade deficits to safeguard free trade, as is explained in Chapter 9, and refrain from relying excessively on monetary policy, as is discussed in Chapter 4.

How the United States Answered Japan's Challenge

On all three fronts of structural reform, it is instructive to start with the real-world experiences of the United States in fending off Japan. This is the story of a pursued country that lost its high-tech leadership and then regained it two decades later. When the United States began losing industries left and right to Japanese competition in the mid-1970s, as is described in Chapter 3, it pursued a two-pronged approach in which it tried to keep Japanese imports from coming in too fast while simultaneously shoring up the competitiveness of domestic industries.

The United States utilized every means available to prevent Japanese imports from flooding the market while pushing for market-opening measures in Japan. These included dumping accusations, the Super 301 clause, various "gentlemen's agreements," currency devaluation via the Plaza Accord of 1985, and an attempt to revamp the Japanese economy via the Structural Impediments Initiative of 1989. The author was directly involved in the U.S.-Japan trade frictions at that time and can say without qualification that the struggle was neither easy nor pleasant (some of the author's experiences are discussed in detail in Chapter 9).

Meanwhile, "Japanese management" was all the rage at U.S. business schools in the 1980s and 1990s. Harvard University professor Ezra Vogel's *Japan as Number One: Lessons for America*, published in 1979, was widely read by people on both sides of the Pacific. The business schools also recruited many Japanese students so they could discuss Japanese management styles in their classrooms. The challenge from a seemingly unstoppable Japan, coupled with the U.S. defeat in the Vietnam War, sent national confidence to an all-time low, while consumption of sushi went up sharply.

Reaganomics and Learning How to Run Faster

The United States was fortunate, however, that the supply-side reforms of President Ronald Reagan—who cut taxes and deregulated the economy drastically starting in the early 1980s—addressed the first of the three challenges of pursued economies by raising the return on capital at home. These policies encouraged innovators and entrepreneurs to generate new ideas and products, especially in the area of information technology.

Reaganomics itself was a response to the stagflation of the 1970s, which was characterized by frequent strikes, high inflation rates, substandard manufacturing quality, and mediocrity all around. It was a reaction against organized labor, which was still trying to extend gains made during the post-LTP golden era without realizing that the United States had already entered the pursued phase in the 1970s with the arrival of Japanese competition. The fact that the United States was losing so many industries and good jobs to Japan also created a sense of urgency that a break from the past was urgently needed.

People with ideas and drive began to take notice when President Reagan lowered taxes and deregulated the economy. These people then began pushing the technological envelope in many directions, eventually enabling the United States to regain the lead it had lost to the Japanese in many high-tech areas. Few Americans in the 1980s thought the nation would ever win back high-tech leadership from Japanese companies like Sony, Panasonic, and Toshiba, yet today, even the Tokyo offices of Japanese companies are full of products from such U.S. brands as Apple, Dell, and Microsoft.

In retrospect, "Japanese management" looked invincible in the 1980s, in part, because Japan was in a golden era with numerous positive feedback loops, whereas the United States was already in the pursued era. Today, few people extol the virtues of Japanese management because Japanese companies, now in the pursued era, are grappling with the same problems that confronted U.S. companies three decades ago. Some of them have already gone bankrupt or have been taken over by companies from pursuing countries. Indeed, the author came up with the concept of pursued economies after noticing that Japanese companies today face problems similar to those that U.S. companies struggled with three decades ago. This also implies that both management and labor must change as the economy moves from one era to the next.

The Need for Labor Market Flexibility in Pursued Economies

Reagan also addressed the second policy challenge of pursued economies by pushing hard for a more flexible labor market. This was symbolized by his decision to fire the civilian air-traffic controllers who had gone on strike in defiance of federal regulations and replace them with military controllers. This bold action, widely supported by the public, finally broke the back of the labor unions that were still trying to extend gains made during the golden era.

Once the country enters the pursued phase, the whole economy must become more flexible to enable its businesses to take evasive action to fend off pursuers. Foreign competitors may suddenly show up from anywhere, often with a vastly different cost structure. When faced with such competition, businesses must downsize or abandon product lines that are no longer profitable and shift resources to areas that remain profitable.

These tough decisions—which must be made without delay—make it difficult for firms to maintain seniority-based wages and lifetime employment because both effectively turn labor into a fixed cost and undermine management's ability to take evasive action. Attaining this flexibility is a new challenge that is unique to the pursued era.

In contrast, during the golden era, when a country is a global leader or is chasing someone without being chased by anyone else, there is typically no need for evasive action. With a promising road ahead and no one visible in the rear-view mirror, businesses take a forward-looking approach and focus on finding good employees and retaining them for the long term. Seniority-based wages and lifetime employment are therefore typical features of the golden era—especially at successful companies—since such measures help maintain a stable and reliable workforce. In the United States, IBM and other top companies had lifetime employment systems during the golden era.

Reagan's deregulation, tax cuts, and anti-union actions enhanced the ability of U.S. businesses to fend off competitors from behind. Even though those measures hurt labor and aggravated income inequality in some quarters, chances are high that without them the post-1990 U.S. resurgence would have been much weaker or faltered altogether. After trying everything from protectionism and currency devaluation to studying Japanese management techniques, the United States concluded that when a country is being pursued from behind, the only real solution is to run faster—that is, to continuously generate new ideas, products, and designs that encourage consumers and businesses to over-stretch.

Supply-Side Reforms Need Time to Produce Results

Although the U.S. success in regaining the high-tech lead from Japan was a spectacular achievement, it took nearly 15 years. Reagan's concepts were implemented in the early 1980s, but it was not until Bill Clinton became president that those ideas bore fruit. The U.S. economy continued to struggle during Reagan's two terms and the single term of George H.W. Bush, who had served as vice president under Reagan.

The senior Bush achieved a number of monumental diplomatic successes, including the end of the Cold War, the collapse of the Soviet Union, and victory in the first Gulf War. Yet he lost his reelection campaign to a young governor from Arkansas named Bill Clinton whose only campaign slogan was, "It's the economy, stupid!" Bush's election loss suggests the economy was still far from satisfactory in the eyes of most Americans 12 years after Reaganomics was launched.

Once Clinton took over, however, the U.S. economy began to pick up—even though few today can remember any of his administration's economic policies. Things were going so well that the federal government was running budget surpluses by Clinton's second term. The conclusion to be drawn here is that while supply-side reforms are essential in a pursued economy, it can take many years for such measures to produce macroeconomic results that the public can recognize and appreciate.

The time needed for structural reforms to produce enough domestic investment opportunities for businesses to over-stretch themselves means the government must operate as "over-stretcher of last resort" in the meantime if the economy is in Case 3 or 4. There is simply no substitute for fiscal stimulus in the short run when the private sector is unable to find sufficient domestic investment opportunities to absorb all the savings generated in the economy.

Structural reform is not a panacea, either. Many economists argued for structural reforms instead of fiscal stimulus in post-1990 Japan and in the post-2008 Eurozone. But both economies suddenly lost steam not because of structural problems, but because they were suffering from post-bubble balance sheet problems. And only a government acting as borrower and spender of last resort can help an economy in a balance sheet recession, as is explained in Chapter 2.

The Challenge of Finding and Encouraging Innovators

With regard to the third challenge—having the right kind of educational system to match human capital requirements in pursued economies—the United States was fortunate to have had a long tradition of liberal arts education that encouraged students to think independently and challenge the status quo. Such thinkers are essential to creating the new products and services that are needed by businesses pursuing Strategy A in advanced countries.

The problem is that not everyone in a society can come up with new ideas or products, and it is not always the same group. It also takes an enormous amount of effort and perseverance to bring new products to market. But without innovators and entrepreneurs willing to persevere, the economy will stagnate or worse. The most important human-capital consideration for countries being pursued, therefore, is how to maximize the number of people capable of generating new ideas and businesses and how to incentivize them to focus on their creative efforts.

Only a limited number of people in any society are able to come up with such ideas. They are often found outside the mainstream because those in the mainstream have few incentives to think differently, and only those with an independent perspective can create something new. Some may also show little interest in educational achievement in the ordinary sense of the word. For those who want to create something new, learning about what was discovered in the past often seems a waste of time. Indeed, many successful start-ups have been founded by college dropouts.

Many innovators and potential entrepreneurs may infuriate and alienate the establishment with their "crazy" ideas. If sufficiently discouraged by the orthodoxy, they may withdraw altogether from their creative activities. Finding these people and encouraging them to focus on their creative pursuits is therefore no easy task.

In this regard, the West's tradition of liberal arts education has served it well. In particular, the notion that students must think for themselves and substantiate their thinking with logic and evidence instead of just absorbing and regurgitating what they have been taught is crucial in training people who can think differently and independently.

At some top universities in the United States, students who simply repeat what their professor said may only receive a "B" grade; an "A" requires that they go beyond the lectures and add something of their own. This training encourages them to challenge the status quo, which is the only way to come up with the new ideas and products that are essential for businesses pursuing Strategy A.

Liberal arts education has a long tradition in the West. It started with the Renaissance and the Enlightenment, when the value of the human intellect was finally recognized after being suppressed for centuries by the Catholic Church. This long struggle to free the intellect from church authorities was not an easy one, and many brilliant thinkers were burned at the stake. Societies that went through this long and bloody struggle therefore tend to cherish the liberal arts tradition.

Societies that did *not* experience such struggles, however, may have to guard against the tendency of the educational hierarchy to worship "authorities" to the detriment of independent thinkers. Once such a hierarchy is established, it becomes difficult for new thinkers to gain an audience, especially when their ideas challenge the orthodoxy. The implication here is that citizens' creativity may not be fully utilized in societies where the educational establishment and other authorities continue to act like the Catholic Inquisitors of the past.

One problem, however, is that a true liberal arts education is expensive. It requires first-rate teachers to guide and motivate students, and those persons with such abilities are usually in strong demand elsewhere. Tuition at some of the top U.S. universities has reached almost obscene levels as a result. Furthermore, the ability to think independently does not guarantee that students will immediately find work upon graduation. As such, this type of education is usually reserved for those who can afford it, which exacerbates the already worsening income inequality in pursued economies as is noted in Chapter 3.

The Need for the Right Kind of Education

In contrast, the cookbook approach to education, where students simply absorb what teachers tell them, is cheaper and more practical in the sense that students at least leave school knowing how to cook. The vast majority of the population is exposed only to this type of education, where there is limited room to express creative ideas or challenge established concepts. Creative minds may be buried and forgotten in such establishments, like the proverbial diamonds in the rough.

In pursued economies, teachers in all schools should be asked to keep an eye out for students who seem likely to come up with something new and interesting. Once found, those students should be encouraged to pursue their creative passions.

The United States always had an excellent system of liberal arts education that encouraged students to challenge the status quo. It was therefore able to maintain the lead in scientific breakthroughs and new product development even as it fell behind the Japanese and others in manufacturing those new products at competitive prices.

In contrast, many countries in catch-up mode adopted a cookbook-style approach to education, which can prepare the maximum number of people for industrial employment in the shortest possible time. When a country is in catch-up mode and pursuing Strategy B, this type of system often appears sufficient because the hard work of inventing and developing something new is already being done by someone else in the developed world.

However, these countries will have to come up with new products and services themselves once they exhaust the low-hanging investment opportunities stemming from urbanization and industrialization. The question then is whether they can modify their educational systems to produce the independent and innovative thinkers and entrepreneurs needed for Strategy A in the pursued era. This can be a major challenge if society has discouraged people from thinking outside the box for too long since both teachers and students may be unable to cope with the new task of producing independent thinkers.

Although people in most societies can recall the names of famous native innovators and entrepreneurs, the issue for national policy makers is whether there are enough people like this to pull the entire economy forward. All the advanced countries are now in the pursued era, and they all need more innovators. Policy makers must therefore work harder to create an environment that will allow innovators to flourish. Countries with large populations may also need more innovators.

The Increased Importance of Education in the Pursued Era

Education also has a bigger payoff in the pursued era because a worker's income depends more on individual abilities than in the golden era, when it was often determined by macroeconomic factors such as GDP growth and by institutional factors such as union membership.

Moreover, businesses in the pursued era will not be investing as much in productivity-enhancing equipment to increase worker productivity as they did in the golden era. Even if they did, those investments would not benefit the workers as they had during the golden era. This means workers must take responsibility for educating themselves and expanding their skill sets if they want to improve their living standards.

The fact that workers are on their own in the pursued era also means inequality will worsen compared with the manufacturing-led golden era if workers do not improve their own skills. This makes education one of the few areas in which policy makers can address the pursued era's inherent tendency to exacerbate inequality.

This inequality problem, both real and perceived, has grown to the point where everything has become more difficult, including the reforms needed to overcome the challenges faced by the pursued economies. The difficulty has arisen in part because low or non-existent wage growth for a large part of the population in pursued economies has made the average person less tolerant and forgiving compared with the golden era, when everyone was enjoying rising wages.

Ensuring equal access to a quality education is one area where policy makers can help reduce inequality in the pursued era. Given

the high social and political costs of inequality in the advanced countries today, addressing this issue with improved educational access
and quality makes good economic sense.

Unfortunately, this is one area where President Ronald Reagan
failed miserably. Although his supply-side and labor-market reforms
were essential for a pursued economy, he swung to the other extreme
on education by drastically cutting federal spending. As Peter Temin
of the Massachusetts Institute of Technology pointed out, this is one
of the key reasons why inequality and the social divide in the United
States have become such a big problem three decades later.[3] If Reagan had understood that improving education is one of the three
necessary policy initiatives for pursued economies, the U.S. social
divide would be much smaller than it is.

Donald Trump made the same mistake. Although his supply-
side reforms and efforts to help domestic manufacturers instead of
Wall Street financiers were laudable, he also cut the federal budget
for education. This worsened the nation's already serious inequality
problems and made it more difficult to implement the policy changes
needed to overcome the challenges of a pursued economy.

The Challenge of Keeping Students in School

Education is also far more important in the de-industrializing pursued era than in the manufacturing-led golden era because most
good jobs in the former are in "knowledge-based" sectors requiring
higher levels of education. In some countries, including the United
States, the challenge in terms of education starts with the need to
keep students in school long enough to learn something useful. Former Fed Chair Janet Yellen noted in a speech on June 21, 2016, that
the median U.S. income is $85,000 for Asian-Americans, $67,000 for
whites, and $40,000 for African Americans.[4] And this order is consist-
ent with the number of years they spent in school.

---

[3] Temin, Peter (2017), *The Vanishing Middle Class: Prejudice and Power in a
Dual Society,* Cambridge, MA: MIT Press, p. 22 and Chapter 10.
[4] Board of Governors of the Federal Reserve System (2016), Monetary Policy
Report, submitted on June 21, 2016, p. 7. https://www.federalreserve.gov/
monetarypolicy/files/20160621_mprfullreport.pdf.

From the author's own experience with both the Japanese and American educational systems, this gap is due, at least in part, to the fact that many, if not most, Asian youth are brainwashed to the extent that the option of *not* studying no longer exists in their minds. The default option is to spend most of their waking hours studying.

When the author attended a Japanese elementary school as a boy, his school happened to have no classes on Saturdays, when nearly all other schools in the country did. When the author left the house on Saturday mornings, he was frequently stopped by adults asking him why he was not in school, as though he were some kind of delinquent. And each time he had to explain that his school had no classes on Saturdays. This shows just how much social pressure there was on every child in Japan to be in school studying five and a half days a week.

When the author moved to the United States at the age of 13 and enrolled in a public junior high school, he was shocked to find that many students there had no intention of studying at all. It came as a surprise because the idea that a 13-year-old could get away with *not* studying was unthinkable for someone from East Asia. And he envied these students because they seemed to enjoy their teenage lives much more than he did.

Fifty-five years later, some of those who neglected their studies might regret their decisions. But 55 years ago, in the midst of the "Golden Sixties," many of them probably thought they could make a decent living without studying so hard. At the time, the United States was in its golden era, and it was quite possible for someone without an advanced degree to buy a three-bedroom house and a car with a V-8 engine, automatic transmission, and power steering.

Many of them saw their parents, who also lacked advanced degrees, still doing relatively well and assumed that the good life was within easy reach. Little did they know that the well-paying manufacturing jobs that generated rising wages for their parents would be lost to pursuing economies and that their lack of education would prevent them from moving higher up on the jobs ladder.

In retrospect, it could be said that the good life experienced during the golden era, when everyone benefited from economic growth, created a false sense of security for many who came to believe it would continue forever. Thus they were caught totally off guard when the United States entered the pursued phase.

Had they grown up in a country where they could see what happens to workers when a country enters the pursued phase, they probably would have been more diligent students. But there was no example for them to follow in the United States and Western Europe because they were the first ones in history to experience this phase of economic development. In a sense, those who did not apply themselves to their studies constitute a lost generation, since it is now too late for many of them to go back to school. These frustrated people blame their plight on visible targets such as immigrants and imports. Many of them also supported Donald Trump's "America First" policies. Their inclination to support extreme-right agendas, however, does not change the fact that they themselves lack the skills today's businesses need. Although their frustrations are understandable and some social safety net must be provided, at the end of the day people must realize that they need to acquire skills that are in demand since the clock cannot be turned back.

The High Price of Asian Educational Achievement

Many Asian-Americans, on the other hand, are the offspring of recent immigrants or are first-generation immigrants themselves. For centuries, China (starting in 598 A.D.) had an imperial examination system that assured upward social mobility for the educated. In Japan, Korea, and Taiwan, the focus on education was such that the largest building in most villages, towns, and cities a century ago was often the public school rather than city hall or mansions for the well-to-do.

With so much emphasis on education, the cultural imprinting to study hard still affects many of their offspring in the United States and elsewhere. Because of this cultural straitjacket on the issue of educational achievement, even the dimmest Asian student ends up studying and acquiring some useful skills. They may not be the most creative or articulate within their respective fields, and aspirations and talents that fell outside the confines of formal education may have been suppressed to the detriment of their self-actualization and true happiness, but at least they earn a decent paycheck.

Indeed, an Organisation for Economic Co-operation and Development (OECD) survey of "life satisfaction" among 15-year-olds in 2015 indicated that Japan ranked 42 out of 47 countries, followed by South Korea, Taiwan, Macau, Hong Kong, and Turkey.[5] In other words, the youth in these countries are having a miserable time. Meanwhile, the same East Asian countries all placed in the top 10 in the latest OECD scientific literacy tests. These results suggest the cultural differences regarding education that the author experienced 50 years ago still hold today—that is, educational achievement in Asia comes at a high cost. But those who study manage to earn a decent living, which pushes up the average income for the group.

For the other two groups, which do not have such a pervasive cultural straitjacket, much depends on the family or environment in which the child is raised. This is because it takes 15 years or more to realize the payoff from education. At a time when it is said that American corporate executives can only see as far as the next quarterly earnings report, it is a tall order for a child to commit to education when the economic payoff of such effort is 12, 16, or even 20 years away. Most students will therefore need a great deal of outside support to continue their long educational journey.

Those from families and communities with a strong commitment to education will naturally go further than those who do not enjoy such support. Even in households where parents are often absent or too busy to help, being a "nerd" is not so painful if the student is surrounded by hard-working classmates. But studying can be very hard for youths who do not receive support and encouragement to stay in school when others like them seem to be having so much fun outside school.

It is these youth who need help, because their eventual inability to contribute to the economy will be a loss to the entire society. They must also be made aware that they are now effectively competing with youth in the emerging world who are studying and working hard to achieve the living standards of those in the developed world.

An advanced degree is not for everyone, of course, but all students need to know what they are good at and what they enjoy doing so they can make appropriate choices given their personal circumstances. The emphasis on personal strengths and circumstances

---

[5] OECD (2017), *PISA 2015 Results (Volume III): Students' Well-Being,* Paris: OECD Publishing, p. 71.

is important because workers in the pursued phase are really on their own, and the chances are high that they will not do well in a field they do not enjoy.

This means counselors advising students at regular intervals might have just as big an impact on the student's (and society's) final educational outcome as teachers and parents. In addition to supporting students who need outside encouragement to further their education, these counselors can help students discover what they are good at and what they enjoy doing so they can be directed to areas where they are likely to succeed. If possible, these counselors should also be trained to spot independent thinkers and encourage them to pursue their ideas further.

The Importance of a Proper Tax and Regulatory Environment

To maximize people's creative potential, countries in the pursued phase must also revamp their tax and regulatory regimes. It must be emphasized that to create something out of nothing and bring it to market often requires so much effort that "any rational person will give up," in the words of Steve Jobs. In a similar vein, Thomas Edison famously claimed an invention is 1 percent inspiration and 99 percent perspiration.

Although some people are so driven that they require no external support, most find outside encouragement important during the long, risky, and difficult journey of producing something the world has never seen before. Financial, regulatory, and tax regimes should therefore do everything possible to encourage such individuals and businesses to pursue their pioneering efforts.

Thomas Piketty cited the retreat of progressive tax rates as the cause of widening inequality in the post-1970 developed world.[6] But the United States, which led the reduction in tax rates, has regained its high-tech leadership while Europe and Japan, which did not go as far as the United States, have stagnated. This comparison suggests that tax and regulatory changes might have to be drastic enough for people to take notice.

---

[6] Piketty, Thomas (2014), op. cit.

The United States is considered one of the most unequal countries in the developed world, with the top few percent owning a large share of the nation's assets. But those at the very top are mostly founders of new companies (Figure 5.1) who have transformed the way people live and work around the world. Except for Warren Buffett, who made his money investing in the stock market, all of them became rich by taking risks and bringing something completely new and useful to the world.

There are some further down the list who made money in largely zero-sum financial or real estate investments or through established companies and inheritance. But in no other country is the list of the wealthiest people dominated by those who have created transformative technologies. The fact that seven of the top eight in the United States are self-made individuals with transformative ideas suggests that inequality has different implications in the United States than in other countries, where the top ranks are dominated by more traditional and established types of wealth.

Figure 5.1 suggests that the gradualist approach preferred by the traditional societies of Europe and Japan may not work well when a drastic push in innovation is required as the economy enters the

Rank	Name	Industry	Net Wealth
1	Jeff Bezos	founder Amazon	$201 B
2	Elon Musk	founder Tesla, SpaceX	$190.5 B
3	Mark Zuckerberg	founder Facebook	$134.5 B
4	Bill Gates	founder Microsoft	$134 B
5	Larry Page	co-founder Google	$123 B
6	Sergey Brin	co-founder Google	$118.5B
7	Larry Ellison	co-founder Oracle	$117.3 B
8	Warren Buffett	chair and CEO Berkshire Hathaway	$102 B

FIGURE 5.1 Richest Persons in the United States

Source: Forbes, "The Forbes 400: The Definitive Ranking of the Wealthiest Americans in 2021," edited by Kerry A. Dolan, https://www.forbes.com/forbes-400/#45b49a177e2f

pursued era. This outcome also suggests that a tax regime that was reasonable when a country was not being pursued may no longer be appropriate when it is.

The Importance of Interpreting Inequality Statistics Correctly

One should also be careful when interpreting data on inequality, which are often presented as though we still live in an agricultural society. The key asset in an agricultural society is land. When data for such societies say the top 10 percent of the population owns 60 percent of the wealth, it is safe to assume that the other 90 percent is either crowded into slums in the remaining 40 percent of the country or is relegated to the status of sharecroppers with no hope for economic advancement.

Today, however, the wealth possessed by the richest individuals in the United States consists chiefly of shares in the companies they founded. For example, 91 percent of Jeff Bezos' wealth consists of shares in his own companies. The ratio is 97 percent for Mark Zuckerberg and 85 percent for Elon Musk. The shares in those companies are valued by the market and the public, not by an expropriation decree issued by a monarchy or a dictator. In other words, it is wealth that is *created* instead of being taken or stolen from others.

An increase in the wealth of these individuals therefore does not entail a decrease in the wealth of others, although that is what is often implied by those presenting such data. Moreover, most people in the advanced countries can lead dignified lives even if they are not especially rich.

In those agricultural societies where land ownership is largely in the hands of a privileged few, land reforms that give ownership rights to former sharecroppers often result in vast improvements in productivity and economic well-being. Similar expropriation policies in advanced countries today, on the other hand, might discourage risk-taking and over-stretching to such a degree that the economies would implode.

There are also certain risks that only wealthy individuals can take. Institutional investors and banks must comply with a host of governance rules designed to prevent the public's money from being exposed to excessive risk. But those rules make it difficult for such institutions to invest in start-ups, where failure rates are high but new ideas are often incubated and hatched.

It is said, for example, that only one in eight start-ups succeed. In other words, investors in this space typically experience seven failures before seeing a single success. Fund managers in banks or pension funds cannot post such a high failure rate and hope to keep their jobs. A rich individual who is accountable only to him- or herself, on the other hand, can allocate a certain amount of his wealth to such investments and wait out the seven failures to reach the one winning bet.

The United States also has an ecosystem of highly successful individuals who help nurture start-ups as venture capitalists. That has allowed the nation to stay ahead of other countries in many areas. While this system tends to make the rich even richer, it actually creates wealth instead of taking it away from someone else.

It is therefore time to treat inequality statistics in the advanced countries with a little more caution. They are not equivalent to land ownership data in agricultural societies.

Better Distribution of Medical Care or More New Medicine?

Another frequently raised inequality issue in the United States is the high cost of medical care. This is important because most Americans, who are brought up in the pioneering spirit of self-reliance, really do *not* want to talk about inequality as long as they are earning a living wage and have a dignified life.

Their rugged sense of self-reliance, however, could be shattered overnight with a catastrophic medical bill. Indeed, a huge share of personal bankruptcies filed in the United States is due to this cause. Even for those who are lucky enough to be healthy and have good health insurance, the fear that they might lose one or both at any time is undermining their faith in the system.

There is a huge room for improvement in the U.S. medical industry, especially in comparison to those available in Japan and some other countries. For example, an appendicitis operation in the United States can easily cost 20,000 dollars when the same operation in

Japan can be done for only 3,000 dollars.[7] Although Japanese doctors frequently complain that they are not paid enough, this one-to-seven difference in cost is adding to the sense of inequality and insecurity among many people in the United States. In other words, if an average American faced Japanese medical bills, his or her sense of inequality would be far less.

At the same time, it is said that almost all new drugs that are brought to the market in the world today are developed in the United States. This is because the United States does not impose a cap on drug prices the way it is imposed in very many other countries, including Japan. As a result, drug companies can recoup the enormous cost of developing a new drug *only* in the United States. This is indeed one of the reasons why the medical cost in the United States is so high.

If the United States imposed a cap just like the one in Japan, chances are high that the research and development on new drugs will come to a standstill, which it almost did when Hillary Clinton tried to devise a national health insurance with a cap on drug prices when her husband was the President of the United States. Some would argue that such a stoppage in medical research would be against the interest of humanity.

This American preference on growth and progress instead of on redistribution served the country well during its golden era because its strong manufacturing-led growth improved the life of everybody and reduced inequality, as is noted earlier. The question is whether the same trade-off is appropriate in a pursued economy where inequality is destined to rise with highly undesirable social consequences.

The Importance of Entrepreneurs in Over-Stretching

A country may have great workers, engineers, accountants, and lawyers, but it is the entrepreneur who brings them together in an enterprise to produce goods and services. Of all the economic resources in a country, entrepreneurial talent is probably the most valuable for

---

[7] Wakakura, Masato (2006), "Kokusai Hikaku: Nihon-no Iryo-hi Wa Yasusugiru" ("International Comparison: Japan's Medical Costs Are Too Inexpensive"), *Voice*, June 2006, Tokyo, PHP Institute, p. 159.

economic growth because without it very little over-stretching takes place. This can be seen from the fact that economies of communist countries that assigned zero value to entrepreneurship all ended up stagnating for decades. The communist disdain for entrepreneurs can be gleaned from the fact that Karl Marx extolled workers to simply overthrow the capitalists and run the factories themselves.

Workers, at least in the short run, may be able to operate the factories because they are the ones actually doing the job. But it is unrealistic to expect them to come up with new products to fend off competitors or to secure financing to put those new products into production, to say nothing of the need to maintain and expand marketing efforts both at home and abroad. After all, these undertakings require extensive knowledge of technology, finance, management, and marketing.

They also require stressful risk-taking at every step of the decision-making process. And many, if not most people, are happy to stay out of such stressful settings if they can help it. But without the ability to address all the issues required to bring new products to market, there is no reason for firms to over-stretch. It is no coincidence that most factories in communist Eastern Europe, Russia, China, and elsewhere ended up producing the same old (and obsolete) items for decades—after all, there was no profit motive to justify taking risks to develop new products and expand the business. By attaching zero value to entrepreneurship and not rewarding risk-taking, Communist countries denied themselves access to such resources and ended up stagnating for decades.

Most capitalists, on the other hand, became capitalists by proving themselves willing and able to address the issues noted above to build a successful business. Since pursued economies always need new drivers of growth, it is vitally important that their governments provide as much opportunities as possible for those who are willing to put up the effort to start something new.

The Renewed Attraction of Socialism and Difficulty of Achieving Public Consensus

Unfortunately for many countries, economic and educational reforms previously mentioned are often derided as "favoring the rich" or "elitist" and rejected out of hand by those with a golden-era mindset.

When an economy is in a golden era with a surfeit of investment opportunities, the rejection of such policies may not lead to a noticeable economic slowdown. But in a pursued economy that needs to outrun its chasers, the inability to fully utilize the innovative and entrepreneurial potential of its people can have devastating consequences. The nation's future growth may well depend on how quickly it can achieve a social consensus on developing growth-friendly infrastructure, such as a liberal arts education system and innovator-friendly financial, regulatory, and tax regimes to maximize the population's innovative capacity.

This may require a new consensus in which those who are unable to think outside the box understand and appreciate the fact that their well-being depends on those who can. Indeed, in the pursued phase the entire society must understand that such thinkers are essential to generating the new investment opportunities at home that will keep the economy out of prolonged stagnation.

This is far from easy, however. As Piketty noted, inequality in the West began increasing in the 1970s and has reached alarming levels in some countries. This increasingly unequal distribution of income is dividing society between the haves and the have-nots and is making it difficult to reach a social consensus of any kind. But without social consensus, the reforms needed to meet the challenges of a pursued economy will not be possible.

It has also been reported that among young people in the United States today, the word *socialism* does not have the same bad connotations it had among the generations that fought the cold war. For example, the January 17, 2020, *Wall Street Journal* wrote that "Fifty percent of adults under 38 told the Harris Poll last year that they would 'prefer living in a socialist country.' That outlook recurs in many more surveys and far surpasses figures from even the radical heydays of the '60s and '70s."[8] This 50 percent probably feels that with a heavy student loan burden, high housing costs, and prohibitive medical bills, the present system is working only for the old and the rich, and that the deck is stacked against them.

---

[8] Ukueberuwa, Mene (2020), "Boomer Socialism Led to Bernie Sanders," *Wall Street Journal,* January 17, 2020. https://www.wsj.com/articles/boomer-socialism-led-to-bernie-sanders-11579304307.

The continued popularity among the young of leftist politicians such as Bernie Sanders and Elizabeth Warren also reflects this dissatisfaction. That means some rebalancing of priorities in the United States is imminent because the weight of these younger voters will only grow in the future. However, that rebalancing must be in the right direction if it is to benefit the public.

This is because the pursued era imposes new constraints and dynamics on the economy that did not exist during the golden era. In particular, the return on capital must be raised in order to create more investment and jobs at home. That means *lower*, not higher, taxes on those who are making investment decisions. This is the opposite of the traditional leftist agenda pursued by the two politicians previously noted. It is indeed ironic that the young people who are complaining about inequality and espousing socialism are also the most avid users of devices and services pioneered by those sitting atop the list of America's richest.

Making Established Political Parties Relevant Again in the Pursued Era

In traditional politics, conservatives push for supply-side reforms such as a balanced budget, lower taxes, and deregulation (i.e., small government), while progressives push for greater expenditures on social programs such as education (i.e., big government). In the golden era, when reasons for businesses to over-stretch were plentiful and the economy was growing rapidly, the lack of supply-side reforms did not appear to slow down the economy in any meaningful way. In other words, this political choice was a matter of preference.

In the pursued era, however, both supply-side reforms and additional spending on education are needed to support economic growth and maintain social unity. In other words, reduced education budgets and a lack of supply-side reforms *will* weigh noticeably on economic growth in the pursued phase.

Some of this can already be inferred from the vibrancy of the U.S. economy, where supply-side and labor market reforms have been implemented, relative to the less-than-impressive growth rates of Japan and Europe, where such reforms have been more gradual. At the same time, the U.S. neglect of education has led to much worse social polarization and political deadlock than in Europe or

Japan. Although the neglect of education during the last four decades in the United States will take decades to correct, access to quality education is where the battle to contain inequality must be fought because workers in the pursued era are really "on their own" and must continue to educate themselves.

More specifically, both conservatives and progressives must adjust their stances to meet the challenges of a pursued economy. For example, the Biden Administration talks a great deal about the importance of creating good union jobs as it seeks to regain the support of blue-collar workers who voted for Trump in 2016. Labor unions had a role to play during the golden era, when the economy was moving along the upward-sloping labor supply curve in Figure 3.1. But in the pursued era, when the global labor supply curve is basically flat at wage level Q, not only do the unions lack the leverage needed to increase wages, but focusing on their demands could also reduce both labor market flexibility and the return on capital at home. Both of these factors will encourage even more firms to relocate production to emerging economies.

The same golden-era legacy problem also afflicts conservatives in America. Until Trump hijacked the Republican Party, it had long been advocating for small government and a balanced budget. The drive to balance the budget had an important role to play during the golden era, when there was a real danger of government borrowing crowding out private-sector investments. But it is extremely problematic in the pursued era, when the private sector as a whole is often a huge net saver even with zero interest rates, meaning the government must serve as borrower of last resort to keep the economy from spiraling downward. This need is even greater when the pursued economy is also in a balance sheet recession.

On a more positive note, progressives' emphasis on infrastructure spending and improving education is essential both to stabilize the macroeconomy and to counter the tendency for inequality to increase in the pursued era. Similarly, conservatives' focus on lower tax rates and deregulation at the microeconomic level is essential during the pursued era because such measures will increase domestic returns on capital and thereby ensure that more investment takes place at home.

That said, a thorough vetting of infrastructure projects is needed to ensure that they are self-financing so that such spending can be sustained over the long run. On education, schools must encourage independent thinking in the liberal arts tradition while directing students to what they are good at so they stay longer in school to learn something useful.

In short, both conservatives and progressives have to readjust their traditional stances to remain relevant in the pursued era. For those who devoted their entire lives to balancing budgets or expanding the power of labor unions, this is a big challenge. But center-right and center-left parties must reinvent themselves to meet the challenges of a pursued economy if they hope to prevent left- and right-wing extremists peddling nonworkable solutions from gaining influence.

Advanced Economies Are Fighting Two Wars

To make matters worse, most advanced economies fell into a balance sheet recession when their housing bubbles burst in 2008. This exacerbated the shortage of borrowers that began toward the end of the 20th century, when these countries entered their pursued phases. The balance sheet recession was followed by the devastating COVID-19 pandemic recession of 2020. Because fiscal stimulus was needed to fight both recessions, these countries are now saddled with a huge public debt.

When faced with such a large public debt, the natural tendency of economists and policy makers with a golden-era mindset is to raise taxes wherever possible to reduce the debt while ignoring the bond market's pleas—expressed in the form of exceptionally low bond yields—*not* to do so. But such wanton tax hikes may discourage businesses from investing aggressively in innovation, thus prolonging the period of subpar economic growth.

That means economies currently emerging from balance sheet and pandemic recessions need to resist the temptation to raise taxes and thereby thwart innovation and over-stretching. They need to resist that temptation if the economy is to gain the escape velocity needed to fend off pursuers. This is particularly important in Japan, where public debt levels are high and an orthodox (i.e., golden-era) mindset still dominates the bureaucracy, academia, and the media.

Most advanced countries today are fighting two wars: one because they are in balance sheet recessions and another because they are being pursued by increasingly sophisticated emerging economies offering attractive returns on capital. They have also been battered, like all other countries, by the COVID-19 pandemic. This means the escape velocity needed for their economies to regain forward momentum is exceptionally high. The leaders of these countries must therefore realize that tremendous effort will be needed to reach that velocity.

Of all the pursued economies, the United States probably comes closest to having achieved a consensus on the need for a growth-friendly tax regime, which is why it attracts innovators from around the world. But with the rich growing ever richer while the remaining 80 percent of the population has seen little income growth for the last 20 years, the temptation to undo what was achieved in the past is growing stronger. The social backlash includes a drive to raise taxes on the wealthy from the left and to block immigration from the right. The anger of the 80 percent was also behind the support Donald Trump and Bernie Sanders received during the 2016 and 2020 presidential campaigns.

The political challenge for pursued countries, therefore, is how to persuade voters to maintain and improve the innovator-friendly tax regimes needed for economic growth when the public debt is so large and inequality so pronounced, with the vast majority of the population experiencing no real income growth for many years.

A Case Study in Bad Taxation: Japan's Inheritance Tax

If a pursued country with an aging or declining population is to sustain economic growth, which is the case for many advanced countries today, it must maximize the productivity of its working-age population, and especially those who are able to create new products and transform them into viable businesses. This is because new, well-paying jobs are likely to come only from new businesses when a country is being pursued. If the country keeps on doing what it has always done, it will be overtaken by emerging economies with younger populations and lower wage costs. Each country in the pursued phase must therefore ask itself whether its tax and regulatory regimes are maximizing the productivity of the people capable of developing new products and services.

In Japan, it has been said that many of the successful people who took risks and worked hard to build and expand businesses are now spending much of their time worrying about inheritance and gift tax liabilities. It is quite sad to see so many capable people with excellent track records talking about such a backward topic when they could be spending their time expanding their businesses and chasing their dreams.

They are worried because the top rates for inheritance and gift tax in Japan are 55 percent and 65 percent, respectively, and the tax-free ceiling was lowered in 2015 to just $300,000 (at an exchange rate of $1 = ¥100). The tax rate starts at 10 percent for assets worth less than $100,000, but climbs rapidly to 40 percent at $1 million. In contrast, the U.S. tax liability on inheritance does not kick in until the amount reaches $11 million, and countries such as Australia have no inheritance tax at all.

The concerns of successful Japanese can be gleaned from the fact that the country's bookstores today are full of books about this tax and how to minimize it. It is also common knowledge that a key reason for the boom in Japan's real estate market is that property offers a way to reduce inheritance tax obligations. The boom underscores just how distorted Japan's allocation of resources is. After all, this is a country where the population is shrinking, and unoccupied homes are a major social problem.

This represents a tremendous waste of human and physical resources that Japan, with its shrinking population, can ill-afford—far too many capable people with a successful track record are distracted by this tax. Individuals who should be expanding their businesses or developing induced pluripotent stem (iPS) cells are instead wasting time and mental focus on managing rental properties, which is something that anyone could do, simply because of the inheritance tax.

As Steve Jobs's remark indicates, few people in any society are able to build a successful business because ordinary people simply cannot withstand the stress. Academics and bureaucrats do not create jobs. Only those with vision who can withstand the stress of building and expanding a business are able to create jobs. As Japan is already suffering from one of the lowest rates of new business formation of any advanced country, the country desperately needs such people.

A shrinking population also means productivity must be raised to maintain the existing level of economic activity. This means resources must be allocated as efficiently as possible to enhance productivity. But in Japan the opposite is happening, and the economy has stagnated as a result.

Taiwan Slashed Inheritance Tax and Gift Tax Rates to 10 Percent

What should be done about this issue? Taiwan's recent experience may offer some clues. The administration of President Ma Ying-jeou implemented bold tax cuts in 2008, slashing the top inheritance and gift tax rates to 10 percent.

Like Japan, Taiwan is being chased by the emerging economies of China and Southeast Asia, and its working-age population began to shrink in 2015. With no language barrier between Taiwan and China, the challenges facing economic policy makers in Taiwan are substantial, which is precisely why they implemented the bold tax cuts noted above.

The Taiwanese authorities initially assumed the lower rates would reduce tax revenues substantially, but in the event, tax receipts did not fall at all (Figure 5.2). Moreover, funds that had been fleeing

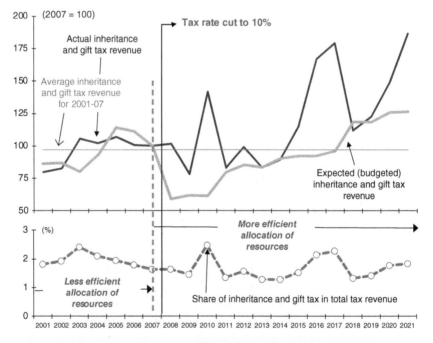

FIGURE 5.2 Taiwan's Inheritance and Gift Tax Cuts Enhanced the Efficiency of Resource Allocation, and Tax Revenues Did Not Fall

Source: Nomura Research Institute, based on data from Ministry of Finance Republic of China, Taiwan

Taiwan for decades because of concerns about the tax and military tensions with Communist China began to return, providing a major support for the Taiwanese economy in the immediate aftermath of the Lehman Brothers' collapse.

Tax revenues did not fall because people who had been spending time and resources to reduce their tax burden decided that at 10 percent it was no longer worth the effort. They decided to pay the 10 percent so they could use their time and resources more productively elsewhere. And because tax revenues did not fall, the lower tax rate did not reduce the funds available for the less fortunate.

From the perspective of the broader economy, the fact that the tax cuts eliminated distortions in the allocation of resources was far more important than any change in tax revenues. All the time and resources that had been devoted to avoiding taxes were now being channeled into more productive pursuits.

If Japan were to lower its highest inheritance and gift tax rates to 10 percent, a great deal of financial and human resources that are either fleeing overseas or going to all the wrong places would come back to where they belong. Such a cut would also encourage the intergenerational transfer of assets in a country where wealth is concentrated in the hands of senior citizens, who typically have a lower propensity to consume. Most importantly, the tremendous distortions in resource allocation that have resulted from efforts to avoid the inheritance tax would disappear as people decide that such efforts are simply not worth their time at a tax rate of 10 percent. While it is difficult to say whether inheritance and gift tax revenues would increase or decrease relative to the current figure of around 2 trillion yen if a 10-percent rate were introduced, even a small decrease would be worth it if the change freed up increasingly precious entrepreneurial resources for forward-looking projects.

The Global Implications of Taiwanese Tax Cut

The revenue-neutral result of Taiwan's drastic cut in inheritance and gift tax rates in 2008 was a pleasant surprise for the local tax authorities. But its implications are far greater because this example proved it is possible to lower tax rates drastically to improve resource allocation in the economy *without* suffering from reduced tax revenues. This implies that similar possibilities may exist in other countries with different tax regimes if the tax authorities in those countries would carefully recalibrate their tax rates to achieve Taiwan-like results.

This also suggests there is a huge potential for tax specialists in all countries to look for similar unexplored possibilities in their own tax regimes. And the key here is that for people to change their behavior, the tax cuts must be large enough to be noticed.

When the West was in its golden era through the 1970s and had no competitors, and when Japan was in its own golden era, chasing the West but facing no competitors of its own, the entire population benefited from economic growth. Given the surfeit of investment opportunities that characterizes the golden era, efficiency losses from the income redistribution function of taxation were not large enough to derail businesses' desire to over-stretch. The fact that golden-era economies were inflationary despite growth-discouraging tax rates and higher interest rates shows just how abundant domestic investment opportunities were.

But now that Japan and the West are being pursued, they will find themselves in a serious predicament if they maintain the golden-era approach to taxation and regulation. The fact that these economies had all suffered from years of near-zero inflation rates despite astronomical monetary easing and zero or negative interest rates indicates just how limited real domestic investment opportunities are.

Tax and regulatory distortions can be found in all countries, even though the source of the distortions may differ considerably. The ultimate goal of regulatory and tax reforms in pursued economies, therefore, should be to minimize the time people spend on tax avoidance and to maximize the time they spend on activities they are good at.

How to Reorganize Society for the Pursued Phase Is an Open Question

How a society should best reorganize itself for the pursued phase has yet to be decided. There are many questions that need to be answered. What are the appropriate labor practices when so many workers are unhappy with wages that have stagnated for the last two decades? What is the best kind of educational system when a traditional liberal arts education is so costly? How should society encourage innovators without appearing unfair to those who are not blessed with similar abilities? How should society help those who were caught off-guard and are now too old to go back to school?

And finally, how should society prepare young people to cope with this unprecedented new environment? All of these represent massive challenges for society and the political system.

There is also a mounting social backlash against measures to encourage innovators and increase labor market flexibility. Even in Taiwan, the top inheritance tax rate was rolled back to 20 percent from the original 10 percent by the new government of President Tsai Ing-wen in 2017. Such setbacks indicate how difficult it is for social institutions to change to match the needs of the new pursued era.

Many authorities, economists among them, are also patiently waiting for a return of the golden era by clinging to a 2-percent inflation target even though the underlying economic realities have changed dramatically since then (this issue is discussed further in Chapter 6). But the delay in implementing the necessary reforms only shortens the distance between the pursued and the pursuing, eliminating the advantages the former had over the latter.

For many traditional societies in Europe and Japan, some sort of shake-up may also be needed to open fields to outside-the-box thinkers. In Japan, decades of economic stagnation and the diminished appeal of established companies are prompting college graduates to consider starting businesses for the first time in many decades. This is a welcome development in a country where tradition and authority still carry a great deal of weight. Some younger engineers in Japanese firms, for example, find it difficult to challenge the achievements of older engineers in the company because such actions can be viewed as a sign of disrespect. Such seniority-based rigidity has discouraged innovation in the country in no small way.

Some European designers are also migrating to the United States and Australia to free themselves from traditional constraints on how and where they can express their creative talents. Tradition-bound societies therefore desperately need new businesses that are open to new ideas and innovations.

If the domestic environment is not producing enough innovators, the government may want to consider importing creative thinkers and innovators from abroad. The immigrant-friendly United States is full of foreign-born innovators competing with each other and with native innovators in universities and the business world.

Generous tax treatment of stock options for innovating companies may also be useful. Since these incentives do not cost the government anything until the private-sector risk-taker actually succeeds, they are cost-effective as well.

If the tax and regulatory incentives are not sufficient, the government itself might have to function as *innovator of last resort* to develop new technologies or open up new fields of research. This is not such a far-fetched idea either. As Richard Duncan pointed out in his *The Money Revolution*, the U.S. government was by far the biggest investor in research and development (R&D) in the country from 1953 to 1979. In the decade that followed the Sputnik shock of 1957, it invested twice as much in R&D as the business sector did. Today the government's investment is just one-third of those investments made by the businesses. Such targeted spending on research by the government is likely to encourage the private sector to follow by launching new businesses that might not have existed unless the government had taken the lead.

Preparing Emerging Economies for the Future

What can emerging economies learn from the experiences of advanced countries today? For those that have yet to enter the middle-income trap, policies essential for growth include providing necessary infrastructure, eradicating corruption, improving education and public health, and adopting a disciplined monetary policy to keep borrowing costs within reasonable limits. These policies must be implemented while pursuing the easier Strategy B so that when wages become high enough to attract competition from other emerging economies, the country will have accumulated sufficient physical and human capital to switch to Strategy A.

Authorities should also operate on the assumption that the rapid growth in tax revenues typical of the golden era will diminish going forward. Projects that must be financed with taxes should therefore be implemented while the economy is still in the golden era. They should also take note of the never-ending rollbacks of the pension-eligible retirement age in nearly all developed countries. These rollbacks prove that the original pension schemes, introduced during these nations' golden eras, were based on overoptimistic assumptions about growth and demographics.

They should also modify and refine their education systems so as not to discourage out-of-the-box thinkers. Even though such people may seem to be of limited value when a country is pursuing other economies, they will become the key drivers of growth when it enters the pursued stage. A nationwide system of liberal arts education should be introduced to encourage students to think independently so that they can one day challenge the status quo and come up with new ideas and products.

Emerging countries that are now enjoying the post-LTP golden era will eventually reach the pursued phase with all its challenges. With so many emerging economies joining the globalization bandwagon, those changes may arrive sooner rather than later. Some of the new entrants to globalization will *lower* the wage level Q for pursued economies, as China probably did when it entered the WTO. That means institutional arrangements such as tax codes and regulations should never be viewed as permanent and may have to be modified as the economy moves from one stage to the next.

On the other hand, historical buildings and neighborhoods with cultural value should not be torn down in the name of modernization. The more rapidly a country develops, the more important this cultural heritage becomes because people in a rapidly changing environment need to be able to put down psychological roots. They need psychological homes where they can reaffirm who they are and whence they came. Historical neighborhoods and monuments also attract foreign tourists, which can help the country earn foreign exchange.

In this sphere, emerging countries should learn from Europe, which attracts a huge number of foreign tourists every year because it kept its beautiful architectural heritage largely intact. Even though Europe's high-tech industries have fallen behind those of America and Asia in some areas, the tourism industry continues to draw millions of American and Asian visitors annually. Income from these nations' architectural heritage was also more stable and reliable, at least until the COVID-19 pandemic, than income from the volatile and extremely competitive high-tech sector.

Emerging countries should also be aware that there is a social backlash against free trade in the developed world originating from both the "lost generation" noted earlier and the disappearance of a mechanism for balancing trade, something that is discussed in greater detail in Chapter 9. The emergence of the "America First" Trump administration and the "Buy American" Biden administration is likely to make it more difficult for emerging countries to access markets in the United States and other advanced economies unless they themselves open their markets to goods from pursued countries.

That means they will have to accept more changes to their own economies, such as higher exchange rates and lower tariffs on imports from advanced countries. And for nations pursuing an export-led growth model based on Strategy B, these changes will have to be made soon if they want to continue enjoying access to the markets of pursued economies.

China's Challenges: Decoupling, Demographics, and Middle-Income Trap

China, the greatest economic growth story of the last four decades, offers a good real-life example of some of the points previously made, as both the middle-income trap and worsening demographics are pressing issues. With a per capita GDP of slightly over $10,000, the country currently finds itself in the middle of the trap (Figure 5.3), while its working-age population began shrinking in

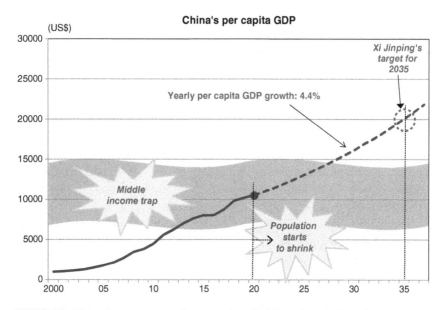

FIGURE 5.3 China Has No Room for Error in Reaching First-World Living Standards

Source: Nomura Research Institute, based on data from IMF, *World Economic Outlook October 2021*

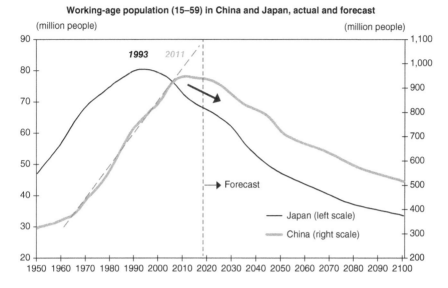

FIGURE 5.4 China May Grow Old before It Grows Rich: Working-Age Population*
Has Started to Contract

*Note: Chinese National Statistical Office defines working-age population as
people aged 15 to 59.

Source: United Nations, Department of Economic and Social Affairs, Population
Division (2019), World Population Prospects 2019, Online Edition

2012 (Figure 5.4). The latest census data, from 2020, imply that the
total population may start to contract as early as 2022. Chinese economists are therefore worried the country will lose its growth momentum due to adverse demographics before it fully emerges from the
trap and joins the ranks of developed economies.

As noted earlier, two necessary conditions must be satisfied for
the export-led model of economic growth to succeed. One is the
ability to make competitive products, and the other is access to foreign markets where those products can be sold. There is no question
that the Chinese have made huge strides toward meeting the first
requirement. Today, the country can make almost everything at high
quality and competitive prices.

But as for the second requirement, Chinese policy makers seem
to be taking access to foreign markets for granted. This is probably
because they have been in the U.S.-led free trade system for over
four decades, and it has become second nature to them. Many of
them may not be aware of how bad the protectionism was globally

before 1945. However, economists in the country need to pay more attention to the question of who will be buying the Chinese products. After all, it is those people who will be doing the over-stretching needed for China's economy to continue growing.

Deng Xiaoping's Decisions Led to the Greatest Economic Growth in Human History

Deng Xiaoping, who spearheaded China's market-opening economic reforms in 1978, understood the importance of securing markets for Chinese-made products. He also had a front-row seat for the bitter U.S.-Japan trade frictions that were unfolding as he opened the Chinese economy to the world in the 1980s. He worried that if Japan and the United States, who were military allies and shared similar values such as democracy and human rights, could get into such an ugly fight, the prospects for U.S.-China trade could not be very bright given the differences in values between the two countries.

To avoid that outcome, he opened the Chinese economy fully to foreign direct investment so that foreign companies investing in China would have a stake in the success of the local economy, something that Japan had utterly failed to do. He also resolved 12 out of 14 ongoing territorial disputes[9] so that his country would be seen as a safe and peaceful member of the world community. He did so because the U.S.-led free trade system is not fully open to countries with territorial ambitions, something that was underscored when Russia's occupation of the Crimean Peninsula in 2014 and invasion of Ukraine in 2022 were met with economic sanctions.

History has shown that Deng Xiaoping's decision to open the economy and end territorial disputes enabled China's economy to grow faster than any nation in history. The Chinese people certainly studied and worked hard to gain the ability to produce competitive products, but it was the political decisions made by Deng Xiaoping that gave his nation access to the markets for those products.

---

[9] Overholt, William (2020), *Myths and Realities in Sino-American Relations*, lecture given for Harvard's Fairbank Center for Chinese Studies on November 12, 2020.

Deng also opened up Chinese society, which resulted in millions of Chinese students going abroad to study at Western universities. They were soon followed by millions more who went abroad as tourists. This was in huge contrast to the totally closed communist societies of Eastern Europe and the U.S.S.R. These differences gave hope to many in the United States that China would soon open its political system as well. The American hope that China would become truly free and open prompted the United States to invite China into the World Trade Organization (WTO), which led to the greatest burst of economic growth in history.

Chinese U-Turn under Xi

When Xi Jinping took control of China in 2013, he not only reasserted authoritarian rule at home, but also reopened many territorial disputes with China's neighbors, backing those claims with both military and economic threats. This change in the nation's stance torpedoed the American hope that China would soon be like them and also clashed with the reason the United States, a reluctant participant in both world wars, had introduced free trade in the first place: to allow countries with similar values to prosper without the need for territorial expansion and the war that often results.

The resulting confrontation with the United States prompted China's leadership to rely more on domestic demand for economic growth, something that has been dubbed the "great domestic" or "dual" economic cycle. It also led to talk of decoupling in both Washington and Beijing.

With 1.4 billion people, there is no question that China has a huge domestic market. The Chinese are also known for their willingness to study and work hard and their entrepreneurial mindset. These positive qualities have led many to conclude that China's economic growth is unstoppable, and that it is just a matter of time before the country overtakes the United States to become the world's largest economy. While that is certainly possible, the analytical framework introduced here suggests it may be difficult for these positives to overcome the negatives coming from the slowdown in exports as tensions with the West increase.

Up to now, China's growth depended heavily on its ability to export at competitive prices. At the height of the export boom in 2006, exports accounted for nearly 35 percent of Chinese GDP. The figure is still around 18 percent today. As long as exports were competitively priced, foreign consumers did the over-stretching for China (even though they themselves thought they were under-stretching), and exports grew rapidly.

With exports effectively selling themselves, Chinese manufacturers kept on expanding via domestic investment, which made huge contributions to employment and economic growth. In other words, the country was in a golden era, and its companies found numerous reasons to over-stretch while pursuing Strategy B. That was possible because they were exporting to people who were richer than themselves.

When the U.S.-China trade war began in 2018, the Chinese Ministry of Commerce claimed that 59 percent of the products subject to Trump's tariffs were actually made by foreign firms in China.[10] In other words, a significant share of Chinese production and employment was still being provided by foreign businesses. This comes as no surprise given that when Deng Xiaoping opened up the Chinese economy in 1978, there was not a single capitalist left in China, and all capital, technology, and management know-how had to be provided by foreign firms. These foreign firms also supplied overseas markets for the products they made in China.

Decoupling from Western markets means Chinese companies will be selling to those who are not so rich, both at home and abroad. As Figure 5.5 shows, "Western" economies (including Japan) account for 56.8 percent of global GDP, while Russia, Africa, and other areas amount to just 25.3 percent (China itself stands at 17.9 percent).

Moreover, per capita GDP in the Western economies is 4.5 times that in non-Western countries. Decoupling would thus imply the loss of many of China's richest customers, leaving behind only the poorer ones. Given that China's own per capita GDP has only recently passed the $10,000 mark, this could sharply reduce the size of the markets in which Chinese companies can sell their products.

---

[10] Regular Press Conference of the Chinese Ministry of Commerce, July 5, 2018. http://english.mofcom.gov.cn/article/newsrelease/press/201807/2018 0702766291.shtml.

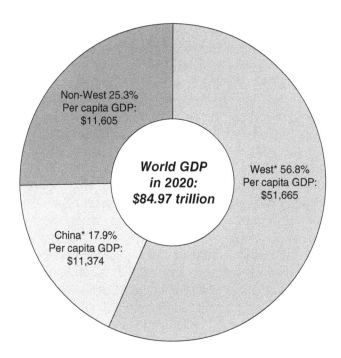

FIGURE 5.5 Can China Afford to Decouple from Western Economies?

*Note: "West" consists of the European Union's 27 countries, Australia, Canada, Japan, New Zealand, Norway, Switzerland, United Kingdom, and United States. "China" consists of Mainland China, Hong Kong, and Macao. "Per capita GDP" refers to average weighted (by GDP) per capita GDP in each group.

Source: Nomura Research Institute, based on data from International Monetary Fund (IMF)'s World Economic Outlook Database for October 2021

China's market is of course important to the West, but with the latter's 56.8 percent share of global GDP far exceeding China's 17.9 percent share, it is clear which would suffer more. China's market is also far less transparent than those of the West.

The Domestic Over-Stretching Required after Decoupling

For the Chinese economy to grow in such an environment, domestic businesses and consumers will have to do the over-stretching themselves. For that to happen, companies will need to continuously come up with new and exciting products capable of wowing consumers. In other words, they must pursue Strategy A despite having fewer—and significantly less wealthy—customers. This makes their situation similar to countries pursuing an import-substitution model of economic growth, as noted earlier.

China has many companies capable of coming up with exciting new products. But the key question for policy makers is whether there are *enough* of them to support an economy of 1.4 billion people and propel it forward. In spite of China's spectacular economic growth over the last 40 years, 600 million people still subsist on a monthly income of RMB 1,000 ($157) or less, and 900 million earn RMB 2,000 or less. As such, the country could still use foreign markets and Strategy B to provide gainful employment for these 900 million people and thereby improve their living standards.

For Chinese companies to develop new products, the government will also have to ensure protection for intellectual property rights—without it, companies will not feel safe in pouring resources into research and development. Since Strategy A is also inherently more risky than Strategy B, the financial system will have to be revamped to ensure greater access to risk capital for these companies. In effect, the Chinese government will have to implement the very sorts of policies the U.S. government has been demanding for years.

While those policy reforms may actually happen, the new environment—with fewer and less wealthy consumers—will be far more challenging than what Chinese companies have grown accustomed to. Economic growth is therefore likely to slow as decoupling progresses. The fact that few countries in the postwar era have had to shift to the more difficult Strategy A when their per capita GDP was still low, and that none of them succeeded in achieving sustained economic growth, suggests that China faces a big challenge.

Moreover, when foreign companies with factories in China begin scaling back their operations in response to lower wages elsewhere (i.e., the middle-income trap) or face higher overseas tariffs on products made in China, someone else will have to take their place to maintain output and employment. Although there are a growing number of capable Chinese companies that can both produce at home and market their products abroad, the issue is the same: Are there enough of them to provide gainful employment for the populace after foreign firms leave?

The Xi administration is also trying to reestablish the predominant role of the Chinese Communist Party (CCP) in society by forcing both domestic and foreign businesses to establish CCP cells inside companies. Such a policy may lower the *perceived* return on capital by reducing the management's freedom to act and thereby reduce the incentives for businesses, both foreign and domestic, to continue investing in the country.

The government is also enacting new laws and regulations, including the new export control laws promulgated in December 2020, that make China an increasingly less attractive destination for production, especially for foreign companies. Although this may be in retaliation to similar moves in the West, it is the opposite of what a country in the middle-income trap should be doing. Instead, the country should be making a conscious effort to increase the domestic return on capital so that both foreign and domestic companies will continue to invest there. Policy makers in China should remind themselves that it is China, not the West, that is facing the middle-income trap.

The Chinese private sector's response to these new regulations has been muted, but they could still have devastating economic consequences. An entrepreneur who might have pursued five new business initiatives each year in the absence of government intervention might now proceed with only two. The missing three cannot be observed since they exist only in the mind of the entrepreneur, but the economy will suffer from a drastic reduction in entrepreneurial over-stretch. Indeed, decoupling could prematurely end China's golden era.

In the short run, the government can always over-stretch to keep the economy from contracting, and the Chinese government appears to be doing so (Figure 5.6). But unless those public works have high enough social rates of return to be self-financing, the burden of financing both the growing budget deficit and the cost of maintaining new projects will eventually force the government to reduce fiscal stimulus. Chinese economic growth could then slow once those fiscal support measures are rescinded unless Chinese companies are successful in continuously coming up with new and exciting products.

As previously noted, China's working-age population—defined as those aged 15 to 59[11]—started shrinking in 2012 just as China was passing the LTP. From a demographic perspective, it is highly unusual for the entire labor supply curve to begin shifting to the left just as a country reaches the LTP. Japan, Taiwan, and South Korea all enjoyed about 30 years of workforce growth after reaching their LTPs. The huge demographic bonus China enjoyed until 2012 is not only exhausted, but has now reversed, as shown in Figure 5.4. That means

---

[11] In most countries, the working-age population is defined as those aged 15 to 64.

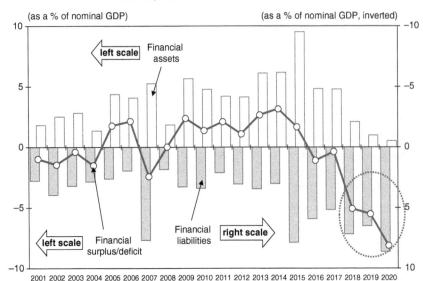

FIGURE 5.6 The Chinese Government Has Been Propping Up the Economy since 2018

Source: Nomura Research Institute, based on data from National Bureau of Statistics China and People's Bank of China

it will not be able to maintain the rapid pace of economic growth seen in the past and, in fact, growth has already slowed sharply.

If the Japanese example is any guide, the decline in total population that is expected to start as early as 2022 will weigh on that portion of economic growth that was made possible by population growth. If China fails to emerge from the middle-income trap before the forward economic momentum from demographic factors is lost, it may—as an aging country with rising social burdens—have difficulty achieving a per capita GDP of $20,000, which seems to be the goal President Xi has set for 2035 (Figure 5.3).

Decoupling does not mean that all of China's trade with the West will disappear overnight. Even in the 1960s, at the peak of the Cold War between the United States and the Soviet Union, the United States and the United Kingdom were importing large numbers of single-lens-reflex cameras from East Germany and using them in public school photography classes. This was because East German cameras were far cheaper than competing products from West Germany and Japan. But that was not enough to make East Germany a prosperous nation.

With help from fiscal policy, the Chinese economy is likely to continue growing for the next few years barring actual military conflict. However, decoupling from the West when the population is aging and domestic wages have already reached a level signaling the middle-income trap could lead to a substantial reduction in growth rates.

In that sense, China has little time to waste—and little room for policy error—if it wants to reach the standard of living noted above by 2035. Like the Japanese economists whose domestic forecasts first looked to the United States, Chinese policy makers must understand who has been doing the over-stretching up to now and who will be doing it in the future if they hope to sustain economic growth after decoupling.

The Economic Destiny of Human Progress

In 5,000 years of civilization, humanity has made tremendous progress in according respect to individuals regardless of their background, creed, skin color, sex, or sexual orientation. Although the process is far from complete and there are some areas where progress has been reversed, the world is far ahead of where it was just 100 years ago. Much of this progress has taken place after countries entered their post-LTP golden eras, indicating that inclusive social reforms have certain economic preconditions.

What, then, is the *economic* destiny of human progress? What is the end game for all the chasing and being chased illustrated in Figure 3.12?

The economic destiny of human progress would seem to be a world in which the opportunity for economic advancement is available equally to everyone on the planet regardless of where they were born or raised. It is a world in which people born in Somalia or Bangladesh will have the same opportunity to advance themselves economically as people born in the United States or Germany. Today, unfortunately, the world remains far from that destination.

A person born in Somalia today would have to study and work exceptionally hard to attain the economic well-being of even less-diligent people born in the United States or Germany. During the golden age of the United States in the 1950s and 1960s, even those with minimal skills could afford a nice house, a big car, and a standard of living that was unthinkable for people on other continents. It is this geographic *inequality* that is being corrected by the process of industrialization and globalization previously described.

During the last three decades, this process of globalization received a huge boost from developments in the information technology (IT) industry that have dramatically lowered the cost of communication. As a result, any job that can be performed outside an office can now be performed anywhere in the world, something that was conclusively proven during the COVID-19 lockdowns. IT has also lowered the stock advantage advanced countries used to enjoy vis-à-vis emerging nations. For example, it was not too long ago that the quality of a university was judged by the number of books in its library. Today, most of the material needed for research in many fields is available on the internet. And this material is accessible from anywhere in the world with an internet connection.

These IT developments lowered the cost of starting or expanding businesses in both emerging and advanced economies. For those willing to put up with the stress of starting and expanding a business, the global marketplace is only an internet connection away, and there are far more business opportunities today than at any time in history.

This also means the easy days are over for those in the advanced countries who do not study or work hard. Their real wages are likely to stagnate or fall if they do not upgrade their skill sets to match and stay ahead of current demand. If governments in pursued countries rely on protectionism to preserve jobs for those with limited skills, the countries themselves may lose their advanced economy status as their industries lose the ability to compete with the rest of the world.

Conclusion

For an economy to grow, someone must over-stretch by spending more than they earn, either by borrowing money or drawing down savings. For consumers to over-stretch, they must be presented with irresistible, "must-have" products. For businesses to over-stretch, they must find attractive investment opportunities worth borrowing money for. The availability of such opportunities depends on, among other things, the stage of economic development and on hard-to-predict technological innovations that lead to new products (Strategy A) or new ways to make existing products more efficiently (Strategy B).

Most emerging economies that have achieved economic growth have followed the export-led Strategy B because they are at the stage of economic development where wages are low and the pursuit of this strategy offers good returns on capital. With consumers in importing countries doing the over-stretching, Strategy B—if the country can offer lower wage costs—is much easier than Strategy A and will allow emerging economies to grow faster than their more advanced counterparts.

For these emerging economies, the developed world's experience suggests they should never assume that the good times, when exports effectively sell themselves, will last forever. They should prepare for the day when they have to switch to Strategy A by consciously upgrading both human and physical capital. As the concept of the middle-income trap suggests, the rapid spread of globalization is also forcing many emerging economies to confront challenges similar to those faced by pursued economies.

Meanwhile, policy makers in the pursued countries must overcome at least three challenges. First, they must recognize that there is a shortage of domestic investment opportunities and that a conscious effort must be made to increase the domestic return on capital with supply-side reforms. Second, they must improve labor market flexibility so that companies can take evasive action to fend off chasers from behind. Third, they must recognize that education is far more important in the post-industrial pursued era than in the manufacturing-led golden era.

In the golden-era political landscape, conservatives pushed for balanced budgets and small government based on the neoliberal tradition along with supply-side reforms such as tax cuts and deregulation. Progressives, on the other hand, pushed for workers' rights, including the right to unionize as well as increased expenditures on infrastructure and social programs such as education.

In the pursued era, the private sector is often a net saver even at zero interest rates because businesses are hard-pressed to find attractive domestic investment opportunities. This means the government must be prepared to operate as borrower of last resort at the macroeconomic level to keep the economy going. Balanced budgets and small government are not appropriate until private sector borrowers are back.

At the microeconomic level, however, economic growth and good jobs will not be forthcoming without businesses investing more at home. This means governments must implement the supply-side reforms such as deregulation and tax cuts to increase the return on capital that are the hallmarks of small government. The government must also address the inherent tendency of inequality to worsen in the pursued era by ensuring that everyone has equal access to quality education.

Political parties must adjust their stances to remain relevant in this new environment. Conservatives will have to drop their insistence on balanced budgets when the private sector is a net saver, and progressives will have to abandon their focus on organized labor and their opposition to supply-side reforms if they hope to attract investment. Making the labor market more flexible also means a better social safety net will have to be provided for workers who might need it.

The tax regime must also be revamped to maximize the creative potential of the population without losing sight of the revenue flow. That will require a carefully calibrated tax structure, meaning that decisions about tax rates should be more a question of technical calibration than a political issue.

Both supply-side and educational reforms take a long time to bear fruit. In the meantime, the government might have to serve as "over-stretcher of last resort" with self-financing public works projects if the private sector remains a net saver. Fortunately, finding such projects should be easier when the private sector is a net saver because government bond yields will fall to very low levels. Such fiscal support must stay in place until another private-sector investment boom arrives.

All of this suggests that economic management in the pursued era is far more demanding than in the golden era. Although some people are longing for the return of the golden era and others are flirting with socialism, none of them will be able to deliver economic growth until they recognize the reality of pursued economies in a global context.

CHAPTER 6

Monetary Policy during the Pandemic and the Quantitative Easing (QE) Trap

The COVID-19 pandemic recession, which struck in early 2020, threw the global economy from Case 3 into Case 2, forcing governments and central banks to make a dramatic policy shift to deal with the life-threatening economic downturn. The subsequent recovery then pushed prices sharply higher because of both supply-side disruptions and Sustainable-Driven Goals (SDGs)-driven higher energy prices, fueling strong inflationary concerns. Those concerns were augmented even further by the Russian invasion of Ukraine in 2022.

When the pandemic hit, people had to stay home to avoid being infected, and millions if not billions of households and businesses suddenly found themselves with drastically reduced incomes. The gross domestic product (GDP) in most countries contracted precipitously as lockdowns, voluntary or otherwise, were implemented. In the second quarter of 2020, the GDP shrank by as much as 8.94 percent in the United States, 11.63 percent in the Eurozone, and 7.95 percent in Japan—the worst figures seen since the Great Depression in the 1930s. The United States, for example, went in just two months from reporting its lowest unemployment rate in 50 years to its highest in 90 years. Only Taiwan, which was the first country to report the existence of the new virus to the World Health Organization (WHO), managed to contain infections from the start of the pandemic and was thereby able to maintain economic activity throughout most of 2020. But even Taiwan was struck by a super-spreader nicknamed "Lion King" in the spring of 2021 and by the Omicron variant in 2022.

This sudden loss of income, in turn, forced affected businesses and households to withdraw savings or borrow money to make ends meet, as they still had to pay rent and other expenditures. These actions caused an abrupt tightening of financial markets, as the savers who used to supply funds to the market began withdrawing their savings, while borrowers who had been absent since 2008 returned in massive numbers to secure working capital. This behavioral shift pushed the economy into Case 2.

As a result, borrowing costs skyrocketed in most markets in early March 2020, further worsening the predicament of businesses already hit hard by the coronavirus. This can be seen from the sudden jump in corporate bond yields in the United States and Europe (Figure 6.1). In Japan, the financial position diffusion index DI in the Bank of Japan (BOJ)'s Tankan survey (Figure 6.2) plunged after the pandemic recession began (see oval at right edge of graph), with the speed of the decline reminiscent of the global financial crisis (GFC) in 2008 (middle oval) and the banking sector "meltdown" in 1998 (left oval).

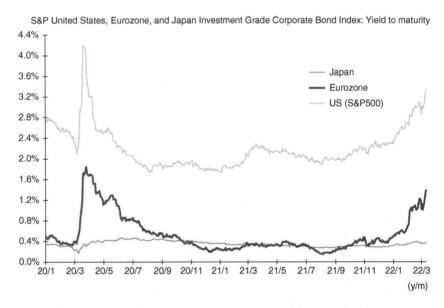

FIGURE 6.1 Corporate Bond Yields Returned to Pre-Pandemic Levels but Increased again in the West due to Inflationary Fears

Notes: Data as of March 11, 2022.

Source: S&P Dow Jones Indices LLC

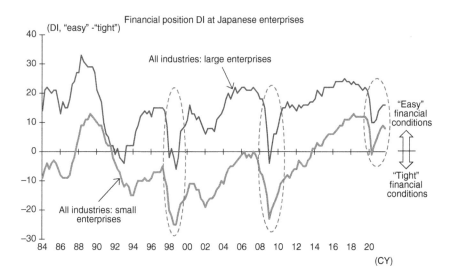

FIGURE 6.2 Financing Challenges of Japanese Enterprises

Source: **BOJ** *Tankan*

But whereas those two crises were triggered by lender-side factors—that is, a financial crisis—the tight financial conditions seen at the beginning of the pandemic were the result of a dramatic drop in borrower revenues.

A weaker economy is usually accompanied by lower interest rates, but this time the opposite happened, and the collapsing economy ushered in sharply higher rates. Central banks responded by acting as lenders of last resort in order to restore the normal workings of financial markets. For the first time since 2008 for the West and since 1990 for Japan, central bank monetary easing became absolutely essential, which was not the case during the pre-2020 balance sheet recessions.

Central banks around the world took up the challenge and injected massive amounts of funds to calm the markets. Even though the COVID-19 shock was not a financial crisis originating with the lenders like the post-Lehman GFC, the amounts provided by central banks this time were far larger than in 2008. These amounts can be seen as the post–February 2020 jump in the monetary base shown in Figures 2.12 to 2.14 and 2.17. In addition, the Fed quickly took interest rates back to zero.

The Fed also provided liquidity *directly* to nonfinancial companies. Such direct lending to the private sector had always been
taboo. But by directly purchasing corporate bonds, the Fed eased
market concerns about businesses' survival and reassured investors,
who then drove bond yields lower. The Fed's concern was that if
businesses were allowed to go under due to revenues lost during the
pandemic, the economy would be unable to recover—and banks'
bad loans would surge—even if a medical solution to the coronavirus was eventually found. As a result of these aggressive easing
measures, corporate bond yields returned to pre-pandemic levels
(Figure 6.1).

Corporate Bond Yield Movements in Japan and Europe Also Relatively Mild

In Europe, the European Central Bank (ECB) not only resumed
quantitative easing (QE), but also began supplying funds at negative interest rates. The yields on Eurozone corporate bonds consequently returned to pre-pandemic levels after blowing out initially
(Figure 6.1). In Japan, the BOJ restarted QE in response to the sudden increase in borrowers.

The central banks' sense of crisis regarding businesses' ability to
endure the pandemic recession was shared by governments, which
implemented a variety of fiscal measures to reduce companies' costs
in the short term, such as the Paycheck Protection Program (PPP)
in the United States. European and Japanese governments' massive
loan guarantee programs have also helped to ease concerns about
companies' ability to survive. The European Union (EU) unveiled a
€750 billion rescue package to be funded by a Euro-wide bond issue,
the first since the creation of the euro.

These measures also prompted governments to become huge
borrowers as they provided financial support to help keep businesses and households viable. The measures had to take the
form of direct payments from the government to individuals and
businesses—as opposed to public works projects—because people could not work in close proximity to each other during the

pandemic. The corresponding expenditures added massively to government budget deficits.

Capital Markets Have Shrugged Off Central Bank Financing of Fiscal Deficits

That raises the question on how to finance the resulting budget deficits. A significant portion of the economic measures implemented thus far—including the $3.9 trillion spent by the United States in 2020—has been effectively funded by central banks' QE, as can be seen by the jump in the post-2020 monetary base previously noted. This had to happen because only central banks can provide the trillions of dollars needed so quickly. Although the private sector has been a large net saver since 1990 in Japan and since 2008 in the West, only a central bank can swiftly provide the sums needed when the government's borrowing requirements jump so suddenly due to what Fed Chairman Jerome Powell called a natural disaster.

While economists have long viewed this sort of de facto central bank financing of budget deficits as taboo because of its tendency to produce pernicious inflation, capital markets have hardly blinked an eye. There were at least five reasons for the market to "think differently" this time.

First, there was little reason to fear inflation during the lockdowns themselves because supply far exceeded demand. In fact, if central banks had not provided support for government fiscal stimulus, economies might well have fallen into a vicious deflationary cycle of bankruptcies and job losses.

Second, the failure of central banks to achieve their own inflation targets despite purchasing huge amounts of government debt under QE since 2008 has taught the markets that QE would not necessarily result in inflation. Although this represented a tremendous loss of face for the central banks and economists who pushed for such policies, it would appear that their failure has helped keep the markets calm during the pandemic.

Third, unlike in an ordinary natural disaster, the economy's capital stock has not been impaired, which means there will be no reconstruction demand after the pandemic has run its course.

Exchange Rates Have Also Held Steady Because Central Banks Acted Together

Fourth, the impact on exchange rates has been minimal since central banks around the world have adopted similar policies. In all past instances where such monetization of the fiscal deficit led to pernicious inflation, it did so by triggering a collapse of the domestic currency in the foreign exchange market, thereby leading to a dramatic rise in the cost of imports. Basically, people feared that central bank "money printing" to finance the government deficit would cause the national currency to lose value, and they rushed to exchange it for other currencies.

This time, however, all central banks are doing the same thing, making it difficult for people to know where to take their money, and exchange rates have been very stable. Although gold and cryptocurrencies did appreciate, this has done nothing to increase domestic inflation rates.

Last but not least, the businesses and households that suffered most from the pandemic were those with little savings. Many went bankrupt as a result. Having realized that it is important to have sufficient savings for a rainy day, those who survived the recession are likely to place a high priority on replenishing savings depleted during the lockdown. Many may go far beyond the pre-pandemic levels of savings, just to be on the safe side, especially with new variants of the virus constantly emerging to threaten the economic recovery.

For some households and businesses, the most important impact of the pandemic for the long term may come from a renewed appreciation of having sufficient savings. This is the opposite of the pre-pandemic mindset in the West, where politicians, academics, and financial types alike bashed the corporate hoarding of cash as a suboptimal use of capital. But those precautionary hoardings helped the companies withstand the pandemic in no small way.

In the new paradigm, share buybacks with borrowed money, which reduced companies' savings and weakened their ability to withstand the pandemic and other external shocks, are likely to be viewed with caution. A renewed appreciation of savings also means post-pandemic economic growth will be weaker but the economies themselves will be more resilient. The probability of an economy returning to Case 3 after the pandemic also increases if its private sector collectively becomes a net saver as it tries to replenish savings that were depleted during the pandemic.

This suggests that central bank financing of fiscal deficits has very different implications during ordinary times and during a pandemic. It is a policy that can be safely employed during a pandemic even if it should be forbidden under normal circumstances.

Inflation Returns

Starting in the spring of 2021, inflation driven by supply constraints became rampant in the United States and Europe as uneven waves of infection hit different parts of the world at different times. Since products made from components fabricated around the globe cannot be completed until all the parts are in place, these rolling waves of COVID-19 disrupted and delayed production and shipments everywhere. It was said, for example, that the shortage of integrated circuit (IC) chips could not be easily addressed because the machines needed to produce those chips also required chips that were in short supply.

For inflation to return on a sustained basis, however, there has to be some improvement in the two factors that pushed the advanced countries into Case 3 in the first place. Those two problems are inferior returns on capital relative to emerging economies and balance sheet concerns following the bubble's collapse, both of which led to an absence of borrowers. There have been signs of improvement in the latter, but little progress on the former. A new factor that emerged during the last two years, the global push toward renewable energy (discussed later), is also likely to result in more domestic investment. But without significant progress on one or both of the two problems previously noted, the economy may still be pulled toward a non-inflationary Case 3 state over the medium term. In the meantime, central banks will have their hands full fighting inflation driven by supply shortages, which do not respond well to monetary tightening.

The Return of Fiscal Stimuli after 50 Years

One key difference between the COVID-19 recession and the post-2008 balance sheet recession is the size of government's fiscal response. In 2008, tens of trillions of dollars in asset value vanished when housing bubbles burst on both sides of the Atlantic. That created a massive and urgent need for the private sector to repair millions of underwater balance sheets, forcing the sector to save as much as 10 percent of GDP per year in the immediate aftermath of the Lehman Brothers' collapse, as is noted in Chapter 2.

In spite of the huge loss of wealth and massive private-sector deleveraging, the best the newly elected Obama administration could manage to extract from the Republican opposition was a two-year, $787 billion package, which comes to about 2 percent of GDP per year. That 2 percent was simply not enough to turn the economy around.

Moreover, there was no follow-up fiscal package because the Republicans, who took control of the lower house of Congress after the mid-term elections in 2010, sought to balance the budget even though the U.S. private sector continued to generate massive excess savings in order to repair its balance sheets for years afterward. The result was a long and painful balance sheet recession that lasted nearly a decade.

This time, the U.S. government administered a fiscal stimulus worth $3.9 trillion—almost 20 percent of U.S. GDP—in 2020 alone. The Biden administration then passed a $1.9 trillion economic support package followed by a $1.2 trillion infrastructure package in 2021. These are massive fiscal programs that even Lawrence Summers warned might incite inflation. There is no doubt that some elements of these large fiscal initiatives have contributed to upward pressure on prices in a recovering economy that is also suffering from supply mismatches. This is also the first time since the war in Vietnam, half a century ago, that concerns over fiscal policy shifted from "too little" to "too much."

The Energy Sector Will Not Return to Pre-2020 World

One sector of the economy that will not return to the pre-pandemic Case 3 world is the energy sector. Because of the recent groundswell of concern over climate change, the business environment for fossil fuel producers has changed drastically. Financial institutions, including central banks, are now under pressure to reduce the flow of funds to fossil fuel–related industries.

This shift in focus to SDGs was bolstered by President Joe Biden, who is deeply worried about the existential threat to humankind posed by climate change. He is also trying to make up lost ground, as his predecessor denied the very existence of the threat and did nothing about it for a full four years. Japan has also announced some fairly ambitious plans, with then–Prime Minister Yoshihide Suga declaring in late 2020 that the nation would be carbon neutral by 2050, effectively eliminating all emissions of carbon dioxide and other greenhouse gases. Europeans are far ahead on this issue, and the Chinese are trying to achieve carbon neutrality by 2060.

But no matter how necessary the transition to renewable energy may be, there is simply not enough renewable energy at present to keep economies going. As a result, the recent move to discourage investment in fossil fuels has already prompted energy shortages in Europe and China, resulting in sharply higher energy prices and stagnant economic growth.

In the past, investments in fossil fuel were carried out in expectation of ever-greater demand for such fuels in the future. But many governments around the world are now stipulating that only electric vehicles may be sold after a certain date. And those new restrictions are likely to spread to other machines and transportation equipment that are currently powered by fossil fuels.

That means those businesses that are contemplating investments in fossil fuel extraction must be able to recover their costs in a drastically shorter time frame. The growing tendency for society to view such action as being morally suspect, if not evil, has also dissuaded many companies from pursuing such projects. As a result of these fundamental changes in the market, supply is falling behind demand, and prices are rapidly rising.

The unfortunate truth is that high prices for fossil fuels are essential in order both to increase investment in renewable energy *and* to justify investment in the fossil fuels that are still needed to avert energy shortages—but whose cost must be quickly recovered. Indeed, it is unrealistic to think the fundamental energy transition the world seeks is possible without high fossil fuel prices.

One must also be realistic about the duration of the transition period. To fully replace fossil fuels with renewable energy will take decades. The only realistic solution that can shorten the time needed to go carbon-free is nuclear power. But as Toyota Motor chairman Akio Toyoda commented on December 17, 2020,[1] Japan would need ten more nuclear power plants if all the cars in the country had to run on electricity. If all the machines in the world that are currently powered by gas, oil, and coal had to run on electricity, the number of additional nuclear power plants needed would be absolutely staggering.

These hard realities are likely to result in bouts of "SDG fatigue" during the long transition period, especially when economies suffer from repeated energy shortages. But such fatigue and the resulting political pushback could easily lengthen the transition period to the detriment of the planet. To avoid such setbacks, it is essential that energy shortages are avoided.

It is difficult to expand the supply of anything, including fossil fuel, when its use is almost certain to face severe restrictions in the near future. The only way to secure a sufficient supply of coal, gas, and oil to keep economies running in the near term while accelerating the deployment of renewable energy in the longer run is to have high fossil fuel prices now. That means high and possibly volatile energy prices are here to stay.

Central banks responsible for price stability must recognize that even if the rest of the economy is trying to return to the disinflationary world that existed before the 2020 pandemic, the energy sector is not. The SDG concerns that emerged during the last two years mean inflationary pressures in energy-related fields are not only not transitory but are actually necessary for the least disruptive transition to renewable energy. The higher energy prices brought about by the Russian invasion of Ukraine may reverse themselves if and when peace returns. But that level is still likely to be higher than the prices seen prior to the pandemic.

That means pursued economies will face high energy prices and reduced purchasing power for years to come. To the extent that the stagflation of the 1970s was triggered by high oil prices, it is possible that a similar phenomenon will be observed as the transition to renewable energy is accompanied by higher energy prices and slower economic growth.

---

[1] Toyotimes, "JAMA Chairman Akio Toyoda Talks Earnestly about Carbon Neutrality in Japan," Toyota Motor Corporation's website, January 8, 2021. https://toyotatimes.jp/en/toyota_news/111.html.

SDG Concerns May Return Economies to Case 1

Over the medium term, SDG concerns could bring far-reaching changes to the global economy that may even push the advanced economies out of Case 3, where they are today, and into Case 1. This is because replacing everything that currently runs on gas, oil, or coal with electrically powered equipment will require huge investments. And both businesses and households are likely to finance a substantial portion of those investments with borrowings.

A greater focus on climate change may also slow down the pace of globalization. Some in Europe and elsewhere are already calling for the erection of barriers against imports from countries that have not done enough to address climate change. Indeed, this could undo some of the globalization that has taken place since the postwar introduction of the U.S.-led free trade system as businesses bring production back home. The concept of pursued economies will also lose some of its relevance if concerns over SDGs slow down the process of globalization. In addition, the recent supply chain disruptions caused by the pandemic may also force businesses to nearshore production. These developments are likely to retard globalization while adding to domestic inflationary pressures.

Normalizing Post-Pandemic Monetary Policy Will Be Challenging

Higher prices brought about by pandemic-driven supply chain disruptions and higher energy prices brought about by climate change concerns are not something a central bank can address. But these higher prices, together with the return of long-awaited fiscal activism, signal a change in the environment surrounding monetary policy.

All unconventional monetary policy since 2008—including QE, forward guidance, and negative interest rates (in Europe and Japan)—has been implemented because the fiscal policy needed to address balance sheet recessions was not forthcoming. The return of fiscal policy—at least in the United States—along with higher energy prices, means central banks should wind down these nonconventional policies and restore their inflation-fighting credentials.

Such credentials are necessary because the fear of inflation is weighing heavily on consumer confidence and on the economy in general. For example, the University of Michigan's consumer confidence index for November 2021 dropped to its lowest level in over a decade—lower even than during the worst of the lockdowns—because of consumer concerns over inflation. Moreover, no matter how confident the Fed might be that prices will eventually stabilize once supply constraints are removed, no one will know for sure for two or three years.

In the meantime, if market participants perceive the Fed to be falling further behind the curve on inflation, they could start selling bonds to protect themselves from inflation, sending long-term interest rates rocketing higher and pushing the economy into recession. If the Fed is no longer credible as an inflation fighter, the chances of such a bond market sell-off will increase sharply. It would also take a great deal of time and effort for the Fed to regain the market's confidence and bring long-term rates back down.

Recognizing this risk, the Fed drastically shifted its stance on inflation and began normalizing monetary policy in late 2021. This process, as indicated in Figure 4.6, will be a huge challenge as it entails raising interest rates while reabsorbing the enormous amounts of liquidity injected into the economy during both the post-2008 balance sheet recession and the post-2020 pandemic recession. To do so, the Fed must sell the government and other bonds it has acquired since 2008. Given the huge amounts involved, this was going to be a difficult and volatile period for the markets even if the real economy had stayed on a recovery path. If this process is not handled correctly, the resulting market volatility could even harm the real economy. But a failure to mop up the liquidity could force the Fed to carry out an even more difficult monetary tightening later on if and when private-sector borrowers return (this point is discussed further a bit later).

This process of normalization was actually attempted and aborted once before by the Fed. When the Fed announced in May 2013 that it was going to begin reducing, or tapering, its purchases of government bonds under QE, the market responded badly and pushed long-term bond yields sharply higher in what came to be known as the "taper tantrum." It took months for the market to regain its composure after that shock.

The tapering was followed by nine interest rate hikes starting in December 2015 along with so-called quantitative tightening (QT) beginning in October 2017. Some of these actions also led to market turmoil. However, the normalization process was aborted when the economy showed modest signs of weakness in the second half of 2019, and was scuttled altogether when the pandemic hit in February 2020.

Market volatility may increase during a post-QE normalization of monetary policy because it will be the first time in history that a recovery starts with massive amounts of liquidity *already* present in the financial sector owing to QE. Since 2008, the Fed has supplied some $5.5 trillion under quantitative easing, and the ECB, Bank of England (BOE), and BOJ have injected €5.28 trillion, £992 billion, and ¥581.8 trillion, respectively (Figures 2.12 to 2.14 and Figure 2.17).

As a result, the U.S. monetary base rose from 6.3 percent of GDP in September 2008 to 27.5 percent in December 2021. The monetary base increased from 9.4 percent to 47.9 percent of GDP in the Euro-zone, from 5.4 percent to 49.3 percent in the United Kingdom, and from 17.1 percent to 122.6 percent in Japan. As a percentage of GDP, these amounts represent a 4.4× increase over the level when Lehman Brothers collapsed for the United States, a 5.1× increase for the Euro-zone, a 9.1× increase for the United Kingdom, and a 7.2× increase for Japan. Multiples over the pre-Lehman era are even larger for reserves in the banking system (Figure 6.3).

These increases in the monetary base imply that if businesses and households were to resume borrowing in earnest (i.e., return to Case 1) and the pre-2008 relationship between monetary aggregates seen in Figures 2.12 to 2.14 were to be restored, credit and the money supply could increase as much as fourfold in the United States, sending the inflation rate sky-high. The only reason these countries have not experienced such runaway inflation is that their economies have been in Case 3, with very weak private-sector borrowing—in fact, businesses and households have been saving money or paying down debt despite near-zero interest rates (Figure 1.1).

That means central banks will have to slash excess liquidity to a fraction of current levels by selling their holdings of government bonds before borrowers return. But that would still be a nightmare for the economy and the bond market because they have never experienced central banks unloading so many bonds in the market. The subsequent fall in bond prices would mean higher borrowing costs for everybody.

Figure 4.6 in Chapter 4 already indicated what would be needed to normalize monetary policy in the United States. It showed that both interest rates and the monetary base will have to be normalized,

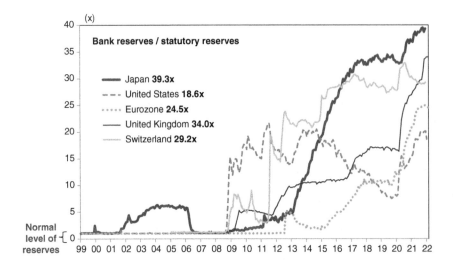

FIGURE 6.3 QE Central Banks Must Reduce Reserves Massively before Borrowers Return to Avoid Credit Explosion

Note: The Bank of England (BOE) and the Fed suspended reserve requirements in March 2009 and March 2020, respectively. Post-suspension figures are based on assumption that original reserve requirements are still applicable.

Sources: Nomura Research Institute, based on BOJ, Federal Reserve Board (FRB), ECB, BOE, and Swiss National Bank (SNB) data

a task that had never been attempted before 2015. Alan Greenspan, who brought down interest rates to 1 percent after the dot-com bubble collapsed in 2001, did succeed in normalizing interest rates by raising the policy rate 17 times starting in 2004, taking it up to 5.25 percent. But he was simultaneously allowing the monetary base to grow, albeit slowly. In other words, at the same time as he was tightening monetary policy by raising interest rates, he was also easing policy by allowing the monetary base to grow. He could do this because he and his predecessors did not implement QE: for him, the normalization process was limited to interest rates.

This time the central banks have to both raise interest rates *and* shrink the monetary base to normalize policy. The difficulty inherent in the latter task is one of the costs of QE (or any central bank financing of budget deficits) and is the reason why central bankers traditionally tried to avoid monetizing fiscal deficits in the first place.

The Need for a Shock Absorber

The difficulty surrounding the task of normalizing the monetary base was acknowledged by the Fed in September 2014 when it reversed the order of policy normalization. Prior to this date, the Fed's official position on unwinding QE was that it would normalize its balance sheet (i.e., shrink the monetary base) first and only then set about normalizing interest rates. But as the challenges surrounding the former became clearer, the order was reversed for the reasons discussed in the following.

To begin with, the bond market had never seen the Fed unload trillions of dollars in government bonds, but it had plenty of experience with rate hikes. By raising interest rates first and normalizing its balance sheet only after rates had returned to sufficiently high levels, the Fed sought to buy itself a shock absorber in case the balance sheet normalization process (or other factors) triggered a collapse of the bond market. In other words, if bond prices tumbled for any reason, the Fed could lower interest rates to soften the shock.

Although the lack of private-sector borrowers in 2015 suggested there was no need to rush the normalization process, central banks that implemented QE must move faster than those that did not. This is because bond yields can surge if the central bank tries to reduce the supply of liquidity just as demand for funds from private-sector borrowers is recovering. Bond yields can also go up if the market starts to believe the central bank has fallen behind the curve on inflation after injecting so much liquidity. Sharply higher bond yields, in turn, will have highly unpleasant consequences for the economy and the market.

If the normalization process is to proceed smoothly, therefore, central banks that have implemented QE must start the process *before* private-sector demand for funds picks up in earnest. This is because bond yields can go up only so much if there are no private-sector borrowers, even if the Fed starts to unload its bonds.

The Fed Is More Concerned about Real Estate than Equities

Another reason for the Fed to normalize monetary policy was the emergence of asset price bubbles in certain sectors, and especially in the U.S. commercial real estate market. As is noted in Chapters 2 and 4, mini-bubbles are possible even in balance sheet recessions because the disappearance of traditional borrowers forces fund managers to buy existing assets that are expected to appreciate. But such bubbles are most unwelcome for central bankers: after all, it was the collapse of the real estate bubble in 2008 that triggered the Western world's worst recession since World War II.

As is noted in Chapter 4, U.S. commercial real estate prices are now 68 percent higher than at the peak of the bubble in 2007 (Figure 4.7). House prices have also exceeded the previous bubble peak reached in 2006 by more than 51 percent. In San Francisco, which has benefited from its proximity to booming Silicon Valley, house prices are now 58 percent higher than at the previous bubble peak.

The central bank's economic support measures during the pandemic have also pushed the price of companies' stock and bonds sky-high, even though many issuers are far less profitable and creditworthy than they were prior to COVID-19. Electric vehicle (EV) maker Tesla, for example, reached a market capitalization that was twice that of Toyota's while producing only one twenty-ninth the number of cars in 2020. In other words, there is a bubble in asset markets driven by central bank liquidity, with investors happy to overlook potential risks. Although it is unfortunate that bubbles were formed, governments and central banks did what they had to do given the lives and livelihoods at stake, at least for the first year of the pandemic.

With asset price bubbles already evident in these markets, it would hardly be surprising if monetary authorities felt pressured to act to avoid a further expansion of these bubbles and their unpleasant aftermath. Whether or not the Fed is able to handle the collapse of mini-bubbles as it pursues normalization depends on the amount of private-sector leverage in the system. If parts of the private sector are highly leveraged, a burst bubble could lead to a bigger mess, while if the leverage is modest, any resulting correction should be manageable.

A look at the U.S. economy from the standpoint of private-sector leverage shows that the household sector, the trigger of the last crisis, has steadily reduced its leverage since then (Figure 2.5). Even in places like San Francisco, where house prices are in bubble territory, most of the high-priced deals are said to involve all-cash offers.

Unfortunately, that is not the case with commercial real estate, where most deals are done with borrowed money. Few businesses buy commercial properties with cash. Fed officials are therefore right-fully concerned about this market and have already imposed strong macro-prudential measures to clamp down on real estate lending since 2016.

Real estate bubbles are not only a U.S. problem. Thanks to the ECB's QE and negative-interest-rate policies, European real estate prices have risen sharply since 2015 (Figure 2.4). In the Netherlands, for example, house prices are already well beyond the previous peak reached in 2007. Even in Japan, real estate prices in popular areas have surged under negative interest rates, astronomical amounts of QE, and the changes to the inheritance tax that are noted in Chapter 5. Prices in the Ginza district in central Tokyo reached a new all-time high in 2017 for the first time since the bubble burst 27 years earlier.

If these bubbles continue to expand and eventually burst, economies will find themselves back at square one facing long and painful balance sheet recessions. That would signal another iteration of the bubble-and-balance-sheet-recession cycle that is noted in Chapter 4 and would also mean that all the efforts to fix the economy since 2008 had been in vain.

The First Attempt at Normalization

As is previously noted, the Fed's first attempt to normalize interest rates after the GFC began on December 16, 2015, when the Federal Open Market Committee (FOMC) unanimously approved the first increase in the federal funds rate in nine years. At the time, the U.S. private sector was still running a huge financial surplus as businesses and households continued to repair their balance sheets. Raising interest rates when the private sector is not borrowing money is a tricky business. Indeed, the Chicago Fed's financial conditions index often indicated an *easing* of borrowing conditions, as is shown in Figure 4.3, in spite of nine policy rate increases from 2015 to 2019. But that did not deter the Fed from raising rates because the key reason for doing so was to provide itself with a shock absorber.

At her press conference on the day of the first hike, Fed Chair Janet Yellen said that "if we do not begin to slightly reduce the amount of accommodation, the odds are good that the economy would end up overshooting both our employment and inflation objectives."[2] She also said that if the Fed were to postpone the normalization process for too long, it "would likely end up having to tighten policy relatively abruptly at some point," thereby increasing the risk of recession.

In a January 6, 2016 interview with CNBC, then–Fed Vice Chair Stanley Fischer declared that market expectations for the pace of tightening were "too low."[3] He also said the Fed needed to proceed with normalization in order to "head off excessively high asset prices," referring to the mini-bubbles in both stocks and commercial real estate. Fischer warned that such high asset prices would be "creating big messes in the markets," which is shorthand for the eventual need to raise interest rates rapidly, triggering a plunge in the value of stocks, bonds, and other assets.

These comments by Fed officials suggest they were fully cognizant of the danger of waiting until the 2-percent inflation target was reached, when the private sector would most likely have already resumed borrowing. The pronouncements also indicate the Fed was actively trying to manage market expectations as it embarked on a difficult journey.

Private-sector demand for borrowings can be expected to increase when balance sheets are repaired, thereby adding to inflationary pressures. Borrowings, however, are unlikely to recover to golden-era levels now that advanced countries are in the pursued phase. Still, even if growth in the money supply and credit were one-tenth of the monetary base multiple, for example, 40 percent instead of 400 percent, inflation rates could still rise to highly unpleasant levels unless the central bank drains the excess liquidity it pumped into the economy under QE.

---

[2] Board of Governors of Federal Reserve System (2015), "Transcript of Chair Yellen's Press Conference, December 16, 2015," p. 10. https://www .federalreserve.gov/mediacenter/files/FOMCpresconf20151216.pdf.

[3] CNBC (2016), "Fed's Fischer: Markets Missing Mark on Future Rates," January 6, 2016. http://www.cnbc.com/2016/01/06/feds-fischer-uncertainty-has-risen-in-markets-unsure-of-n-korea-news-impact.html.

QE Trap: Tug-of-War between Monetary Authorities and Markets

Even with the precautions previously noted, the first rate hike in nine years sparked tremendous market volatility in early 2016, with the Dow falling as much as 12 percent from its peak. Volatility picked up not only because many market participants had gotten addicted to easy money, but also because the Fed started tightening when the inflation rate was still well below target.

But the Fed's determination not to fall behind the curve on both asset prices and the general level of prices was demonstrated when John Williams, then president of the San Francisco Fed, said late in March 2016 that the 30 percent decline in share prices on Black Monday in October 1987 had had little impact on the real economy. He also cited economist Paul Samuelson's quip that the stock market has predicted "nine out of the last five recessions" in an attempt to emphasize that the stock market and the real economy are not the same thing.[4] Vice Chair Fischer also noted that the U.S. economy was largely unaffected by large swings in equity prices in 2011. The fact that these remarks came out as soon as markets regained their composure underscores the sense of urgency at the Fed regarding the normalization of monetary policy and suggests it was hard at work on managing expectations of further rate hikes.

First Iteration of QE Trap

The January 2016 turmoil was the first domestic iteration[5] of what the author dubbed the "QE trap" in his previous book[6]—a repeated tug-of-war between investors and the monetary authorities. In this

---

[4] Williams, John C. (2016), "The Right Profile: Economic Drivers and the Outlook," a presentation to Town Hall Los Angeles, February 18, 2016. http://www.frbsf.org/our-district/files/Williams-Speech-The-Right-Profile_Economic-Drivers-and-the-Outlook.pdf.

[5] The "taper tantrum" of 2013 was a similar market reaction, but the Fed was only reducing the degree of accommodation at the time, i.e., it was not yet *tightening* monetary policy.

[6] Koo, Richard C. (2015), *The Escape from Balance Sheet Recession and the QE Trap*, Singapore: John Wiley & Sons, 2015, Chapter 6.

trap, a central bank that has implemented QE but is now raising interest rates has to take a step back if the rate increase results in market turmoil. But once the market regains its balance, the central bank resumes its drive to normalize monetary policy. That, in turn, prompts another round of volatility. This sort of back-and-forth iteration of conflict between the markets and the authorities has been observed frequently since then.

Figure 6.4 illustrates the possible behavior of long-term interest rates in two scenarios: one in which the central bank has engaged in QE (thick line) and one in which it has not (thin line). When a central bank takes interest rates to zero after a bubble bursts but does not resort to QE, long-term government bond yields will still fall sharply because the economy is weak and government is the only borrower issuing fixed income assets denominated in the home currency. This

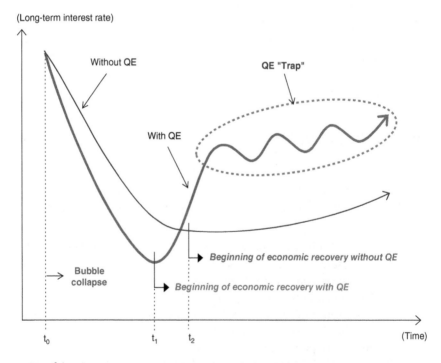

FIGURE 6.4 QE "Trap" (1): Long-Term Interest Rates or Exchange Rates Could Go Sharply Higher When QE Is Unwound

fall in government bond yields is the self-corrective mechanism of economies in balance sheet recessions that is noted in Chapter 2.

Once the economy begins to show signs of life after a few years, the central bank will raise short-term rates at a pace deemed appropriate given the extent of the economic recovery and inflation. Bond yields will rise gradually in line with both the short-term interest rate and the recovery in private-sector loan demand. At that point, people will be happy and relaxed because the recovery has finally arrived. This is the usual pattern of monetary policy normalization and bond yields in an economic recovery.

A central bank that has implemented QE, meanwhile, faces a very different set of circumstances. In this case, long-term rates will fall further and faster at the outset than in the non-QE case because the central bank is also buying huge quantities of government bonds. Such low rates are likely to support asset prices via the portfolio rebalancing effect and bring about economic recovery a little sooner (t_1) than in the economy where there was no QE (t_2).

Once the recovery is within sight, however, the market starts to gird for trouble as rate hikes and an eventual mop-up of excess liquidity by the central bank appear increasingly likely. Market participants must brace themselves because there is over $3.66 trillion in long-term bonds that the central bank must sell off to drain the excess reserves, as noted earlier.

If the Fed has to sell those bonds, bond prices will fall and yields will go up. If it holds on to the bonds until maturity, the Treasury will have to sell an equivalent amount of bonds on the Fed's behalf to absorb the excess liquidity (this is explained further a bit later). And if the Fed wants to postpone the normalization of its balance sheet, it will have to raise interest rates that much faster and higher to stay ahead of the curve on inflation. The resulting rise in interest rates may also trigger a stock market crash.

To the extent that market participants have become addicted to QE—known in the market as the "central bank put"—the reverse portfolio rebalancing effect (i.e., the negative wealth effect) brought about by the central bank's normalization of monetary policy would be equivalent to going through painful withdrawal symptoms. From the standpoint of the policy authorities, however, withdrawal symptoms alone are not cause enough to discontinue treatment of the patient. While treatment may be paused temporarily if symptoms become too severe, it will need to resume as soon as the market stabilizes lest the central bank fall behind the curve. It was precisely this kind of mindset that underpinned the previously noted remarks by Stanley Fisher and John Williams in March 2016.

Global QE Trap

There is also an international dimension to the QE trap. Indeed, the strengthening of the dollar since the Fed's September 2014 announcement of its intention to normalize interest rates can be seen as a manifestation of a *global* QE trap.

Soon after the Fed's announcement, the BOJ eased policy again and the ECB began indicating it would follow with its own version of QE. The prospect of higher interest rates in the United States and lower interest rates in Japan and Europe then prompted a rush of capital outflows from these two regions into the U.S. bond market in search of higher yields. Those inflows pushed the dollar sharply higher but also prevented a rise in long-term U.S. interest rates, thereby propping up the bubble in U.S. commercial real estate.

Between the summer of 2014 and the beginning of 2016, the dollar climbed as much as 48 percent against the Mexican peso and as much as 37 percent against the Canadian dollar (Figures 6.5 and 6.6). Not only are both countries key U.S. trading partners, but many U.S. companies have factories in one or both. U.S. workers who must compete with factories in these countries were therefore rightfully worried about such a major appreciation of the U.S. currency.

Presidential candidates Donald Trump and Bernie Sanders capitalized on this situation. Their stances against free trade have proved very popular among the blue-collar workers who have suffered as the dollar rises. Trump even proposed levying a 35 percent duty on imports from Mexico to help U.S. workers and companies fighting imports from that country.

Calls for protectionism became so loud in 2016 that even Hillary Clinton was forced to declare her opposition to the current form of the Trans-Pacific Partnership (TPP), an agreement she herself had helped negotiate. Her uncharacteristic shift can be attributed to the fact that the U.S. dollar's substantial appreciation made the free-trade argument a difficult one to sell in the United States. Indeed, when she accepted the Democratic Party's presidential nomination in 2016, the entire arena was filled with signs exclaiming "No to TPP!"

FIGURE 6.5 Mexican Peso versus U.S. Dollar

Source: FRB

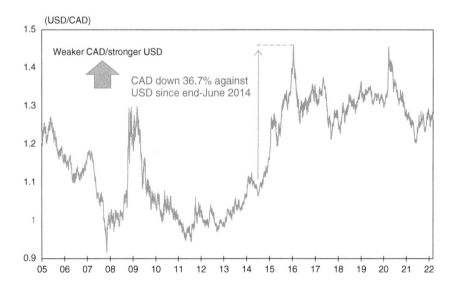

FIGURE 6.6 Canadian Dollar versus U.S. Dollar

Source: FRB

Since protectionism can quickly destroy world trade, the Fed had to curb its rate hikes until the presidential election was over. In this round of the QE trap, therefore, the Fed had to temper its response because of the surging dollar rather than falling stock prices or rising bond yields.

The stock market's surprisingly strong reaction to the Trump victory in November 2016 and the remarkable stability of the dollar during the Trump years gave the Fed a window of opportunity to raise interest rates eight times in the next two years, thereby making up for time lost during the election campaign. How the dollar remained stable during the Trump years in spite of eight rate increases by the Fed is explained in Chapter 9. The rate hikes gave the Fed the shock absorber it needed to embark on the main event, that is, the normalization of its bloated balance sheet.

The Difficulty of Normalizing the Central Bank Balance Sheet

If normalizing interest rates with QE is difficult, normalizing the central bank's balance sheet is no easier. Some have argued that this process should be relatively straightforward since banks have the excess reserves supplied under QE to buy the bonds being sold off by the central bank, but there is an asymmetry involved here.

When the central bank was acquiring the bonds under QE, there was no private-sector demand for borrowings. That means interest rates were low and bond prices were high. But when the time comes for the central bank to sell the bonds, both the economy and private-sector demand for borrowings have presumably recovered. Interest rates will therefore be higher and bond prices lower. The fact that the central bank is selling bonds at a time when the private sector also wants to borrow means interest rates could go much higher than when the central bank was a buyer. The situation can be further exacerbated if the central bank is viewed as being behind the curve on inflation. That is also why the Fed wanted to undo QE in 2017, *before* private-sector borrowers returned and when the asymmetry problem was minimal.

Many in the market, however, became complacent after Ben Bernanke assured them the Fed would hold the bonds until maturity.

He indicated that instead of selling bonds to absorb excess liquidity, the Fed would mop up the liquidity by *not reinvesting* the proceeds of maturing bonds it held. Hearing this, many in the market assumed that nothing terrible would happen to the bond market even if the Fed normalized its balance sheet, as long as it did not sell the bonds. But this complacency is also problematic.

When a government bond matures, the government usually issues a refunding bond to obtain funds from the private sector to pay the holder of the maturing security. Because of the huge quantity of government bonds issued in the past, the market for refunding bonds in both Japan and the United States is three to four times the size of that for newly issued debt to finance government expenditures.

Ordinarily the issuance of refunding bonds is not thought to produce significant upward pressure on interest rates because the proceeds will be paid to private-sector holders of maturing government debt who are likely to reinvest those funds in government debt again. In other words, the money will stay in the bond market. Bond market participants therefore relax when they hear that the U.S. Treasury is issuing refunding bonds as opposed to new-money bonds, because they know the former have a largely neutral impact on the market.

In contrast, investors grow tense when a new-money bond is issued because fresh private-sector savings will have to be found to absorb the bond—this money, after all, will be used to build roads and bridges and will not be coming back to the bond market. In other words, new-money bonds can add to upward pressure on interest rates.

But if the maturing government debt is held by the central bank, which will not reinvest the redeemed funds, the funds raised from the private sector by the Treasury via the issuance of refunding bonds do not flow back to the bond market. Instead, they go to the central bank, where they disappear. This, of course, is how the Fed normalizes its balance sheet by absorbing excess liquidity in the market. That means these refunding bonds—despite their name—have the same impact on interest rates as new-money bonds. In other words, they exert the same upward pressure on interest rates as if the central bank had sold its bond holdings directly on the market.

The Fed Tackled the QE Exit Problem Head-On

On June 14, 2017, the Fed announced it would tackle this difficult issue of unwinding QE, now dubbed *quantitative tightening* (QT), head-on with a concrete plan. Under this scheme, the Fed would initially stop reinvesting $6 billion a month in Treasury securities and $4 billion a month in mortgage-backed securities (MBS), raising those amounts by $6 billion and $4 billion every three months until they reached $30 billion and $20 billion, respectively. From that point on, the Fed would continue not reinvesting $50 billion a month until the level of excess reserves in the banking system had been brought down to a desirable level.

Figure 6.7 shows a projection for the amount of reserves remaining in the market under the Fed's June 2017 schedule. In making this projection, it was assumed that required reserves (the heavy black line) would continue to grow along the trend lines established between January 2015 and May 2017. Although the Fed had not announced what level of reserves would ultimately be appropriate, the June 2017 schedule indicated that excess reserves in the U.S. banking system (as defined at that time) would have been totally removed by July 2021, or 46 months after the start of QT.

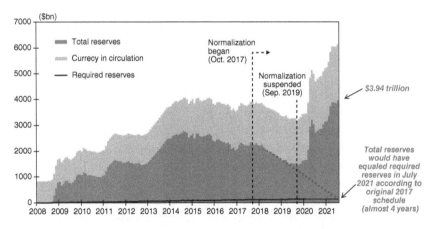

FIGURE 6.7 Balance Sheet Normalization Envisioned by the Fed in 2017

Notes: Reserve requirement has been suspended since March 2020, but for the above calculation, it is assumed that the requirement that was in effect in February 2020 remains in force.

Source: Nomura Research Institute, based on FRB data; estimates by Nomura Research Institute

Chair Yellen, who started QT, said at her press conference on June 14, 2017: "My hope and expectation is that . . . this is something that will just run quietly in the background over a number of years, leading to a reduction in the size of our balance sheet."[7] She quickly repeated the phrase "something that runs quietly in the background" and compared the process to watching paint dry in order to re-direct the market's attention away from the QT. While this is naturally what the Fed would like to see happen, there are a number of potential problems.

The Fed commenced QT in October 2017, which marks the start of the U.S. government's 2018 fiscal year. Figure 6.8 shows the amount of additional private savings that would be required under the Fed's plan to discontinue its reinvestments. The required funds from the private sector amounted to some $300 billion in FY2018 and to

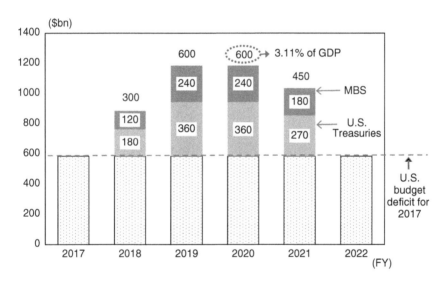

FIGURE 6.8 Additional Private Savings Required to Offset the Fed's 2017 Quantitative Tightening

Notes: U.S. fiscal accounting year runs from October to following September. MBS = mortgage backed securities.

Source: Nomura Research Institute

---

[7] Board of Governors of Federal Reserve System (2017), "Transcript of Chair Yellen's Press Conference, June 14, 2017," pp. 16–17. https://www .federalreserve.gov/mediacenter/files/FOMCpresconf20170614.pdf.

$600 billion in both FY2019 and FY2020. The $600 billion figure is roughly equal to the entire federal budget deficit for FY2017. In other words, removing QE in those two years was to have the same impact on interest rates as doubling the 2016 federal deficit.

It is difficult to describe the likely hit to bond market supply/demand from an effective doubling of the fiscal deficit as "just running quietly in the background." Even with a shock absorber already in place, this process is likely to put upward pressure on interest rates and may even lead to a steep drop in bond prices. But if QT *did* run quietly in the background, that would also mean the original QE had had no real impact on the market or the economy.

In spite of these concerns, the QT that commenced in October 2017 went relatively smoothly, proving that the original QE had not been all that effective. And it was ineffective because the U.S. private sector was a large net saver throughout this period. In other words, very few individuals and businesses actually borrowed those funds to increase consumption and investment. Many bond market participants apparently also failed to notice that some of the refunding bonds sold by the Treasury were refunding bonds in name only. Inflows of capital from abroad probably helped as well.

QT came to an abrupt halt when a forecasting error at the New York Fed open market desk on September 17, 2019, caused short-term interest rates to spike.[8] Although this accident probably had little to do with QT itself,[9] the Fed stopped the process just to be on the safe side. The Fed also reversed the normalization of interest

---

[8] For details, see Gara Afonso, Marco Cipriani, Adam Copeland, Anna Kovner, Gabriele La Spada, and Antoine Martin, "The Market Events of Mid-September 2019," *Federal Reserve Bank of New York Staff Reports No. 918*, March 2020. https://www.newyorkfed.org/medialibrary/media/research/staff_reports/sr918.pdf.

[9] QT may have had an indirect impact to the extent that it forced the Fed to pay interest on excess reserves (IOER) starting in late 2008 in order to maintain the effectiveness of its interest rate policy as banks would have no incentive to lend below the rate that they can get on IOER. Before the IOER was offered, banks earned interest on excess reserves by offering those funds in the interbank market (explained in Chapter 8), which increased the liquidity of the market. But the IOER reduced the incentive for banks to do so and that may have reduced the liquidity of the interbank market and pushed the short-term rates higher.

rates and lowered rates twice when signs of weakness in the economy appeared in the second half of 2019.

The advent of the pandemic recession a few months later forced the Fed to reverse course by bringing interest rates back down to zero and restarting the massive QE program, as noted at the beginning of this chapter. But the Fed's sustained QE during the pandemic made the eventual normalization of monetary policy that much more challenging.

No Theoretical Consensus on How to Wind Down QE

Another challenge for central banks normalizing monetary policy is that the economists who encouraged them to adopt QE never provided any theoretical framework indicating how these policies should be wound down. As a result, there is no consensus among academics, market participants, or the authorities on what conditions should be satisfied before starting to unwind QE or at what pace it should be wound down.

The complete absence of a theoretical framework means any decision to exit the policy will almost certainly be criticized in hindsight by academics, market participants, and authorities as being either too early or too late. And this pushback actually happened inside the Fed with its introduction of a "new approach" in August 2020 (this is discussed a bit later).

With no theory to guide the timing of this move, the real question for central bank officials is whether they would prefer to be criticized for being too early or too late *ten years from now*. All indications up to August 2020 suggest that the Fed decided that, if it is going to be criticized no matter what it does, it would rather err on the side of being too early. The loss function in this case is that a premature exit will result in a more gradual subsequent recovery, but an exit that is too late could cause the economy to overheat and asset bubbles to form, forcing the Fed to engage in an abrupt tightening that could plunge the U.S. economy back into a 2008-like balance sheet recession.

This preference for being too early is fully reflected in the Fed's 2013 decision to begin tapering QE when inflation (measured by the core personal consumption expenditures deflator) was running at just 1.1 percent, and to carry out its first rate hike in 2015, when the inflation rate was only 1.3 percent. The subsequent eight rate hikes were also implemented when inflation was less than 2 percent. These actions indicated that 2 percent was the upper limit on inflation and underscored how afraid the Fed had been of falling behind the curve on inflation, at least until August 2020.

Symmetric Inflation Targets Are Both Ineffective and Dangerous

But in the midst of the pandemic recession in August 2020, the Fed introduced a "symmetric" inflation target based on a "new approach," whereby it would not immediately tighten monetary policy even if the inflation rate hit 2 percent. This new forward guidance, which suggested the Fed was now willing to err in favor of being too late, seemed to be a response to the dire economic straits the United States faced due to the COVID-19 pandemic. Criticism by orthodox economists unhappy with the Fed's continued failure to reach its own 2-percent inflation target may also have played a role in the switch.

But the Fed was failing to reach the target not because it had the wrong policy, but because the economy was fundamentally in Case 3, which is characterized by a lack of borrowers. This shortage of borrowers, in turn, originates from balance sheet problems or inferior returns on capital. These are issues the central bank has little control over. In other words, the announcement of a symmetric target was unlikely to increase borrowing because that was not where the problem lay.

When the inflation rate moved sharply higher in 2021, the Fed scuttled the symmetric target and moved to normalize monetary policy. The fact that bank lending had picked up meaningfully in the fourth quarter of 2021 probably added to the Fed's inflation concerns. U.S. bank lending expanded at a double-digit annualized pace starting in the fourth quarter of 2021 (Figure 6.9). After a short slowdown at year-end due most likely to the spread of the Omicron variant, loan growth has picked up again in the new year, suggesting that U.S. borrowers may be coming back.

As noted earlier, the Fed had to shift its stance because if bond market participants viewed it as having fallen behind the curve on inflation, they would sell bonds to protect themselves from inflation.

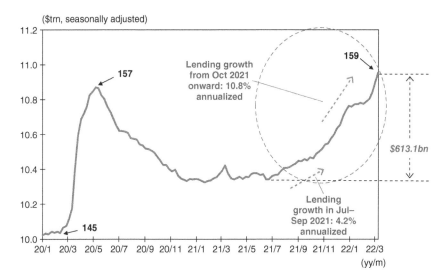

FIGURE 6.9　Credit Creation in the United States Increasing Starting in Q4 2021

Loans and leases at U.S. commercial banks

Note: Numbers in the graph correspond to numbers shown in Figure 2.12.

Source: Nomura Research Institute, based on FRB, "H.8 Assets and Liabilities of Commercial Banks in the United States"

The resulting crash in bond prices and surge in yields would not only slow down the economy but might also crash the asset market. This would be the "big mess" scenario that Fischer was trying to avoid back in 2016. Realizing this risk, Chairman Powell jettisoned the "new approach" and started normalizing monetary policy in November 2021 in the face of a rapidly increasing inflation rate.

Post-2022 QT Clearly Framed as Inflation-Fighting Tool

In this new round of normalization, it is worth noting that the QT has been framed very differently. At his March 16, 2022, press conference, Chairman Powell was asked whether the Fed is already behind the curve on inflation, that raising rates by a quarter-point at each FOMC meeting would be enough to curb a consumer price index (CPI) inflation rate of 7.9 percent. One reporter even added that the last time CPI inflation had been at 7.9 percent, in July 1981, the Fed's policy rate was 19.2 percent.

Chairman Powell responded to such concerns by noting that this time the Fed would not only raise rates but would also engage in QT early on and urging reporters to keep that in mind. These remarks indicate that the Fed, after falling behind the curve on inflation in terms of interest rates, is trying to make up for that delay by moving quickly ahead with QT. In other words, the QT is now front and center of the monetary normalization process.

He then added that while the pace of QT would be faster this time than in October 2017, the method used would be similar ("familiar"). In fact, he used the word *familiar* three times in a row. This is an indication that the Fed is hoping to minimize the rise in long-term interest rates by taking the same approach to QT as it did last time—an approach that the bond market is accustomed to.

But the last experiment with quantitative tightening was conducted preemptively at a time when private-sector borrowing demand was weak and inflation was subdued, which meant there was little reason why long-term interest rates should rise. The Fed also discouraged the market from paying attention to QT.

This time, in contrast, inflation is already running high, and private-sector borrowing demand is starting to exhibit sharp growth, perhaps in response to the fall in real interest rates deep into the negative range as a result of sharp increases in inflation rates. The Fed is also asking the market to pay more attention to the QT which will be implemented at a much faster pace than the previous QT. In other words, many of those factors that kept long-term rates low during the previous episode of QT are no longer available for the post-2022 QT.

Put differently, central banks that did *not* pursue QE could play around with a symmetric target for a while because there were only minuscule excess reserves in the banking system and the probability of a sudden explosion in credit creation was low. The three lines in Figures 2.12 to 2.14 and 2.17 all moved together before Lehman's collapse because excess reserves in the banking system were minimal and liquidity provided by the central bank (i.e., the monetary base) served as a constraint on the growth of the money supply and credit. Indeed, the most famous battle against inflation in the United States, led by Paul Volcker in October 1979, was successful precisely because the Fed tightened the supply of liquidity, which forced short-term interest rates as high as 22 percent.

But central banks that implemented QE do not have the luxury to wait. With so much excess reserves in the banking system, there is no longer any constraint on credit creation when borrowers return. That means they can rein in inflation only with higher interest rates because the option of limiting reserves does not exist. To avoid what Yellen called an "abrupt tightening," which has the potential to push bond yields sky-high, central banks that unleashed QE must normalize monetary policy *before* credit creation gets underway in earnest.

"We Are All Japanese Now"

What exactly is the Fed's "new approach"? From the tone of Chairman Powell's earlier speeches, it appears that many at the Fed felt it had been a mistake to begin normalizing monetary policy in December 2015 and that this approach had led to unnecessary economic weakness and the failure to reach the 2-percent inflation target. For example, Fed Governor Lael Brainard said on June 1, 2021, that "in the previous monetary policy framework, the customary preemptive tightening based on the outlook to head off concerns about future high inflation likely curtailed critical employment opportunities for many Americans and embedded persistently below-target inflation."[10]

The proponents of this new approach with a symmetric target are basically saying that, if the public's pre-1979 inflationary mindset could be eradicated with drastic monetary tightening, it should be possible to extinguish today's deflationary mindset, along with the economic weakness it fostered, by allowing the economy to experience high enough inflation for long enough. In other words, instead of focusing on the balance sheet problems and pursued economy issues that led to deflationary conditions in the first place, they are saying the economy will recover if only the public's deflationary sentiment can be eliminated.

Interestingly, the ECB came to the same conclusion when it revised monetary policy in July 2021 following an 18-month review. Key changes included a pledge to ease monetary policy forcefully

---

[10] Brainard, Lael (2021), "Remaining Steady as the Economy Reopens," at The Economic Club of New York, New York, NY (via webcast), June 1, 2021. https://www.federalreserve.gov/newsevents/speech/brainard20210601a.htm.

when inflation or interest rates approach zero, the replacement of the existing inflation target of "below, but close to, 2 percent" with a symmetric target that pays equal attention to readings falling above and below 2 percent, and a pledge to refrain from preemptive inflation-fighting policies.

These new monetary policy approaches adopted by the Fed and the ECB are analogous to BOJ Governor Haruhiko Kuroda's "bazooka" policy, unveiled in 2013, in which he repeatedly declared the bank would not consider normalizing monetary policy until the rate of inflation was consistently above 2 percent. In that sense, the Fed and the ECB belatedly joined the BOJ to create a world in which "We are all Japanese now."

The fact that consumer confidence had dropped to a 10-year low late in 2021 with the return of inflation (albeit supply-driven inflation) and that long-term interest rates also started moving higher suggests there are serious problems with the argument presented above. The first is that proponents of this view believe central banks can affect people's expectations and behavior without policy makers acting to address balance sheet problems or the inferior returns on capital that have led to excess savings in the private sector. Although this view is held by many economists, the evidence provided in earlier chapters suggests it is little more than wishful thinking.

The second problem, which became alarmingly clear with the onset of inflation in 2021, is that the new approach strips the central bank of its inflation-fighting credentials. Indeed, central banks that implemented negative interest rates, massive QE, and symmetric inflation targets were all trying to establish themselves as *deflation fighters*. Many prominent academic economists—including Paul Krugman, a Nobel laureate—have also argued that "the central bank needs to credibly promise to be irresponsible"[11] so that more people will expect inflation, resulting in lower expected real interest rates. The statement from Governor Brainard previously presented also highlights a belief that the Fed's earlier practice of trying to suppress inflation in advance—that is, its "inflation-fighting" stance—had been a mistake.

---

[11] Krugman, Paul (2011), "Credibility and Monetary Policy in a Liquidity Trap (Wonkish)," *New York Times*, March 18, 2011.

When inflation arrived, central banks realized they had zero credibility as inflation fighters because they have been combating deflation for the last twelve years. But the combination of high inflation and an absence of central bank with inflation-fighting credentials had the potential to trigger a bond market sell-off and a surge in long-term interest rates that would be disastrous for the economy. Chairman Powell's sudden hawkish shift on inflation in late 2021 was probably based on the view that the Fed needed to emphasize its determination to prevent such a scenario by reinventing itself as an inflation fighter.

The dramatic shift in the Fed's stance also served to highlight the uselessness of a symmetric inflation target. The idea that having a long enough period of high inflation will rid people of their deflationary mindset ignores the risk that such a policy may bring about a bond market crash. And if the bond market crashes, the economy may go down with it. Fortunately, Chairman Powell realized this danger and changed course before it happened, but the risk remains depending on what happens to inflation.

The third problem with the new approach concerns the question of how much stronger the U.S. economy[12] would be if the Fed had not begun normalizing policy in 2015. The Chicago Fed's national financial conditions index largely shrugged off the nine rate hikes that began in 2015 and the QT that commenced in 2017 (see circled portion at lower right in Figure 4.3). In fact, it indicated that financial conditions remained highly accommodative and were not weighing on the economy up until the pandemic. The U.S. unemployment rate also fell steadily, from 5.0 percent in December 2015 to a 50-year low of 3.5 percent in February 2020, and stock prices continued to post new all-time highs during this period.

Financial conditions failed to tighten because the U.S. economy has been in Case 3, and businesses and households were both large net savers because they were still repairing their balance sheets. This also means that when businesses and households are repairing their balance sheets, they do *not* respond to movements in interest rates, whether up or down. That, in turn, implies that U.S. economic activity probably would not have been any stronger if the Fed had kept policy accommodative in 2015 and beyond. The lack of borrowers in

---

[12] Neither the ECB nor the BOJ have tried to normalize monetary policy since 2008.

the real economy also forced fund managers at financial institutions to continue investing excess private savings in existing assets, leading to rising asset prices.

This conclusion can also be inferred from the experiences of the BOJ and the ECB. Not only have they not even mentioned the possibility of normalizing monetary policy, but they actually took their policy rates into negative territory. Moreover, the BOJ has been implementing what the Fed would call a symmetric inflation target since 2013.

Nevertheless, private-sector borrowing in both regions experienced almost no pickup in growth during this period (Figures 2.13 and 2.17), indicating that their private sectors were not responding to interest rates either. The continued stagnation of these economies suggests that, contrary to Governor Brainard's previous comment, the U.S. economy probably would not have been any stronger if the Fed had chosen not to normalize policy starting in 2015.

The fourth problem with the new approach concerns the costs that delaying policy normalization would have had in the United States. Asset price bubbles would probably have grown even larger with continued zero interest rates and ever-greater market liquidity. The Fed's quantitative tightening drained $660 billion in liquidity from the market between October 2017 and September 2019. If this liquidity had stayed in the market, it would most likely have been used to purchase existing assets given the shortage of borrowers in the real economy.

Even though the Fed began normalizing monetary policy in 2015, stock prices have continued to post fresh all-time highs, and commercial real estate prices are now 68 percent higher than they were at the previous peak in 2007. Both would probably be even higher today without the post-2015 normalization of policy. With rising house prices already a major driver of the inequality that has divided U.S. society, few would view further expansion of the housing bubble as a desirable policy outcome.

Housing prices are also becoming a major social issue in the Eurozone. When the ECB talked to people from different walks of life during its 18-month review of monetary policy,[13] according to

---

[13] Lagarde, Christine (2021), "Interview with Financial Times," *Interview with Christine Lagarde, President of the ECB, conducted by Martin Arnold on 11 July 2021*, July 13, 2021. https://www.ecb.europa.eu/press/inter/date/2021/html/ecb.in210713~ff13aa537f.en.html.

President Christine Lagarde, the concern over house prices was so great that the Bank had to promise to pay greater attention to the cost of housing when making monetary policy decisions.

Bubbles Create Both Financial and Macroeconomic Problems When They Burst

Yet mid-2021 comments by senior Fed officials suggest they are surprisingly unconcerned about the potential for the bubble to burst. They argue that the risk of another Lehman-like event is low because U.S. financial institutions are much better capitalized than they were in 2008.

There is no question that U.S. banks are better capitalized now than in 2008. But when a bubble bursts, it creates two problems, as is noted in Figure 6.10. One is the financial crisis triggered when financial institutions that participated in the boom suffer capital impairments and begin to distrust each other. The other is the balance sheet recession that results when asset prices plunge but the debt used to acquire them remains, forcing an over-indebted private sector to

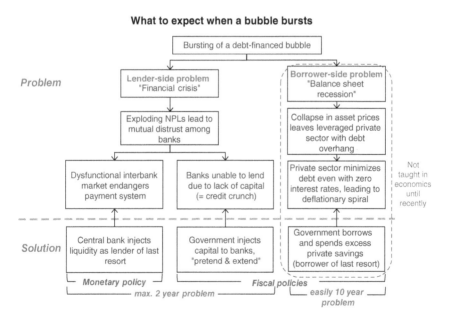

FIGURE 6.10 Well-Capitalized Banks Will Not Prevent Balance Sheet Recession

begin paying down debt. The former is a financial problem related to lenders, while the latter is a macroeconomic problem related to borrowers. And the central bank bears responsibility for both.

Financial Crises Can Be Contained in about Two Years If Properly Addressed

The 2008 GFC created a great deal of financial turmoil: Lehman Brothers went bankrupt, Merrill Lynch was rescued by Bank of America, Morgan Stanley needed help from Mitsubishi UFJ, and the economy struggled under a credit crunch. Nevertheless, the seize-up in financial markets—as indicated by the sharp increase in the Chicago Fed's financial conditions index triggered by the Lehman shock—had largely subsided by 2010, a little more than two years later (Figure 4.3). Growth in banks' assets and liabilities also began to normalize in about two years (Figure 8.11), and conditions in the interbank market returned to normal around the same time (Figure 8.12).

This was because the authorities responded appropriately with the measures prescribed for Case 2 in Chapter 1. The U.S. government, for example, injected capital via the Troubled Asset Relief Program (TARP) in October 2008 and allowed banks to roll over impaired commercial real estate loans with the Policy Statement on Prudent Commercial Real Estate Loan Workout ("pretend and extend") in October 2009.

In Japan, the government responded to the nationwide banking crisis in 1997, which was triggered by the failure of Hokkaido Takushoku Bank, by injecting capital into the banks and offering generous loan guarantees to borrowers. The debilitating credit crunch that was causing so much economic pain began to ease about two years later, in 1999 (see Figures 6.2 and 8.7). The point is that even a major financial crisis, which is a lender-side problem, can be contained in about two years if appropriate policies are implemented.

Recovery from Balance Sheet Recessions Takes Far Longer than Two Years

The same cannot be said for balance sheet recessions, which involve borrower-side problems. Both Europe and the United States suffered balance sheet recessions lasting nearly a decade after Lehman went under. Economic growth and inflation remained depressed even though the Fed and the ECB took interest rates to zero and engaged in truly astronomical amounts of quantitative easing.

As is explained in Chapters 1 and 2, a key reason for this is that individual households and businesses are all behaving responsibly by trying to restore their financial health, and there is no way they can do anything else. But when everyone deleverages at the same time, it creates the unintended consequence (i.e., the fallacy-of-composition problem) of a disappearance of borrowers and triggers a deflationary spiral.

Both Fed Chairman Ben Bernanke and Vice Chairwoman Janet Yellen were cognizant of this danger and managed to save the economy by repeatedly warning Congress that the United States would fall off a "fiscal cliff" if it pursued fiscal consolidation. In contrast, policy makers in the Eurozone were ignorant of this danger and proceeded to push their economies off the cliff. In the ensuing collapse, Spain's unemployment rate surged to 26 percent and Greece's GDP plunged by 27 percent.

These experiences indicate that a balance sheet recession will continue until the majority of people have finished repairing their balance sheets, a process that can easily take a decade because of the fallacy-of-composition problem that makes balance sheet repairs doubly difficult. Having banks that are well capitalized increases the probability that the two-year lender-side problems will be relatively mild, but they do nothing to mitigate the 10-year borrower-side problems, which can be extremely painful.

Calling the Post-2008 Economic Downturn the GFC Was a Mistake

Unfortunately, the economics profession was completely oblivious to the concept of a balance sheet recession when Lehman Brothers failed and the GFC ensued in 2008. Even today, few understand the dangers inherent in such a recession.

In retrospect, it was a major mistake to have dubbed the post-2008 economic downturn the "global financial crisis," or GFC. Even though the long and painful recession had some elements of a financial crisis during the first two years, the far bigger problem was that millions of household and business balance sheets were underwater and required nearly a decade to repair. But because it was called the GFC, most commentators looked only at what was happening in the financial sector and ignored what was happening to the balance sheets of households and businesses. Those businesses and individuals with impaired balance sheets also had every reason to hide that fact until their financial health is restored, as is mentioned in Chapter 2. The fact that most commentators in academia and the markets in 2008 were totally unaware of the ailment called balance sheet recession made them pay even less attention to the impaired balance sheets of the private sector.

As is noted in Chapter 1, it was Mikhail Gorbachev who said, "You cannot solve the problem until you call it by its right name." The post-2008 debacle should have been called the Great Balance Sheet Recession, or GBSR, instead of the GFC. But because it was dubbed the GFC, most people never paid attention to the most important driver of the recession. That has left open the possibility that the world will repeat the mistake of underestimating the devastating impact of balance sheet repairs by the private sector after a bubble bursts.

Chairman Powell's comment that we need not worry too much about elevated asset prices because banks are now better capitalized than in 2008 reflects this sort of complacency. Both house prices and commercial real estate prices (Figure 4.7) have now risen well beyond their previous bubble peaks. If these bubbles burst, the U.S. economy will be back to square one, facing years of painful balance sheet recession all over again.

The ECB's Policy Review Was Far from Adequate

European house prices are also far above the bubble-era highs in many parts of the continent (Figure 2.4). In spite of the growing danger that another bubble is in the making, the ECB policy review unveiled in July 2021 did not even mention that private-sector balance sheet problems were a key reason why the Eurozone economy has been depressed since 2008 (this point is explained further in Chapter 7). Instead, it argued that the slump was attributable to a lower real equilibrium interest rate resulting from "a decline in productivity growth, demographic factors and persistently higher demand for safe and liquid assets in the wake of the global financial crisis."[14] Here, "real equilibrium interest rate" refers to the rate of interest that will allow policy makers to consistently achieve their inflation target.

Looking at the cited factors one by one, productivity growth has declined because a private sector facing balance sheet problems was forced to change course and shift from forward-looking capital investment to backward-looking balance sheet repairs. A similar slowdown in productivity growth was also observed in Japan in the years after the bubble burst in 1990.

The demographic factors noted next simply cannot explain the dramatic change in private-sector behavior that occurred around 2008, as shown in Figures 2.6 and 2.7.

As for the third factor cited—an apparent preference for safe assets—this merely reflects the private sector's inability to take on risk after personal and corporate financial health had been impaired. In other words, the ECB is looking only at the superficial phenomena of an economic slowdown and is trying to attribute them to financial factors such as lower equilibrium interest rates and a preference for safe assets without indicating why those phenomena emerged in the first place. That raises the likelihood that the Eurozone will repeat the mistake of underestimating the danger posed by runaway asset prices and subsequent private-sector deleveraging.

Large and Expensive Rate Hikes Are Required to Contain Inflation

The fifth problem with the new approach involves Chairman Powell's claim that the Fed has all the tools it needs to deal with inflation. He is probably referring to the success of former Chairman Paul Volcker in stamping out inflation at the end of the 1970s. As noted earlier, however, Volcker tamed inflation by restricting the supply of liquidity to control the money supply and allowing the federal funds rate to find its own equilibrium.

---

[14] European Central Bank (2021), "An Overview of the ECB's Monetary Policy Strategy," *Strategy Review*, July 2021. https://www.ecb.europa.eu/home/search/review/html/ecb.strategyreview_monpol_strategy_overview.en.html.

At the time, liquidity supplied by the Fed was indeed a constraint on credit creation by private-sector financial institutions. When the Fed reduced the supply of liquidity, the tightening impact manifested itself immediately in the form of skyrocketing interest rates (Figure 4.3). The resultant federal funds rate of 22 percent shocked the economy into a recession and killed inflation.

But today the Fed has unleashed $3.66 trillion in excess reserves, and liquidity is no longer a constraint on credit creation. If the Fed wanted to achieve the same tightening effect as seen in October 1979, it would first need to take back or neutralize the $3.66 trillion in the banking system. If the Fed used the same QT schedule employed last time, starting in October 2017, it would need six years and eight months to remove the excess reserves from the system. In other words, the immediate response of interest rates observed when the Fed tightened liquidity in 1979 cannot be expected to repeat itself. Indeed, the existence of this huge pool of excess liquidity may be one reason why the Chicago Fed's national financial conditions index did not respond to the Fed's nine rate hikes starting in December 2015.

If the Fed wants to achieve the same tightening effect observed in the late 1970s, it will have to raise interest rates substantially and pay that same high rate on all the excess reserves that banks have with the Fed, that is, the $3.66 trillion figure previously noted. This is to ensure that banks have no incentive to lend this money out to the private sector once borrowers return. In other words, the Fed will have to operate as the "borrower of *first* resort" to neutralize the $3.66 trillion in the banking sector.

The interest paid on excess reserves held by commercial banks in their accounts at the central bank is called interest on excess reserves (IOER). If the federal funds rate required to contain inflation happens to be 3 percent, the 3 percent the Fed pays on that $3.66 trillion will cost it $110 billion a year. Because the Fed's revenue is returned to the Treasury at the end of each year, that $110 billion increase in IOER will result in an equal reduction in government revenue, and the annual federal budget deficit will increase by $110 billion.

Central banks will try to justify this additional interest expense by saying they have been earning huge amounts of interest income on the bonds acquired via QE over the years, which benefited taxpayers. While that may be true, the low-yielding bonds held by central banks will suffer capital losses if inflation returns and they are forced to raise rates. The central banks themselves are also likely to experience negative spreads when the interest rate they pay on excess reserves exceeds the low yields on government bonds acquired via QE.

Few central bank governors will want to explain to taxpayers that their year-end bill has increased by $110 billion because the central bank needs this money to prevent commercial banks from lending to the private sector. The IOER will also increase excess reserves in the banking system by the same amount. Yet the longer the central bank hesitates to raise rates due to a fear of political blowback, the more inflation will accelerate.

This mechanism, in which taxpayers bear the cost of rate hikes, has never been an issue in the past because QE was never tried to this extent before 2008. As can be seen in Figure 6.11, excess reserves in the U.S. banking system is about $ 3.66 trillion,[15] which is 1952 times larger than the $1.876 billion in August 2008 just before the Lehman collapse. This means IOER before QE was negligible. Today, if a central bank that implemented QE fails to pay IOER, it will lose control over credit creation and inflation when borrowers return. The point is that the Fed may have been successful in

IOER = Interest on Excess Reserves (Interest on Excess Reserves at Private-Sector Banks Paid by Central Bank)

	Increase in excess reserves since August 2008	As % of GDP in 2021	Notional interest rate	Annual IOER (increases fiscal deficit)
United States	$3.66trn	15.9%	3%	$109.8bn
Japan	¥465.6trn	85.9%	2%	¥9,312.7bn
Eurozone	€3.66trn	29.8%	2%	€73.12bn
United Kingdom	£0.95trn	40.9%	3%	£28.4bn

FIGURE 6.11 The Cost of Raising Interest Rates without Ending QE = IOER

Note: The BOE and the Fed suspended their reserve requirements in March 2009 and March 2020, respectively. The above figures are based on the assumption that original reserve requirements in August 2008 in the United Kingdom and in February 2020 in the United States are still applicable.

Sources: Nomura Research Institute, based on BOJ, FRB, ECB, and BOE data

[15] Based on the definition of excess reserves that was in place in August 2020.

eradicating inflation 40 years ago, but there is no guarantee it will be able to achieve the same result with the same tools now that it has created $3.66 trillion in excess reserves.

With the $3.66 trillion in excess reserves reducing the effectiveness of conventional monetary tightening, the Fed may actually have to induce some of Stanley Fischer's (highly unpleasant) "big mess" scenario by implementing rate hikes and QT faster so that the negative wealth effect of falling asset prices will weigh on the economy and inflation. To the extent that the QE was supposed to stimulate inflation by raising asset prices, a determined QT should dampen inflation by lowering asset prices.

It is said that those who manage to *avoid* a crisis never become heroes. For someone to become a hero, there must first be a crisis, and the person who predicted it and saved those who followed him will become a hero after thousands have perished. But before the crisis strikes, the future hero is criticized for wasting time and resources preparing for it. That is the plot line for all the Hollywood action movies. The whole point of the Fed's 2015 normalization efforts was to remove excess liquidity in the banking system *before* borrowers (and therefore inflation) returned, thereby avoiding the need to raise interest rates abruptly and belatedly.

For better or worse, borrowers did not return, and the Fed's post-2015 normalization was heavily criticized, as shown by the quote from Brainard previously cited. But if the Fed had succeeded in removing the excess liquidity, it would have regained the power and mobility Volcker had in his battle against inflation, putting it in a very credible position as an inflation fighter to combat price increases that are now unfolding in the United States.

A post-pandemic surge in pent-up demand has combined with supply mismatches and energy shortages to push prices significantly higher. Furthermore, market participants will not know whether this surge is temporary or not until several years have passed. In the meantime, the markets may experience a bond market sell-off that could make everything more difficult. At such times, nothing calms the market better than a central bank with strong inflation-fighting credentials. To regain that credibility, central banks must raise interest rates and implement QT to demonstrate their commitment to controlling inflation, even if those actions roil the markets (= QE trap) in the short run.

The Total Cost of QE May Outweigh Benefits

The potential for the exit from QE to raise bond yields and exchange rates prematurely and dampen economic activity means the total cost of QE cannot be determined until the normalization of monetary policy is completed. When the costs and benefits are examined over the course of the policy's lifetime, those initial benefits may well turn out to be small relative to the subsequent costs of unwinding the policy.

Ultimately, central banks that implemented QE will probably be forced to use all the tools at their disposal to either sterilize or drain excess liquidity when borrowers return. Those tools would include tougher capital, liquidity and reserve requirements as well as moral suasion to keep banks from lending to the private sector. In other words, some sort of "financial repression" may be necessary when borrowers return. Central banks are also likely to use reverse repos, pay interest on reserves, and offer term deposits with higher interest rates so that they can act as borrowers of *first* resort to discourage commercial banks from lending to businesses and households.

The problem is that none of these remedies is simple or inexpensive. For example, raising the reserve requirement will be one of the most direct ways of sterilizing the excess reserves in the banking system. But for this policy to work smoothly, excess reserves must be distributed more or less evenly across the banks. Unfortunately that is not the case, which makes it difficult to use this tool to tighten monetary policy.

In comparison to economies that did not implement QE, those that did may end up recovering more slowly because interest rates and exchange rates rise sooner. Economies that did not resort to QE may even turn out to have greater cumulative GDP over the course of the cycle (including the unwinding of QE) than those that did. In that sense, the jury is still out on QE. As Milton Friedman said, there are no free lunches. How to unwind trillions of dollars of QE without sending bond yields or exchange rates to punitive levels is therefore the single most important challenge monetary authorities in the West and Japan face today.

QE—or any central bank financing of budget deficits—should be used only in dire emergencies such as the COVID-19 pandemic, where the government needs quick access to a large amount of money to save people's lives and livelihoods. The central bank must also operate as lender of last resort when there are lender-side problems, such as in a financial crisis. But the high cost of exiting from QE means it should *not* be used in most other circumstances, including balance sheet recessions.

The Fallacy of Helicopter Money Argument

Unfortunately, old beliefs die hard. Both the Fed's new approach and the ECB's recent adoption of a symmetric inflation target suggest that orthodox economists are still influential. Even though fiscal policy is the correct remedy for problems caused by a lack of borrowers (Cases 3 and 4), orthodox economists who never considered the possibility of a private sector shift to minimizing debt, together with those who are fixated on the size of the public debt, continue to advocate for more monetary policy, which was designed to address problems caused by a lack of lenders (Cases 1 and 2). In spite of the utter failure of zero and negative interest rates, inflation targeting, forward guidance, and massive QE to increase borrowings and lift inflation rates (Figures 2.11 to 2.14 and 2.17), these monetary policy "true believers" have pushed hard for further easing, including a symmetric inflation target.

Their remarkable faith in the efficacy of monetary policy may have its origins in the concept of helicopter money. The belief that an economy will invariably improve if only money is dropped from the sky serves as the intellectual foundation for these economists' conviction in monetary policy. Masazumi Wakatabe, the current Deputy Governor of the BOJ and one of the most ardent proponents of monetary easing in Japan, declared confidently that "the question of how to increase nominal GDP always has an answer: helicopter money."[16] These economists believe that, since dropping money from helicopters will always revive the economy, slightly less extreme policies, such as QE and inflation targeting, will also stimulate it.

---

[16] Wakatabe, Masazumi (2016), "Herikoputa Mane to wa Nanika (3)" ("What Is Helicopter Money?"), *Nikkei*, June 20, 2016.

Four Versions of Helicopter Money (1): Dropping Money from the Sky

An overview of the helicopter money debate shows that the actual policies being discussed can be classified into four main types. The first is helicopter money in the literal sense of dropping money from helicopters. Would this work?

In Japan, at least, it would be yet another complete failure. When the typical Japanese finds a 10,000-yen note lying on the ground, she will turn it in to the nearest police station rather than spend it. A helicopter money policy can work only if people in the country have little sense of right and wrong.

A more fundamental defect in the argument for helicopter money is that it focuses exclusively on the logic of buyers while completely ignoring the logic of *sellers*. Many people may indeed try to go shopping with money that has fallen from the sky, but there is no reason for sellers to accept such money. No seller in her right mind would exchange products and services for money that had fallen from the sky.

Sellers are willing to take money in exchange for goods and services only because they believe the supply of money is strictly controlled by the central bank. If the authorities actually began dropping money from helicopters, shops would raise prices dramatically, close their doors, or demand payment in foreign currency or gold. The economy would then collapse. Indeed, history shows that the first area in which trouble is likely to arise is the foreign exchange market, where the value of the currency would plummet, causing import prices to spike. There is no economy so wretched as one in which the people no longer trust the national currency.

It is astonishing that economists arguing in favor of helicopter money have never considered sellers' perspectives. Once they realize what is going on, there is no reason for them to accept money falling from the sky. The argument that monetary policy is effective because helicopter money, the ultimate form of monetary accommodation, always works is complete nonsense that ignores the other half of the economy, the sellers. Taking monetary accommodation to such extremes will lead to the economy's collapse, not its recovery. There is no case in recorded history of an economy without a credible national currency outperforming an economy with one.

Four Versions of Helicopter Money (2): Direct Financing of Government Deficits

Some proponents of helicopter money would say that the helicopter money policies now being discussed do not actually involve dropping money from the sky but rather call for direct financing of government fiscal expenditures by the central bank. The argument here is that if fiscal expenditures help the economy, direct central bank financing of the government should help it even more.

There are two problems with this view. First, as is noted in Chapter 2, the government does *not* need the central bank's help to finance fiscal stimulus when the economy is in Case 3 or 4, except in emergencies such as the COVID-19 pandemic. The funds needed to finance the stimulus can be found in the financial market in the form of surplus private-sector savings. And fund managers at financial institutions are more than happy to lend to the government because it is the only borrower left[17] issuing high-quality fixed income assets. That, in turn, takes government bond yields down to extremely low levels.

The second reason why this kind of helicopter money will not work is identical to the reason why QE failed to deliver the inflation anticipated by the three central bank governors as is noted in Chapter 2. Fiscal stimulus itself will provide a large boost to the economy and is absolutely essential when the economy is in Case 3 or 4. But the "direct" part of the direct financing of fiscal stimulus by the central bank cannot stimulate the economy or raise inflation any more than the indirect QE.

While direct financing by the central bank will increase reserves in the banking system, those reserves will become trapped in the system in exactly the same way that QE-supplied reserves have been trapped, as shown in Figures 2.12 to 2.14 and 2.17. That is because the private sector is a net saver. In other words, how the central bank acquired the government bonds is irrelevant. Both growth and inflation had stagnated in Japan (since 1990) and the West (since 2008) for so long despite astronomical monetary easing because the private

---

[17] This is not necessarily the case in the Eurozone, as is explained in Chapter 7.

sector, facing a huge debt overhang, stopped borrowing after an asset bubble burst.

During a national emergency such as the COVID-19 pandemic, however, the government may need to borrow money in a hurry to help affected households and businesses. In such cases, only the central bank can meet the government's borrowing requirements, and central banks around the world fulfilled that mission. But that was basically a Case 2 situation requiring a lender of last resort. And even here, the central bank will eventually have to normalize monetary policy by removing excess liquidity supplied during the crisis.

Four Versions of Helicopter Money (3): Direct Cash Handouts to Consumers

A third version of helicopter money involves distributing money directly to consumers without requiring that it pass through financial institutions. This approach at least acknowledges the difficulty (previously noted for the second version of helicopter money) when the economy is in Case 3 or 4—namely, that liquidity injected by the central bank cannot leave the financial sector and enter the real economy without the help of private-sector borrowers.

In this scenario, a consumer might open her mailbox one morning to find an envelope from the central bank containing thousands of dollars in cash. While that discovery may bring momentary joy, she might well feel a chill down her spine once she realizes that everyone around her has received a similar envelope. Unless the amount involved is small or there is absolutely no reason for inflation to pick up (e.g., if the country is in the midst of a pandemic-driven lockdown), the entire nation would quickly panic as people lost confidence in the central bank and no longer had any idea how much the national currency was worth.

Regardless of what the recipients of such cash might wish to do, sellers of goods and services would be forced to protect themselves, with stores putting up signs requiring payment in either foreign currency or gold. This is no different from the nightmare scenario in which money is actually dropped from helicopters.

Many countries distributed cash to their citizens during the COVID-19 pandemic that began in 2020. But those payments were made by the government, not by the central bank. And governments were able to make such payments after much public debate among lawmakers on how best to stop the deflationary spiral of bankruptcies and job losses. Furthermore, because all countries faced the same problem at the same time, there was no reason for the exchange rate to collapse, as noted in the beginning of this chapter. In other words, the government could distribute cash because there was no reason for a pernicious inflation to take hold in a pandemic-driven recession characterized by depressed demand.

Four Versions of Helicopter Money (4): Government Scrip and Perpetual Zero-Coupon Bonds

A fourth version of helicopter money involves the government (instead of the central bank) printing money or replacing the government bonds held by the central bank with perpetual zero-coupon bonds. Those proposing this policy hope that fiscal stimulus financed by government scrip or perpetual zero-coupon bonds, which are not viewed as government liabilities, will elicit spending from people who are currently saving because of concerns about the size of the fiscal deficit and the likelihood of future tax increases.

In economics, the public's purported reluctance to spend in response to fiscal stimulus because of worries about future tax hikes is called Ricardian equivalence. *Equivalence* here refers to the possibility that deficit spending or tax cuts will have only a limited stimulative impact on the economy because the public will begin saving more to prepare for the future tax increases needed to pay for the spending increases and tax cuts.

But if this proposition is valid, it also implies that consumption will *increase* each time the government raises taxes since higher taxes mean lower deficits in the future. The fact that this phenomenon has never been observed in the real world suggests the theory is nothing more than empty conjecture. The author himself has not met a single person who would refrain from purchasing something because of the fear that taxes will eventually go up in response to increased government fiscal stimulus today. Even the economists who talk endlessly about Ricardian equivalence do not practice it themselves.

On the contrary, there are many cases in history where government over-stretching led to economic recovery and growth because of the positive fallacy of composition and feedback loops as noted in Chapter 5. And that is especially true for economies in Case 3 or 4 when the fiscal multiplier is very high as demonstrated by the New Deal policies during the 1930s and by the military spending during World War II. If the common perception of fiscal stimulus is based on this historical record, people may actually spend more money once they see that the government is coming to their rescue with a fiscal stimulus because they will expect their incomes to be increasing soon. In such circumstances, it makes no sense for economists to expect people to act based on Ricardian equivalence. That means few, if any, would be enticed to spend money simply because the government is using scrip or zero-coupon perpetual bonds (instead of conventional bonds) to finance its expenditures.

Huge Exit Problems for Zero-Coupon Perpetuals and Government Scrip

The issue of mopping up reserves to normalize monetary policy becomes even more challenging with the fourth version of helicopter money. Perpetual zero-coupon bonds are absolutely worthless, which means the central bank cannot sell them to the private sector to mop up the excess liquidity. With nothing worthwhile to sell, the only way for the central bank to drain the excess reserves created by its purchases of perpetual zero-coupon bonds is to ask the government to issue an equivalent amount of conventional interest-bearing bonds, or to issue such bonds itself.

The same would be true when trying to absorb reserves created by the issue of government scrip. Once this scrip starts circulating, it becomes part of the monetary base, and draining it from the system in order to normalize monetary policy requires that the central bank either sell its bond holdings or ask the government to issue new bonds.

If the government is to issue bonds to mop up reserves created by zero-coupon perpetuals or government scrip, it must do so with the understanding that it will not spend the proceeds of the issuance. If it spends them, the absorbed liquidity will flow back into the economy, defeating the whole purpose of draining the reserves—to keep inflation in check. Meanwhile, the government will still have to pay interest on those bonds.

When the bonds issued to absorb the liquidity mature, the government will need to utilize the unused proceeds of the bonds previously noted to redeem the bonds while issuing an equal amount of new bonds to quickly reabsorb the liquidity just released to the private sector via the redemption. Since this cumbersome process will have to go on forever, the government may just decide to issue perpetual (but not zero-coupon) bonds to absorb the liquidity for good.

Economists who recommend the issuance of government scrip or perpetual zero-coupon bonds say the key advantage of this approach is that it does not lead to an expansion of government liabilities. However, that is true only at the outset: these instruments will become the equivalent of government liabilities when the economy eventually recovers, and the liquidity released to the market via these instruments will have to be absorbed by the bond-issuing government.

MMT Steps into the Spotlight Ahead of the 2020 U.S. Election

Attention has also focused on so-called Modern Monetary Theory (MMT) after some of the Democratic candidates in the 2020 U.S. presidential election expressed interest in the theory. The theory holds that a government cannot default on its debts if those debts are denominated in a currency issued by its central bank. This means that—as long as there is no inflation—the government can implement whatever policies are needed without worrying about budget deficits if only the central bank continues to buy the bonds issued to fund those policies. MMT advocates not only acknowledge the importance of fiscal policy, unlike those who single-mindedly push for more monetary easing via methods such as helicopter money, but also want to mobilize monetary policy to allow governments to administer even more fiscal stimulus.

There are several reasons why this theory has attracted so much attention at this juncture. First is the fact that none of the advanced countries had seen an acceleration of inflation until the spring of 2021 despite massive central bank purchases of government bonds for over a decade under QE. Second, wealth inequality and stagnant incomes have become major social issues in many countries. There is even a concern that these societies—and perhaps democracy itself—will become dysfunctional unless governments spend more on needed social programs. To politicians who are concerned about these issues, MMT appeared attractive because it might allow them to spend more to address these issues.

MMT Expectations versus Reality

The problems with this theory, however, are almost identical to those of the second version of helicopter money previously noted. First, the primary condition required for this theory to work is that there is *no inflation*. In other words, this theory had no role to play through the 1980s, when advanced economies were in the golden era and inflation was a pressing issue for policy makers. With the economy booming in Cases 1 or 2, there was also no need for the kind of fiscal stimulus that MMT claims to enable. Nor has it had any role to play since the spring of 2021, when supply constraints pushed inflation rates sharply higher.

When a nation is in Case 3 or 4—either because it is in the pursued phase or in a balance sheet recession—the economy will fall into a deflationary spiral unless someone outside the private sector, that is, government, steps up to borrow and spend those excess private-sector savings. The proponents of MMT would then argue that direct central bank financing of government borrowing would enable governments to run *even larger* budget deficits, thereby stimulating the economy and helping to rectify social problems.

The MMT proponents are correct in saying that in a deflationary environment, the government should administer greater fiscal stimulus both to help the economy and address pressing social issues. After all, post-1990 Japan and the post-2008 Western economies faced deflation not because central banks implemented the wrong policies, but because governments did not borrow enough to fill the deflationary gap opened up by the private-sector savings surplus. Governments even threw fiscal policy into reverse at times, as when Eurozone governments pursued austerity starting in 2010 or when the Japanese government raised its consumption tax in April 1997, April 2014, and October 2019.

Larger Fiscal Deficits Do Not Require MMT When Private Demand for Borrowing Is Weak

The question is whether this requires the use of MMT, that is, central bank financing of government budget deficits. The answer is no, because the funds required for fiscal stimulus are already sitting in the financial sector in the form of excess private-sector savings. The amount of fiscal stimulus required to generate economic recovery is equal to the size of the private savings surplus that created the deflationary gap in the first place. That surplus also means those savings will flow into bonds issued by the sole remaining borrower—the government—driving bond yields down to levels that would have been inconceivable during the golden era, when the economy is mostly in Case 1 or 2.

The most appropriate policy response in such circumstances is for the government to borrow the excess savings of the private sector and use this money to fund self-financing public works projects so that it can avoid the costly QT and QE trap when the economy recovers. There is no need for the government to use unconventional tools such as MMT or QE except in a dire emergency, like the COVID-19 pandemic.

Change in Private-Sector Borrowing Should Be a Key Metric for Judging Effectiveness of Monetary Policy

Proponents of MMT and QE would respond to the preceding by saying that central bank purchases of government bonds will help contain the rise in interest rates that typically accompanies fiscal stimulus. It is true that when the central bank becomes a new purchaser of government bonds, bond prices rise and yields fall. But higher or lower interest rates by themselves have a net neutral impact on the economy; all they do is transfer income from lenders to borrowers, or vice versa. Since the gains of one group are equal to the losses of the other, the net effect of interest rate changes themselves on the economy is neutral.

The reason why lower (or higher) interest rates are helpful in stimulating (or cooling down) the economy is that people respond to them by increasing (or decreasing) borrowing to finance investment and consumption. It is those changes in borrowing that influence the level of economic activity. No matter how large the movement in interest rates may be, its net effect on the economy is likely to be negligible if it is not accompanied by changes in private-sector borrowings. The key metric in judging the effectiveness of monetary policy, therefore, should be its impact on private-sector borrowings, not on interest rates.

The Fed dropped interest rates to zero immediately after the failure of Lehman Brothers in September 2008. But the economy failed to respond for a long time afterward because the private sector was actually *reducing* its borrowings until 2011 (Figure 2.12) in order to repair damaged balance sheets. A rapid increase in borrowings is also unlikely when the economy is in the pursued phase. Indeed, these two reasons are precisely why there is so much excess private-sector savings in the first place.

Interest rates did decline in all of the countries that had their central banks buy government bonds under QE. And both the BOJ and the ECB congratulated themselves on this achievement in their 2016 and 2021 reviews of monetary policy, viewing it as evidence that unconventional monetary accommodation had worked. However, private-sector borrowing did not pick up in any of these countries (Figures 2.13 and 2.17), which is why they found it so hard to achieve their inflation targets.

MMT proponents have also argued that lower interest rates will reduce the government's interest expense. But any decline in the government's interest expense will lower the private sector's interest income by an equivalent amount, which means the net economic impact is neutral.

Furthermore, central bank purchases of government bonds will crowd out private-sector fund managers' purchases, squeezing the earnings of financial institutions and the incomes of pensioners relying on interest income to make ends meet. That will also force fund managers to purchase existing assets, which could push the economy into an unproductive cycle of bubbles and balance sheet recessions, as is noted in Chapter 4. Except in dire emergencies like the COVID-19 pandemic, therefore, fiscal stimulus should be funded not by the central bank but by the private savings surplus that created the deflationary gap in the first place.

The Shape and Form of the QE Trap Depends on Actions of Other Central Banks

The sharp pickup in inflation originating from COVID-driven supply constraints and higher energy prices is forcing central banks to rescind QE and normalize monetary policy. However, the size and shape of the QE trap they face during the normalization process may well depend on the actions of other central banks.

If a central bank is the first to exit QE, it is likely to attract inflows of foreign capital seeking higher yields, which will strengthen the currency while keeping bond yields from rising too much. This is exactly the sort of QE trap the Fed faced when it became the first to announce a normalization of monetary policy in September 2014.

If a central bank is the last to normalize, it may benefit from a weaker currency while other central banks are exiting from QE. This is what the BOJ was hoping to achieve when Governor Kuroda repeatedly insisted the BOJ would not consider normalizing policy until inflation had sustainably reached the 2-percent target. But his hopes for a weaker yen were dashed when President Trump started arguing for a reduction of the U.S. trade deficit. How his talk of the trade deficit kept the dollar from appreciating despite higher US interest rates is described in Chapter 9.

The central bank that exits last is also likely to face higher bond yields because at that point in time neither domestic nor foreign investors will be eager to buy its bonds—after all, other countries are already offering much higher yields. If the BOJ is the last to wind down QE, therefore, it will not be able to count on foreign capital inflows to keep bond yields low.

With Japan's public-sector debt already the largest in the world, some investors may question the ability of the nation's finances to withstand higher JGB yields. The interest paid on excess reserves (Figure 6.11) may also add significantly to what are already very large fiscal deficits in Japan when the BOJ normalizes interest rates. Certain investment funds may try to profit by short-selling Japanese Government Bonds (JGBs) given the huge amounts of bonds the BOJ will have to sell to normalize monetary policy. Such selling could develop into a fiscal crisis if not handled correctly. These risks suggest that the best time for the BOJ to exit QE is now, when inflation rates are still low. As the Fed's successful post-2017 QT proved, the policy that had no impact on the way in (i.e., no pickup in inflation) should have no adverse impact on the way out as long as external conditions remain the same.

Normalization is also more challenging for Japan because its central bank bought over ¥30 trillion in domestic equities via exchange-traded funds (ETFs). Unwinding those holdings would almost certainly have an adverse impact on the Japanese stock market. The ultimate effect on interest and exchange rates of ending QE therefore hinges in part on when other central banks decide to wind down their own versions of QE.

With all central banks facing the same global inflationary threat due to pandemic-related supply shortages and the higher energy prices driven by the concern over climate change, the optimal scenario would be for the three main central banks to exit QE at the same time to minimize destabilizing capital flows between these markets.

Will Borrowing during the Pandemic Help Relieve Debt Trauma?

In Japan, the COVID-19 pandemic has forced many companies to resume borrowing (to secure working capital) for the first time since 1990. This represents a major shift for businesses that had been paying down debt to repair damaged balance sheets after the bubble burst in 1990. This painful experience left them traumatized over debt even after they had finished cleaning up their balance sheets.

As a result, they continued to shun borrowings and instead adopted the "cash flow management" approach whereby all investments must be financed by ongoing cash flow. But such a management philosophy is not good for economic growth because there is no over-stretching in the form of increased borrowings. That has kept a damper on Japan's economic growth.

It will be a major step forward if the pandemic helps these traumatized corporate executives to overcome their aversion to debt. And psychological traumas need to be cured only once.

Neither Monetary nor Fiscal Stimulus Comes Cheap

Some may argue that while monetary accommodation via QE or helicopter money leaves excess liquidity that must eventually be mopped up, a continuous reliance on fiscal stimulus will also generate public debt that must be paid back. Although the two outcomes sound similar, their impact on the economy is actually very different.

First, when the economy is in Case 3 or 4, fiscal spending works from day one by keeping both GDP and the money supply from shrinking. By preventing a decline in GDP, it gives the private sector the income (and jobs) it needs to repair damaged balance sheets. Government borrowing also keeps the money multiplier from turning negative in the face of private-sector deleveraging. That prevents the money supply from shrinking as it did during the Great Depression. Indeed, when the government is the only borrower, the effectiveness of monetary policy hinges on the size of its borrowings.

When GDP is prevented from falling, nonperforming loan problems in the banking system are contained because those with income can still service their debts. Government borrowing also offers a destination for surplus savings, which, in turn, provides interest income to depositors, pensioners, and financial institutions. Government borrowings also absorb excess private-sector savings which, in the absence of such borrowings, might have ended up fueling asset bubbles. That, in turn, prevents the private sector from squandering its savings on bubbles.

Government bond yields also fall to very low levels when the government is the only remaining borrower, which makes many infrastructure projects self-financing (or nearly so) if properly chosen and executed. For projects that are self-financing, debt repayment problems will not arise even if the public debt number grows. Last but not least, undertaking necessary infrastructure spending when the economy is in Case 3 and interest rates are extremely low provides massive cost savings for future taxpayers.

When the private sector regains its financial health and the economy returns to Case 1, financial markets will tell the government to change course via the signal of higher interest rates. Once the recovery in private-sector borrowings is confirmed from flow-of-funds data and discussions with financial market participants, the government should start raising taxes and cutting spending to match the increase in private-sector borrowings.

If the higher interest rates are *not* accompanied by an increase in private-sector borrowings, as happened during the so-called taper tantrum in 2013 and other instances of the QE trap, the fiscal authorities should just stay put. The higher rates in this case may simply reflect market indigestion due to factors unrelated to borrowing demand.

In contrast, monetary accommodation via QE, helicopter money, or negative interest rates will have little impact on the real economy in Case 3 except via the actions of the misinformed foreign exchange and stock market participants as noted in Chapter 2 who may push for a lower exchange rate and higher stock prices, believing that their economies are still in Case 1 or 2.

Lower exchange rates brought about by monetary easing, however, are effectively a beggar-thy-neighbor policy when other trading partners face the same balance sheet or pandemic problems. The United States, which benefited from lower exchange rates when it became the first country to implement QE, suffered from a strong dollar (Figure 2.20) and consequent bouts of protectionism as other nations introduced their own versions of the policy.

Both former ECB President Draghi and BOJ Governor Kuroda have argued that the policy of negative interest rates is working because bond yields have fallen since it was introduced. In both cases, however, there has been virtually no pickup in private-sector borrowing. And since there has been no increase in borrowing or over-stretching, economic growth has not accelerated.

The continued sluggishness in borrowing is to be expected—after all, if there were any borrowers left in the economy, they would have resumed borrowing long before interest rates had fallen to these levels. Unless one believes that the last 20 or 30 basis point decline in interest rates will suddenly trigger a huge increase in borrowings, it is difficult to make the case that negative interest rates will bring about a recovery.

More recently, it appears that even the market participants noted in Chapter 2 who responded enthusiastically to monetary easing in the early years of GFC are becoming more cautious. This is probably because their expectations of QE-induced increases in the money supply and inflation rate never materialized. In other words, central banks can fool people for only so long.

The fact that the central bank is crowding out private-sector *lending* to the only borrower left—the government—deprives pensioners, depositors, and financial institutions of interest income. Banks also suffer from the prolonged recession as more borrowers become unable to service their debts. The health of financial institutions and the livelihoods of pensioners are undermined even more by negative interest rates. In addition, precious time and political capital is wasted when the policy debate is devoted to basically ineffective monetary policy.

In the end, an overreliance on monetary policy may only result in scared depositors, angry pensioners, and worried financial institutions without producing any of the growth in borrowing for real investments needed to lift the economy. Some financial institutions may become so desperate for yield under zero or negative interest rates that they take on risks they are ill-equipped to assume.

The September 2021 Beige Book[18] survey of regional US economic conditions issued by the twelve regional Federal Reserve Banks contained a comment that said: "loan pricing remained competitive, with multiple respondents (i.e., banks), citing concerns regarding too much liquidity and margin compression". Another comment said: "loan growth was a challenge" and that "business loan standards loosened slightly on balance". The December report of the same year said "Liquidity remained elevated and banks continued to report difficulties in finding investments to deploy excess funds." If the only way monetary easing can boost private-sector borrowing is by lowering banks' margins and lending standards, that is a clear indication that the policy has reached its limits.

The benefits of monetary easing in Case 3, therefore, are likely to be limited to a few mini-bubbles in certain asset classes (the so-called portfolio rebalancing effect) and their secondary effect on the real economy. If those bubbles grow large enough and eventually burst, the economy is back to square one, facing years of painful balance sheet recession all over again. And economies in the pursued era are far more vulnerable to this cycle of bubbles and balance sheet recessions than economies in the golden era.

If and when economic growth or inflation returns—for whatever reason—a central bank that has implemented QE or helicopter money policies will face the challenging task of regaining its credibility as an inflation fighter by selling bonds to drain excess reserves

---

[18] Board of Governors of the Federal Reserve System. (2021a) "The Beige Book: August 2021," released September 8, 2021. https://www.federalreserve.gov/monetarypolicy/files/BeigeBook_20210908.pdf

(or having the government sell refunding bonds on its behalf) or immobilizing the reserves by paying a higher rate of interest on them (IOER). All of these options would entail costs for taxpayers. If the central bank had to normalize its balance sheet in a hurry (=QT), yields are likely to go higher and become more volatile, which could adversely affect both financial markets and the economy.

In addition, central banks that have implemented QE or helicopter money policies cannot afford to be seen as falling behind the curve on inflation. That means that if they want to avoid the worst aspects of the QE trap, they may have to start tightening much earlier than central banks that stayed away from these unconventional easing measures. In the worst case, QE, which was not helpful in raising the number of borrowers on the way in, may actually hamper the return of borrowers on the way out by pushing interest rates higher as part of the QE trap.

The point here is that neither fiscal stimulus nor monetary stimulus comes cheap, but a cost-benefit comparison shows fiscal stimulus to be far more desirable—and often absolutely essential—when the economy is in Case 3 or 4. When the economy is in the pursued phase or in a balance sheet recession, policy makers must mobilize the nation's best and brightest to identify and implement viable—if not self-financing—public works projects. This will not only help the present generation but also provide necessary infrastructure for future generations at the lowest possible cost.

When the economy is in Case 1 or 2, of course, the opposite is true, and monetary policy should play the central role in maximizing the economy's potential. In this case, the use of fiscal policy to support the economy should be discouraged except under emergency situations.

Harvard University professor Kenneth Rogoff argued that negative-interest-rate policies would work better if cash, or at least large-denomination bills, were banned entirely.[19] But that would impose major inconveniences on society just so that some economist's ill-conceived monetary policy remedy might work slightly better. Instead of forcing the public to endure such a disruption—which could also hurt the economy through a loss of efficiency—economists

---

[19] Rogoff, Kenneth S. (2016), *The Curse of Cash,* Princeton, NJ: Princeton University Press.

should realize that monetary policy worked well in the past because the advanced economies were all in a golden era characterized by strong private-sector demand for borrowings, but is not working now because those same economies are experiencing balance sheet recessions and are in the pursued phase, with limited domestic investment opportunities.

Albert Einstein once said "stupidity is when you keep doing the same experiment but keep on hoping for a different outcome." Monetary easing policies such as zero interest rates, negative interest rates, QE, forward guidance, and inflation targets have all failed to produce results within the expected timeframe when the economy is in Case 3 or 4. Instead of continuously doubling down on monetary policy, it is time for policy makers to question the fundamental assumptions behind these failed policies and to look for policies that may actually work.

CHAPTER 7

Europe Is Repeating Mistakes of the 1930s

The Failure of Economics in the 1930s and the Rise of National Socialism

When the pandemic-driven recession hit the Eurozone in early 2020, many elected leaders and their voters were horrified to find that they had no fiscal or monetary policy levers with which to fight the swiftest and deadliest economic collapse in living memory. That sense of helplessness had the potential to undermine the already precarious electoral support for the European Project, which first came to light with the Eurozone crisis that began in 2010.

Member states willingly ceded sovereignty over monetary and exchange rate policy to the European Central Bank (ECB) when they adopted the Euro. But they also lost sovereignty over fiscal policy—not only because of the limitations imposed by the Stability and Growth Pact (SGP) and the subsequent Fiscal Compact, but also because of the ease with which capital can flow between the Eurozone's 19 different government bond markets—all of which use the same currency.

Under this arrangement, the unique position government bonds hold in each country as the highest-rated fixed income asset denominated in the national currency is lost since there are 18 other government bonds denominated in the same currency. Having 18 close substitutes means any member government deviating from the norm established by the best fiscal performer among the 19 countries is punished by capital outflows and higher interest rates.

This loss of fiscal sovereignty has been the key driver of poor performance of Eurozone economies since 2008 as well as the emergence of extreme-right anti-euro political parties in many member countries. And that was long before the onslaught of COVID-19. This alarming development manifested itself first in the 2010 Eurozone crisis, which left many voters with the impression that their elected officials had no monetary or fiscal policy levers to alter their economic future as long as they remained in the currency union. It is even more worrying that this political disillusionment is happening in economic circumstances very similar to those prevailing when similar far-right groups appeared in the 1930s.

It was already noted in Chapter 3 that Communism was a byproduct of the extreme inequality created in the course of industrialization before an economy reached the Lewis Turning Point (LTP). In contrast, the far-right National Socialism, or Nazism, was a result of extreme economic hardship brought about by an inept policy response to a balance sheet recession. In other words, it was policy makers' inability to understand that their economies were in Case 3 or 4 that led to that tragic outcome.

When the New York stock market bubble burst in October 1929, all of those who had leveraged up during the bubble started paying down debt at the same time. This can be seen in the sharp fall in loans outstanding after 1929 in Figure 2.15. But since there was no one on the other side to borrow and spend, the U.S. economy fell into the $1,000–$900–$810–$730 deflationary spiral and lost a full 46 percent of nominal gross national product (GNP) in just four years in an event that came to be known as the Great Depression. In 1933, the U.S. unemployment rate was more than 25 percent nationwide and exceeded 50 percent in many major cities.

The problem is that the economics profession never considered this type of recession until several years after 2008 because it never allowed for the possibility of a private sector that sought to minimize debt. The entire theoretical toolkit of economics, built over many decades, was predicated on the assumption that the private sector always seeks to maximize profits.

Because recessions driven by private-sector attempts to minimize debt had never been considered by economists, the public was totally unprepared for the balance sheet recessions that hit them in 1929 and again in 2008. Even Keynes, who argued for an increase in government spending in 1936, seven years after the Great Depression began, failed to free himself from the notion that the private sector is always maximizing profits.

With no-one in 1929 aware of the ailment called a balance sheet recession, it did not occur to political leaders of the time that the government should mobilize fiscal policy and act as borrower of last resort. On the contrary, most economists and policy makers, who never considered the possibility that the economy could be in Cases 3 or 4, argued strongly in favor of a balanced budget, believing that the private sector was still maximizing profits.

When the recession began in 1929, both U.S. President Herbert Hoover and German Chancellor Heinrich Brüning insisted that government should balance its budget as quickly as possible. The Allied Command, the victors of World War I, also demanded that the German government balance its budget and continue to make reparation payments. That was the worst possible policy for this type of recession because the economy would quickly fall into a deflationary spiral if the government abandoned its role as "borrower of last resort." Soon enough, the German economy fell into a deflationary spiral that caused the unemployment rate to soar to 28 percent.

Although the Americans had only themselves to blame for getting caught up in a bubble, Germany was still recovering from the traumatic hyperinflation that followed its defeat in World War I and was very much dependent on U.S. capital when the New York stock market crashed. The extent of its reliance on American capital can be inferred from the saying in Germany in the 1920s that train passengers in the first-class cabin do not speak German at all, those in second class speak a little, and those in the ordinary cars speak it very well indeed. With American capital rushing back to the United States after the crash and the Allied powers demanding both a balanced budget and reparation payments, the German economy had no place to go but down.

The extreme hardship and poverty this mistaken policy imposed on the German people forced them to find a way out. With only a limited social safety net in the 1930s and the established center-right and center-left political parties largely beholden to orthodox economics and insisting on a balanced budget, the only choice left for the German people to alter their course after four years of terrible suffering was to vote for the National Socialists, who argued against both austerity and reparation payments.

The Nazis, considered by most Germans to be a gang of racist hoodlums just a few years earlier, thus ended up winning 43.9 percent of the vote and securing the chancellorship in 1933. It was not as if nearly half the German population woke up one morning and suddenly began hating immigrants and Jews. What happened was that they finally lost faith in established parties that remained beholden to fiscal orthodoxy. People voted for the Nazis because the established parties, the Allied governments, and the economists had proved totally incapable of rescuing them from the four years of horrendous poverty that followed the crash of 1929. The Nazis were swept to power because economists of that period failed to understand the horror of the balance sheet recession that had led to so much suffering for the German people.

For better or for worse, Adolf Hitler quickly implemented the speedy, sufficient, and sustained fiscal stimulus needed to overcome a balance sheet recession—the construction of the autobahn expressway system was among the many public works projects undertaken by the Nazi government. That started the positive feedback loop of fiscal stimulus that can be expected when the economy is in Case 3. By 1938, just five years later, Germany's unemployment rate had fallen to 2 percent.

This was viewed as a great success by people both inside and outside Germany—in contrast, the democracies of the United States, France, and the United Kingdom continued to suffer from high unemployment as policy makers were unable to think outside the box of orthodox economics insisting on balancing the budget. The U.S. unemployment rate, for example, was still 19 percent in 1938. The stark contrast between this and Germany's 2 percent rate made Hitler seem like an attractive alternative, and even those who used to look down their noses at the ranting lance corporal from Austria began to worship the man.

Germany's spectacular economic success also led Hitler to think that perhaps this time the nation could win a war—its economy, after all, was in a virtuous cycle and generating the taxes needed to support rearmament efforts, while the U.S., U.K., and French economies were in a vicious cycle of unattended balance sheet recessions with ever-dwindling tax receipts and military budgets.

That is what led to the cataclysm of World War II. Nothing is worse than a dictator who has the wrong agenda but the right economic policy. And the problem was made far worse in the 1930s by democracies' inability to switch to the right economic policy until hostilities began.

Once war broke out, the democracies were finally able to introduce the same sorts of policies Hitler had implemented six years earlier. In other words, Allied governments started acting as borrower and spender of last resort by procuring massive numbers of tanks and fighter planes, and the U.S. and U.K. economies jumped back to life, just as the German economy had done six years earlier.

This happened because companies that received large government orders to build fighter planes or warships were able to borrow from banks to expand their capacity. They could do so even if their balance sheets were not yet presentable because they already had the most credible buyer in the world for their products, the government. That started a virtuous cycle of over-stretching by businesses that led to rapid growth. The combined productive capacity of the Allies soon overwhelmed that of the Third Reich, but not before millions had perished.

Every country has its share of xenophobic persons who blame immigrants and foreigners for society's problems. But their ability to garner enough votes to emerge victorious in Germany despite the region's democratic traditions and high levels of education suggests that ordinary people who traditionally voted for parties espousing democratic values switched allegiance in desperation. It has been observed time and again that when survival is at stake, respect for individuals and human rights is often thrown out the window. And that is when things can go wrong in a big way.

The Nazis' initial successes and the tragedies that followed were attributable largely to a lack of understanding of balance sheet recessions among the period's economists and policy makers. Had Allied governments and the Brüning administration understood the mechanics and dangers of balance sheet recessions and administered sufficient fiscal stimulus to fight deflationary pressures in Germany, most Germans would never have voted for an extremist like Hitler.

If Allied governments had also administered sufficient fiscal stimulus after 1929 or even 1933 to prevent deflationary spirals in their own economies, Hitler's success would not have appeared so spectacular by contrast. And if stronger Allied economies had been able to present a credible military deterrent, Hitler might have thought twice about starting a war. The failure of economists to understand balance sheet recessions in the 1930s therefore contributed significantly to the Nazis' initial success and all the human suffering that followed.

History Is Repeating Itself since the Global Financial Crisis (GFC) in 2008

Fifty million lives were lost in World War II, and readers may think such a tragic mistake could never be repeated. Unfortunately, that is not the case, especially in Europe.

When housing bubbles burst on both sides of the Atlantic in 2008, the Western economies fell into a severe balance sheet recession, with private sectors increasing savings or paying down debt in spite of zero or negative interest rates.

Figure 7.1 illustrates the financial position of the household sector in Eurozone countries that experienced housing bubbles. It shows that households in these countries were either borrowing huge sums of money (i.e., were running a financial deficit) or reducing savings to invest in houses during the bubble, but after the bubble burst, they all began saving (i.e., were running a financial surplus)—some to a massive extent—in spite of zero interest rates. That puts these economies squarely in Cases 3 and 4.

The plight of the Spanish and Irish household sectors is noted in Chapter 2. Their nonfinancial corporate sectors have also been going through very difficult times since 2008. The Spanish nonfinancial corporate sector, shown in Figure 7.2, has been a significant net saver since 2008 despite low or even negative interest rates. It is particularly worth noting that the white bars for the nonfinancial corporate sector in Figure 7.2 frequently went below zero starting in 2008.

White bars below zero are a bad sign because they usually indicate that a credit crunch or a steep drop in income is forcing the

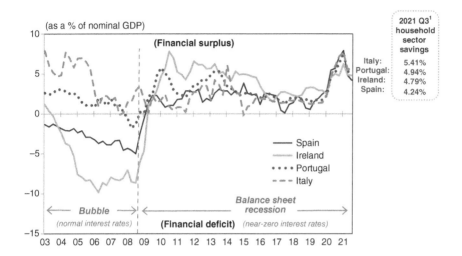

FIGURE 7.1 Eurozone Household Sectors[1] Are Savers in Post-Bubble Era

Notes: 1. All entries are four-quarter moving averages. For the latest figures, four-quarter averages ending in 2021 Q3 are used.

Sources: Based on the flow of funds data from Banco de España; National Statistics Institute, Spain; the Central Bank of Ireland; Central Statistics Office Ireland; Banco de Portugal; Banca d'Italia; Italian National Institute of Statistics, and the International Monetary Fund (IMF)

sector to draw down *past* savings to make ends meet. That means Spain was suffering from both balance sheet problems (shaded bars above zero) and a credit crunch (white bars below zero). In other words, the Spanish economy was often in Case 4 if not in Case 3 from 2008 to 2016.

The Spanish economy did better from 2016 until the pandemic recession hit in 2020, but the recovery was not fueled by domestic demand, as both the household and corporate sectors remained net savers. Instead, it was driven by a sharp contraction in the nation's external deficit as imports shrank faster than exports. And that was made possible by reduced domestic demand and the increased competitiveness of Spanish industry due to years of painful internal deflation. This latter possibility is discussed later in regard to the path of unit labor costs in Figure 7.9.

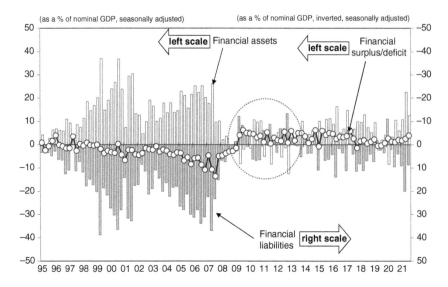

FIGURE 7.2 Spanish Nonfinancial Corporations

Notes: Seasonal adjustments by Nomura Research Institute. Latest figures are for 2021 Q3.

Sources: Nomura Research Institute, based on flow of funds data from Banco de España and National Statistics Institute, Spain

The Spanish corporate sector remained in financial surplus (i.e., was a net saver) for years after 2008 in spite of zero or negative interest rates. This aversion to borrowing may be a result of the painful credit crunch that struck Spain during the Eurozone crisis. Corporate treasurers who have lived through a credit crunch typically become extremely averse to borrowing, and such trauma can last for years.

The Irish nonfinancial corporate sector was also mostly a net saver (Figure 7.3) from 2008 until 2018. The fact that the Irish household sector was a huge net saver (Figure 2.7) suggests the Irish economic growth observed from 2016 to 2019 was also a result of lower wages due to internal deflation (see Figure 7.9), coupled with the country's tax haven status.

Greek households (Figure 7.4) were not as highly leveraged as their Spanish or Irish counterparts even though Greek house prices also soared (Figure 2.4). Nevertheless, the sector has been paying down debt since 2010, as indicated by the shaded bars above zero. This is a natural reaction for any sector caught in a bubble bust.

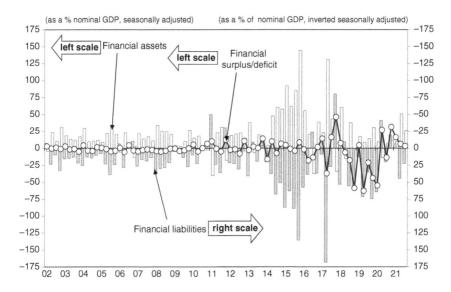

FIGURE 7.3 Irish Nonfinancial Corporations

Notes: Seasonal adjustments by Nomura Research Institute. Latest figures are for 2021 Q3.

Source: Nomura Research Institute, based on flow of funds data from the Central Bank of Ireland and Central Statistics Office, Ireland

What is really disturbing about the Greek household and non-financial corporate sectors is that they have been drawing down financial assets since the end of 2009, as indicated by the white bars below zero (circled areas in Figures 7.4 and 7.5). As noted earlier, white bars below zero are very bad signs, because they indicate that people are drawing down past savings to make ends meet. Such withdrawals are typically triggered by a credit crunch involving troubled financial institutions or by a significant fall in income. With Greek gross domestic product (GDP) down nearly 30 percent from 2008 (Figure 7.6), it is understandable that many Greek households and nonfinancial corporations are being forced to dis-save just to pay for daily necessities. That means the low savings figures for Greece in Figure 1.1 are due not to strong investment but rather to weak income.

One reason Greece's GDP fell so sharply was that the International Monetary Fund (IMF), which was called in to help the country following the deficit-fudging scandal in 2010, had no understanding

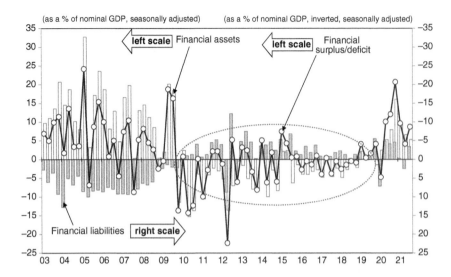

FIGURE 7.4 Greek Households Deleveraging but also Drawing Down Savings to Survive

Notes: Seasonal adjustments by Nomura Research Institute. Latest figures are for 2021 Q3.

Sources: Nomura Research Institute, based on flow of funds data from the Bank of Greece and Hellenic Statistical Authority, Greece

of balance sheet recessions at the time (it does now). The IMF forced the country to engage in draconian fiscal consolidation in the hope that this would win back creditors' trust. Although that would be the right course of action for a country in an ordinary fiscal crisis, Greece was also in a balance sheet recession, and the austerity measures triggered the $1,000–$900–$810–$730 deflationary spiral, causing nominal GDP to contract by nearly 30 percent (Figure 7.6).

The Greek government lost the market's trust when it was revealed that its pre-2009 government had been fudging the budget deficit numbers and the actual deficit was much larger than reported. However, the IMF and the EU also lost their credibility in the eyes of the Greek people when the economic package they imposed not only failed to meet its own growth projections, but also ended up depressing the nation's GDP by nearly 30 percent. Now that both sides have made one massive mistake each, it is time for them to call it even and move forward.

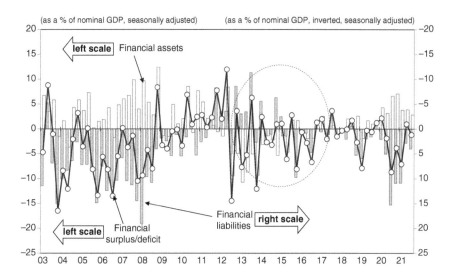

FIGURE 7.5 Greek Nonfinancial Corporate Sector also Drew Down Savings during Crisis

Notes: Seasonal adjustments by Nomura Research Institute. Latest figures are for 2021 Q3.

Sources: Nomura Research Institute, based on flow of funds data from the Bank of Greece and Hellenic Statistical Authority, Greece

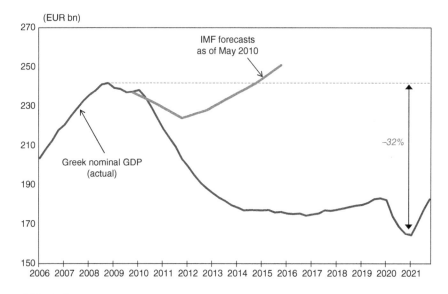

FIGURE 7.6 Greece's Nominal GDP Falls Far below IMF Forecasts

Source: Nomura Research Institute, based on Hellenic Statistical Authority, Greece; IMF, "IMF Executive Board Approves €30 Billion Stand-By Arrangement for Greece" May 9, 2010

Germany's Balance Sheet Recession Preceded Others by Eight Years

In contrast to the peripheral countries previously noted, Germany, the largest of the Eurozone countries, experienced no housing bubble (Figure 2.4). Not only that, but German house prices actually fell 8 percent while house prices in other parts of the Eurozone rose sharply, all under the same low interest rates.

This happened because Germany had entered a balance sheet recession eight years *earlier*, in 2000, when the dot-com bubble burst. This can be seen from Figure 7.7, which shows that German households not only stopped borrowing money after 2000, but also started paying down debt. And that was happening even after the ECB took interest rates down to their lowest level in the postwar period.

This change in household behavior happened because German households and businesses, who are usually very conservative, apparently lost their heads during the dot-com bubble in the Neuer Markt, the German equivalent of the Nasdaq, which went up tenfold from 1998 to 2000 (Figure 7.8).[1] When the bubble burst and the market lost 97 percent of its value, the financial health of Germany's private sector was devastated. Businesses and households went on to save as much as 10 percent of GDP in the wake of bubble burst, tipping the economy into a severe balance sheet recession.

Seeing that the German economy was in trouble, but not realizing that it was in a balance sheet recession, the ECB promptly brought interest rates down to a postwar low of 2 percent to help the largest economy in the Eurozone, but to no avail. This inability to revive Germany's economy with record-low interest rates led to the notion that the country was "the sick man of Europe."

The Germans, without realizing that their problems were rooted in the balance sheet, began to push for structural reforms in a plan known as Agenda 2010. Because balance sheet recessions were not taught in economics, German economists and policy makers simply assumed that traditional monetary easing was not working because of structural problems. It was the same mistake Japan had made a decade earlier, and for exactly the same reason.

---

[1] The Neuer Markt changed its name to TecDAX on March 24, 2003.

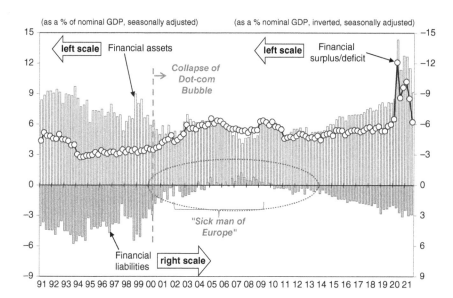

FIGURE 7.7 German Households Stopped Borrowing Altogether after Dot-Com Bubble

Notes: Seasonal adjustments by Nomura Research Institute. Latest figures are for 2021 Q3.

Sources: Nomura Research Institute, based on flow of funds data from Bundesbank and Eurostat

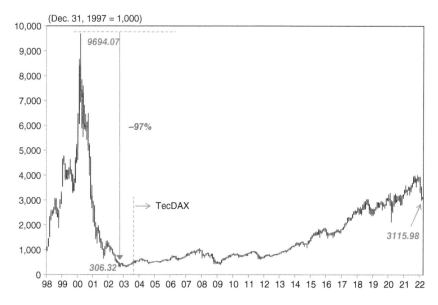

FIGURE 7.8 Neuer Markt Collapse in 2001 Pushed German Economy into Balance Sheet Recession

Sources: Bloomberg and MarketWatch, as of March 14, 2022

However, structural issues that existed decades before 2000 cannot explain the sudden shift in German private-sector savings behavior starting in that year (Figure 7.7). This fundamental misdiagnosis created huge distortions in the Eurozone economies after 2000 and again after 2008, when Germany began demanding that other economies in the currency bloc implement the same structural reforms it had carried out even though those economies were all suffering from balance sheet—not structural—problems.

While Germany was struggling with both a balance sheet recession and painful structural reforms that were no cure for the recession, Eurozone countries that had avoided the dot-com bubble and had clean balance sheets responded enthusiastically to the ECB's monetary easing. In other words, the postwar-low interest rate of 2 percent designed to help the German economy was of no help to that country because its economy was in Case 3 with no private sector borrowers, but the same rate was far too low for the rest of Europe, which was in Case 1 with plenty of private sector borrowers. In no time, many of these countries found themselves engulfed in huge housing bubbles.

The fact that Germany was in a balance sheet recession while the other countries were experiencing housing bubbles also opened up a large competitive gap between the two. Slow money-supply growth in Germany, which was suffering from a balance sheet recession, led to stagnant wages and prices, while rapid money-supply growth in the rest of the bubble-ridden Eurozone resulted in sharply rising wages and prices. That made Germany highly competitive relative to the rest of Europe.[2]

The housing boom in the rest of Europe and improved competitiveness at home allowed the Germans to rapidly increase their exports within the region. With the rest of Europe doing the overstretching for Germany, the country was able to overcome its balance sheet recession.

When the global housing bubble burst in 2008 and the rest of Europe plunged into a balance sheet recession, Germany was already emerging from its own balance sheet recession. This lack of

---

[2] Readers interested in seeing how the competitiveness issue evolved in the post-2008 Eurozone are referred to Chapter 5 of the author's previous book, *The Escape from Balance Sheet Recession and the QE Trap* (2015), for a more detailed discussion.

synchronization between the German economy, the largest in the Eurozone, and the rest of the bloc, combined with policy makers' lack of awareness of the economic disease called a balance sheet recession, created prolonged difficulties for the Eurozone that lasted over 10 years.

If the private sector as a whole is saving, someone outside the private sector must borrow and spend those savings to prevent the economy from falling into a deflationary spiral. Unfortunately, in spite of dramatic increases in private-sector savings after 2008, the concept of balance sheet recessions was still not in economic textbooks, and powerful figures on both sides of the Atlantic started pushing for fiscal consolidation in a repeat of the 1930s.

In the United States, this move was spearheaded by the Tea Party faction of the Republican Party, and in the Eurozone, it was the Germans, led by Chancellor Angela Merkel and Finance Minister Wolfgang Schäuble, who pushed for austerity. In the United Kingdom, Prime Minister Gordon Brown was cognizant of balance sheet recessions and administered the required fiscal stimulus, but he was soon voted out of office in favor of David Cameron, who opted for draconian austerity measures.

Fortunately for the United States, policy makers from Ben Bernanke to Larry Summers recognized soon after the GFC that they were facing a balance sheet recession, the same economic ailment that had afflicted Japan since 1990. They then employed the expression "fiscal cliff" to persuade Congress not to engage in premature fiscal consolidation. Although the United States came close to falling off the fiscal cliff on several occasions, it ultimately managed to avoid that predicament and recovered faster than other countries, even though it had been the epicenter of the GFC.

Defective SGP Invites Extreme-Right Political Parties

In the Eurozone, where policy makers remained unaware of the ailment called a balance sheet recession or the need for government to act as borrower of last resort in such situations, one country after another fell off the fiscal cliff, with devastating consequences. The SGP that created the euro also made no provision whatsoever for this type of recession and actually prohibited governments from borrowing more than 3 percent of GDP *regardless* of how much the private sector was saving.

In other words, Eurozone governments were prevented from acting as borrower of last resort beyond 3 percent of GDP.

The Spanish private sector saved an average of 7.64 percent of GDP in the 13 years after 2008 Q3 (Figure 1.1). But since the government was allowed to borrow only 3 percent of GDP, savings equal to more than 4 percent of GDP leaked out of the nation's income stream, tipping the Spanish economy into a horrendous recession.

Moreover, weakened economies saw tax receipts fall and budget deficits rise to more than 3 percent of GDP. An increase in the budget deficit due to economic weakness is referred to in economics as an automatic stabilizer because it forces government to increase borrowing and spending, which helps stabilize the economy.

But instead of utilizing this stabilizer function by expanding government borrowing to match the increase in private-sector savings, Eurozone governments were forced by the SGP to *reduce* their borrowing to 3 percent of GDP. Instead of mitigating the recession, these government actions made it far worse. The Spanish unemployment rate shot up to 26 percent, and many other countries suffered a similar fate. With center-left and center-right political parties alike insisting on the fiscal consolidation mandated by the SGP and the Fiscal Compact—not unlike German center-left and center-right political parties in the early 1930s—average citizens grew increasingly destitute and desperate.

Shockingly, the SGP offers no advice on how a government should address this kind of deflationary gap because it assumes that situations like Cases 3 and 4 can never happen. This is not surprising given that the SGP was ratified in 1998, when no one outside Japan knew anything about balance sheet recessions. But when the housing bubbles burst in 2008, triggering Europe's balance sheet recessions, policy makers were left with no tools to stop the deflationary spiral, resulting in deep recessions and tremendous human suffering not unlike what Germany experienced during the 1929–33 period. It is this fundamental defect in the SGP that nearly destroyed the Eurozone economies starting in 2008.

Predictions of Eurozone Crisis Are Ignored

This disastrous outcome was perfectly predictable given the SGP's limitations. The author tried to warn Europeans in his 2003 book, *Balance*

Sheet Recession: "Since fiscal stimulus is the most effective—if not the only—remedy for a balance sheet recession, as soon as the symptoms of balance sheet recessions are observed in Europe, the EC Commission is strongly advised to take action to free the Eurozone economies from the restrictions of the Maastricht Treaty.[3] Failure to do so may result in Europe falling into a vicious cycle with an ever-larger deflationary gap. Indeed, of the three regions—Japan, the United States, and Europe—Europe is by far the most vulnerable when it comes to balance sheet recessions because of the restrictions placed on it by the Maastricht Treaty."[4] Although the importance of the book was noted by Joseph Ackermann, the CEO of Deutsche Bank at the time, and was featured in the bank's report to its clients, the warning went unheeded, and one Eurozone economy after another fell into a prolonged balance sheet recession after 2008, exactly as predicted.

The author then warned about the political consequences of this problem in his 2008 book *The Holy Grail of Macroeconomics*, arguing that ". . . forcing a country or region in a balance sheet recession to balance the budget out of misguided pride or stubbornness will not benefit anyone. Indeed, forcing an inappropriate policy on a nation already suffering from a debilitating recession can actually put its *democratic* structures at risk by aggravating the downturn."[5] This warning, too, was ignored, and extremist parties have gained ground in all of these countries, just as predicted.

By May 2014, people had become so desperate that nationalist anti-EU parties shocked the political establishment with victories in European Parliament elections in the United Kingdom, France, and Greece. The United Kingdom also voted itself out of the EU in 2016, with some arguing that "the only continent that had lower growth rates than Europe was Antarctica!" These results underscore just how many people are unhappy and distrustful of the European political and economic establishment because of this critical defect in the SGP.

---

[3] This is the original treaty that led to the creation of the euro and SGP.

[4] Koo, Richard C. (2003), *Balance Sheet Recession: Japan's Struggle with Uncharted Economics and its Global Implications*, Singapore: John Wiley & Sons (Asia), p. 234.

[5] Koo, Richard C. (2008), *The Holy Grail of Macroeconomics: Lessons from Japan's Great Recession,* Singapore: John Wiley & Sons (Asia), p. 250.

The gains made by Eurosceptics prompted both the establishment and the media to warn about a loss of momentum in the fiscal consolidation and structural reform efforts they consider essential to the region's economic revival. The powers-that-be have labeled the triumphant Eurosceptics "populists" and are desperately trying to paint them as irresponsible extremists.

All of the anti-EU parties that performed well in elections have elements of nativism in the sense that they blame immigrants for many of their countries' domestic problems. They are also irresponsible in that there is no reason why stricter controls on immigration would meaningfully improve the lives of people suffering from devastating balance sheet recessions.

Policy Makers Need to Ask Why Eurosceptics Made Such Gains

On the other hand, the establishment's claim that it has pursued responsible policies deserves to be critically reexamined. Most countries in Europe fell into severe balance sheet recessions after the housing bubble collapsed, yet not a single government has recognized that and responded appropriately. To make matters worse, establishment policies have centered on fiscal consolidation, which is the one policy a government must *not* implement during a balance sheet recession. That mistake has had devastating consequences for the people of Europe.

Moreover, the establishment has made the situation worse by mistaking balance sheet problems for structural problems. While every Eurozone country, as a pursued economy, needs to address a variety of structural problems to stay ahead of its pursuers, the recessions that started in 2008 were due mostly— perhaps about 80 percent—to balance sheet problems, with structural issues responsible only for the remaining 20 percent or so. After all, it is difficult to attribute the sudden collapse of these economies in 2008 and their subsequent stagnation to structural factors that had existed for decades prior to that. Furthermore, these economies were all responding normally to conventional macroeconomic policies until 2008 (2000 in Germany), indicating that there were no structural problems then.

As is noted in Chapter 5, all advanced countries are facing two challenges: they are being pursued and they are in balance sheet recessions—and, more recently, pandemic recessions. Structural reforms are necessary to address the former, but fiscal stimulus is needed to deal with the latter. Of the two, the latter is far more urgent because a balance sheet recession can destroy an economy very quickly, as demonstrated by the United States during the Great Depression in the 1930s. In a sense, the present situation is more serious than that of the 1930s because policy makers then only had to deal with a balance sheet recession.

As is noted in Chapter 5, structural reforms often take a decade or more to produce macroeconomic results and are no substitute for fiscal stimulus when the economy is in a balance sheet recession. Political leaders, therefore, must make it clear to voters that structural policies are needed to stay ahead of the pursuing countries, but if the economy is in a balance sheet recession, fiscal stimulus is urgently needed to offset the deflationary pressures coming from private-sector deleveraging. And that should not be too difficult to explain with charts like those in Figures 2.6 and 2.7.

The situation also varies from one country to the next. In Spain and Ireland, which experienced particularly large bubbles, balance sheet problems are responsible for a greater percentage of the ongoing economic weakness, while in Italy, which did not see a major bubble, the issues are probably more structural in nature.

Regardless of national differences, the Eurozone as a whole is in Case 3, with its private sector saving 5.11 percent of GDP on average since 2008 (Figure 1.1) in spite of negative interest rates. Since the economy is suffering from a lack of borrowers, governments must do the opposite of what the private sector is doing—they must support the economy by borrowing and spending the 5.11 percent of GDP worth of excess private-sector savings.

No Official Recognition of the Disease

Unfortunately, neither the European Commission (EC) nor the ECB seems cognizant of the danger posed by this alarming surplus of private-sector savings. As a result, they continue to demand fiscal consolidation and structural reforms from member countries while ignoring the most urgent need, which is to re-inject excess private-sector savings into the economy's income stream. For example, former ECB President Mario Draghi demanded at the beginning of each and every one of his press conferences that all Eurozone members observe the fiscal consolidation goals mandated by the SGP and the subsequent Fiscal Compact. That means he believed the Eurozone economy was in Case 2, where lenders and not borrowers are the constraint on growth.

His belief that the economy is in Case 2 led the ECB to introduce long-term refinancing operations (LTROs), targeted LTROs (TLTROs), quantitative easing (QE), and a negative-interest-rate policy—all of which are designed to increase *lending*, on the assumption that there is an ample supply of willing borrowers. Although some of these ECB policies did help the Eurozone economy move from Case 4 to Case 3 (but not completely, as is explained in Chapter 8), the actual credit extended to euro-area residents over the last 13 years increased by a minuscule 16 percent, as shown in Figure 2.13.

Since those who created the euro never anticipated Cases 3 and 4, fiscal policy was effectively banned in the Eurozone, leaving monetary policy as policy makers' only tool for addressing recessions. It was what Draghi called "the only game in town." As a result, when Germany first fell into a balance sheet recession in 2000, the ECB had to ease monetary policy by lowering interest rates to a postwar low of 2 percent—thereby creating bubbles elsewhere in the Eurozone—to help the country. When the bubbles burst and those countries fell into balance sheet recessions in 2008, the ECB had to ease even further by taking interest rates below zero in a feeble attempt to help the rest. But fighting balance sheet recessions in one part of the Eurozone by creating bubbles elsewhere is no way to run a currency union.

The SGP Should Have Forced Countries in Case 3 to Use Fiscal Stimulus

Put differently, if Germany had used fiscal stimulus to fight its post-2000 balance sheet recession, the housing bubbles and subsequent balance sheet recessions the Eurozone suffered would not have been nearly as bad as they were. This is because the ECB would not have felt the need to bring interest rates to a postwar low to prop up the German economy, and higher interest rates would have meant smaller housing bubbles in the rest of Eurozone.

This suggests that, in order to make the single currency work, the SGP should have required member governments to combat balance sheet recessions within their borders using domestic fiscal policy. This would have insulated ECB's monetary policy and the other member economies from the influence of bubbles and balance sheet recessions in individual countries.

Restricting the use of fiscal policy when an economy is in Case 1 and 2 is fine. But when a country is in Case 3, the SGP should require it to mobilize fiscal policy with EU support and blessing so that its balance sheet problems do not distort the economic policies of countries that did not participate in the bubble.

The Eurosceptics have made gains not because they are populists, but because the established center-left and center-right parties' mistaken policy choices dragged the economy down and devastated so many lives. After waiting fruitlessly for many years, voters realized the situation was not going to improve as long as the established parties remained in power. For people whose lives had been destroyed by their governments' inaction (or worse) on the deflationary gap, the first step toward a solution was to free their countries from the fiscal straitjacket imposed by the defective SGP—hence the surge in support for anti-EU parties. And those are exactly the circumstances under which Adolf Hitler and the National Socialists came to power in Germany in 1933.

Germans, Who Suffered Most after 1929, Have Ironically Made Others Suffer since 2008

It is truly ironic that it is the Germans who are imposing this fiscal straitjacket on the Eurozone even though they were the first victims of a similar fiscal orthodoxy in 1929 when Allied governments imposed austerity measures on the Brüning administration. Those demands devastated the German economy and pushed its unemployment rate up to 28 percent, as noted earlier. If anything, it is the Germans who should be warning about the dangers of austerity when an economy is in Case 3. The Germans also appear to have forgotten how quickly their own economy recovered with fiscal stimulus after 1933.

Perhaps Germans today are so appalled by the brutality of the Nazi regime that everything Hitler did is now rejected out of hand. This kind of total repudiation of a person or an era can be dangerous because people who were never taught what he did *right* to win the hearts of the German people will be naïve and unprepared when the next Hitler comes.

With so many far-right political parties winning votes in countries suffering from balance sheet recessions, the people of Europe must urgently be made aware of this economic ailment. Without a proper understanding of the disease, member countries may find their economic crises accompanied by a crisis in democracy.

Social safety nets today are far more extensive than they were in the 1930s, making modern democracies more resistant to such recessions and policy mistakes. Indeed, social safety nets themselves are a form of fiscal stimulus that did not exist in the 1930s. Nevertheless, people's mistrust and unhappiness could eventually explode if complacent politicians, economists, and bureaucrats continue to implement misguided policies.

European Recovery Is Led by Internal Deflation

Economies do adjust given sufficient time. In spite of the misguided policies previously described, some European economies began to show signs of life from around 2016 until the onslaught of the pandemic. But that was a result of a painful *internal deflation* that made them more competitive relative to the outside world. Figure 7.9 shows that unit labor costs in high-unemployment countries like Spain, Ireland, Portugal, and Greece have all fallen quite substantially from their peaks. According to the Organisation for Economic Co-operation and Development (OECD), unit labor costs fell 14.5 percent from their previous peak in Greece, 8.6 percent in Spain, and 8.0 percent in Portugal. In Ireland, they plunged 42.9 percent from the high, although this decline may have been exaggerated by discontinuities in the Irish GDP data.

In contrast, German unit labor costs rose 42.8 percent from their low in 2006 Q4 as the country recovered from its post-2000 balance sheet recession. This divergence in unit labor costs made peripheral countries quite competitive vis-à-vis Germany and the rest of the world. The fact that post-2016 Spanish growth came from imports

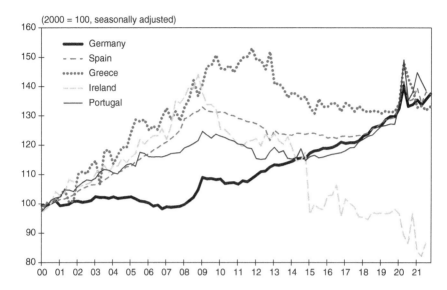

FIGURE 7.9 Euro Crisis Depressed Unit Labor Costs in Peripheral Countries

Source: Nomura Research Institute, based on OECD data

falling faster than exports indicates that it was indeed an internal deflation story. Although the ECB often talks about the importance of achieving the 2-percent inflation target, it was actually this painful internal deflation that allowed Eurozone's hardest-hit countries to recover in the absence of fiscal stimulus.

COVID-19 Exposes Defects in Eurozone Structures Again

It was against this backdrop that the COVID-19 pandemic struck Europe in 2020. When the economy was hit by the lockdowns, Eurozone voters realized once again that they had no monetary or fiscal policy levers to fight the devastating recession and public health crisis. This was in stark contrast to non-Eurozone governments, which could combat the pandemic and the recession it triggered by borrowing—especially from investors who must hold high-quality fixed income assets denominated in the domestic currency. In the United Kingdom, the Bank of England even offered to lend directly to the government on an emergency basis. These countries also have the option of allowing their exchange rates to weaken.

Support for the European project began to dissolve as more voters began to realize that their helplessness stemmed from their membership in the Eurozone. Support for the euro in Italy, which had held up during the Eurozone crisis, fell dramatically when the pandemic struck.

Fortunately, the EU seems to have learned from its mistakes during the Eurozone crisis and opted to suspend the Fiscal Compact limits on fiscal deficits during the pandemic, something the author had strongly recommended in his 2003 book. Furthermore, Angela Merkel and Emmanuel Macron recognized that the lack of fiscal response to the pandemic represented an existential threat to the European project. The two leaders then led the negotiations on a €750 billion euro-wide fiscal package to help the helpless. The two leaders recognized that if Eurozone voters felt their elected representatives were powerless to address the pandemic as long as they remained in the Eurozone, support for the euro and for democracy itself might crumble.

The two leaders overrode opposition from the Netherlands and a few other countries and weathered four days of tough negotiations to broker a package under which the EU would borrow €750 billion under its own name to help member countries hit hard by the pandemic. This one-off package was at least able to mitigate the suspicions held by many that they were doomed as long as they stayed in the Eurozone.

Whether this euro-wide fiscal package eventually leads to fiscal union remains an open question. If that were to happen, and the region's government bond markets were unified into a single market, the problem of capital flight between government bond markets mentioned at the beginning of the Chapter would disappear. That would allow the Eurozone, at least collectively, to wield fiscal policy like any other country. However, the fact that the arduous negotiations took four days and produced only €390 billion in grants—the actual "rescue" portion of the package—suggests a true consensus has yet to form on the question of fiscal union.

Even if they believe fiscal union is still far off, Eurozone leaders probably concluded that if the euro project is to be preserved, voters must never be left feeling helpless again. To ensure that voters feel empowered to decide their own future, the euro's institutional framework needs to be modified. Such discussions have already started.

The Euro's Institutional Defect

As noted at the beginning of this chapter, Europeans who voted to join the common currency more than two decades ago believed they were only giving up sovereignty over monetary policy. But as subsequent events have shown, they have effectively lost sovereignty over fiscal policy as well. That left national governments unable to respond to voter demands, placing their economies and democratic institutions at risk. This unintended consequence of the euro has both institutional and market-driven causes that must be addressed.

The institutional cause is that the SGP, which caps the fiscal deficits of member countries at 3 percent of GDP, never considered that an economy could be in Cases 3 or 4. In other words, it never envisioned a world in which the private sector was saving more than 3 percent of GDP at a time of zero interest rates. Proponents of the SGP, along with most of the economics profession, assumed the private sector would be borrowing, not saving, at such low interest rates.

But when the housing bubble burst on both sides of the Atlantic in 2008, the private sectors of all affected countries—both inside and outside the Eurozone—rushed to deleverage, saving far more than 3 percent of GDP after central banks had lowered interest rates to zero or even negative levels. Spain's private sector, for example, has been saving over 7 percent of GDP on average since 2008. And if someone is saving 7 percent of GDP, someone else must borrow and spend that 7 percent to keep the national economy from contracting. However, the SPG allowed the Spanish government to borrow only 3 percent of GDP, opening up a deflationary gap equal to 4 percent of GDP and plunging the country into a horrendous recession and internal deflation.

An obvious way to rectify this institutional defect would be to allow member governments to borrow more than 3 percent of GDP when the private sector is saving more than 3 percent of GDP at zero interest rates. This is a necessary condition—but not a sufficient condition—for rectifying the problems unique to the Eurozone.

Capital Flight Is at the Core of Eurozone Problems

This is because even if the SGP is revised in this way, member governments will still face an unforgiving market-driven constraint that has drastically undermined their fiscal policy sovereignty. As noted in the beginning of this chapter, this constraint stems from the fact that all government bonds issued by member governments are denominated in the same currency.

As is explained in Chapter 4, if the private sector in a non-euro country is a huge net saver—that is, if it is running a large financial surplus—in spite of zero interest rates, pension funds and other institutional investors who are entrusted with those savings but are unable to take on substantial foreign exchange risk or put all their money into equities will rush to purchase government bonds. The government, after all, is the only borrower left who is issuing highly rated fixed income assets denominated in the home currency.

This rush brings government bonds yields down to levels that would have been unthinkable when the economy was in Cases 1 and 2. If the government then carefully selects infrastructure projects capable of earning a social rate of return higher than the super-low yield on government bonds, the projects themselves will be self-financing. That allows the government to utilize the nation's savings to fight recessions without burdening future taxpayers. This is the self-corrective mechanism of economies in Cases 3 and 4 that is first noted in Chapter 2.

Eurozone investors, in contrast, can choose from 19 different government bond markets because they are all denominated in the same currency. That means there is no assurance that Spanish savings will be invested in Spanish government bonds or that Portuguese savings will be used to buy Portuguese government bonds.

During the Eurozone crisis that started in 2010, a huge amount of private-sector savings from the peripheral countries went into German government bonds, pushing yields on Bunds to unthinkably low levels while raising the yields on peripheral governments' bonds (Figure 7.10). That happened because the German economy was coming out of a (balance sheet) recession with a shrinking budget deficit, while other member countries were entering a (balance sheet) recession with expanding budget deficits. The foreign exchange risk that ring-fenced government bond markets and channeled excess domestic savings to their own government bond markets in non-Eurozone countries during balance sheet recessions could not do the same in the Eurozone. In other words, the self-corrective mechanism of economies in Cases 3 and 4 does not function very well in the Eurozone.

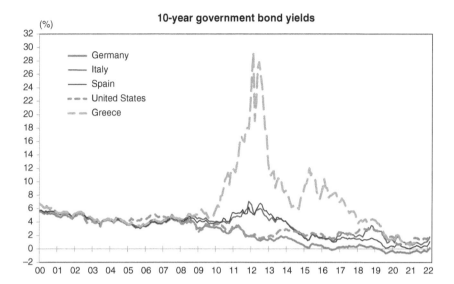

FIGURE 7.10 Eurozone-Specific Capital Flight Led to Eurozone Crisis

Source: Nomura Research Institute, based on data from ECB and Federal Reserve Board (FRB)

That also means the 19 government bond markets end up competing with each other, since investors can dump the debt of any member country that is running large fiscal deficits in favor of bonds issued by other governments that are fiscally better behaved. This often led to the perverse outcome of healthy economies in no need of money being flooded with funds, while countries in balance sheet recessions and desperately in need of funds for fiscal stimulus to counter recessions were unable to borrow, even when their own private sectors are generating plenty of savings.

Market-Based Fiscal Discipline Created a Backlash against Euro

Under this framework, the only options for the Eurozone were (1) to have Germany, the region's fiscal poster child, run much larger budget deficits and thereby enable the other 18 members to do the same, or (2) to have the less fiscally fortunate nations trim their deficits and draw closer to Germany. Germany rejected the first alternative, forcing the other countries with excess savings problems into option (2) with devastating consequences.

This was amply demonstrated during the 2010 Eurozone crisis, when investors sold off the government bonds of many peripheral countries even though every country except Greece was generating *more than enough* private-sector savings at home to finance its budget deficit. In other words, if those countries had been outside the Eurozone, they could have weathered the recession in the same way that the United States or Japan did. However, the sell-off in their government bond markets has prevented Eurozone governments from tapping their own national savings to fund necessary fiscal stimulus.

During the crisis, some unscrupulous U.S.- and U.K.-based investment funds made the situation worse by shorting peripheral government bonds while flooding the media with talk of so-called redenomination risk, that is, the imminent disintegration of the European Monetary Union (EMU). This attack on the euro was contained only when ECB President Draghi declared he would do "whatever it takes" to defend the EMU. Another sell-off was also observed in the Italian government bond market in 2018, when a newly elected government wanted to increase its fiscal spending by about 0.4 percent of GDP. The point is that the threat of such capital flight means no member country can utilize fiscal policy to a greater extent than the Eurozone's best fiscal performer, which at present happens to be Germany.

This loss of fiscal freedom due to "market pressure" persisted even after the constraints of the SGP and the Fiscal Compact were removed in spring of 2020. As the coronavirus spread rapidly throughout the region, the EU declared that the constraints of the Fiscal Compact could be ignored until June 2021. Member countries, however, were still unwilling to take major fiscal action because of concerns about a potential sell-off of their government bonds.

This Eurozone-specific, market-imposed fiscal straitjacket has robbed member countries of their fiscal sovereignty. And if member countries cannot utilize the savings generated by their own private sectors to fight economic downturns, voters will feel they are not in control of their economic destiny and will lose confidence in democratic structures and the euro.

Fiscal Dis-Union Is Needed to Make Monetary Union Work

One way to address this issue is to replace the current limit on fiscal deficits with a rule allowing only *citizens* of a country to hold bonds issued by the government, so that, for example, Portuguese government bonds could be held only by Portuguese citizens. While such a rule might sound outrageous at first, it would not only eliminate the capital flight problem previously described and restore full fiscal sovereignty to member governments, but would also help normalize ECB's monetary policy.

Allowing only the citizens of a country to hold its government's bonds solves the Eurozone-specific problem of capital flight among government bond markets. Institutional investors who need to buy the highest-rated fixed income assets will purchase their own government's bonds, thereby allowing governments to use the savings of their own private sectors to combat balance sheet recessions.

Under this fiscal dis-union scheme, Eurozone residents would lose the right to buy the government bonds of other member countries, and member governments would no longer be allowed to sell their bonds to foreigners. But this would be a small price to pay for the restoration of fiscal sovereignty.

This new regime would also make the financing of fiscal deficits an entirely *internal* matter for individual countries: if a member government goes bust, only its own citizens will be affected. That would remove the justification for Brussels or any other outsiders to meddle in the fiscal policy of member nations, thereby bolstering the democratic institutions of member governments as they regain the ability to respond to voter demands on recessions and public health crises with their own fiscal policies.

This internalization of fiscal policy will also impose discipline on individual governments because they will no longer be able to blame their troubles on the whims of international investors (such as the unscrupulous investment funds noted earlier) or supranational institutions such as the EU and the IMF. This is as it should be: a government that cannot even persuade its own people to hold its bonds has no reason to expect foreigners to buy those bonds instead. That should be welcome news for Germans and others who have been unhappy with the prospect that they might be forced to rescue countries that opted for profligate fiscal policies.

All efficiency gains from the free movement of capital within the Eurozone will also be retained by the private sector because the proposed capital controls apply only to one asset class that lies outside the private sector: government bonds. And foreign holdings of government bonds have never proved to be the best use of capital.

With minimal capital flight and short-term interest rates controlled by the inflation-fighting ECB, bond yields are also likely to stabilize. Because capital flight will be minimal, bond yields in countries that experienced capital outflows in the old framework are likely to decline, while those in countries that experienced capital inflows will go up.

Transitioning to and enforcing the new framework will involve additional costs. A separate arrangement will also have to be made to allow the ECB to hold member governments' bonds for the conduct of monetary policy. But these are not insurmountable issues. Even if some investors manage to find ways around the new rule, the destabilizing capital flight that has plagued the Eurozone for so long will be minimized as long as most institutional investors abide by it.

Fiscal Dis-Union Will also Normalize Monetary Policy

This proposal would also provide massive relief to the ECB, which has been forced to carry out numerous unconventional monetary policies such as QE and negative interest rates precisely because the defective SGP and the above mentioned capital flight prevented member governments from employing fiscal policy to provide necessary support for their economies.

Even though the ECB did everything it could, there is no reason for monetary easing to work when borrowers have disappeared because of balance sheet problems and the economy is in Cases 3 and 4. This loss of monetary policy effectiveness has been amply demonstrated by the ECB's failure to meet its inflation target for 12 consecutive years starting in 2008 despite massive amounts of QE (Figure 2.13) and negative interest rates.

When a recession is caused by a lack of private-sector borrowers, the government must act as borrower of last resort to keep the economy going, and the proposal above would allow Eurozone member governments to perform that role for the first time. That would free the ECB from a burden it could never bear and allow it to exit from the ineffective and potentially costly unconventional monetary easing measures it has been forced to implement. That should be welcome news for the Germans and others who were unhappy with the central bank's "excessively" accommodative policies. In other words, the proposed framework will help normalize not only the fiscal policies of Eurozone member countries, but also the monetary policy of the ECB.

Differentiated Risk Weights as an Alternative to Fiscal Dis-Union

Another less drastic way to keep savings from leaving the country would be to assign lower risk weights to institutional investors' holdings of domestic government bonds relative to foreign government debt. In other words, institutions would be required to hold more capital against holdings of foreign government bonds than against holdings of domestic government bonds, even if they are denominated in the same currency. This could be justified on the grounds that investors should know the risk characteristics of their domestic bond market best.

In this way, Spain's excess savings would be encouraged to flow into Spanish government bonds and Portugal's savings into Portuguese government bonds. The resulting inflow of domestic savings into domestic government bond markets would lower bond yields and provide these countries with the fiscal space they need to engage in necessary fiscal stimulus. Indeed the fiscal dis-union proposal mentioned above should be reinforced with differentiated risk weights so that it will work even better.

The point is that any country that is suffering from a recession caused by excess private-sector savings should be able to finance the necessary fiscal stimulus if it can channel the excess savings that triggered the recession into its own government bond market. The low government bond yields that result should also make many public works projects self-financing if they are carefully chosen. If fiscal dis-union or differentiated risk weights enabled Eurozone governments to utilize this self-corrective mechanism of economies in Cases 3 and 4, then member governments would be no worse off than non-Eurozone governments in their ability to support an economy suffering from a shortage of borrowers.

Recycling Peripheral Savings Back to Peripheral Countries

There is also an option, at least in theory, of recycling departed savings back to the country of origin. For such recycling to work smoothly, however, countries like Germany that are experiencing capital inflows must borrow those funds and then re-lend them to countries like Spain in some sort of automatic arrangement. It has to be automatic so that bond market participants would not have to worry about bond yields being pushed higher by uncertainties surrounding the recycling.

That means net-inflow countries such as Germany would have to quickly determine how much to borrow and recycle back to Spain, Portugal, and so on. But the politics of such a mechanism—including the question of how much to borrow and who will assume the risk—are likely to be difficult to resolve.

The €750 billion package agreed to in July 2020 can be considered a kind of recycling program. The fact that it took the shock of over 100,000 COVID-19 deaths in Europe and more than four full days of arduous negotiations suggests that this approach to recycling is not easy.

If recycling is politically too cumbersome and difficult, perhaps it should be reserved only for truly region-wide challenges like the recent pandemic and Russian induced energy crisis. For day-to-day fiscal operations, fiscal dis-union reinforced with differentiated risk weights should be used to keep recession-inducing excess savings from leaving the country.

Misplaced Fear of "Diabolical" Feedback Loop

Unfortunately, because of the negative feedback loop observed between sovereign and banking crises during the Eurozone debacle that started in 2010, many Eurozone officials are not at all enthusiastic about allowing domestic financial institutions to hold more of their own government's bonds. Indeed, their current inclination is to make it more difficult for domestic banks to do so. But that will make it even harder for member countries to use their own excess private-sector savings to fight balance sheet recessions.

Moreover, this fear of the negative feedback loop is totally misplaced because the origin of the loop is the fundamental inability of Eurozone governments to use fiscal policy to tackle balance sheet recessions. This inability *guarantees* that Eurozone economies in balance sheet recessions will implode when a debt-financed bubble bursts, which, in turn, will exacerbate banking sector problems. The banking problems arise not only because banks have lent money to bubble participants, but also because the imploding economy makes it difficult for *all* borrowers to service their debts. And the same inability to use fiscal policy also prevents the governments from helping their banks, making the situation doubly worse.

When investors realize that the government is unable to stop either the implosion of the economy or the explosion of nonperforming loans (NPLs) in the banking system, they become rightfully scared and move their money to safer locations abroad, resulting in capital flight and higher government bond yields at home. The higher bond yields then force even more austerity on the government, which further exacerbates problems in the economy and the banking sector in a vicious cycle.

The correct way to address this "diabolical" feedback loop is to allow governments to combat balance sheet recessions with fiscal stimulus from the outset, thereby averting the vicious cycle. Once the economy stabilizes, the authorities can repair the banking system with the time-honored measures that are explained in Chapter 8. With no implosion of the domestic economy or the banking system, excess savings in the country will head toward the nation's own government bonds instead of toward higher-priced, lower-yielding foreign government bonds.

Making Monetary Union Work without Fiscal Union

Making monetary union work without fiscal union was never meant to be straightforward. And the "price" of regaining full fiscal sovereignty in a monetary union is fiscal dis-union. Whether that price tag is too high for member countries to regain fiscal freedom should be decided by the voters.

Amending the SGP in the manner recommended here would not be easy either. The *Financial Times'* Martin Wolf, commenting on the author's dis-union proposal, wrote that while the proposal itself was interesting, legal and bureaucratic hurdles would make implementation and enforcement problematic.[6] But the EU has already made numerous supposedly impossible procedural changes in response to EMU challenges, including the inauguration of the banking union and the introduction of capital controls during the crisis in Cyprus. The recent €750 billion EU fiscal package was also supposed to be "impossible."

The dis-union proposal should also be good news for Germans and others concerned about the endgame for the ECB's "crazy" monetary easing policies. The proposed measures would also free Germany from both the pressure to implement more fiscal stimulus and the fear of rescuing profligate member countries. In other words, Germany and other frugal countries in northern Europe should support the present proposal because it gives them everything they have been demanding.

Unlike those who argue that the euro project was a disastrous experiment that should never have been tried, the author believes the euro is one of humanity's greatest achievements, with bright and dedicated people from across the region striving for years to make it work. And it worked quite well before 2008, when most economies were in Cases 1 and 2.

The Eurozone ran into massive problems when it fell into Cases 3 and 4, when fiscal policy became absolutely essential, as predicted by the author in his 2003 book. That means the fundamental cause of the crisis is the Eurozone's inability to deal with economies in Cases 3 and 4, not the absence of fiscal union, lack of progress in structural reforms, or insufficient fiscal stimulus in Germany.

All that is needed in the Eurozone is to ensure that member countries suffering from recessions caused by excess private-sector savings—even at zero interest rates—are able to channel those savings into their own government bond markets, thereby enabling member governments to use those savings to fight recessions. If government expenditures are directed to carefully selected, self-financing projects made possible by low bond yields, there will be no increase in future taxpayers' burden, either.

It is hoped that the EU, the ECB, and member governments will open their eyes to the deflationary danger posed by their private

---

[6] Wolf, Martin (2015), "A Handy Tool—But Not the Only One in the Box," *Financial Times*, January 4, 2015. https://www.ft.com/content/0d3f41dc-86bf-11e4-8a51-00144feabdc0.

sectors' large financial surpluses and implement the fiscal measures proposed here before it is too late. If they do, European voters will no longer be left feeling helpless and can then be expected to resume voting in a direction more conducive to the proper functioning of democracy. The United Kingdom may also rethink its ties with the Eurozone when the latter starts to demonstrate robust growth.

The German Model Is Not for Everyone

At the opposite extreme, the Germans have been obsessed with the notion that the government budget must be balanced. But this obsession ignores the iron law of macroeconomics—namely, that if someone is saving money, someone else must borrow and spend those savings to keep the national economy from contracting. The German preference for balanced budgets—known as *schwarz nul,* or black zero—makes sense only if the German private sector is not a net saver or if foreigners are willing to borrow and spend Germany's savings by running trade deficits with the country. The fact that the German private sector has been a huge net saver (i.e., has been running a financial surplus) to the tune of 6.72 percent of GDP on average for the last two decades means it is foreigners who have propped up the economy. In other words, Germany kept its economy going by running huge trade surpluses with the rest of the world.

Under ordinary circumstances, such large and continuous trade surpluses would have pushed the country's exchange rate sky-high and reduced its export competitiveness and income growth. But Germany's membership in the Eurozone has virtually eliminated this currency appreciation risk and allowed the country to continue exporting. That allowed the country to export its way out of post-2000 balance sheet recession, something that Japanese could not do ten years earlier because the yen kept on appreciating with Japan's large trade surpluses. Although President Donald Trump once complained loudly about the German exchange rate and U.S. trade deficits with the country, he could do nothing about it because Germany belonged to the euro.

Even if there is nothing on the horizon that might dislodge Germany from the plush position it has found for itself in the Eurozone, it makes no sense for the country to insist that other member countries follow its lead. The German model is not a model for other countries or for the world. First, if all other Eurozone members became like Germany, the region would be running such a large trade surplus that the exchange rate of euro would rocket higher, destroying the export competitiveness of Germany and everyone else. Second, by definition, all countries cannot run trade surpluses at the same time. The German model is a partial equilibrium model that works only for Germany in the Eurozone, not a general equilibrium model that works for everyone.

Nothing on the horizon is likely to dislodge Germany from the unique position it currently enjoys, but the country should be mindful of the fact that it has that position precisely because other countries are *not* behaving like it does. It should also work harder to help others in the Eurozone because the disintegration of the bloc has the potential to hurt Germany more than other members.

Three Problems with Milton Friedman's Call for Free Markets

When Milton Friedman, Nobel Laureate and neoliberal champion of free markets, monetary policy, and small government, visited Japan in the 1950s and spoke to economist Kazushi Nagasu, he had strong things to say about the plight of his people: "I am a Jew . . . I do not think I need to tell you what kind of horrible deaths Jewish people had to face. The real drive behind my argument for free markets is the bloodied cries of Jewish people who perished under Hitler's and Stalin's regimes, and their message is that the best way to happiness is to have a framework that brings people together where states, races and political systems have no influence."[7]

Although many sympathize with Friedman and agree that a free market provides that ideal framework, he is wrong on at least three counts. The first is his assumption that markets driven by a profit-maximizing private sector can never go wrong. But every several decades the private sector loses its head in a bubble—something observed most recently in the dot-com bubble that burst in 2000 and the housing bubble that imploded in 2008.

During a bubble, the private sector engages in a frenzy of speculation and ends up misallocating trillions of dollars of resources, the

---

[7] Uchihashi, Katsuto (2009), "Shinpan Akumu-no Saikuru: Neo-riberarizumu Junkan" ("Cycle of Nightmares: The Recurrence of Neoliberalism"), updated version, in Japanese, *Bunshun Bunko*, Japan, pp. 88–89.

scale of which no government could ever hope to match. In other words, markets work well when businesses and households have cool heads, but not when a bubble has formed. And bubbles are easier to form in the pursued era than in the golden era when Friedman was formulating his theories.

When the bubble bursts, the private sector comes to its senses and realizes it must remove its debt overhang by minimizing debt. But when a large part of the private sector is engaged in debt minimization at the same time, the economy falls into a devastating fallacy-of-composition problem called a balance sheet recession.

This is where Friedman made his second mistake. He argued that monetary policy—whereby the central bank supplies liquidity and lowers interest rates—should be mobilized to counter recessions. That was the right policy to employ when he was developing his theories in the 1950s and 1960s, as the United States was in a golden era and its economy was in Case 1 or 2. But once the economy enters a balance sheet recession or the pursued phase and the private sector stops borrowing money, the economy is in Case 3 or 4, and monetary policy is no longer effective. It stops working because an absence of borrowers even at zero interest rates prevents funds supplied by the central bank from entering the real economy.

His third mistake was that his emphasis on small government caused him to oppose the use of fiscal stimulus, which to him symbolized big government and intervention by the state. But in a balance sheet recession, the government *must* act as borrower (and spender) of last resort. There is no other way to keep the economy out of a deflationary spiral and give the private sector the income it needs to pay down debt and rebuild its balance sheet.

Friedman's overriding emphasis on the supremacy of markets, monetary policy, and small government allows no room for government to act as borrower of last resort. But it was the failure of the Brüning government to do just that that led to Germany's economic collapse and paved the way for Adolf Hitler's rise to power in 1933. The failure of the French, U.K. and U.S. governments to act as borrowers of last resort not only enhanced Hitler's reputation, but also prevented those governments from presenting a credible deterrent to his rapidly expanding military. To prevent the tragedy of another Holocaust, it is essential that the public be taught what a balance sheet recession is and how to fight it with fiscal stimulus.

CHAPTER 8

Money and Banking in the Other Half of Macroeconomics

When a bubble bursts, the economy typically faces an absence of both borrowers and lenders (Case 4). The absence of borrowers causes a balance sheet recession, which is a macroeconomic phenomenon. The absence of lenders causes a credit crunch, which is a financial phenomenon. Depending on the nature and size of the bubble and the subsequent policy response, one can also happen without the other.

Lenders disappear from the scene because they lent money to participants in the bubble, many of whom became insolvent or unable to service debts after the bubble burst. The post-bubble balance sheet recession will also reduce the incomes of those who were not involved in the bubble. That, in turn, undermines their ability to service their debts. The resultant increase in nonperforming loans (NPLs) erodes banks' capital, leaving them unable to lend. Many lenders may find themselves effectively bankrupt as well.

Two Banking System Externalities

When banks are unable to function fully because of impaired balance sheets, the broader society suffers in two ways. First, banks are at the core of the payment system. Because everything from utility bills to college tuition is paid via the banking system, a breakdown here can have a devastating economic impact. Banks' second function is to ensure that saved funds are borrowed and spent, thereby keeping the economy going. A failure of this intermediation function will also lead to the sort of $1,000–$900–$810–$730 deflationary spiral discussed earlier.

On the first point, banks have to make hundreds of thousands of payments on behalf of depositors for a wide variety of purposes every day. In making those payments, banks are merely *passive* executors of requested transactions. They have no prior knowledge of when a depositor will purchase something or what the price will be.

Banks also receive a large number of payments on behalf of depositors from depositors at other banks. But there is no guarantee that the payments they receive one day will match the payments they have to make to other banks on the same day. To help them deal with this significant daily uncertainty, interbank markets and central banks were created to ensure that banks always have enough funds to meet payment requirements.

The interbank market was created to allow banks with net inflows to lend their surplus reserves to banks experiencing net outflows. Since the aggregate inflows and outflows for the banking system should sum to zero, a fully functioning interbank market should keep the payment system from running into difficulties.

But when a bubble bursts and many borrowers go bankrupt, banks begin to distrust each other because they are all saddled with large and growing portfolios of NPLs. When banks are saddled with many NPLs, those with net inflows refuse to loan out excess funds on the interbank market because they worry the borrower may go under without repaying the loan. A dysfunctional interbank market thereby threatens the continued functioning of the payment system, which is crucial to the economy.

To counter this vulnerability, central banks were created to serve as lenders of last resort to the banks. If a bank faces an excessively large outflow of funds (or the interbank market becomes dysfunctional), it can go to the central bank to borrow the funds needed to make the payment. Since the advent of central banks, virtually all payments between banks have been settled through accounts they have with the central bank. In the United States these are known as "fed funds."

Regarding the second function of banks, bank capital may fall below the required minimum when losses are incurred on NPLs. When that happens, banks must abstain from lending because their capital is not considered sufficient to absorb the associated risks. And when such capital problems prevent many banks from lending, the economy faces a predicament known as a credit crunch.

The entire economy suffers when banks are unable to lend the savings entrusted to them because saved funds cannot re-enter the economy's income stream even if there is a plentiful supply of borrowers. Indeed, this lender-side problem can also trigger the $1,000–$900–$810–$730 deflationary spiral. These lender-side difficulties, when coupled with borrowers' debt overhang problems, throw the economy into Case 4.

The potential for a dysfunctional banking system to damage the entire economy means there are large externalities to the banking business. Since banks' continued functioning is essential to the economy, government cannot treat them like any other private-sector business. That is why banks in every country are closely supervised by the government.

When problems arise in the banking sector, the government and the central bank are expected to implement the sorts of policies that are described under Case 2 in Chapter 1 to ensure that banking functions are maintained. For example, if the interbank market has become dysfunctional, the central bank is expected to act as lender of last resort to help banks experiencing net outflows. If the NPL-induced credit crunch is bad enough to threaten a deflationary spiral, the government must inject capital into the banks to enable them to resume lending.

Japan recapitalized its banks in 1998–99, and the United States did the same with Troubled Asset Relief Program (TARP) in 2008. Although such capital injections tend to be extremely unpopular because they seem to favor banks over other private-sector businesses, they usually succeed in restoring banks' lending function within a few quarters. The point is that the remedies for a financial crisis are well known and, once implemented, will usually resolve lenders' problems within a year or two. Once the banking system resumes functioning, the economy moves from Case 4 to Case 3.

While central bank monetary policy is largely useless in bringing back borrowers facing balance sheet problems or inferior returns on capital issues, it is absolutely essential in helping lenders emerge from a financial crisis. Lenders' and borrowers' problems are summarized in Figure 6.10.

Are Eurozone Banking Problems Still Unresolved?

When Lehman Brothers' failure triggered the global financial crisis (GFC) in 2008, both the West and Japan faced massive banking-sector problems. While the United States, United Kingdom, and Japan implemented the kinds of measures previously noted to address the banking crisis in the first two years, the Eurozone continued to struggle with these problems for years after the GFC.

The primary cause of the Eurozone's banking-sector problems is that the economy itself continued to struggle for the reasons that are noted in the previous chapter. In particular, the Stability and Growth Pact (SGP) prevents member governments from borrowing more than 3 percent of gross domestic product (GDP) even though their private sectors have been saving 5 to 10 percent of GDP since 2008 in order to repair balance sheets damaged by the housing bubble's collapse. But if the private sector in aggregate is saving 7 percent of GDP, as is the case in Spain today, and the government is allowed to borrow only 3 percent of GDP, the remaining 4 percent will leak out of the economy's income stream and become a deflationary gap. With governments unable to fill that gap, it is hardly surprising that problems in the economy and banking sector persist. The fact that the Eurozone's 19 government bond markets are all denominated in the same currency has also created horrendous capital flight problems noted in Chapter 7 that ordinary countries never had to face.

GDP can be maintained if the government can borrow and spend the private sector's excess savings. If it is maintained, businesses and households will have the income needed to service their debts even if they are technically insolvent. And if borrowers continue to service their debts, banks' NPL problems will remain manageable. Many borrowers might actually succeed in working through their debt overhang given sufficient time.

Japanese banks in 1997 went through an experience similar to that of European banks after 2008 as a result of premature fiscal consolidation. Under pressure from the International Monetary Fund (IMF), the Ryutaro Hashimoto administration opted for austerity when the private sector was still saving more than 5 percent of GDP to repair balance sheets damaged when the bubble burst in 1990. Japan's economy promptly fell into a classic $1,000–$900–$810–$730 deflationary spiral starting in April 1997 and contracted for five straight quarters. That proved to be the final blow for both borrowers and lenders who had done everything they could to service debt for seven years after the bubble burst, and a nationwide banking crisis and credit crunch erupted in October 1997.

That forced the Japanese government to mobilize all the policy tools at its disposal, including a recapitalization of the banking sector, to overcome the crisis. Even with all those efforts, it still took until 1999, nearly two years later, for things to return to normal (this point is discussed further a bit later with regard to Figure 8.6). The point is that the macroeconomic background is very important when dealing with banking crises, and the Eurozone banking crisis is no different.

Two Eurozone Misunderstandings Regarding Japanese and U.S. Banking Problems

Banking crises are frequent occurrences in post-bubble economies, but the Eurozone authorities have also made a number of mistakes in handling the crisis that delayed the recovery in both the banking sector and the real economy. In particular, they have not only failed to make the crucial distinction between ordinary and systemic banking crises, but have also misunderstood the lessons offered by Japan and the United States. Even worse, they have forcefully implemented policies based on those misunderstandings.

The Eurozone authorities believed that Japan's long economic slump occurred because banks and the government were unwilling to address NPL problems, at least until the arrival of Koizumi administration in 2001, more than 10 years after the bubble burst in 1990. In the United States, they thought the economy recovered so swiftly after 2008 because monetary authorities required banks to quickly dispose of their NPLs in accordance with market principles. Those two views led the European authorities to conclude that their own banks also needed to dispose of NPLs swiftly in order to hasten the economic recovery.

Unfortunately, both of those beliefs were fundamentally incorrect, and they resulted in a sluggish recovery for the European banking system and economy.

Japanese Banks Began Writing Off Bad Loans Early On

Many Western pundits over the last two decades have attributed Japan's economic stagnation to banks' tardiness in writing off bad loans. But this view is completely mistaken, as I noted at the time. How this myth was created and disseminated by certain unscrupulous Wall Street types is discussed later in the chapter.

The first political leader in Japan to raise the issue of NPLs following the bursting of the bubble in 1990 was Prime Minister Kiichi Miyazawa, who argued in 1992 that a quick resolution of this problem using public funds would reduce the future cost to taxpayers. Unfortunately, ignorant Japanese media pundits, business leaders, and politicians rejected Miyazawa's plan not only because bank rescues are politically unpopular in any country, but also because they had no understanding of how to handle a banking crisis since Japan had not experienced such a crisis since the war.

Fortunately, this rejection only delayed the clean-up process by about two years. Japanese banks began setting aside huge provisions against NPLs in 1995 (Figure 8.1). Consequently, some 80 percent of the bad loan losses had already been provisioned against *before* Junichiro Koizumi became prime minister in 2001. It is simply not true that Japanese banks were reluctant to provision against their NPLs until Koizumi arrived.

Why NPLs Did Not Decline Even as Provisions Rose

In spite of this, most overseas analysts continue to believe that Japan was slow to address its bad loan problems because the official data on NPLs showed them increasing until 2001 (Figure 8.2). But, in fact, this was only on paper: Japan's tax authorities, out of a desire to bolster revenues, refused to acknowledge the bad loans as NPLs long after they had been designated as such by both the banks and the Ministry of Finance's banking bureau.

Banks were therefore forced to keep the loans on their books and provision against them using *after-tax* earnings. This ridiculous state of affairs had to continue until the tax authorities finally recognized individual NPLs as losses based on their own definition of what constitutes a total loss, a process that took years. The point

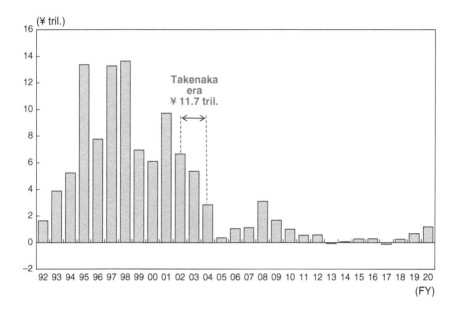

FIGURE 8.1 Japanese Banks' Losses on Bad Loan Disposals

Note: Includes commercial banks only; investment banks, insurance companies, and other financial institutions are not included.

Source: Financial Services Agency, Japan, "FSA Publishes the Status of Loans Held by All Banks as of the End of March 2021, Based on the Financial Reconstruction Act"

is that Japan's NPL statistics did not reflect the loan-loss provisions already made by the banks.

Faced with such a ridiculous tax regime, the Ministry of Finance (MOF) banking bureau came up with a "grand bargain" in 1998 to provide an incentive for banks to proceed quickly with NPL disposals. This "bargain" allowed Japanese lenders to count as capital (deferred tax assets) the taxes they had paid and would eventually recoup—and which would not have been due if the tax authorities had properly classified the loans as NPLs from the outset.

The scheme worked, and Japanese banks effectively wrote off problem loans by increasing provisions while piling up deferred tax assets as capital. This led to an unusual situation in which deferred tax assets increased massively after 1998 (Figure 8.3) and accounted for a substantial portion of Japanese banks' capital (Figure 8.4).

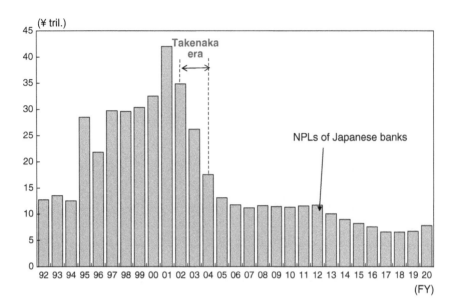

FIGURE 8.2 Japanese Banks' NPLs

Note: Includes commercial banks only; investment banks, insurance companies, and other financial institutions are not included.

Source: Financial Services Agency, Japan, "FSA Publishes the Status of Loans Held by All Banks as of the End of March 2021, Based on the Financial Reconstruction Act"

Heizō Takenaka, the Koizumi administration's financial services minister in 2002, did not bother to understand the tax issues behind this grand bargain, and created great turmoil by demanding that banks reduce their deferred tax assets to levels in line with those in the United States in what became known as the "Takenaka shock." He appeared totally unaware of the different tax treatment of NPLs in Japan and the United States, where tax authorities accept the NPL designations of banks and the banking authorities. His action fomented unnecessary confusion and triggered a nationwide credit crunch. The point is that Japanese banks did not delay their bad loan disposals to the extent suggested by some official statistics or by overseas commentators.

Takenaka and other self-proclaimed "reformists" who dominated the Japanese media in the late 1990s also pushed strongly for bailins, which would have forced large depositors and bond holders to

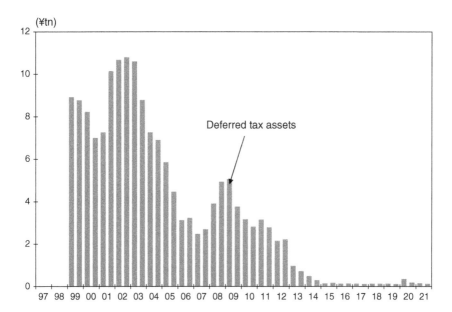

FIGURE 8.3 Deferred Tax Assets of Japanese Banks Jumped after "Grand Bargain" in 1998

Source: Nomura Research Institute, based on data from Japanese Bankers Association

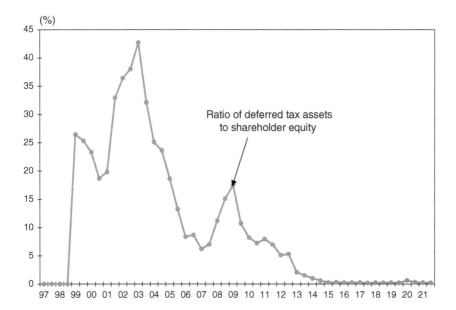

FIGURE 8.4 Deferred Tax Assets' Share of Japanese Bank Capital Soared after 1998

Source: Nomura Research Institute, based on data from Japanese Bankers Association

accept losses during bank failures. They argued that pressure from depositors and other creditors would force banks to improve their management. This approach is not dissimilar to the views of Jeroen Dijsselbloem of the Netherlands, the chairman of the Eurogroup of finance ministers from 2013 to 2018 who also pushed for bail-ins. Takenaka and company even concocted the fake notion that Japan's adoption of bail-ins was an "international commitment"[1] in their attempt to dismantle the blanket deposit guarantee implemented in 1995. Although some discipline imposed by depositors on bank management is useful under certain circumstances, forcing depositors to accept losses via bail-ins would have been nothing short of national suicide in a country where commercial real estate prices had fallen 87 percent nationwide (Figure 2.1) and all of its banks had rock-bottom credit ratings (Figure 8.5).

By then, no Japanese bank was rated above D minus in Moody's financial strength ratings,[2] and most were at the lowest rating of E, when banks are generally expected to be rated B or higher. With all of the nation's lenders carrying such rock-bottom ratings, any bank closure accompanied by a bail-in would have triggered a massive panic among large depositors at all banks. A panic would have ensued as large depositors had no place to go because all the other banks would have had credit ratings just as low as the bank that was shut down.

A bank run precipitated by small depositors can be handled easily by having the central bank bring in and display stacks of bills to depositors waiting outside the bank offices. But if large depositors at all banks, most of which are corporations keeping funds in the banks to pay their workers, are simultaneously forced to withdraw cash to protect themselves, catastrophe will result.

This sort of madness was only narrowly averted when the author personally persuaded Shizuka Kamei, then serving as chairman of the Liberal Democratic Party's Policy Planning Committee, to postpone the introduction of bail-ins in December 1999. And not a single country raised objections to Japan extending its blanket deposit guarantee, in complete contradiction to the prediction made by the likes of Takenaka, who argued that Japan will be punished for not

---

[1] The Japanese term was *kokusai-koyaku*.

[2] Moody's stopped publishing these ratings in 2015.

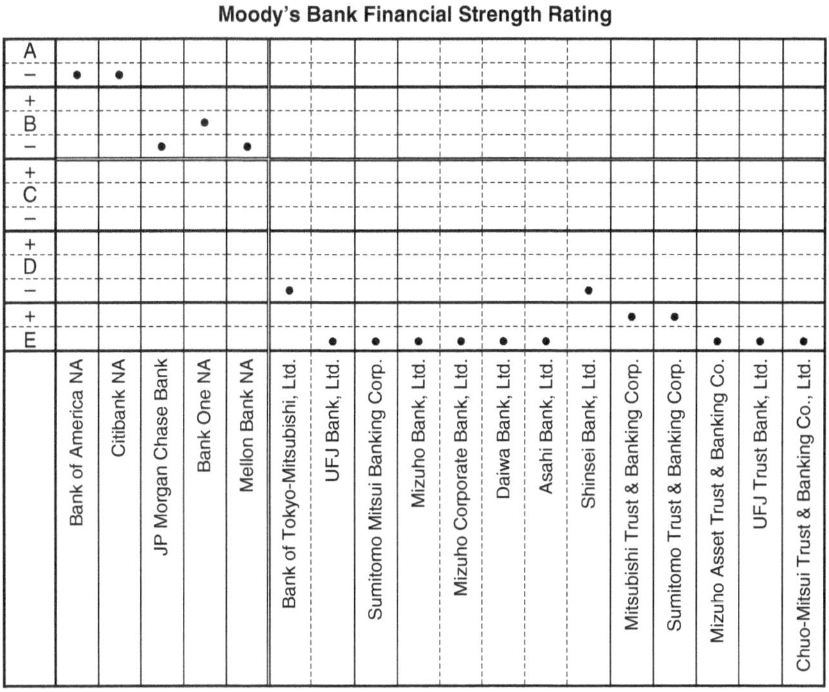

Moody's Bank Financial Strength Rating

Rating	Bank of America NA	Citibank NA	JP Morgan Chase Bank	Bank One NA	Mellon Bank NA	Bank of Tokyo-Mitsubishi, Ltd.	UFJ Bank, Ltd.	Sumitomo Mitsui Banking Corp.	Mizuho Bank, Ltd.	Mizuho Corporate Bank, Ltd.	Daiwa Bank, Ltd.	Asahi Bank, Ltd.	Shinsei Bank, Ltd.	Mitsubishi Trust & Banking Corp.	Sumitomo Trust & Banking Corp.	Mizuho Asset Trust & Banking Co.	UFJ Trust Bank, Ltd.	Chuo-Mitsui Trust & Banking Co., Ltd.
A																		
−	•	•																
+																		
B				•														
−			•		•													
+																		
C																		
−																		
+																		
D																		
−						•							•					
+														•	•			
E						•	•	•	•	•	•	•				•	•	•

FIGURE 8.5 Credit Ratings of Japanese Banks in 2002 Were Too Low to Implement Bail-Ins by Removing Blanket Deposit Guarantee

Note: As of November 1, 2002.

Source: Moody's

meeting its (nonexistent) "international commitment." Interestingly, when Takenaka himself became Financial Services Minister from 2002 to 2005, he did not implement a single bail-in.

The Real Cause of Japan's Slump Can Be Traced to Borrowers, Not Lenders

As for the impact of Japan's banking crisis on the real economy, the Bank of Japan (BOJ) has for decades been asking 10,000 large and small businesses for their views on the "lending attitude of financial institutions" in its quarterly Tankan survey (upper portion of

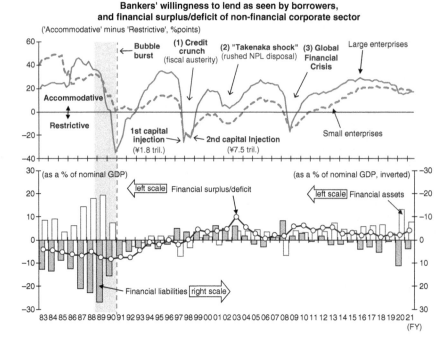

FIGURE 8.6 Japanese Banks Were Willing Lenders, with Three Exceptions

Notes: Shaded areas indicate periods of BOJ monetary tightening. For the latest figures in the lower chart, four-quarter averages ending in 2021 Q3 are used.

Sources: Bank of Japan, "Tankan," "Flow of Funds Accounts;" Cabinet Office, Japan, "National Accounts"

Figure 8.6). According to this survey of corporate borrowers, Japanese banks have been willing lenders for most of the last 30 years. The only exceptions were three credit crunches, each of which was triggered by factors outside the banking sector.

The first credit crunch, in 1997, was caused by the economic collapse that resulted directly from austerity programs implemented by the Hashimoto administration under pressure from the IMF, as noted in Chapter 2. The second crunch was a result of the maddening demand by Financial Services Minister Takenaka to undo the grand bargain reached in 1998, as previously noted. The third crunch was sparked by the Lehman Brothers collapse and the subsequent GFC, which originated in the United States. At all other times Japanese banks were willing lenders, at least in the view of the 10,000 corporate borrowers surveyed by the BOJ. By 2019, just before the onslaught of the COVID-19 pandemic, bankers' willingness to lend— especially to small and medium-sized firms—had returned to levels last seen during the bubble era.

Nevertheless, the bar graph at the bottom of Figure 8.6[3] shows that businesses not only did not borrow during this period, but were actually paying down debt from 1995 to 2012 (shaded bars above zero) in spite of zero interest rates. Even though some businesses have resumed borrowing since 2013, indicating that their balance sheets have been cleaned up, the corporate sector as a whole remained a net saver to the tune of 2.9 percent of GDP on average from 2013 to 2020. That means Japan's non-financial corporate sector has been refusing to borrow even though banks have been willing lenders and companies have completed their balance sheet repairs.

This indicates that the main reason for the weakness in Japan's economy was that borrowers disappeared *faster* than lenders: businesses that could not find attractive investment opportunities at home or whose balance sheets had been damaged when the bubble burst were all saving money or paying down debt in spite of zero interest rates. Even after their balance sheets are repaired by 2013, many were so badly traumatized by the painful deleveraging experiences that they continued to stay away from borrowings. Indeed, the Japanese corporate sector has been a net saver to the tune of 1.86 percent of GDP on average over the last 30 years despite zero interest rates (Figure 4.2). Japan's economy has been stuck in Case 3 since 1991 except for the three brief credit crunches previously noted, when it found itself in Case 4.

Japan certainly had banking problems. But that was not the main cause of the country's economic stagnation because borrowers disappeared faster than lenders. In such a situation, fixing the banks would not have boosted the economy because borrowers, not lenders, were the constraint on growth. Unless there is a credit crunch, therefore, policy makers in such circumstances should focus on fixing the economy first. It is interesting to note that this phenomenon of borrowers disappearing faster than lenders was also observed in the United States during the Great Depression according

---

[3] This is the same chart as shown in Figure 4.2.

to a survey of 3,438 manufacturers conducted by the National Conference Board in 1932.[4]

The IMF, which was surprised to learn the truth about Japan's banking problems after the author pointed it out with the preceding charts in a meeting held at its Washington, D.C., headquarters in 2009, flew him as a speaker to a seminar titled, "How Japan Recovered from Its Banking Crisis: Possible Lessons for Today" at the annual meeting of the IMF and the World Bank in Istanbul on October 6, 2009. The goal was to try to foster a proper understanding of what actually happened in Japan when the West was suffering from a similar banking crisis following the collapse of Lehman Brothers in September 2008.

Unfortunately, people will believe anything if it is repeated often enough, and in spite of the IMF's efforts in Istanbul, most people in Europe continue to argue that Japan offers a cautionary tale in its reluctance to deal with bad loans. And it is this incorrect belief that has been hampering the recovery of the European banking system. Japan addressed the banking crisis much sooner than is commonly believed in the West, but that did not help its economy recover because the main driver of the recession was a lack of borrowers.

U.S. Rescue of Commercial Real Estate Went against Market Principles but Led to Recovery

Turning to the United States in the post-2008 era, it is shocking to note that many European banking officials actually believe the U.S. economy recovered so quickly after 2008 because U.S. authorities forced banks to swiftly address their NPL problems. The truth, however, was just the opposite. In particular, European officials appear to be completely unaware of the "Policy Statement on Prudent Commercial Real Estate Loan Workouts" that was jointly implemented by the Federal Reserve, the Federal Deposit Insurance Corporation (FDIC), and the Office of the Comptroller of the Currency (OCC) on October 30, 2009,[5]

---

[4] For details, please see Koo, Richard C. (2008), *The Holy Grail of Macroeconomics: Lessons from Japan's Great Recession*, Singapore: John Wiley & Sons. pp. 99–100.

[5] https://www.federalreserve.gov/boarddocs/srletters/2009/SR0907.htm.

in an attempt to rescue both the banks and the commercial real estate market. The U.S. authorities also announced a blanket deposit guarantee at the outset of the Lehman crisis so that nobody in the country will have to worry about bail-ins in a bank failure.

By October 2009, commercial real estate prices in the United States had already plunged 40 percent from their peak[6] (Figure 4.7), and the refinancing crisis for commercial real estate loans was so bad that many thought the commercial real estate would be the next pillar to fall after the residential housing market. A collapse of the commercial real estate market at that juncture would have completely devastated the U.S. economy and its banks and made the recovery many times more difficult and expensive.

Faced with this massive crisis, the three U.S. banking authorities noted above took the highly unusual step of asking banks to roll over existing commercial real estate loans even when the loan's outstanding balance far exceeded the value of the underlying collateral. This request, known by banks as the "pretend and extend" policy, succeeded in averting a crisis in the commercial real estate market. This is clearly indicated by Figure 4.7, which shows that the policy not only stopped the prices from falling, but also sparked a recovery in that market.

Together with President Obama's $787 billion fiscal stimulus package for the real economy, "pretend and extend" laid a foundation for the subsequent banking recovery. It also cost U.S. taxpayers nothing. Today, U.S. commercial real estate prices are 68 percent higher than at their 2007 peak. The point is that, instead of forcing banks to recognize losses quickly, as assumed by the European banking authorities, U.S. banking authorities actually asked the banks to pretend that everything was fine so that they could continue to extend their loans to commercial real estate borrowers.

---

[6]This is the amount of price decline policy makers and market participants were looking at in October 2009. This data series was subsequently revised in September 2017, and the amount of decline shown in Figure 4.7 reflects the revised data, not the data policy makers were basing their decisions on in October 2009.

Volcker's "Pretend and Extend" Saved the World during Latin the American Debt Crisis

October 2009 was by no means the only time U.S. banking authorities had resorted to a "pretend and extend" policy. A similar policy was adopted during the Latin American debt crisis, which erupted in 1982. This crisis, which started in Mexico but soon spread to all Latin American borrowers, was at the time the country's worst postwar financial crisis and left seven of the eight largest U.S. banks insolvent and hundreds of others in equally bad shape.

The author was personally involved in helping to resolve this crisis as the Federal Reserve Bank of New York economist in charge of syndicated eurodollar loans, the instrument U.S. banks used to lend money to Latin American borrowers. He can attest that the United States survived the crisis only because Fed Chairman Paul Volcker announced a "pretend and extend" policy on the day the crisis erupted and kept it in place for a full *seven* years thereafter.

When Mexico went belly up in August 1982, Volcker immediately requested all U.S. banks with more than $1 million in exposure to the country to continue rolling over loans that came due, even though Mexico was effectively bankrupt. This was necessary because if one bank had been allowed to leave Mexico with whatever dollars the country still had, all the other banks would have tried to do the same, resulting in a complete collapse of both the banks and the Mexican economy.

Volcker also quickly assured banks that the authorities would *not* treat those loans as bad loans (even though they were). This assurance was necessary to free the banks from the regulatory requirement to write off NPLs, which would have caused another massive fallacy-of-composition problem and made the crisis far worse. If all banks had tried to dump their impaired Mexican assets in the market at the same time, there would have been no buyers, and the prices of the assets would have collapsed (as happened with collateralized debt obligations (CDOs) containing subprime mortgages in 2008). The resultant free-fall in asset prices, which would have forced the banks to mark down those assets that are still on their books, would have further aggravated the crisis in a vicious cycle. This policy of forbearance, which was also enacted jointly by the Fed, the FDIC, and the OCC, remained in place for seven years, giving U.S. banks the time they needed to rebuild their capital and balance sheets.

How difficult that seven years was for the banks and the Fed can be gleaned from an incident in 1987 when Citibank, which instigated the Latin American lending craze in the first place in the late 1970s, managed to recapitalize itself to the point where it could write off its Latin American NPLs. When it announced its intention to do so, Paul Volcker publicly disparaged the move as being selfish and unwelcome. He had to do so to ensure that other banks, which were still struggling, did not feel pressured to follow Citibank. Had they been forced to follow Citi's lead, the whole rescue package could have disintegrated then and there. Citibank went ahead and wrote off its Latin American debt anyway, but this incident was not lost on the Fed.

In 1991, Citicorp experienced a serious capital shortage when an insurance company it had lent money to went bankrupt. The bank then tried to negotiate with the Fed to modify the accounting treatment of the incident so that the capital shortage would not look so bad. The Fed, remembering the bank's selfish action in 1987, flatly denied the request, forcing Citicorp to scurry for capital at short notice. Luckily for the bank, Prince Alwaleed of Saudi Arabia was willing to put up the money needed to keep it afloat.

But this incident shows how difficult that seven years was for the Fed and the banks. When the entire banking system is on the brink of collapse, what might be the right thing to do under ordinary circumstances, such as writing off NPLs, can become the worst thing to do because of the fallacy-of-composition problems. And the banking authorities must recognize those pitfalls immediately and move quickly, as Paul Volcker did in 1982 and again in 1987 with the Citibank action.

In 1989, after lenders had finally regained their financial health sufficiently to absorb their Latin American losses, the authorities introduced Brady bonds to bring the saddest chapter in postwar U.S. banking history to an end. While many have heard of the bonds, few are aware of the crucial measures, including the "pretend and extend" and forbearance policies, that U.S. authorities implemented in the preceding seven years to prevent a full-blown crisis.

These two examples from 1982 and 2009 show that while the U.S. banking authorities seek market-based solutions when banking problems are limited in scale, that approach goes out the window during a systemic crisis, when many banks are confronting the same problem at the same time. U.S. policy makers then opt for pragmatism above all else.

Eurozone Fails to Distinguish between Ordinary and Systemic Banking Crises

European officials seem curiously unaware of the crucial distinction between ordinary and systemic banking crises. In an ordinary crisis, where only a small number of banks are in trouble, the European authorities' preferred, market-based solution of quickly disposing of NPLs is appropriate. This is because the rest of the banking system and the economy can absorb the shock. But in a systemic banking crisis where many banks are affected simultaneously, such a solution can easily result in massive self-defeating fallacy-of-composition problems.

In the systemic case, it is crucial to save *all* banks so that no fallacy-of-composition problems can manifest themselves. This is neither an easy nor a popular decision to make as righteous pundits will decry the moral hazard issues involved in saving badly managed banks. But only those who predicted the crisis and warned the public in advance have any right to talk about moral hazard. Everyone else, who did not see the crisis coming, is part of the problem, not part of the solution. And there were not many individuals in Europe who saw the GFC coming and warned the public beforehand.

Unfortunately, no one in post-2008 Europe wanted to make the above unpopular decision. The resultant failure to save all banks led to prolonged banking problems and depressed economy for nearly a decade.

This fundamental failure to make a distinction between ordinary and systemic banking crises in Europe was made worse by the authorities' ignorance of the U.S. use of "pretend and extend" policies in both 1982 and 2009 to address systemic banking crises. This misreading of events in the United States, coupled with a mistaken belief that Japan's prolonged slump was caused by an unwillingness to write off bad loans, prompted European banking authorities to push for quick NPL disposals, bail-ins, and high capital asset ratios in the midst of a massive systemic crisis. Such policies only exacerbated the banking sector paralysis because the quick disposal of NPLs reduced bank capital while forced bail-ins scared away potential providers of capital to the banks.

Even without forced bail-ins, there are far fewer providers of capital in a systemic banking crisis since so many financial institutions are facing similar problems. That increases the cost of capital if it is available at all. But expensive capital will increase the pressure on banks to cut lending. If banks reduce lending in order to economize on capital and achieve required capital-to-asset ratios, the credit crunch that is already choking the economy will only grow worse. The resultant weakness in the economy then aggravates banks' NPL problems in a vicious cycle.

Visualizing the Eurozone Credit Crunch

The systemic nature of the European banking crisis and the extent to which banks were economizing on capital (leading to a credit crunch) can be observed using flow-of-funds data. Figure 8.7

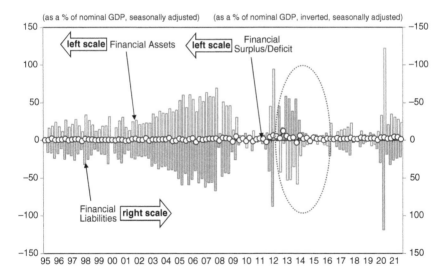

FIGURE 8.7 Credit Crunch in Spanish Financial Sector

Notes: Seasonal adjustments by Nomura Research Institute. Latest figures are for 2021 Q3.

Sources: Nomura Research Institute, based on flow of funds data from Banco de España and National Statistics Institute, Spain

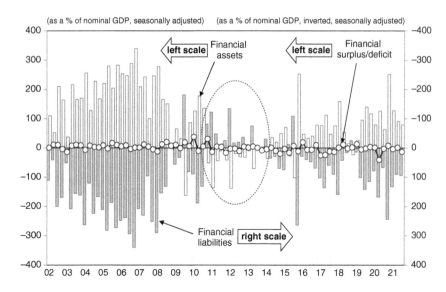

FIGURE 8.8 Credit Crunch in Irish Financial Sector

Notes: Seasonal adjustments by Nomura Research Institute. Latest figures are for 2021 Q3.

Source: Nomura Research Institute, based on flow of funds data from Central Bank of Ireland and Central Statistics Office, Ireland

provides flow-of-funds data for the Spanish financial sector. It shows that while the initial shock triggered by the Lehman bankruptcy in 2008 was not that severe, the situation grew much worse starting in 2012 during the Eurozone crisis when the shaded bars went above zero and the white bars went below zero (the circled area) for nearly four years. In effect, banks were reducing both assets (i.e., loans) and liabilities in order to economize on capital and enhance their capital ratios. But those actions made the credit crunch much worse than it already was and devastated the Spanish economy.

Irish banks were particularly hard hit when that nation's housing bubble burst. This can be seen in Figure 8.8, which shows white bars below zero and shaded bars above zero from mid-2010 through the end of 2013 (the circled area).

In Portugal, which did not experience a large housing bubble, banks were relatively calm until the Eurozone crisis hit in 2012 (Figure 8.9). The white bars then moved deeply below the

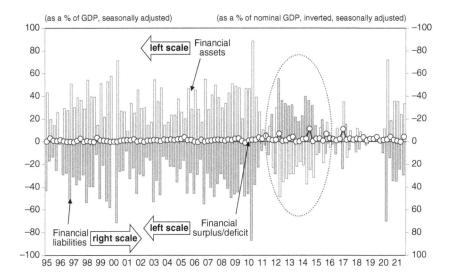

FIGURE 8.9 Credit Crunch in Portuguese Financial Sector

Notes: Seasonal adjustments by Nomura Research Institute. Latest figures are for 2021 Q3.

Source: Nomura Research Institute, based on flow of funds data from Banco de Portugal

zero line and the shaded bars deeply above the zero line until the end of 2015 (the circled area), indicating a huge contraction in Portuguese banking activity during this period.

Even in Germany, which had no housing bubble, banks shrank their balance sheets after 2008 (Figure 8.10) because many of them were caught holding U.S. CDOs containing toxic subprime loans. German banks bought CDOs in response to the disappearance of domestic private-sector borrowers after the dot-com bubble burst in 2000, as is noted in the previous chapter. Indeed, the post-2008 reaction of German banks was far more violent than when they faced the collapse of the dot-com bubble and the crash of the Neuer Markt back in 2000. In most quarters from 2008 to 2013, the white bars were below zero and the shaded bars were above zero (the circled area), a distressing state of affairs that had seldom been observed in the past.

In comparison, the turmoil in the U.S. financial sector was much milder and more short-lived, as shown in Figure 8.11, even though it received far more press attention because it was the epicenter of the

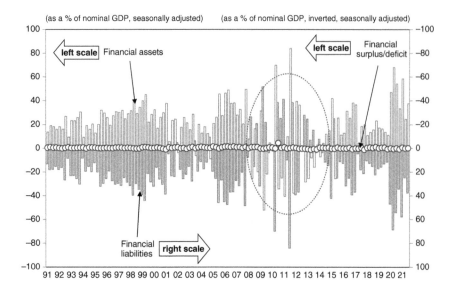

FIGURE 8.10 Post-2008 Turmoil in German Financial Sector

Notes: Seasonal adjustments by Nomura Research Institute. Latest figures are for 2021 Q3.

Sources: Nomura Research Institute, based on flow of funds data from Bundesbank and Eurostat

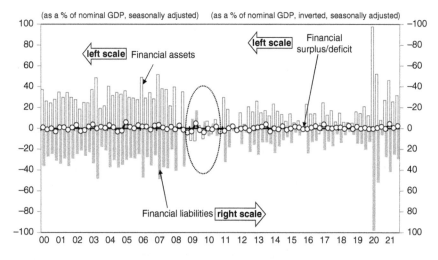

FIGURE 8.11 Lehman-Triggered U.S. Financial Crisis Was Over in Two Years

Notes: Latest figures are for 2021 Q3.

Sources: Nomura Research Institute, based on flow of funds data from Federal Reserve Bank (FRB) and U.S. Department of Commerce

GFC. Indeed, after a modest disruption immediately following the Lehman collapse (the circled area), the situation was more or less back to normal by the end of the eighth quarter. This demonstrates that even a financial crisis of the magnitude of the GFC can be contained in about two years with a proper policy response.

With so many national banking systems trying to economize on capital by trimming financial assets (i.e., loans) at the same time, it is obvious that the Eurozone was suffering from a massive systemic banking crisis and not an ordinary banking crisis. The correct way to address such a credit crunch is for the government to relax capital requirements by postponing their imposition date or to inject capital directly into the banks, as Japanese and U.S. authorities did in 1998–99 and in 2008, respectively. The imposition of bail-ins was also totally counterproductive under the circumstances.

The Japanese and U.S. decisions also indicate that if the policy choice is between ending the credit crunch and fixing the banks, the authorities must end the credit crunch first. Allowing it to continue means saved funds are not being borrowed and spent, resulting in an ever-weaker economy. A weaker economy, in turn, makes it difficult for borrowers to service their debts, thus increasing banks' NPLs and undermining efforts to fix the banks.

Unfortunately, European banking authorities continued with their market-fundamentalist orthodoxy, simultaneously demanding higher capital ratios, bail-ins, and quick disposals of NPLs. The result was a sustained credit crunch with extremely slow loan growth (Figure 2.13) and a weaker economy.

The Right Way to Inject Capital

If capital is to be injected in a systemic banking crisis, it must be injected into many banks simultaneously to avoid the issue of stigma.[7] The government must also ensure that the injected capital is used to support lending and not to write off NPLs. This is important because cleaning up NPLs and ending the credit crunch are two *contradictory* goals: the faster banks dispose of their bad loans, the more their capital will shrink, impeding efforts to lend. While both are ultimately

---

[7]Those banks that received capital may be viewed by the public as badly managed and dangerous, and such perceptions can actually worsen the banking crisis.

desirable goals, the authorities—given the choice—should strive to end the credit crunch first for the reasons previously noted.

The government should then allow banks to use their earnings to write off NPLs over the medium term. When the author spearheaded the effort to recapitalize Japanese banks starting in late 1997 via numerous television and parliamentary appearances, he had to make sure the fresh capital was used to support lending and not to dispose of bad loans.

The preceding also means that there should be little or no conditions attached to capital injection unless it is a case of forced nationalization. This is important because if the conditions attached are too onerous, banks would rather cut lending to meet capital requirements than accept government's money to maintain lending, but that will make the credit crunch even worse. In other words, capital injection will not solve the problem it is supposed to solve.

This is exactly what happened to Japan in March 1998. When the original capital injection legislation was drafted, the author made sure that it contained minimal conditions for injection so that the banks would take the money. Then the U.S. Treasury Department, which apparently had no understanding of the complexity of these issues, demanded that the Japanese government attach strict conditions to capital injections. The Department apparently knew nothing of the lessons learned from the capital injection to American banks made by the Reconstruction Finance Corporation in 1933. Against the objection from the author, the Japanese government added tons of conditionalities to capital injection when it was offered to the banks.

As feared by the author, not a single Japanese bank raised hands to take the money. The banks concluded that it is better to economize on capital by cutting lending instead of accepting onerous conditions from the government in exchange for capital. But that only made the credit crunch worse.

Realizing the mistake, the government quickly dumped most of the conditions, and the banks finally took the money (¥1.8 trillion) that stopped the credit crunch from worsening. However, that was not good enough and another bigger injection was made in March 1999 (¥7.5 trillion) to finally end the crunch. How the first injection stopped the crunch from getting worse, and the second injection ended it are shown in the upper graph of Figure 8.6.

The author also recommended that NPL disposals proceed *slowly* in Japan to avoid the fallacy-of-composition problem of everybody selling distressed assets at the same time. That advice was based on his involvement in the rescue of American banks in the 1982 Latin American debt crisis. This public stance made the author very unpopular with U.S. investment houses and their asset-stripper friends who sought to buy Japanese assets on the cheap. They were hoping that if Japanese banks were all forced into a fire sale of distressed assets, prices would collapse, and they would be able to buy the assets at huge discounts.

On the other hand, the author received support from Volcker, who published a piece in leading Japanese economic journal *Toyo Keizai*[8] arguing that the government should establish a *speed limit* on the pace of bad loan write-offs to prevent the fallacy-of-composition problems described earlier. His recommendation (and mine) is, of course, the exact opposite of what Eurozone officials are demanding of banks today.

As the previous examples indicate, banking authorities face a minefield of contradictions and fallacy-of-composition problems when addressing a systemic banking crisis. But few people in the Eurozone today seem capable of drawing a distinction between an ordinary banking crisis involving only a few banks and a systemic crisis involving a large number of lenders. Until those distinctions are drawn and the contradictions addressed, the Eurozone is likely to experience a sustained credit crunch and subpar economic performance.

Ghosts of American Asset Strippers Are Killing European Banks

The irony here is that it was mostly American asset strippers and their Wall Street friends in the 1990s who disseminated the belief that the Japanese economy had stagnated because banks were not writing off

---

[8]Volcker, Paul A. (2001), "Jinsoku na Furyo-saiken Shori ga Hitsuyo daga Shori no Seigensokudo wa Daiji" ("Prompt Disposal of NPLs Is Needed, but So Is Setting a Speed Limit"), *Shukan Toyo Keizai*, June 23, 2001, p. 58.

their NPLs fast enough. They spread these misinformation because they had come to Japan to buy distressed assets on the cheap but were unable to purchase them at attractive prices. Disappointed, they started telling the Western media and policy makers that the Japanese economy was not recovering because banks were not writing off their NPLs fast enough.

Western journalists posted in Japan had no knowledge of how the United States had handled the 1982 Latin American debt crisis. Moreover, most had a poor command of the Japanese language. This forced them to rely on Western financial institutions for their stories since they never knew whether the person who picked up the phone at a Japanese institution would speak English. As a result, not only did Western journalists fail to get the Japanese side of the story, but they were bombarded with stories from Western asset stripers and investment bankers who insisted the Japanese economy was doomed until its banks cleaned up their NPLs. Those stories ultimately reached Washington, where equally uninformed officials began repeating the story invented by self-interested American asset strippers.

It was also quite astonishing to see so many high-ranking U.S. officials and academics making these arguments about Japan without realizing that the United States had had to use the same "pretend and extend" policy when it faced problems of a similar scope during the 1982 Latin American debt crisis. Indeed, the ignorance of U.S. officials, academics, and investment bankers (but not commercial bankers) regarding the "pretend and extend" policies of 1982 and 2009 is appalling. The only banking crisis with which they seemed to be familiar was the 1989 savings and loan crisis, which was tiny in comparison with the Latin American debt crisis. Those same officials and economists then went on to lecture the Japanese—and other Asians after the 1997 Asian currency crisis—on what to do in a banking crisis without knowing anything about their *own* nation's crises.

Japanese banks are now considered some of the healthiest in the world, and Mitsubishi-UFJ bank was able to rescue Morgan Stanley in the midst of the Lehman crisis. But economic growth remains slow because private-sector borrowers are still in short supply (Figure 2.3). This fact suggests that those who blamed the banks for the nation's economic stagnation 25 years ago largely misunderstood the situation. The Japanese economy has been sluggish not because of a lack of lenders, but because of a lack of borrowers.

The irony in all of this is that the self-serving pronouncements by American asset strippers talking their book on Japanese NPLs 20 years ago has convinced unsuspecting post-2008 Europeans that they must rush ahead with NPL disposals, further compromising their response to the systemic banking crisis. True to form, asset strippers and investment bankers are also telling European officials to speed up NPL disposals so that they can buy distressed European assets on the cheap. Since that is part of the job description of asset strippers, one cannot expect them to recommend a gradualist approach to bad loan disposals. But just as Volcker warned the Japanese in 2001, European officials charged with looking after the broader economy should have the courage to consider the gradualist option during a systemic banking crisis.

"Too Big to Fail" Had Little to Do with GFC

Not all of the U.S. authorities' post-2008 policy responses were on the mark. In particular, their emphasis on "too big to fail" and the orderly dissolution of such institutions missed the key lessons of the systemic banking crisis. An absence of legal provisions for an orderly dissolution of nonbanks such as Lehman and AIG was *not* responsible for the severity of the crisis. The GFC would have unfolded even if there had been a textbook-perfect resolution of Lehman.

The crisis in September 2008 got so bad not because Lehman was too big to fail, but rather because every other financial institution suffered from the same problems as Lehman. In particular, no one knew the value of their huge CDO holdings because the market for those securities had completely evaporated. In other words, no one knew how big their losses were or even whether they were still solvent. When all financial institutions face the same problem at the same time, everyone distrusts everyone else because they know that others are in the same boat. It was this tremendous uncertainty and mutual distrust that made the GFC so devastating.

The mutual distrust among U.S. banks got so bad that the interbank market became largely dysfunctional, forcing many lenders to borrow reserves from the Fed to make payments. This can be seen in Figure 8.12, which shows that borrowed reserves skyrocketed to

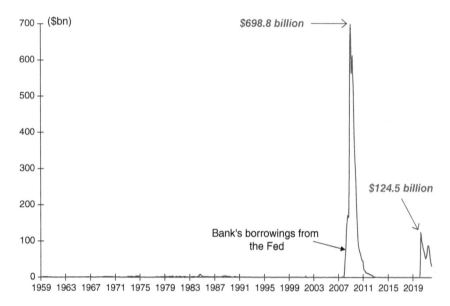

FIGURE 8.12 Banks Use Borrowed Reserves Only in Emergencies

Source: Board of Governors of the Federal Reserve System

$700 billion during the GFC from about $200 million just prior to it. This 3,500-fold increase indicates just how dysfunctional the interbank market had become at the time of the Lehman crisis, when banks simply could not trust each other.

Problems of this magnitude do not happen often, but when they do, the authorities must have the power to implement "pretend and extend" policies the way Volcker did during the Latin American debt crisis in 1982. In the wake of the GFC, the U.S. authorities implemented the blanket deposit guarantee and the "Policy Statement on Prudent Commercial Real Estate Loan Workouts" previously noted also because they understood that they were facing a systemic banking crisis.

The sudden increase in borrowed reserves seen since 2020, on the other hand, is a result of the COVID-19–driven recession forcing businesses to secure working capital in a hurry. The sudden return of borrowers who had to secure working capital to survive the lockdowns strained the financial market as seen in Figure 6.1 and pushed the economy into Case 2.

Remembering Volcker's Actions in 1982

As noted earlier, the 1982 crisis engulfed a huge number of financial institutions around the world via their participation in syndicated loans. With hundreds of banks around the world holding claims on Latin American borrowers that were collapsing in value, the situation resembled the more recent GFC.

On the day the crisis erupted, Volcker made a superhuman effort to contain it by calling the heads of central banks around the world and requesting that they instruct their banks to stay with the Latin American borrower while maintaining their credit lines with American banks, knowing full well that both were insolvent. The crisis erupted on a Friday morning (New York time) in August 1982, and the 13-hour time difference meant that most people in Japan had already left the office. When Volcker, after many emergency meetings and conversations with other central bank governors, called BOJ Governor Haruo Maekawa, it was already well past midnight in Tokyo, and only a handful of people remained at the bank.

It fell to Mr. Shuzou Aoki, who happened to be still working, to answer the call from the chairman of the Federal Reserve. To the harried and agitated Fed chairman, Aoki could only say that the governor had left for the day and on his way to his country home in Karuizawa, which was a four-hour drive from Tokyo in those days, and there were no mobile phones in 1982.

A flabbergasted Volcker yelled at the BOJ official, "If you cannot get Governor Maekawa on the phone in the next few hours, there will be no U.S. banks left on Monday!" Shocked, Aoki worked desperately to find a way to contact Maekawa and have him call the Fed chairman. When he finally succeeded, Volcker told Maekawa that Mexico and American banks needed all the help Japanese banks could offer.

While Volcker in Washington, D.C., was frantically calling foreign central bank governors and asking them to instruct their banks to continue lending to Mexico and U.S. institutions, hundreds of other Federal Reserve staff were calling U.S. banks, urging them to continue lending to the bankrupt state of Mexico. The author recalls that the instruction from Washington at the time was, "Do not let a single U.S. bank with an exposure of more than one million dollars to Mexico leave Mexico." Although these efforts succeeded in avoiding a GFC-like outcome with tens of millions of jobs lost, the legality of the U.S. authorities' actions was perhaps questionable. After all, government bank supervisors are not authorized to ask a bank to continue lending to a bankrupt borrower.

Volcker had the courage to save the world first and worry about the legality of his actions later. A lesser central bank governor might have worried about overstepping his authority and desisted from taking the necessary actions until it was too late. This problem seems to be particularly acute in the Eurozone, where national banking authorities must consult so many different institutions before acting—witness the situation in Italy in the spring of 2017. Such powers should be explicitly granted to national banking authorities at the first indication of a systemic banking crisis so that they can act without delay.

Obsession with Too-Big-to-Fail May Constrain Future Policy Actions

Unfortunately, that is not the direction that U.S. legislators went after Lehman. Instead, they were obsessed with the need to constrain too-big-to-fail financial institutions while limiting the range of actions the Fed might be able to take at times of crisis. Talking about "too big to fail" is politically popular because no one likes big banks or fat bankers. But if Lehman were an isolated case, it would never have morphed into a global crisis that eventually claimed 8 million jobs on either side of the Atlantic.

This can be seen from the May 1984 collapse of Continental Illinois Bank, the seventh largest bank in the country, which represented the largest bank failure in postwar U.S. history. But the repercussions of this event were nothing like the turmoil created by Lehman's failure. And that was because the cause of Continental's failure was very much limited to the bank itself: no other banks were suffering from similar problems. In other words, it was not a systemic banking crisis.

What is needed in a systemic crisis is an explicit granting of emergency powers to the banking authorities so that they can move quickly to save *all* banks. Lesser minds may object to such policies, citing moral hazard and the cost to taxpayers. But the extraordinary actions taken by Volcker prevented a debilitating credit crunch and economic collapse even though most of the largest U.S. banks remained technically insolvent for nearly seven years. His actions also cost the U.S. taxpayer nothing. In fact, most people in the world outside of Latin America had no idea that a massive, seven-year global banking crisis was unfolding beneath the surface.

Volcker's actions in 1982 also proved that the bail-ins championed by the likes of Jeroen Dijsselbloem, chairman of the Eurogroup of finance ministers, are by no means the only way to save taxpayers' money. On the contrary, by keeping the economy functioning despite massive problems in the banking sector, "pretend and extend" policies in 1982 and 2009 probably boosted GDP and overall tax revenues by billions if not trillions of dollars compared with the European bail-in approach. And on both occasions, the relatively strong economy made possible by these policies gave the banks the income they needed to repair their balance sheets over time.

Unfortunately, the Dodd-Frank rules enacted after 2008 make it more difficult for the Fed to take the kind of actions Volcker took back in 1982. The proponents of the new rules apparently believe that the risk of another Lehman-like crisis can be minimized by placing constraints on systematically important financial institutions (SIFIs). But that assumes that everything is always fine, apart from the reckless actions of a few "too-big-to-fail" institutions—which is nonsense.

During the subprime crisis, it was not just SIFIs, but everyone, including the rating agencies as well as bank regulators at the Federal Reserve, the FDIC, and the Comptroller of the Currency at the Treasury Department, was wrong. When former Fed Chairman Alan Greenspan described the GFC as a "once-in-a-hundred-year event," it proved only that he and his staffers were oblivious to the danger of having so many financial institutions holding complex CDOs filled with toxic subprime mortgages. When so many people are proven wrong at the same time,[9] a policy to help everyone is needed to prevent the total collapse of the system. And that is basically what Volcker did back in 1982. Blaming the GFC on SIFIs is populism, not responsible policy. And in

---

[9] The Federal Reserve Bank of New York, the only federal government agency with the ability to assess country risk in the 1970s, began warning American banks not to increase their exposure to Latin America in 1979 but the warning was largely ignored.

the Eurozone, pragmatism is needed above all else. They could also use someone like Volcker who is willing to take unpopular actions in order to save the economy, jobs, and taxpayers.

Are Reserve Requirements and Money Multipliers Obsolete?

Leaving NPLs, the rest of this chapter is devoted to the somewhat wonkish topic of how money is created in the banking system because it has implications not only for how policy makers should respond to crises, but also for the changing relationship between monetary aggregates and the level of economic activity as the economy moves from the golden era to the pursued era. Readers who are not interested in this debate between economists are welcome to skip to Chapter 9.

In previous chapters, frequent references were made to the concept of the *money multiplier*, and this term will be explained fully in the following. But a number of economists have objected to the use of concepts such as money multipliers and reserve requirements, arguing that they are no longer useful in understanding monetary policy. Some even say they were *never* applicable, arguing that money was never created the way it was taught in textbooks. In particular, economists who believe bankers actually create money out of thin air tend to argue that reserve requirements and the money multiplier are irrelevant concepts.

This point has been made by M. McLeay, A. Radia, and P. Thomas at the Bank of England (2014)[10] as well as by Z. Jakab and M. Kumhof (2015)[11] and R. Werner (2016),[12] among others. The latter two actually

---

[10] McLeay, Michael, Radia, Amar and Thomas, Ryland (2014), "Money Creation in the Modern Economy," *Bank of England Quarterly Bulletin 2014 Q1*, pp. 14–27. https://www.bankofengland.co.uk/-/media/boe/files/quarterly-bulletin/2014/money-creation-in-the-modern-economy.pdf.

[11] Jakab, Zoltan and Kumhof, Michael (2015), "Banks Are Not Intermediaries of Loanable Funds—And Why This Matters," *Bank of England Working Paper*, No. 529. https://www.bankofengland.co.uk/-/media/boe/files/working-paper/2015/banks-are-not-intermediaries-of-loanable-funds-and-why-this-matters.pdf.

[12] Werner, Richard A. (2016), "A Lost Century in Economics: Three Theories of Banking and the Conclusive Evidence," *International Review of Financial Analysis,* 46: pp. 361–379.

examined how banks account for money-lending transactions. Kumhof, who worked for Barclays Bank, and Werner, who worked with Raiffeisenbank, concluded that when a banker grants a loan, he simply credits the bank account of the borrower with the amount of the loan *without* any corresponding debits. From this they concluded that bankers create money out of thin air (or with the stroke of a pen), and that this action has little to do with the availability of reserves in the banking system.

But these economists failed to ask what happens when the borrower actually uses the loaned funds. When the loan is used to purchase a car, for instance, the car dealer must be paid. If the seller insists on cash payment, the borrower must withdraw the required amount from the bank that granted him the loan (Bank A) in bills and coins. That means Bank A must either have that cash on hand or obtain it from the nearest branch office of the central bank.

In the first case, Bank A will have to debit its cash holdings. In the second case, it will have to debit its account at the central bank when it receives the cash. It is at this point, perhaps days or weeks *after* the loan is granted, that the debit corresponding to the loan appears in the bank's books.

If the car is purchased with a check drawn on Bank A, the seller will deposit the check with his bank (Bank B). Bank B will then present the check to Bank A for payment, and Bank A will debit its account at the central bank by the amount of the purchase and credit the same amount to Bank B's account at the central bank. It is at this point that the debit corresponding to the granting of the loan appears in the bank's books if the car was purchased with a check.

It is only after Bank B acknowledges that its account at the central bank has received the funds from Bank A that the transaction is considered complete. This time lag is the reason why it takes a few days for funds deposited with a check to become available for the depositor to use.

What this means is that, even though the debit corresponding to the granting of the loan may only appear days or weeks after the loan is granted, the bank *must* have sufficient cash on hand or reserves at the central bank to fund the loan. Otherwise, it cannot make any payments or grant any loans.

The authors just noted would probably respond by arguing that reserves do not represent a constraint on bank lending because they are available from the central bank "on demand." Although it is true that banks can borrow reserves from the central bank by posting high-quality collateral, both the availability of such collateral and the stigma attached to such borrowing (see the following) discourage banks from relying on the central bank as a source of reserves except in emergencies.

In the United States, reserves borrowed from the Fed by commercial banks are called "borrowed reserves," a data series that was used earlier in the lower graph of Figure 2.15 and in Figure 8.12. If the preceding authors are correct, borrowed reserves should have grown more or less in line with bank loans. Figure 8.12, which tracks borrowed reserves since 1959, indicates not only that there was no growth in borrowed reserves, but that they represented just 0.86 percent of total reserves held by the banks even before quantitative easing (QE) was introduced in 2008. This means 99.14 percent of the reserves held by banks are obtained from private-sector sources who are willing to entrust their money with the bank, such as depositors, bond holders, and shareholders. But there is no guarantee that they will *always* trust the banks, as the history of bank runs amply demonstrates. And bank runs happen when people suspect that a bank does not have enough reserves to make payments.

Within this framework, large banks, which generally have full access to the interbank market, can be expected to turn to the central bank for borrowed reserves far less often than smaller regional banks, which may have only limited access to the interbank market.

During his time at the Federal Reserve Bank of New York, the author was involved in a project to familiarize the U.S. offices of foreign banks with access to the Fed discount window. The discount window is where banks put in their requests to borrow funds from the Fed. At the time, money center banks, a group that includes the domestic offices of foreign banks, were allowed to access the discount window up to three times per month, while smaller regional banks could do so up to six times each month.

If a bank exceeded that maximum, the Fed would send a team of bank supervisors to audit it and determine the cause of its reserve management problems. Since a Fed audit, like a tax audit, is not a pleasant affair, banks did their best to ensure they had adequate reserves. There was also a strong stigma attached to borrowing from the Fed because frequent borrowing implied the institution was poorly managed. These maximums were considered guidelines, inasmuch as banks were granted almost unlimited access to the discount window in the case of a systemic crisis, as seen in the wake of the Lehman crisis (Figure 8.12).

To borrow from the Fed, banks also had to post high-quality collateral to ensure that taxpayers' funds were not placed at risk. Although many economists with no experience in bank supervision, including those on the payrolls of central banks, often talk as though reserves are freely available from the central bank at the going interest rate, any bank that borrows from the central bank faces myriad costs, and those who borrow too often will face highly unpleasant audits. This explains why borrowed reserves constituted only 0.86 percent of bank reserves in the United States before QE was launched in 2008.

More recently, the guidelines previously noted have been relaxed for banks in "good standing" with the Fed. The Fed has also introduced the Standing Repo Facility (SRF) to make it easier for qualified institutions to access short-term funding from the central bank, and is trying to remove some of the stigma attached to the use of its discount window for banks in good standing. But the "good standing" designation presumably means the bank is meeting its reserve and other requirements most of the time.

The notion that a bank can create money out of thin air because the central bank is always ready to provide reserves "on demand" is therefore nonsense. At the moment the loan is granted, there is no corresponding debit at the bank because the money has not moved. But as soon as that loan is used to make a payment, the debit appears, either in the form of reduced reserves at the central bank or reduced cash holdings at the bank office that granted the loan. Because banks do whatever they can to avoid borrowing from the central bank, only banks with plenty of nonborrowed reserves grant loans.

For individual loan officers, however, the availability of reserves is not a major concern unless the bank is in serious difficulty or the requested loan amount is exceptionally large. This is because the need to hold reserves applies to the *entire* bank, not to individual branches. As such, only people working in the head office's treasury department closely monitor the bank's reserve positions. Others are likely to have no idea where the bank's reserves stand. However, if the requested loan is large enough, even loan officers who do not normally check with headquarters would probably call the treasury department to make sure the loan can be funded.

Perhaps the silly notion held by some economists that banks create money out of thin air could have been avoided if government regulators had required banks to have two reserve accounts at the central bank, one for general payments and the other for loan withdrawals. As soon as a loan is granted (but not paid out), the bank would move the amount of the loan from the general reserve account K to the loan reserve account L, and when the loan is paid out, it would be paid out from the reserves in account L. That way, there would be a visible debit to correspond with the granting of the loan for academic economists to see. In real life, banks make no distinction within the reserve account because debits from loan withdrawals are no different from the hundreds of other withdrawals the bank has to process every day on behalf of depositors.

The vast majority of these payments are settled through the accounts that banks maintain with the central bank. When outflows exceed inflows, the bank's reserves with the central bank are drained, while reserves increase if the reverse is the case. Whether the bank has sufficient reserves or not is therefore a hugely important issue in running a bank.

Because banks earn next to nothing for processing a massive number of payments every day, they are allowed to earn interest by lending the deposits entrusted to them. That provision creates an incentive for banks to lend as much as possible to maximize interest income. But if they lend too much, they may run into ugly payment problems. Government regulators have therefore imposed reserve requirements to ensure that banks do not lend excessively and jeopardize their role as payment processors. These requirements are generally set at a low level because inflows and outflows tend to even themselves out over time, especially at the larger banks.

In Japan, an officer at the Bank of Japan who is responsible for overseeing a particular bank will monitor the institution's progress in meeting its reserve requirements. When the bank appears likely to fail the requirement, the officer will make a phone call a few days before the end of the reserve maintenance period to ensure that the bank makes the necessary adjustments.

It was noted earlier that only banks with sufficient reserves grant loans. Although most well-managed banks can extend loans most of the time, they will stop lending altogether when they feel their supply of reserves is exhausted or uncertain. At such times, banks put aside their profit-maximizing motive and stop granting loans so that remaining reserves can be earmarked for the more urgent purpose of making payments. Banks also refrain from lending when they feel that their capital is insufficient to absorb the risk associated with lending. Such a shift away from lending results in painful credit crunches.

Credit crunches were observed in the United States in the early 1990s following the savings and loan debacle, in Japan during its banking crisis from 1997 to 1999, and in Western economies after the GFC in 2008. The post-2008 credit crunch continues today in some parts of the Eurozone. At such times, when many banks are unable to lend, monetary authorities must act quickly to recapitalize the banks or, if there are plenty of borrowers, allow banks to use "fat spreads" to recapitalize themselves, as is noted with regard to Case 2 in Chapter 1. They should also provide sufficient reserves as lender of last resort to ensure the payment system does not run into difficulties. The authorities should push the banks to dispose of NPLs only after the debilitating credit crunch has subsided.

In the post-2008 world, where central banks have flooded the system with excess reserves via QE, most banks have no problem meeting their reserve requirements. Indeed, the United Kingdom suspended its reserve requirement when the Bank of England embarked on its massive QE program in 2009. The Fed also suspended its reserve requirement when it launched its own QE program in response to the pandemic in 2020.

But reserve requirements will become relevant again when the private sector finishes repairing its balance sheet and resumes borrowing. Indeed, some in the United States are already arguing that a higher reserve requirement might be needed—together with higher interest rates, tighter liquidity, and capital requirements—if the unwinding of QE (i.e., QT) that is described in Chapter 6 turns out to be too slow to contain inflationary pressures in the economy.

Individually, Banks Are Financial Intermediaries, but Collectively, They Are Money Creators

So how does money get created in this system? The money supply is defined as the aggregation of all bank accounts plus notes and coins in circulation. The money creation process starts when the central bank decides to inject reserves into the banking system by purchasing government bonds or other financial assets from a private-sector entity. For example, if the central bank buys government bonds from an insurance company, (1) the central bank credits the account that the insurance company's bank (Bank E) has with the central bank by the amount of the purchase, and (2) Bank E credits the account that the insurance company has with the bank by the same amount. Since the money supply includes all amounts held in private sector bank accounts, transaction (2) increases the money supply.

Many journalists and even economists use the term *printing money* to refer to the money creation process. In reality, however, the process starts when the central bank credits Bank E's account with the central bank with a keyboard input in transaction (1). In other words, no printing of any kind is involved in the modern money-creation process.

The amount of coins and bills in circulation is decided entirely by society's demand for cash. For example, in the transaction involving Bank A and the car dealer noted earlier, if the dealer who sells the car to the borrower from Bank A wants to be paid in cash, the borrower will have to get the cash from Bank A. If Bank A does not have enough cash on hand, it will have to obtain those bills and coins from the nearest branch office of the central bank *in exchange* for its reserves with the central bank. In other words, Bank A's reserves with the central bank will decrease by the amount of cash withdrawn. When the cash is withdrawn from Bank A to pay for the car, that transaction will reduce the balance of the borrower's bank account with Bank A while increasing bills and coins in circulation by the same amount, leaving the total money supply unchanged.

The amount of funds commercial banks have with the central bank, together with notes and coins in circulation, is called the monetary base and is shown in the top lines in Figures 2.12 to 2.14 and 2.17. Transaction (1), which increases Bank E's balance with the central bank, also increases the monetary base.

Because transaction (1) boosts the reserves Bank E has with the central bank, the bank can grant loans to earn interest income *if there are willing and qualified borrowers*. If such a borrower presents itself, the bank will grant the loan by (3) crediting the borrower's bank account by the amount of the loan. Since the money supply includes all bank accounts, transaction (3) will also expand the money supply. The loan amount is capped by the increase in reserves from transaction (1) minus the larger of either (a) required reserves or (b) whatever sum bankers consider it appropriate to keep within the bank.

When the borrower then uses the borrowed money to buy a smartphone from a phone retailer, the retailer's bank (Bank F) will (4) credit the retailer's account by the amount of the purchase, which increases the money supply, while the borrower's Bank E will (5) debit the borrower's account by the same amount, which reduces the money supply. Bank E will also debit its account at the central bank by the amount of the smartphone purchase and credit Bank F's account with the central bank by the same amount. Bank E's reserves at the central bank are reduced, while Bank F's reserves at the central bank are increased.

Transactions (3) and (5) therefore cancel each other out in terms of their impact on the money supply. That leaves only the increase in the money supply due to transactions (2) and (4).

Bank F, which now has more reserves with the central bank, will try to lend the money (minus the reserve requirement) to earn interest income *if there is a willing and qualified borrower*. If such a borrower shows up and borrows the money to buy furniture, the initial increase and subsequent decrease in the borrower's bank account will offset each other, but (6) the increase in the furniture store's bank account will remain, thereby increasing the money supply. This also means the furniture store's bank (Bank G) will try to lend the inflow of reserves *if there are any willing and qualified borrowers*.

This process will not continue forever because banks cannot lend out all incoming reserves—after all, the insurance company, car dealer, or furniture store may want to withdraw money for their own purposes. The reserve requirement prescribes the minimum amount banks must set aside to prepare for the possibility of withdrawals. When the full amount of reserves supplied by transaction (1) is set aside as required reserves by Banks E, F, G, and so forth, the process of money supply creation has reached its apogee.

The Variability of the Money Multiplier and Its Policy Implications

The ratio of total bank deposits created (i.e., the sum of transactions (2), (4), (6), ...) to the initial injection of reserves (1) is called the *money multiplier*, a term that is first seen in this book in Chapter 2.

This ratio will reach its maximum value if there is strong demand for loans and all reserves are fully set aside for meeting reserve requirements.

This process of money creation will come to a halt much sooner if banks do not have enough capital to lend, as previously described (Cases 2 and 4), or if the demand for loans from qualified borrowers is insufficient or nonexistent (Cases 3 and 4). For economies in Cases 3 and 4, where the private sector as a whole is either paying down debt or saving money, this money creation process will not only fail to engage but may actually go into reverse, triggering the kind of money supply shrinkage observed during the first four years of Great Depression (Figure 2.15). As noted in Chapter 2, this shrinkage was reversed only when the government showed up as borrower of last resort with its New Deal program in 1933 (Figure 2.16).

In the golden era, with strong demand for borrowings to finance productivity- and capacity-enhancing investments, the money multiplier is mostly stuck at its maximum value. That makes it easy for monetary authorities to predict the response of economic activity to monetary policy changes because any change in central bank supplied liquidity will have an immediate and predictable impact on economic activity through the growth in credit. It was no coincidence, therefore, that the Fed treated the money supply as a leading indicator of the economy.

But in the pursued phase or during a balance sheet recession, when demand for loans becomes very weak, the multiplier is likely to be a fraction of its maximum potential value. It may actually turn negative at the margin if the private sector as a whole is paying down debt, as happened during the Great Depression. The fact that it is not stuck at its maximum value as in the golden era also means it can fluctuate. That makes it difficult to predict the impact of changes in monetary policy on the economy.

For example, the astronomical QE carried out by central banks after 2008, which basically involves central banks engaging heavily in transaction (1) to expand the monetary base, all failed to produce inflation because the private sector started to minimize debt, and transactions (3) and beyond hardly materialized. An absence of borrowers, therefore, is synonymous with a near-zero money multiplier at the margin. And that is when monetary policy is least effective.

But if borrowers return for any reason, the same amount of reserves that was not inflationary earlier may suddenly become highly inflationary as the money multiplier is pushed higher. It was this prospect that prompted the Fed to start normalizing monetary policy in 2021 Q4 when bank lending began to increase rapidly, as is noted in Figure 6.9.

As long as the money multiplier is not at its maximum, loan officers should be able to grant loans without worrying about whether there are sufficient reserves. If the multiplier is at its maximum but there is still unmet demand for loans, lending rates are likely to be bid up while banks compete with each other for deposits. These phenomena have been observed in many countries during their golden eras, especially before interest rates were fully deregulated.

How the Money Supply Lost Its Role as Leading Indicator of Economic Activity

In his testimony to Congress on February 23, 2021, Fed Chair Jerome Powell said that ". . . when you and I studied economics a million years ago, M2 and monetary aggregates generally seemed to have a relationship to economic growth. Right now . . . the growth of M2 . . . does not really have important implications for the economic outlook. M2 was removed some years ago from the standard list of leading indicators . . . and . . . that classic relationship between monetary aggregates and economic growth . . . just no longer holds." This statement seems to have much to do with the fact that in the pursued era (1) the money multiplier is low and variable because of weak loan demand, and (2) a large portion of borrowings is used to finance purchases of existing assets instead of funding activities that add to GDP.

As is noted in Chapter 5, for an economy to grow, someone must over-stretch, that is, spend money above and beyond their income. If everyone spent only as much as they earned, the economy would be stable, but it would not grow. And it is borrowings that allow people to spend more than they earn. That means there should be a connection between borrowings and economic growth. If the borrowings to finance real activities are not growing, it is difficult to expect the economy to achieve rapid growth.

"A million years ago," during the golden era, a large portion of businesses' borrowings was indeed used to finance productivity- and capacity-enhancing investments. In other words, the growth of lending was closely related to over-stretching activities that added to GDP. Since growth in loans (transactions (3) and (5) in the previous example), which are a bank asset, goes hand-in-hand with growth in the money supply (transactions (2), (4), and (6)), which is a bank liability,[13] growth in the money supply and economic activity were closely correlated.

In today's pursued economies, the dearth of attractive investment opportunities in the real economy means not only that demand for borrowings is weak, but that the borrowing that does take place is often used to finance purchases of existing assets that do *not* add to GDP. For example, according to estimates compiled by the Institute of International Finance in 2017, the percentage of funds that corpo- rations procured from banks and the bond market that was actually used to finance capital investment, thereby directly boosting economic growth and inflation, was 25 percent in Japan but just 3 percent in the United States and the Eurozone.[14] The rest was used to buy back shares, to refinance existing debt, or to provide working capital, all of which make only small contributions to economic growth or inflation.

This means the growth in borrowing to finance real activity is even smaller than the growth in credit shown in Figures 2.12 to 2.14 and 2.17. If borrowings are increasingly used for purposes that do not add to GDP, the correlation between the growth in lending (and money supply) and the growth in economic activity is increasingly weakened. That may explain why the money supply is no longer a good indicator of economic activity in advanced countries today.

Data Is Needed on "Operating Loans" as Distinct from "Financing Loans"

If this analysis is correct, the government should collect data sepa- rately for loans taken out to finance real consumption and invest- ment and for loans taken out to finance purchases of existing assets.

---

[13] Please recall the discussion on Figure 2.13 in Chapter 2.

[14] Institute of International Finance (2017), *Capital Market Monitor,* March 2017, Chart 6.

If we were to borrow some terms from the leasing industry and call the former an "operating loan" and the latter a "financing loan," the former should provide a leading indicator of economic activity going forward because it will be an indicator of over-stretching by businesses, which is essential for economic growth. Financing loans, on the other hand, may be a useful indicator of future asset prices.

Viewed in this way, it appears that the share of financing loans is increasing relative to the share of operating loans as economies move from the golden era to the pursued era. And that is because there is less demand for operating loans in pursued economies. Since the funds used for financial loans tend to stay in the financial sector—as the seller of the asset must invest the proceeds in some other asset—the increase in the share of such loans is likely to exert less upward pressure on interest rates than a similar increase in operating loans. This is another reason why interest rates are lower and "financial capitalism" is a bigger problem in the pursued era than in the golden era.

Governments should collect these data from both banks and capital markets so that everyone will have a better idea of what is really happening in the economy and markets.

Money Creation Does Not Mean Wealth Creation

The preceding discussion should make it clear that while individually banks are financial intermediaries because they only lend out funds that are entrusted to them by depositors (less the reserve requirement), collectively they are creating large amounts of bank deposits because of their ability to lend money under the fractional reserve banking system. It also means the fractional reserve system is necessary (but not sufficient) to ensure that saved funds are borrowed and spent, thereby keeping the economy going.

Finally, it should be noted that this process of money creation does not make society any richer. The increase in the money supply is matched by an increase in the debt of those who borrowed to purchase the car, smartphone, or furniture. The net increase in wealth from the money creation process is therefore zero. If the borrowed money is used to finance over-stretching by businesses and households, it will lead to economic growth. But that is the result of the productive use of borrowed funds and not of money creation itself.

CHAPTER 9

Backlash against Globalization and Conflict between Free Trade and Free Capital Flows

Backlash against Globalization in Pursued Countries

The disappointment and despair felt by many in the Eurozone is due largely to glitches in the Stability and Growth Pact (SGP) and the design of the euro, which have prevented member governments from responding correctly to balance sheet recessions. However, there is also a widespread sense of frustration among those in advanced countries over income inequality and stagnant wages, along with a general feeling of helplessness. Indeed, the establishment figures and "experts" responsible for the Great Recession are losing credibility everywhere. Even in the United States, where the economy is doing better than most, Donald Trump, a complete outsider, was elected president in 2016 because of his opposition to free trade and other establishment policies. In some countries, the social backlash against the establishment has become large enough to threaten not only social cohesion but also those nations' democratic institutions.

One reason for this frustration and social backlash in the advanced economies is that these countries are experiencing the pursued phase for the first time ever. As is noted in Chapter 5, many were caught off guard, having assumed the golden era that they enjoyed into the 1970s would last forever. It is no surprise that those who have seen no improvement in their living standards for many years but still remember the golden era, when everyone was hopeful and living standards were steadily improving, would long for the "good old days."

The June 2016 Brexit vote, where older people tended to vote for an exit from the European Union (EU) while younger people voted to stay, suggests that the older generation is still hoping for a return of "great" Britain, when the country was second to none. In the United States, Trump's "Make America Great Again" movement was supported largely by blue-collar white males who long for the life they enjoyed during the golden era, when U.S. manufacturing was the undisputed leader of the world.

Participants in this social backlash view globalization as the source of all evil and are trying to slow down the free movement of both goods and people. Trump and others like him are openly hostile to immigration and are arguing in favor of protectionism. They have also scuttled agreements such as the Trans-Pacific Partnership (TPP) that seek even freer trade.

In response to this backlash, the establishment has continued to argue the virtues of globalization and free trade, claiming that people like Trump and their policies will ruin the global economy. However, the establishment's arguments offer nothing new, are unable to explain why there is so much opposition and political polarization in the first place, and provide no remedy for the anger and dissatisfaction felt by so many people.

Mistakes in Textbook Economics' View of Trade Triggered Social Backlash

This chapter argues that even though free trade and globalization have improved the lives of billions of people on this planet, economics contains a number of incorrect notions regarding trade that have prevented policy makers from taking the actions needed to safeguard the gains from globalization while minimizing its costs. It is because of these mistaken notions that global imbalances and the social reaction against free trade have grown as large as they have.

These mistaken notions include (1) an incomplete understanding of the conditions needed to benefit from free trade, (2) inconsistencies between the so-called investment/savings (I/S) theory of trade balances and the reality, (3) insufficient appreciation of the conflict between capital flows and trade flows, and (4) the unrealistic assumptions behind the so-called impossible trinity or policy trilemma. Each of these is discussed in detail in the following text. Once the causes of each problem are identified, remedies to contain trade imbalances and the social backlash are offered.

Free Trade Theory Is Incompletely Taught

On the first point, regarding free trade, economists have traditionally argued that while free trade creates both winners and losers within the same country, it generates significant overall welfare gains for both trading partners because the gains of the winners are greater than the harm suffered by the losers. In other words, there should be more winners than losers from free trade (strictly speaking, this is about amounts and not the headcount, but it is assumed that the latter is a close approximation of the former). With more winners than losers, the political backlash from the losers should be containable as well. The task for policy makers, according to this view, is to ensure that the losers are looked after so that free trade can continue to benefit the entire society.

This conclusion, however, is based on a key assumption that was never mentioned in textbooks: that imports and exports will be largely balanced as free trade expands. If this assumption holds, or if the country is running a trade surplus, the number of winners will be greater than the number of losers, just as the theory suggests. But when that assumption does not hold and a nation continues to run trade deficits, free trade may produce far more losers than the theory would suggest.

The last time the United States had a balanced trade was in 1980, or more than four decades ago. It has run huge trade deficits every year since then (Figure 9.1), annually increasing the ranks of those who consider themselves losers from free trade.

By the November 2016 U.S. presidential election, there were apparently enough losers from free trade, together with other groups, to put the openly protectionist Trump into the White House. This was by no means the result of Trump's demagoguery: Hillary Clinton was nominated as the Democratic candidate for president in an arena covered by banners saying "No to TPP," the most advanced free-trade

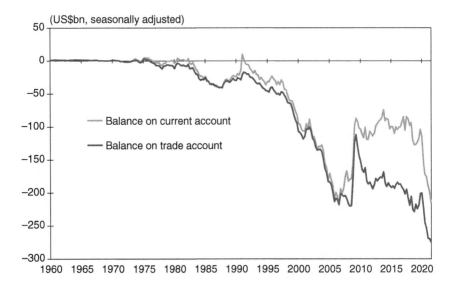

FIGURE 9.1 U.S. Trade and Current Account Deficits Reach Alarming Levels

Source: Nomura Research Institute, based on data from U.S. Bureau of Economic Analysis

agreement in history and a pact that she herself had negotiated. Bernie Sanders was also openly critical of free trade from the outset of the campaign. In other words, none of the candidates was in favor of free trade.

In 2020, Joe Biden, who defeated Trump in the presidential election, strongly advocated a "Buy American" policy that also runs contrary to the principles of free trade. With no candidates in favor of free trade in 2020 either, it would appear that the social backlash against free trade in the United States has grown very large indeed.

Trade and current account balances are important because they represent a transfer of income from one country to another. Exports are added and imports subtracted when calculating a country's gross domestic product or GDP. As indicated in Figure 9.1, the U.S. trade deficit amounted to almost $922 billion a year by 2020,[1] or about 4.4 percent of GDP. The U.S. current account deficit, which

[1] U.S. Bureau of Economic Analysis, "U.S. International Transactions, Third Quarter 2021," December 21, 2021. https://www.bea.gov/sites/default/files/2021-12/trans321.pdf.

includes trade in services, amounted to some 2.9 percent of GDP in the same year. The United Kingdom ran a trade deficit totaling more than 6.0 percent of GDP in 2020.[2] This means that a great deal of income and many jobs were transferred from these deficit countries to countries running surpluses.

Deficit countries receive goods made by the surplus countries, so it is not a loss in an accounting sense. But the fact remains that deficit countries lose income and jobs. People who lose their jobs will seek other jobs elsewhere, but they are likely to earn less than before because the expertise acquired in their previous job is unlikely to be fully utilized in their new job. Their reduced income also means lower savings. These people then join the ranks of those who view themselves as losers from free trade.

Many, if not most, economists will argue that the focus should be on the current account, which includes trade in services, instead of the trade account. And U.S. current account deficits have, in fact, been somewhat smaller than its trade deficits (Figure 9.1). But in terms of social impact, a trade deficit is equivalent to a manufacturing deficit, and the viability of the manufacturing sector plays a major role in inequality, as is noted in Chapter 5. In other words, without looking at trade deficits, one might not fully appreciate the driver of protectionist pressures in U.S. politics.

The election results indicated that a free-trade regime with no mechanism for reducing trade imbalances is approaching its limits. It will take a nondemocratic regime to maintain free trade when a large portion of the population no longer feels that free trade is working for them.

This also means that the 70-year postwar era, when Americans did so much over-stretching for the world economy, is coming to an end. How the surplus countries that benefited from the U.S. trade deficits of the last 40 years respond to the end of this era is crucial in determining whether the peace and prosperity that free trade enabled will continue. This point is discussed later in the chapter.

---

[2]Office for National Statistics, U.K., "UK Balance of Payments, The Pink Book: 2021," October 29, 2021. https://www.ons.gov.uk/economy/national accounts/balanceofpayments/bulletins/unitedkingdombalanceofpaymentst hepinkbook/2021#trade.

Importance of Trade and Current Account Balances

The International Monetary Fund (IMF) and others have been warning countries for decades that an external deficit of more than 3 percent of GDP is unhealthy. Unfortunately, those warnings have originated largely from concerns over the *financing* of the external deficit (discussed later), not its human toll. In other words, as long as the financing of these deficits appeared sustainable, the IMF and governments made little effort to balance the trade account.

Many establishment economists and commentators have also continued to argue in favor of free trade despite the strong backlash against it. But in many cases, the commentators themselves are from industries that are winners from free trade and globalization. In the United States, the media, academia, and financial sector, together with Silicon Valley, the defense industry, and Hollywood, are globally competitive and are trying to expand their businesses abroad. In other words, free trade is in their own interest.

The fact that the openly protectionist Trump was elected in 2016, however, suggests they are not the only industries in the United States. It was Trump's political genius that allowed him to recognize that there is a huge group of unhappy losers from free trade in the United States, and that establishment economists have largely assumed them away based on the theory of free trade, which says winners always outnumber losers.

On the other hand, as is noted in the discussion of the import-substitution model of economic growth in Chapter 5, outright protectionism is likely to benefit the working class in the short term only. In the long run, history has shown repeatedly that consumers and businesses lose reasons to over-stretch in such an environment, resulting in economic stagnation. Protected industries also fall behind in terms of competitiveness and technological advances, leaving the economy vulnerable to more dynamic competitors. A developed nation that relies on protectionism to save jobs may even fall off the list of "advanced" economies.

Disappearance of Trade-Balancing Mechanism

The next question is why trade imbalances grew as large as they did and why nothing was done about it. Large and continuing trade imbalances were not expected when the United States launched the free-trade system with the General Agreement on Trade and Tariffs (GATT) in 1947. At the time, the underlying assumption was that any large trade imbalances could be addressed by the movement of gold and occasional adjustments in exchange rates. Exchange rates themselves were initially fixed against the U.S. dollar under the Bretton Woods agreement, and the dollar was set at a relatively high level to help Europe and Japan recover from the devastation of the war. The dollar was also tied to gold.

As Japanese and European industry recovered from the devastation of the war and regained their competitiveness, these countries began to run trade surpluses with the United States. But each exchange rate adjustment under this "fixed-until-adjusted" regime turned out to be very cumbersome and created a great deal of turmoil, starting with the devaluation of the British pound in the 1960s. The U.S. government was also alarmed by outflows of gold.

The world then moved to a floating exchange-rate system in the 1970s that was no longer tied to gold. As a result, the yen/dollar exchange rate, which had been set at 360 under the Bretton Woods agreement, fell to 175 by 1978 based on the adjustment mechanism described later. The dollar also fell from 4.0 Deutschmarks in 1969 to just 1.72 Deutschmarks in 1980.

These adjustments were driven by the following sequence of transactions. A Japanese manufacturer that sells its products in the United States receives the proceeds of those sales in dollars. The company must then sell those dollars on the foreign exchange market to obtain the yen it needs to pay its domestic employees and suppliers. Similarly, U.S. companies that earn yen by selling their products in Japan must sell those yen to buy dollars to pay their domestic workers. However, Japan's large trade surplus with the United States means that dollar selling and yen buying by Japanese exporters to the United States is far greater than dollar buying and yen selling by U.S. exporters to Japan, leading to substantial upward pressure on the yen versus the dollar.

It is this upward pressure on the yen that pushed the yen/dollar rate from 360 in early 1970 to 175 in 1978, during a period when importers and exporters were the main players in the foreign exchange market. This appreciation of the yen and the mark in the foreign exchange market reduced the competitiveness of Japanese and West German products in the United States and kept trade imbalances from growing too large. In other words, these exchange rate adjustments served to reduce trade imbalances in the original free trade system.

Free Capital Flows Ended Exchange Rates' Ability to Rectify Trade Imbalances

That all changed in 1980 when, without fully considering the implications, the United States, Europe, and Japan began liberalizing cross-border capital flows, prompting a major shift in the makeup of foreign exchange market participants. For the first time since the war, this liberalization allowed portfolio investors in these countries to invest in each other's assets, including bonds, stocks, and real estate.

To purchase those foreign assets, investors first had to enter the foreign exchange market to obtain the necessary foreign currency. The liberalization of capital flows therefore led to a sharp influx of portfolio investors into the market. Today it is said that only about 5 percent of foreign exchange trading is directly related to trade flows, while the remaining 95 percent consists of financial flows.

Moreover, U.S. interest rates have been consistently higher than those in Japan (Figure 9.2) and West Germany, which has led to

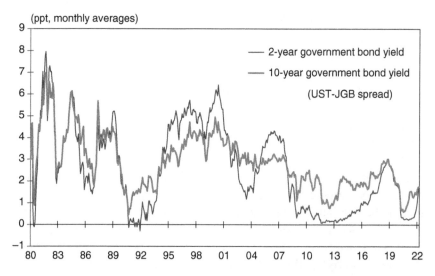

FIGURE 9.2 Yield Spread between U.S. and Japanese Government Bonds Always Favored U.S. Dollar

Note: Two-year Japanese government bond (JGB) yield based on semi-annual compound yield; 10-year JGB yield based on average accepted yield through 1982 and secondary market yield on on-the-run issues from 1983 onward.

Source: Ministry of Finance, Japan Bond Trading, and Federal Reserve data

massive capital inflows to the U.S. bond market from Japanese and European investors. Investors in those countries who wanted to buy higher-yielding U.S. bonds first needed to acquire dollars to purchase those bonds. The resulting dollar buying overwhelmed the net dollar selling resulting from the U.S. trade deficit and sent the dollar higher against other currencies. As a result, the dollar shot up to 280 yen in 1982 and to 3.30 Deutschmarks in 1985 despite large and sustained U.S. trade deficits with both countries. This development also meant that the foreign exchange market lost its traditional role of helping rebalance national trade accounts starting in 1980. Meanwhile, large and sustained U.S. trade deficits continued to increase the number of people who viewed themselves as losers from free trade.

So how strong is the dollar? According to the easy-to-understand "Big Mac index" maintained by *The Economist* magazine and as first noted in Chapter 5, the U.S. currency is heavily overvalued against every global currency except the Swiss franc, with the overvaluation amounting to 15 percent for the euro and fully 42 percent for the Japanese yen (Figure 9.3). The Big Mac index is based on a single product from a single company, and other indices might produce slightly different results, but the general picture would likely be the same. The fact that the dollar has been so expensive on a purchasing power parity basis is a key reason why the United States continues to lose its manufacturing base to the rest of the world. It is also why the number of Americans who feel they have been harmed by free trade continues to grow.

In spite of an overvalued dollar and sustained trade imbalances, the economics profession justified this free movement of capital that began in the 1980s with the neoliberal notion that anything that increases the freedom of the private sector should improve its welfare. These changes were also implemented without careful thought on the part of political leaders and economists. And it is those carelessly implemented aspects that are causing the backlash to globalization we see today. This also means that the term *globalization* as used today actually has two components: free trade and the free movement of capital.

Of the two, it was argued in previous chapters that the free-trade regime introduced by the United States after 1947 led to unprecedented global peace and prosperity. Although free trade produces winners and losers, creating a need to help the latter, the degree of improvement in real living standards since 1945 has been nothing

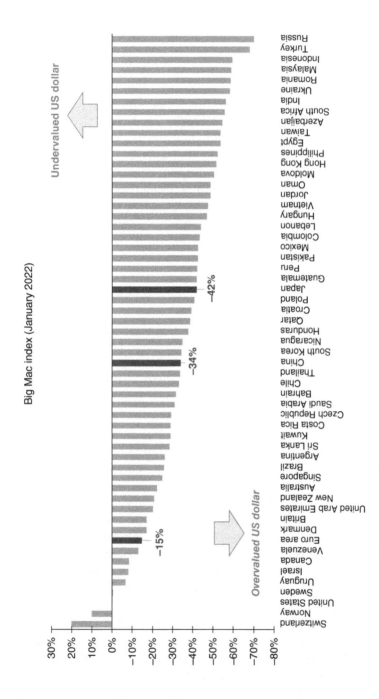

FIGURE 9.3 U.S. Dollar Overvalued against Most Currencies

Source: Compiled by Nomura Research Institute (NRI) from *The Economist*, "Big Mac index" (https://github.com/TheEconomist/big-mac-data/find/master)

short of spectacular in both pursued and pursuing countries. It is said, for example, that an average U.S. resident today is better off than the Queen of England in 1900 thanks to massive advances in technology and free-trade-driven competition, which made air conditioners, automobiles, and smartphones affordable for ordinary people.

The same cannot be said for the free movement of capital, the second component of globalization. Manufacturing workers and businesses in many pursued economies are insecure not only because imports are surging, but also because exchange rates driven by portfolio capital flows of questionable value (explained later) are no longer acting to equilibrate trade. The backlash from these groups is now threatening the very existence of free trade.

Influence of Trade and Capital Flows on Foreign Exchange Market

To better understand the relationship between trade and capital flows, let us take a step back and consider a world in which only two countries—the United States and Japan—are engaged in trade, and each country buys $100 in goods from the other. The next year, both countries will have $100 earned from exporting to its trading partner, enabling it to buy another $100 in goods from that country. The two nations' trade accounts are in balance, and the trade relationship is sustainable.

However, if the United States buys $100 in goods from Japan but Japan buys only $50 from the United States, Japan will have $100 to use the next year, while the United States will have only $50, and Japanese exports to the United States will fall to $50 as a result. Having earned only $50 from the United States, the Japanese may also have to reduce their purchases from the United States the following year. This means the trade relationship is not sustainable and the resulting negative feedback loop may push trade into what is called a contractionary equilibrium.

When exchange rates are added to the equation, the Japanese manufacturer that exported $100 in goods to the United States must sell those dollars on the foreign exchange market to buy the yen it needs to pay domestic suppliers and employees. However, the only entity that will sell it those yen is the U.S. manufacturer that exported $50 in goods to Japan.

With $100 of dollar selling and only $50 of yen selling, the dollar's value versus the yen will be cut in half, as noted in the preceding example. The strong yen then makes Japanese exports to the United States less competitive, and the weak dollar makes U.S. exports to Japan more competitive. This is how exchange rates adjust to equilibrate trade. It also describes the trading regime that existed until the end of the 1970s.

Continuing with this example, if Japanese portfolio investors such as life insurers and pension funds wanted to invest in higher-yielding U.S. Treasury bonds and bought the remaining $50 that Japanese exporters wanted to sell, there would then be a total of $100 in dollar-buying demand for the $100 the Japanese exporter seeks to sell, and exchange rates would not change. If Japanese investors continued buying $50 worth of dollar-denominated investments each year, exchange rates would remain the same despite the ongoing $50 U.S. trade deficit with Japan.

If Japanese investors decided to invest more than $50 in dollar assets each year, the dollar could actually appreciate against the yen in spite of the sustained $50 U.S. trade deficits. It was precisely such capital inflows into the United States that pushed the dollar from a low of 175 yen in 1978 to a high of 280 yen in 1982, and from a low of 1.72 Deutschmarks in 1980 to a high of 3.30 Deutschmarks in 1985.

Although such capital inflows may continue for a long time, the foreign investors are effectively lending money to the United States. And there is no guarantee that this financing of the U.S. trade deficit by foreign investors will continue forever. At some point, the money will have to be paid back to foreign life insurance holders and pensioners. This is the financing issue of external deficit the IMF and the others are concerned about, as mentioned earlier.

Unless the United States sells goods to Japan, there will be no U.S. exporters to provide Japanese investors with the yen they need when they eventually sell their U.S. bonds to pay yen obligations to Japanese pensioners and life insurance policyholders. Unless Japan is willing to continue lending to the United States in perpetuity, therefore, the underlying 100:50 trade imbalance will manifest itself and move the exchange rate when the lending stops.

At that point, the value of the yen will increase, resulting in large foreign exchange losses for Japanese pensioners and life insurance policy holders. Hence, this scenario is also unsustainable in the long run. The United States, too, would prefer a healthy relationship in which it sells goods to Japan and uses the proceeds to purchase goods from Japan to an unhealthy one in which it funds its purchases via constant borrowing.

Economics Profession Allowed Trade Imbalances to Continue

In the real world, there are not just two countries trading with each other but over *two hundred*. Cross-border capital flows from portfolio investors around the world also dwarf foreign exchange transactions by exporters and importers. Oil exporters with small domestic markets further complicate the situation. In this complex multilateral environment, it is neither possible nor desirable to balance each and every bilateral trade account.

The complexity of the actual world, however, does not change the fundamental fact that a country running a deficit is losing income and jobs and must borrow from abroad to maintain its exchange rate and imports. That means there must be a balance between the complex realities of the multilateral trading (and investing) world and the political need to prevent the number of losers from free trade from increasing to the point where the whole system is at risk of collapsing from a protectionist assault.

Instead of seeking this balance, however, governments allowed the dollar to remain strong based on robust demand for dollar-denominated assets from foreign portfolio investors. To make matters worse, many economists, making the faulty assumption that the winners from free trade always outnumber the losers, argued that governments should not even *try* to adjust the exchange rate in defiance of market forces.

There is also an understanding among monetary authorities in the advanced countries that there is something "sacred" about market-determined exchange rates and that governments should not meddle in the workings of the foreign exchange market. Moreover, many economists claimed that exchange rates were not effective in reducing trade imbalances because of the so-called investment/savings theory of trade described later.

The dollar therefore remained strong despite sustained U.S. trade deficits and an ever-expanding group of losers from free trade. The result has been the powerful political backlash against free trade and globalism we see today.

Trade Imbalance Is *Not* Decided by Investment/Savings (I/S) Balance

Moving on to economists' second misconception about the source of trade imbalances, many economists in the West, together with the Chinese government recently and the Japanese government 30 years ago, argued that these imbalances are at bottom a reflection of the I/S balance in the two nations. Their view is that the United States is running large trade deficits because investment exceeds savings—or, to put it differently, because consumption exceeds production—and that it makes no sense for the United States to complain when nations like Japan and China, where savings exceeds investment, step up to fill the supply shortfall.

According to this view, trade balances are largely decided by the I/S balances of individual countries. It is therefore futile to address trade imbalances with exchange rate adjustments or market-opening measures in the surplus countries because such measures have only a limited short-term impact. Professor Ryutaro Komiya of the University of Tokyo, who championed this theory in Japan 30 years ago, publicly advised Japanese trade negotiators not to take seriously the U.S. demands to open Japan's market. He argued that there was no reason for Japanese negotiators to heed such pressure when U.S. demands ran counter to economic theory on trade and when many prominent academic economists in the United States opposed their own government's position.

According to this view, the United States must save more and spend less if it wants to reduce its trade deficit. Since that could push the country into a recession, many U.S. political leaders shied away from seeking a smaller trade deficit. The trade deficit remained unaddressed, and the losers from free trade were ignored and allowed to proliferate until they finally elected Trump president in 2016.

I/S Balance Theory Cannot Explain What Happened to the U.S. Economy

The argument that the U.S. trade deficit is the result of too much consumption and too little production, and that somehow Americans are living beyond their means, has convinced many. After all, a trade deficit *does* signify that a country's consumption is greater than its production.

The problem is that there are numerous reasons why consumption might exceed production, and the I/S theory is just *one* of them. Moreover, this theory—which is dominant in the discipline of economics—has been totally inconsistent with what is happening in the U.S. economy.

The theory implies that Japan and China are supplying products that the United States cannot supply in sufficient quantities for itself. But if that were the case, the U.S. industries still producing those products would be operating at 100 percent capacity, and both businesses and employees in those sectors would be celebrating their good fortune.

But that is the opposite of what has actually happened. When Japanese exports to the United States surged some 50 years ago, U.S. industry was capable of supplying huge quantities of automobiles, steel, television sets, and many other products. However, those products were driven out of the market by Japanese rivals, forcing tens of thousands of U.S. manufacturers into bankruptcy and causing the loss of millions of jobs. U.S. manufacturers simply could not compete with quality imports sold at lower prices because of an excessively strong dollar. Instead of enjoying good fortune, as suggested by the I/S balance theory, they all went out of business.

This trend continued as economies like Taiwan, South Korea, Mexico, and finally China began to increase their exports to the United States. In other words, what actually happened to U.S. industry was the opposite of what the I/S balance theory had predicted.

U.S. consumption ended up being greater than production because the dollar was overvalued, not because U.S. manufacturers did not have enough capacity to produce those products. The two different causes of trade deficits are summarized in Figure 9.4.

While the economists espousing I/S balance theory place little emphasis on exchange rates, nothing is more important than the exchange rate for exporters and importers deciding whether or not to go ahead with a trade deal. No matter how strong domestic demand may be, if the product cannot be sold at a price consumers are willing to pay, there is no point in exporting it. And the exchange rate is one of the most important determinants of the final selling price in the importing country.

In other words, even if the economy is very strong, only products that clear all of the final selling price hurdles will actually cross the

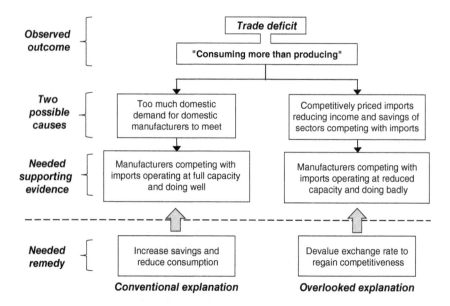

FIGURE 9.4 Inappropriate Exchange Rates Are Largely Responsible for Trade Imbalances

border and be sold in the country. That means a strong economy is neither a necessary nor a sufficient condition for imports to grow. Given the same exchange rate, a country will import more when domestic demand is strong than when it is weak, but it is not the case that strong domestic demand will always result in greater imports regardless of the exchange rate.

On the other hand, even a weak economy will import products that can be sold more cheaply than the domestic competition. That means price-competitive imports, which are heavily dependent on the exchange rate, are both a necessary and a sufficient condition for imports to grow (and for exports to decline). It is also for this reason that the export-led growth model based on Strategy B mentioned in Chapter 5 worked so well for many emerging economies.

Individual Savings Result in Collective Dis-Saving

When imports grow for this reason, those making goods that compete with those imports will lose jobs and income. As incomes decline, so do savings, and production will fall below consumption. But this happens not because people opted for a profligate lifestyle, as implied by the I/S balance theory, but because consumers in the importing nation wanted to *save* money by buying less expensive imports—the antithesis of a profligate lifestyle. But collectively, these consumers' purchases of imports eliminate the jobs and reduce the incomes of those employed by local industries competing with imports.

That means there is a fallacy-of-composition problem behind this type of trade deficit: while individually people are trying to save money by buying cheaper imports, collectively they end up *dis-saving* because of the drop in income and savings of those employed by sectors competing with imports. And this happens because an overvalued dollar allows trade deficits to continue in the United States. Proponents of the I/S balance theory of trade seldom mention exchange rates, but they are of crucial importance for real-world exporters and importers.

Long-Term Structural Impact of Exchange Rates

Exchange rate fluctuations are also perfectly capable of changing the entire structure of the economy. When the dollar strengthened sharply in the first half of the 1980s, rising to a high of 280 yen and 3.30 Deutschmarks, it was said in the United States that industries that would have disappeared in 30 years had disappeared in just five. In other words, even Americans expected that some light industries such as textiles would eventually relocate to lower-wage countries, but they never expected them to disappear so fast.

The same phenomenon was observed in Japan in the 1990s. When Japanese manufacturers were confronted with the shocking exchange rate of 79.75 yen/dollar in April 1995, many simply gave up and moved their factories overseas. Although many in Japan also expected that some industries would eventually have to move abroad, they never expected the relocation process triggered by the ultra-strong yen in April 1995 would be so abrupt. Since then, many former industrial regions of Japan have begun to resemble the U.S. Rust Belt.

Irreversibility of Factory Relocation in Medium Term

A complicating factor is the element of irreversibility that characterizes this process of moving production overseas. Many U.S. factories that moved offshore prior to the Plaza Accord of September 1985 never returned even though the accord succeeded in cutting the value of the dollar in half, from 240 to 120 yen, by 1987. Similarly, many of the Japanese factories that left the country after the yen surged to 79.75 yen/dollar in April 1995 never came back even though the Japanese currency fell back to 147 yen/dollar three years later.

This indicates that once a business experiences a devastatingly high exchange rate, the repercussions continue long after the exchange rate returns to a more reasonable level. In other words, once an unthinkable exchange rate like the 79.75 yen/dollar rate of April 1995 becomes a reality, it changes the "realm of possibilities" for all exporters and importers for many years even if the actual exchange rate remains at that level for only a few seconds.

Once domestic suppliers disappear altogether due to the over-valued domestic currency, subsequent imports of products that are no longer produced at home will depend in part on the strength of domestic demand, much as the I/S balance theorists have postulated. This suboptimal legacy effect of exchange rates can stay with the economy for many years.

Even in such circumstances, however, returning to a trade-equilibrating exchange rate is desirable because it will stop the losers from free trade from endangering what is left of free trade. For example, the nationwide protectionist pressures seen in the United States prior to the Plaza Accord in 1985 completely disappeared after the accord had halved the value of the dollar in 1987, even though many industries that left the country before the accord never returned. Protectionist pressures in the United States did not return to the levels seen in 1985 until the dollar started strengthening against other global currencies in the global "quantitative easing (QE) trap" that started in September 2014, as is noted in Chapter 6.

Export "Push" Is Often More Important than Import "Pull"

While proponents of the I/S balance theory of trade emphasize the role of strong U.S. domestic demand in pulling in imports, actual U.S. trade is often driven by the marketing *push* of foreign exporters eager to enter the U.S. market. The amount of effort postwar Japanese manufacturers had to exert to establish a foothold in the U.S. market while overcoming both racism and the bitter animosity of a former enemy was legendary. But they were willing to put in that effort because the U.S. market was not only the largest, but also the most transparent in the world and had relatively few nontariff barriers.

This contrasted with the markets of Japan and many other countries that were often open only on paper, at least until recently. During the U.S.-Japan trade frictions 30 years ago, Japanese trade negotiators argued that their market was fully open and that U.S. exports to Japan were so limited because U.S. companies were not trying hard enough. But for companies that must maximize their return on capital, it is difficult to justify moving into a market that is known to be difficult for foreign companies to enter, especially when there are other markets offering higher returns on capital.

The author can attest to the difficulty of entering the Japanese market in the 1990s because he was directly involved in the U.S.-Japan trade frictions at the time. As an American citizen residing in Japan, who had also worked for the Federal Reserve as an economist, the author was asked by the U.S. Embassy in Tokyo at the height of U.S.-Japan trade frictions to explain the U.S. trade position to Japanese television audiences, as he was a frequent guest on a number of programs.

After receiving extensive briefings on various issues from embassy staff, the author made a case for U.S. exporters in numerous nationally televised debates with Japanese economists and policy makers. The author covered disputes on everything from auto parts to semiconductors and the Fuji-Kodak rivalry. While Japanese trade negotiators were openly claiming that the Japanese market was open, the reality was far different.

At the height of the trade frictions, the author found an American car with right-hand-drive on the streets of Sydney, Australia. Since he was familiar with that particular model of car, he bought it and imported it to Japan both to find out what sort of nontariff trade barriers there really were and to thwart criticism of U.S. automakers by Ministry of International Trade and Industry (MITI, now METI) officials for not producing right-hand-drive cars to match the Japanese market.

The author encountered a mind-boggling range of trade barriers that can be condensed into two numbers. First, it cost $2,000 to rent an entire container to transport the car 5,000 kilometers from the port of Sydney, Australia, to the port of Yokohama, Japan. Meanwhile, it cost $9,000 to clear all the nontariff barriers erected against imported cars and have the vehicle shipped from Yokohama to the author's residence 50 kilometers away in Tokyo. Some of the exasperating nontariff barriers the author encountered during the import process were mentioned by Walter Mondale, the U.S. Ambassador to Japan, in speeches at the time.

This experience indicated that even though top Japanese bureaucrats were very smart, they had no idea of the kind of trade barriers that existed on the ground. The difficulty of entering the Japanese domestic market was also demonstrated by the existence of many so-called export-only companies in Japan, as is noted in Chapter 5.

Having spent time on the front lines of the trade dispute between pursuing and pursued countries, the author will never forget the intense mutual hostility that characterized U.S.-Japan trade frictions from the mid-1980s to the mid-1990s. Not only did the author receive his share of death threats, but the trade frictions ultimately began to resemble a racial confrontation.

In all of these encounters, the author, in addition to discussing individual trade cases, argued that if Japan continued to resist pressures to open its market while at the same time running huge trade surpluses with the United States, the trade imbalances would eventually push the yen sky-high and force Japan's best industries to leave the country.[3] This prediction unfortunately came true in April 1995, when the yen appreciated to 79.75 yen/dollar.

This happened because the loud and very acrimonious U.S.-Japan trade frictions in the early 1990s scared many Japanese portfolio investors into thinking the United States might want to devalue the dollar even further. That fear made them hedge their long-dollar positions (by selling dollars forward) or refrain from buying dollar assets, leaving the exchange rate to be determined largely by trade flows. The resulting strength in the yen then started a wholesale exodus of Japanese manufacturers from the country. Some of those factories also relocated to the United States, which finally cooled down the decade-long U.S.-Japan trade frictions.

About the only time the I/S balance theory of trade so strongly espoused by economists is relevant is when there is a large demand shock—such as those following the Lehman Brothers collapse in

---

[3] Koo, Richard (1994), *Yoi-Endaka, Warui-Endata (Good Strong Yen and Bad Strong Yen)*, Toyo Keizai Shinpousha, Tokyo.

2008 and the COVID-19 pandemic in 2020. At such times, the near-collapse of the U.S. economy did cause a substantial reduction in its imports. The stoppage of many investment projects around the world after 2008 also drastically reduced Japanese exports, which were dominated by capital goods.

Similarly, China's massive 4-trillion-yuan fiscal response to the Lehman crisis in November 2008 did increase its imports substantially, which was a huge help to the world economy at that time. Although these abrupt changes in demand can be used to explain changes in imports and exports, relying on the I/S balance alone to explain the overall trade imbalance is poor economics.

When U.S.-Japan trade frictions were at their worst in the early 1990s, the Japanese side demanded that the United States reduce its large budget deficits to improve its I/S balance and reduce its trade deficit. Many Western economists were making the same argument, equating the U.S. budget deficit to a nation living beyond its means. But by the second half of the 1990s, the U.S. government was running large budget surpluses, yet the country's trade deficit had almost doubled. This indicates the U.S. trade deficit was driven by factors other than fiscal deficits. In spite of such glaring errors and the inconsistency between what was predicted by the theory and what actually happened, the proponents of I/S balance theory remain influential within the economics profession, making it difficult for policy makers to address trade imbalances with adjustments to exchange rates.

The preceding experience showed that free trade could create more losers than winners if a country is allowed to run deficits for an extended period of time, and that the I/S balance theory of trade was inconsistent with the facts on the ground. The post-1980 driver of trade imbalances has been the exchange rate misalignment brought about by cross-border capital flows. To fight the destructive backlash against free trade and globalization, therefore, policy makers must ensure that capital flows do not push exchange rates in a direction that will worsen trade imbalances. That, in turn, requires a good understanding of the drivers of cross-border capital flows.

Unfortunately, this is the third area in which poorly conceived economic theory has prevented policy makers from taking appropriate actions to limit trade imbalances. In particular, insufficient recognition of the inherent conflict between free capital flows and free trade flows has resulted in many inconsistent policies over the years.

Open Capital Markets Are a Relatively New Phenomenon

The major economies opened their markets to cross-border capital flows only four decades ago. U.S. financial markets were not liberalized until the *Monetary Control Act of 1980*, which started the deregulation of interest rates. The Monetary Control Act itself was a response to the double-digit inflation the U.S. economy was suffering in the late 1970s, which made it difficult to maintain administered interest rates.

Before this act, there had been a raft of controls and regulations that insulated U.S. financial markets from the rest of the world. These included Regulation Q, which controlled domestic interest rates; Eurodollar reserve requirements, which discouraged arbitrage between domestic and offshore markets; and the Fed's discouragement of domestic financial institutions from offering foreign-currency-denominated financial products to U.S. retail customers.

The deregulation of Japan's capital markets also started in 1980, when the Foreign Exchange Law was amended to allow, in principle, investments in foreign assets for the first time. Washington pushed hard for Japan to open its capital markets via the so-called Yen Dollar Committee, based on the mistaken notion that it would attract more foreign capital to Japan and strengthen the yen. It was mistaken because as soon as the floodgates were opened in the early 1980s, the capital that flowed *out* of Japan in search of higher yields elsewhere completely overwhelmed the foreign capital that flowed into the country, resulting in a significant decline in the value of the yen as noted earlier.

Many European countries also started removing controls on cross-border portfolio flows starting in the 1980s. These liberalization efforts accelerated in the 1990s as part of preparations for the single currency.

The point is that, even in advanced countries, it was only in the last 40 years that cross-border capital flows really got off the ground. This also means that capital flows had not been liberalized when the founders of macroeconomics such as John Maynard Keynes, Sir John Richard Hicks, and Paul Samuelson were writing from the 1930s through the 1970s.

Capital Flows Distort Trade Flows

When financial markets and cross-border capital flows are liberalized, market forces move capital around so as to equalize expected returns in all markets. To the extent that countries with strong domestic demand tend to have higher interest rates than those with weak demand, money will flow from the latter to the former. Such flows strengthen the currency of the former and weaken the currency of the latter. They may also add to already strong investment activity in the former by keeping interest rates lower than they would be otherwise, while depressing already weak investment activity in the latter by pushing interest rates higher than they would be otherwise.

To the extent that countries with strong domestic demand tend to run trade deficits and those with weak domestic demand tend to run trade surpluses, these capital flows will exacerbate trade imbalances between the two by pushing the deficit country's currency higher and pushing the surplus country's currency lower. In other words, these flows are not only inconsistent with the interests of individual countries, but are also detrimental to the attainment of balanced trade between countries. The widening imbalances then intensify calls for protectionism in the deficit countries. These destabilizing flows are summarized in Figure 9.5.

Furthermore, the equalized rate of return on capital obtained in this way might not be in the best interest of any individual country. For example, if market forces are trying to equalize global interest rates at, say, 3 percent, countries requiring rates either above or below 3 percent will suffer. Indeed, the market-driven 3 percent rate of interest may not be in the interest of *any* individual economy.

In the world that existed before efforts to liberalize capital flows commenced in the early 1980s, trade was free, but capital flows were regulated, so the foreign exchange market was driven largely by trade-related transactions. The currencies of trade surplus nations therefore tended to strengthen, and those of trade deficit nations to weaken. That encouraged surplus countries to import more and deficit countries to export more. In other words, the currency market acted as a natural stabilizer of trade between nations.

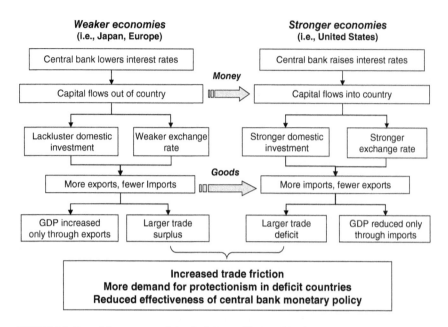

FIGURE 9.5 Free Movement of Capital Can Kill Free Trade

Today, the capital flows that dominate the foreign exchange market seek to equilibrate investment returns across countries in accordance with market principles. Not only has the world lost a mechanism for balancing trade, but capital flows have frequently moved exchange rates in such a way as to increase global imbalances, as described in Figure 9.5.

If imbalances and job losses prove too much for the deficit country to tolerate, either the market or politicians will act, usually with unpleasant consequences. The market reaction may include a collapse of the deficit country's currency (the dollar fell from 360 yen in 1971 to 79.75 yen in 1995). The resultant foreign-exchange losses incurred by surplus-country investors could wipe out earlier gains and put a temporary stop to the sorts of capital flows illustrated in Figure 9.5.

But once investors in the surplus countries get over their losses in a couple of years, they will see that the U.S. trade deficit is declining with a weaker dollar. They will then conclude that "the dollar has fallen enough." This will prompt a resumption of the kind of capital flows indicated in Figure 9.5, and they will not stop until another crash forces another temporary suspension. Indeed, the world may repeat this foolish cycle of destabilizing capital flows and financial crashes for decades without any benefits or efficiency gains accruing to the countries involved.

If politicians are forced to act, it can lead to protectionism and a collapse of global trade, as exemplified by the Smoot-Hawley Tariff Act, which triggered the global depression in the 1930s. More recently, with no mechanism for balancing trade left, continued growth in the U.S. trade deficit and the number of losers from free trade helped usher in the protectionist policies of President Trump.

As noted in Chapter 6, after the Fed announced its intention to normalize monetary policy in September 2014, the dollar appreciated over 20 percent on a trade-weighted basis and more than 60 percent against the Mexican peso at one point (Figure 6.5) as portfolio investors sought the potentially higher interest rates of the United States. Such a large and abrupt appreciation of the dollar made life difficult for U.S. manufacturers and their employees and contributed in no small way to the election victory of Trump, who openly argued in favor of protectionism. This means that the increased demands for protectionism prior to the 1985 Plaza Accord and the increased demands for protectionism led more recently by Trump were both driven by capital flows that pushed the value of the dollar higher in spite of huge U.S. trade deficits.

Efficiency Gains from Capital Flows?

Some may argue that there must be efficiency gains for the global economy if capital is earning a higher return abroad. Although that may be true for carefully executed direct investment flows (discussed later) and intracountry capital flows, the outcome is not so clear for portfolio flows when different countries and currencies are involved. Japanese investors ended up incurring huge foreign-exchange losses when the dollar fell from 240 yen in 1985 to 80 yen in 1995. The Chinese also sustained massive losses on their dollar investments when the RMB appreciated 37 percent against the dollar between 2005 and 2015. Large European investments in the United States from 2001 to 2003 also cost investors dearly as the euro climbed sharply higher against the dollar. Similarly, U.S. investors with foreign-currency assets suffered heavy losses when the dollar became the strongest currency in the world starting in September 2014. These investors all expected to make money by investing abroad, but all they had left at the end of the day was massive foreign-exchange losses.

It is also difficult to argue that the massive purchases of U.S. Treasuries by the Japanese starting in the 1980s and by the Chinese starting in the 1990s were the best use for those funds. When the average American is living far better than the average Japanese or Chinese, it makes no fundamental sense for the latter two to be lending money to the former. Richard Cooper (1997)[4] has also argued that there are many cases of cross-border capital flows that are hard to justify on efficiency grounds, among them flows driven by differences in tax laws and accounting treatment.

The point is that the massive capital flows that are influencing exchange rates are of dubious value because it has *never* been proven that such flows actually improve the welfare of all concerned. Economists and financial market participants who pushed for ever-freer capital flows simply *assumed* based on neoliberal tenets that whatever increases the freedom of the private sector will result in a better allocation of resources. Although that is largely true in a closed economy, a positive result is not assured in an international context with multiple currencies where labor is not allowed to move freely (this last point is discussed further later).

Capital Flows Are Undermining Effectiveness of Monetary Policy

The rapid expansion of cross-border flows is also complicating the implementation of monetary policy. Today, it is just as easy for Japanese households to invest their savings in U.S. dollars as it is for Croatian households to arrange home mortgages in Japanese yen. The ease with which these transactions can be undertaken would have been unthinkable just 20 years ago.

---

[4] Cooper, Richard N. (1997), "Should Capital-Account Convertibility Be a World Objective?" in Peter B. Karen et al. (ad.), "Should the IMF Pursue Capital-Account Convertibility?" *Essays in International Finance 207*, Princeton NJ: Princeton University International Finance Section, May 1998, pp. 11–19.

Indeed, the pre-2008 housing bubbles in Europe were made possible to some extent by people taking out home mortgages in Japanese yen or Swiss francs in what was known as the "carry trade." This refers to investments financed with borrowings in foreign currencies offering lower rates of interest. Even if the European Central Bank (ECB) tried to rein in housing bubbles in Spain and other Eurozone countries by raising interest rates, home buyers borrowing in yen would not be affected, because the interest rates they pay are determined by the Bank of Japan (BOJ).

Higher euro interest rates due to ECB tightening, however, will widen the interest rate differential between the euro and the yen in favor of the former. That, in turn, lifts the euro against the yen by enticing capital away from the yen and into the euro. The weaker yen reduces the liabilities of those Europeans borrowing in yen, emboldening even more people to fund their investments with borrowed yen. In other words, the growth of mortgages denominated in Swiss francs and Japanese yen undermined the effectiveness of ECB policy in the Eurozone.

When the Fed announced its intention to normalize monetary policy in September 2014, the United States was already nearing full employment, and some assets were displaying bubble-like characteristics. Commercial real estate prices in particular had already returned to their pre-crisis peak and were still moving higher, as shown in Figure 4.7. Any central banker in such circumstances would want to begin tightening monetary policy to forestall inflation and prevent an asset price bubble.

What followed, however, was vastly different from what the Fed expected. When the Fed announced in September 2014 that it would normalize interest rates, Japan and Europe were still in the process of expanding QE and lowering interest rates. As a result, massive amounts of funds left those two regions for the United States in search of higher yields. U.S. funds that had flowed out of the country after the global financial crisis (GFC) in 2008 in search of higher yields in emerging markets also began to return.

Those capital inflows pushed the dollar sharply higher while putting downward pressure on long-term U.S. bond yields. Instead of monetary tightening resulting in higher bond yields and putting the brakes on a commercial real estate bubble, domestic and foreign appetite for U.S. debt kept Treasury yields low and provided further fuel for the bubble in commercial real estate. Commercial real estate prices are now 68.3 percent higher than at the height of the bubble in 2007 and are 68.9 percent higher than in September 2014 (Figure 4.7).

The same capital inflows also transformed the dollar into the world's strongest currency, which made life difficult for both U.S. exporters and companies competing with imports. As a result, the already alarmingly large U.S. current account deficit expanded further, fueling protectionist pressures from both workers and businesses.

The United States, which wants and needs stronger exports and a cooler commercial real estate market, is getting the opposite because of cross-border capital inflows, while Japan and Europe have the same problem in reverse. Both are running large external surpluses while suffering from weaker domestic demand, which is why they eased monetary policy in the first place. But monetary easing prompted capital outflow to the United States, weakening their currencies and encouraging their exporters to export more.

National Policy Objectives Are Inconsistent with Free Capital Flows

No economics textbook offers any guidance as to what the Fed or the BOJ should do under these circumstances. This is because most of the academic literature on so-called "open economies" dealt with open trade in goods only and seldom included open trade in capital. In other words, the economics profession has never envisioned a world with a globalized financial market, in which anyone, anywhere can borrow and invest in any currency at any time. But that world is here today. The world economy is truly in uncharted waters.

In this world, central banks that set low interest rates end up stimulating investment outside their borders via the carry trade, while those setting higher rates end up attracting a disproportionate share of global savings. At the moment, the BOJ and the ECB find themselves in the former position with negative interest rates, while the Fed is in the latter position with a strong dollar. This is not a problem specific to any individual country. It is a problem for *all* central banks in a globalized financial market.

Moreover, the adverse exchange rate movements created by these capital flows have caused global imbalances to reach alarming levels and pushed desperate working families in deficit countries into the protectionist camp. No economist would argue that such a world is desirable on the grounds of either efficiency or equity. If no one wanted this outcome, how did it come about?

It came about because the opening of capital markets in these countries brought their financial sectors together into a single global market, while governments and labor markets remained strictly local. The conflict stems from market forces trying to integrate the world's economies into a single market, but the people and governments of individual countries have no intention of becoming a single country.

Many Different Countries, One Financial Market

To see this, assume that Japan and the United States were planning to become one country. Their relationship would then be like the one that exists between the states of California and New York, and no one would give a second thought to trade imbalances between the two, no matter how large they might become.

The balance of trade between states like California and New York is not an issue because people, capital, and goods are free to flow between the two. If New York has a booming economy but California is in recession, people will move from California to New York in search of better job opportunities. Similarly, if investment opportunities are more attractive in California than in New York, capital will flow from New York to California in search of higher returns.

Even if people are not so free to move, the federal government in Washington, D.C., can use its powers to redistribute income from areas experiencing an inflow of income (i.e., a trade surplus) to areas experiencing an outflow of income (i.e., a trade deficit). This is possible because both California and New York are part of the United States.

With all factors of production free to move between New York and California, it also makes no sense for the two states to have separate monetary policies. Given the ease with which money can move between them, any difference in interest rates would immediately result in massive arbitrage that would equalize rates.

Today, capital is moving between countries *as though* they were going to become a single nation. That is why investors pay so little attention to the huge current account deficits of the United States or the current account surpluses of Japan (which they themselves created). It also explains why monetary policy is losing its effectiveness at the national level, in the same way that New York and California cannot have separate monetary policies.

The problem, however, is that neither Japan nor the United States has any plans to merge into a single nation. Both set limits on immigration that restrict the free movement of labor between the two countries. They also have different value systems, different languages, and different traditions. In other words, they are and will remain separate nations. The fundamental disconnect of free capital flows comes from the fact that countries are trying to remain independent while their financial markets are behaving as though they were about to merge into a single nation.

When policy makers and economists in the advanced countries were pushing for free capital flows in the late 1970s and early 1980s, they *should* have asked voters whether this was the outcome they wanted to see. No such vote was taken because no one was thinking that far ahead. But today the world is living with the consequences of the decisions made then.

To make matters worse, many policy makers and economists are still unaware of how the world got into this mess in the first place. For example, Trump and others blame free trade for today's problems, but it is actually the free movement of capital that is causing these huge global imbalances.

The calls for protectionism and the rhetoric against free trade in the United States would have been much more manageable if the value of the dollar had not risen as much as it did after September 2014. To the extent that capital flows are allowed to exacerbate the external imbalances of individual countries, trade frictions and imbalances are likely to remain important political issues for years to come.

Financial Types Have No Choice Either

The financial market participants behind these capital flows are also unable to act any differently since they are part of the market forces that are bringing national markets together by directing funds to where expected returns are the highest, even though such actions may worsen global imbalances and add to protectionist pressures at some later date. Their actions can also undermine the effectiveness of their own central banks as the higher interest rates meant to dampen domestic investment end up attracting more investment funds from abroad, while the low interest rates intended to stimulate domestic investment end up causing domestic investment funds to move overseas.

As chief economist of a research institute associated with the largest investment bank in Japan, the author's main job is to brief the bank's global investor clients. Based on his own involvement with the pre-1995 U.S.-Japan trade frictions, the author often notes that trade imbalances are a potentially important determinant of exchange rates. But in the period before 2016, the typical reaction of many younger investors was to stare back in disbelief. They could not imagine that trade-related transactions, which account for only about 5 percent of total foreign exchange transactions, could have such an impact. Portfolio investors had also paid virtually no attention to trade or current account imbalances during the two decades from 1995, when U.S.-Japan trade frictions finally subsided, to November 2016, when Trump was elected president of the United States.

Instead, they were interested mainly in the direction of monetary policy in various countries and the resultant changes in interest rate differentials. This is in spite of the fact that monetary policy has lost much of its effectiveness in the advanced economies (Figures 2.12 to 2.14 and 2.17), all of which are in the pursued phase and are suffering from balance sheet recessions or their aftermath.

It is indeed fascinating to note that, regardless of where they reside, investors are all looking at basically the same economic, market, and policy indicators when making investment decisions. The questions the author is asked by investors in New York are no different from those he hears in Singapore, Frankfurt, Tokyo, or London. They really are part of one huge global market working to equalize returns on capital.

A New Realization in Foreign Exchange Market?

Foreign exchange market participants had ignored massive U.S. trade deficits and supported the dollar based on a belief that sustained deficits on this scale do not matter. However, Trump's election victory and the social backlash he represented seem to have influenced the behavior of foreign exchange market participants since 2016.

The fact that the dollar has not strengthened against the Japanese yen and some other currencies during Trump's four-year term in spite of the Fed's push to normalize monetary policy may reflect a new realization among foreign exchange market participants that trade imbalances *do* matter. For example, until the day Trump was elected the 45th president of the United States, most foreign exchange analysts were predicting the dollar would strengthen to 130 or 135 yen from around 110 yen at the time. Their view was based on the assumption that the Federal Reserve would continue to normalize (raise) interest rates while the BOJ and ECB maintained extremely accommodative stances, thereby widening interest rate differentials in favor of the dollar.

These analysts' forecasts for U.S., Japanese, and European monetary policy proved correct: the United States raised interest rates eight times between the 2016 election and the first half of 2019, while the negative Japanese and European policy rates were unchanged. Despite this 200-basis-point increase in interest rate differentials in favor of the dollar, the yen/dollar exchange rate averaged around 110 yen to the dollar all the way to the onset of the COVID-19 pandemic.

This 25-yen difference between the projected yen/dollar exchange rate of 135 and the actual rate of 110 probably reflects a renewed understanding among foreign exchange traders that trade imbalances do matter, especially under a president like Trump. After all, they do not want to be caught long dollars when the U.S. president starts talking (or tweeting) down the dollar in an attempt to reduce the trade deficit. If the president actually began talking down the dollar, it could easily fall 5 to 10 percent against the yen or euro in a matter of minutes, resulting in huge foreign exchange losses for those who were long dollars.

The fear of such tweets probably reduced the number of Japanese portfolio investors who were buying dollars. That, in turn, allowed yen buying by Japanese exporters to keep the yen strong despite a widening interest rate differential that should have stengthened the dollar.

The Biden administration, which has not said much about trade imbalances, appears to be allowing the foreign exchange market to revert back to its old and problematic ways, and the dollar has been strengthening rapidly, especially against the yen, in response to monetary policy tightening by the Fed.

Converse of Optimal Currency Theory Is Needed

There is a rich literature in economics on the theory of optimal currency areas. It argues that if two regions have free movement of capital, labor, and goods, they should adopt a common currency. It also states that, if there is to be a common currency, there should also be free movement of capital, labor, and goods. In areas such as the Eurozone, where governments have invested a great deal of time and effort to enable the free flow of capital, labor, and goods, a single currency will provide major benefits for all concerned.[5] Globally, however, governments making such efforts are the exception rather than the rule.

Theory and reality are at greatest odds when it comes to the flow of people because immigration remains a thorny issue in most countries. Even if immigration were fully liberalized, differences in language, race, religion, and culture would continue to hamper the free movement of people. The world consists of 200 independent nations mostly because there are 200 different and often mutually exclusive value systems and national identities. The barriers created by the differences in these values cannot be overcome by economic exchanges alone.

Nor is it realistic to expect the advent of a world government capable of redistributing income across national borders. As long as nations have no intention of becoming a single country or giving up an important part of their sovereignty to a "world government," trade imbalances—which signify the transfer of income from deficit to surplus nations—will remain a major political issue.

Although individual governments and the IMF seek to reduce trade imbalances, their efforts often run contrary to financial markets' trend toward a unified market. Indeed, the IMF itself sometimes seems schizophrenic, with one part of the organization pushing for freer movement of capital while the other is fighting trade imbalances brought about by the same. This disconnect between free capital flows and the trade tensions resulting from a lack of political integration will be with us for decades.

---

[5] One exception is the problem of capital flight among the Eurozone's 19 government bond markets, as is explained in Chapter 7.

The key question facing the world economy today, therefore, is really the *converse* of the optimal currency area concept. In other words, if the free movement of one or more factors of production is not achievable, should the remaining factors be allowed to move freely? More specifically, if labor is not allowed to move freely across national borders, should capital be allowed to do so?

Answering this question in full would probably require volumes of research. More specifically, policy makers and scholars must reexamine the costs and benefits of the unrestricted opening of capital markets instead of blindly assuming that anything that increases the freedom of the private sector is good for the economy. Although the economics profession has proved that open trade in goods improves the welfare of the concerned economies, it has *not* demonstrated that open trade in capital will produce the same result when there are multiple currencies involved and other factors of production are not free to move.

The Case for Government Intervention in Foreign Exchange Market

But policy makers facing protectionist threats today may not have the luxury of waiting for the findings of such research: they may have to act now to protect free trade and preserve world peace. To the extent that the explosion of cross-border capital flows during the past four decades contributed to larger global imbalances and more calls for protectionism, they may want to consider placing some restrictions on those flows. Realistically speaking, however, the genie is already out of the bottle, and putting global capital flows back into that bottle will be extremely difficult.

As a second-best solution, policy makers may wish to mull more direct government involvement in the foreign exchange market if capital flows themselves are to be left to the private sector. For example, they may want to consider implementing something similar to the Plaza Accord of 1985 to periodically realign exchange rates in order to forestall protectionism and prevent destructive cycles of capital flows and financial crashes.

As is noted earlier, a strong dollar in the summer of 1985 left the U.S. administration facing widespread calls for protectionism.

Only a handful of U.S. companies were still competitive against the Japanese when the dollar was hovering around 250 yen, or against the Germans when the dollar was at 3.30 Deutschmarks. Indeed, it was said at the time that only two U.S. companies, Boeing and Coca-Cola, were still in favor of free trade, while everyone else was opposed to it. President Ronald Reagan, a strong believer in free trade, had to convene a meeting of the G5 countries on September 22, 1985, to establish the Plaza Accord, which was designed to save free trade by weakening the dollar.

Although initially markets were highly skeptical that governments had the ability to move exchange rates, the G5 (later G7) countries succeeded in halving the value of the dollar to 120 yen and 1.63 Deutschmarks by the end of 1987. By 1988, the Accord had completely neutralized the protectionist threat in the United States. Although the dollar did return briefly to 160 yen in 1990, it never exceeded that level ever since, indicating that forceful government action can have a lasting impact.

Can Governments Escape from Policy Trilemma?

The problem is that Plaza Accord–like government interventions are considered "politically incorrect" in the neoliberal climate that permeates the economics profession, where any market restrictions or interventions undertaken by the government are viewed with suspicion. But these economists are operating on the false assumption that the losers from free trade will never outnumber the winners. With the losers from free trade already having huge influences on national elections, policy makers no longer have the option of standing by and doing nothing.

If capital flows are to remain free, policy makers must prevent the losers from free trade from outnumbering the winners by ensuring that trade balances do not get out of whack. Ironically, under the current regime of liberalized capital flows and a hands-off policy toward foreign exchange rates, protectionist measures are the only tool policy makers have to "defend" free trade by keeping trade imbalances within politically or socially acceptable bounds.

This leads to the fourth problematic notion in economics that has discouraged policy makers from taking action in the foreign

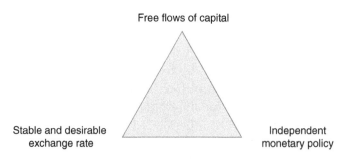

FIGURE 9.6 Policy Trilemma

exchange market to limit trade imbalances. This concept, which Maurice Obstfeld called the policy trilemma (Figure 9.6), states that a government cannot influence exchange rates if the central bank maintains an independent monetary policy focused primarily on the domestic economy and capital flows remain free, as they have been since 1980. Economists' objection, otherwise known as the impossible trinity, says that of the three policy goals of free capital flows, independent monetary policy, and a stable exchange rate at a desirable level, national authorities can achieve only two out of the three.

For example, if the authorities want to lower the exchange rate while maintaining free capital flows, the central bank must reduce interest rates to prevent inflows of foreign capital, which could cause the currency to rise. In other words, they are no longer free to choose monetary policy.

Similarly, if they decide to raise interest rates in order to stamp out inflation while continuing to allow the free flow of capital, they cannot avoid the currency appreciation that will result when those high interest rates attract inflows of capital from abroad. They therefore lose control over exchange rates.

This thesis was originally proposed by Canadian economists like Robert Mundell when that country was liberalizing its capital flows with the United States in the 1960s. Economists then used this theory to argue against the U.S. government use of exchange rates to address trade imbalances.

For those who have studied this theory, it seems pointless, even reckless, for the U.S. government to try to lower the value of the dollar in a world where capital flows remain free and the Fed is pursuing an independent monetary policy. After all, the theory says this is impossible.

Trilemma's Implicit Assumption Is Not Consistent with Foreign Exchange Market Reality

Although the trilemma is taught in universities around the world, it is based on an assumption that does not hold in the actual foreign exchange market. The theory assumes that currency market participants are almost exclusively portfolio investors who make investment decisions based solely on interest rate differentials. In other words, exchange rates in the theory are determined almost entirely by interest rate differentials between the countries.

But in the real world, portfolio investors also draw on a wide variety of economic and political indicators when those indicators seem relevant to their investment decisions. There are also many other participants in the foreign exchange market, including importers, exporters, and central banks.

This distinction among different categories of market participants is important because importers and exporters do not have the choice of *not* participating in the foreign exchange market, whereas portfolio investors do. Those involved in exports and imports need to buy and sell foreign currency to conduct their business. If the United States is running trade deficits with Japan, that means the dollar selling and yen buying stemming from U.S.-bound goods is greater than the yen selling and dollar buying stemming from Japan-bound goods, putting upward pressure on the yen as noted earlier. In other words, as long as the United States is running a trade deficit with Japan, there will always be upward pressure on the yen and downward pressure on the dollar from exporters and importers in the two countries.

Portfolio investors, on the other hand, are not required to enter the foreign exchange market or buy dollar assets. If Japanese investors think they can make money by investing in dollar-denominated assets, they will acquire dollars in the foreign exchange market. Otherwise, they will not. They may also choose to invest in foreign assets denominated in nondollar currencies. This is in huge contrast to the situation at importers and exporters, who have no choice but to sell their foreign exchange earnings for domestic currency in the case of exporters and vice versa for importers.

If trade imbalances become a political issue, thereby increasing the risk that the U.S. administration may want to weaken the dollar in the future (as happened after the Plaza Accord of 1985), portfolio investors would reduce their allocations to dollar-denominated assets or hedge their existing exposure to dollar assets (by selling dollars forward) in order to reduce their foreign exchange risk. When many portfolio investors stop buying dollars in the foreign exchange market or begin hedging their long-dollar positions, the relative importance of importers and exporters in the foreign exchange market increases. Since the latter group is putting upward pressure on the yen, the reduced influence of the former group means the yen will move higher against the dollar.

As noted earlier, this is why the dollar did not appreciate against the yen under President Trump—something most foreign exchange analysts were forecasting prior to his election in November 2016. That means the U.S. government *was* successful in keeping the exchange rate from appreciating even with free capital flows and an independent monetary policy focused on the domestic economy.

Trilemma Is Irrelevant When Desired Exchange Rates Help Rectify Imbalances

This event demonstrated that the policy trilemma noted by economists disappears when the authorities seek an exchange rate that will help to rectify trade imbalances. In other words, the trilemma is only valid if the authorities seek an exchange rate that serves to *exacerbate* trade imbalances.

The G5 nations succeeded in slashing the yen/dollar exchange rate from 240 when the Plaza Accord was signed in September 1985 to 120 at the end of 1987 because authorities sought an exchange rate that would help reduce trade imbalances. Hence, there was no policy trilemma. U.S. interest rates were much higher than Japanese rates throughout this period (Figure 9.2), but investors were reluctant to buy U.S. assets in the face of sustained and severe trade frictions between the United States and Japan. Sustained trade frictions pushed the yen/dollar exchange rate down to 79.75 in April 1995.

On the other hand, if the authorities in a trade-surplus country like Japan try to keep the value of their currency low—as the BOJ is doing today—the policy trilemma will manifest itself very strongly, and monetary policy autonomy will be lost. To prevent the yen from appreciating, the BOJ must keep interest rates low. In other words, the trilemma is relevant when the monetary authorities want to push exchange rates away from trade-equilibrating rates.

Many economists have cited this trilemma and the I/S balance theory of trade when questioning U.S. government moves to reduce trade deficits. However, the problem is with the theories themselves and not with U.S. policies.

Determining Trade-Equilibrating Exchange Rate Is No Easy Task

Deciding what constitutes the trade-equilibrating exchange rate is not easy, of course. After all, this is largely a zero-sum game, and no country wants to be stuck with an uncompetitive exchange rate. The current "hands-off" market-determined exchange rate regime adopted by the developed countries is in some sense a cop-out by policy makers who find it impossible to agree on an exchange rate. But given the groundswell of protectionism, policy makers simply cannot leave the exchange rate to the whims of international investors and speculators who care little about trade imbalances or the loss of ordinary workers' jobs.

Although agreeing on an exchange rate (or a range for an exchange rate) is a difficult political decision, purchasing power parity provides an idea of how overvalued a currency is. According to the "Big Mac index" shown in Figure 9.3, the U.S. dollar is overvalued against every global currency except the Norwegian krone and the Swiss franc, with the overvaluation amounting to 15 percent for the euro and fully 42 percent for the Japanese yen.

The fact that the dollar is so expensive on a purchasing power parity basis is a key reason why there are so many losers from free trade and so many calls for protectionism in the United States. It should therefore be in the interest of all U.S. trading partners to keep the dollar in a range where the number of U.S. losers from free trade decreases rather than increases. That is the only way to save the free trade system that has been so beneficial for humanity since 1947.

It should be noted that even a trade-equilibrating exchange rate does not guarantee that all industries in the country will survive. It is simply the rate that equates the total value of imports and exports. Industries that cannot survive at that exchange rate will still have to relocate.

Even if exchange rates are adjusted to equilibrate trade, there will be grievances from workers in pursued countries. This is because exports from those countries are likely to be more capital- and technology-intensive, while those from pursuing countries are likely to be more labor-intensive. Consequently, even if trade is balanced, the pursued countries end up "importing labor" because of the higher labor content of their imports. However, that is still far better than the situation today, where deficit countries could continue losing income and jobs to surplus countries for decades because no mechanism exists to equilibrate trade.

Central Bank Intervention Is Effective If It Sides with Trade-Driven Flows

In addition to the trilemma, which discouraged the U.S. government from playing a more active role in the foreign exchange market, many market participants have argued that even if central banks intervene in the foreign exchange market on behalf of governments, their actions are bound to be ineffective because private capital flows are now so much larger than the amounts central banks can mobilize. This argument has also discouraged policy makers from using exchange rate adjustments to address trade imbalances.

The impact of such interventions, however, can far exceed the actual amounts of money being mobilized if central banks side with trade-driven foreign exchange flows and coordinate their actions. Siding with trade-driven flows means buying the currencies of surplus countries and selling the currencies of deficit countries.

Central banks are the only foreign exchange market participants who do not have to worry about profits and losses. When they side with trade-driven flows and start pushing exchange rates in such a direction as to reduce trade imbalances, private-sector participants, who *do* have to worry about losing money, get scared. After all, they are in the market to make money, not to prove how strong they are.

Upon seeing central banks charging in their direction, many would prefer to avoid confrontation because central banks have potentially *unlimited* ammunition when they are pushing exchange rates in such a direction as to reduce trade imbalances. This is because the central bank of a deficit country wishing to weaken its currency can "print" potentially unlimited amounts of its own currency and sell it on the foreign exchange market to depress the currency's value.

To avoid such confrontations, investors who have been betting on an appreciation of deficit-country currencies will quickly square their positions by selling those currencies and buying back the currencies of surplus countries. Their selling multiplies the impact of the central bank's initial sale of the deficit-country currency and pushes exchange rates in the desired direction.

The best example of this was in the two years after the Plaza Accord of September 1985, when G5 central banks successfully pushed the overvalued U.S. dollar down from 240 yen to 120 yen. This also offers confirmation that the policy trilemma does not apply when the central bank is pushing exchange rates in a direction that serves to reduce trade imbalances.

In contrast, central bank interventions that go against trade flows tend to be ineffective or easily overpowered by the market. For example, if the central bank of a trade-deficit country wants to strengthen its currency, it must sell its holdings of foreign currency and buy its own currency. Since its holdings of foreign currency are limited, market forces can easily overwhelm a central bank when traders see its ammunition being depleted. This is how George Soros triumphed over the Bank of England (BOE) in 1992. The point is that central banks do have the power to influence exchange rates if they are moving them in a direction that serves to correct trade imbalances.

The "Asian Plaza Accord" and the Responsibility of Surplus Countries to Sustain Free Trade

It was noted at the beginning of this chapter that the 70-year postwar era, in which a generous United States helped the world economy grow by purchasing the world's products while running large trade deficits (i.e., over-stretching), is coming to an end. In this new and potentially conflict-ridden era, the response of surplus countries that have benefited from earlier U.S. generosity will be critical in determining how the global trading system evolves. If they want to avoid a 1930s-like breakdown in global trade and maintain access to the U.S. market, they must act consciously and decisively to reduce the number of Americans who view themselves as being losers from free trade.

One way to do this would be for China, Japan, South Korea, and Taiwan, which together account for 45.0 percent of U.S. trade deficits (Figure 9.7), to band together and revalue their currencies by, say,

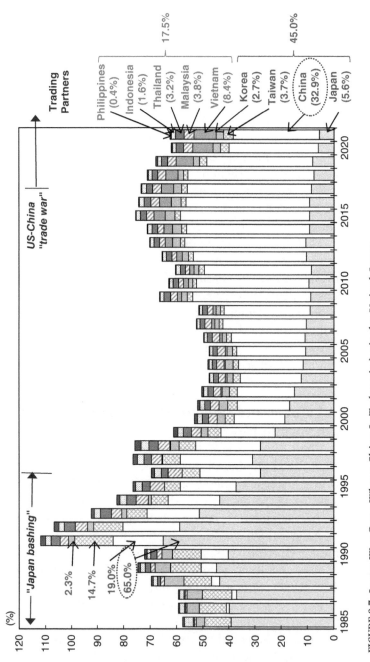

FIGURE 9.7 Japan Was Once Where China Is Today vis-à-vis the United States

Source: U.S. Census Bureau

20 percent against the U.S. dollar in what might be described as an Asian Plaza Accord. By acting together, they could push their currencies much higher than if they acted individually because intra-Asian trade would not be affected. It would be even better if the Association of Southeast Asian Nations (ASEAN) countries, which together account for another 17.5 percent of the U.S. trade deficit, could be brought on board. Such a multilateral adjustment would reduce both U.S. trade deficits and the number of Americans who view themselves as losers from free trade.

These four countries have various political issues among themselves. However, they all have one serious problem in common: their huge trade imbalances with the United States. This issue is also difficult to address individually because other countries might try to take advantage of an exchange rate initiative undertaken by a single country. Working together, they should be able to solve the problem.

It was previously noted that the strong protectionist pressures seen in the United States just before the Plaza Accord was signed in September 1985 were no longer an issue in Washington by the time the Louvre Accord was signed in February 1987. Instead of allowing highly arbitrary tariff-based protectionism to wreck the global trade system, it would be far better for surplus countries to jointly realign their exchange rates and thereby safeguard the free-trade system that has benefited them and the rest of humanity since 1947.

Surplus Countries Opening Markets Is Preferable to Currency Appreciation

There is actually one more action many surplus countries can take before embracing currency appreciation, and that is to open their domestic markets to imports. But before addressing that topic, it would be useful to see why countries covet a trade surplus.

Because exports are added and imports are subtracted when calculating the GDP, there is a feeling among some policy makers that a trade surplus is essential to sustained economic growth. The fact that the Asian countries that achieved rapid growth did so with exports under Strategy B by running large trade surpluses implies that a trade surplus is good for growth. Many countries are also trying to keep their exchange rates low in order to remain competitive for the same reason. Based on these notions, many fear that the loss of trade surpluses necessarily means lower economic growth. But is that actually the case?

GDP is compiled by adding consumption, investment, net exports, and net government spending. Net exports can decline for two reasons: a decrease in exports or an increase in imports. A fall in net exports due to reduced exports implies a decline in production and employment and a weaker economy overall.

But if the decline in net exports is due to higher imports, someone in the country must have increased consumption or investment in the process. If the imports are mostly consumer products, consumption has grown. If they are mostly capital goods, investment has grown. In either case, GDP will increase even if net exports have shrunk. Greater consumption or investment also implies an improvement in living standards. For the same decline in the trade surplus, therefore, an increase in imports is better than a decline in exports. If a country must reduce its trade surplus, it is better to open the domestic market to more imports than to accept a higher exchange rate, which reduces exports.

Politically, it is often more difficult to open the domestic market because of vested interests in the protected industries. Opening the market also hurts weak industries that have no place to go, whereas currency appreciation affects strong, globally competitive industries that may be able to withstand the shock by outsourcing. Politicians can also get away easier with exchange rate appreciation because they can always claim that they are not in control of the foreign exchange market.

But the country as a whole suffers if it moves toward a contractionary equilibrium with currency appreciation instead of an expansionary equilibrium with market-opening measures. The economy will experience reduced long-term growth if currency appreciation expels the best industries, leaving only protected sectors with dim future prospects. Living standards will also suffer as people are forced to pay much higher prices while income growth stagnates with a fall in exports.

When trade frictions between the United States and Japan flared up in the 1980s and continued into the 1990s, Japan fiercely resisted U.S. pressure to open its market based on the I/S balance argument noted earlier in the chapter. This resulted in an appreciation of Japan's currency from 240 yen/dollar in 1985 to 80 yen/dollar in

1995, forcing the country's best industries to move overseas. The resultant hollowing-out of manufacturing contributed in no small way to the nation's subsequent economic stagnation.

If Japan had acceded to U.S. demands to open its market, the probability is high that the exchange rate would have stayed well above 100 yen/dollar and that many industries that left the country would have remained. If the market-opening measures had boosted Japanese consumption, they would also have increased living standards and GDP by the same amount, even if the trade surplus declined.

Japan did learn from the disastrous 1990s and took a very different approach when the Trump administration demanded a correction of the U.S.-Japan trade imbalance in 2017. Instead of rejecting demands for market-opening measures, the Shinzo Abe administration decided to buy nearly 150 extremely expensive F-35 fighter planes (about $220 million each) to calm the trade dispute. By offering a big answer to a big problem, Abe succeeded in reducing trade tensions and kept the exchange rate from appreciating.

For Japan and other countries that need to import oil, some bilateral surpluses with non-oil-producing countries are needed to earn enough foreign exchange to pay for their oil. But this argument cannot be used as justification for a trade surplus. If the domestic market is fully open to imports, then the only way to reduce the surplus is to allow the exchange rate to rise, but most surplus countries today still have a long way to get there.

When doing nothing about the trade imbalance is no longer an option, surplus countries should seek an expansionary equilibrium by opening their domestic markets to imports instead of allowing their exchange rates to rise, thereby creating a contractionary equilibrium for both themselves and the world.

Adjustments to Exchange Rates Can Lead to Capital Flight

Although a central bank can influence the exchange rate if it is trying to reduce trade imbalances, its actions may come at a high cost if they trigger capital flight. To understand this risk, imagine a world in which the U.S. government openly started to push for a weaker dollar. In the face of such overt government action, anyone holding dollar assets, including U.S. investors, would probably consider dumping those assets in exchange for foreign-currency assets and buying back the dollar assets later, after they have become cheaper in foreign currency terms.

If those investors sold the U.S. bonds they held, bond prices would be pushed lower, sending yields higher and putting highly unpleasant pressure on U.S. financial markets and the economy. Indeed, this sort of capital flight could lead to sharply higher bond yields and the dreaded "big mess" scenario that is noted in Chapter 6, something the Fed has been trying to avoid at any cost.

Although largely forgotten by both market participants and academics, such a disastrous capital flight actually occurred 35 years ago in March 1987, roughly a year and a half after the start of the Plaza Accord. By then the dollar had fallen from 240 yen in September 1985 to an all-time low of just over 150 yen, and from 2.84 Deutschmarks when the Plaza Accord was signed to just 1.82 Deutschmarks. U.S. authorities were satisfied with the extent of the adjustment. To indicate their satisfaction, the G7 countries in February 1987 concluded the Louvre Accord, which basically stated that the dollar had fallen enough. After the agreement was signed, the Japanese government busily assured investors, who had suffered huge foreign-exchange losses on their U.S. bond holdings, that 150 yen marked the bottom for the dollar.

But a few days before the all-critical Japanese fiscal year-end on March 31, the dollar suddenly slipped below 150 yen, shocking Japanese investors who had refrained from selling the dollar in the belief that 150 yen marked the bottom. Feeling betrayed and panicked, they dumped U.S. bonds, exchanged dollars for yen, and bought JGBs, sharply widening the interest rate differential between the two bond markets starting on the day the dollar fell below 150 yen (Figure 9.8).

U.S. policy makers and market participants, who seldom look to Asia for answers, initially had no idea what was happening and blamed the sudden increase in U.S. bond yields on domestic inflationary fears. From his vantage point in Japan, the author could see what was happening and quickly telephoned his former colleagues at the Federal Reserve Bank of New York to inform them that the long-feared capital flight was now unfolding, knowing that Paul Volcker, the Fed chairman, had been worried about this risk from the outset of the Plaza Accord. The author told U.S. authorities that, by looking at what was happening to (1) the yen/dollar exchange rate, (2) U.S. Treasury

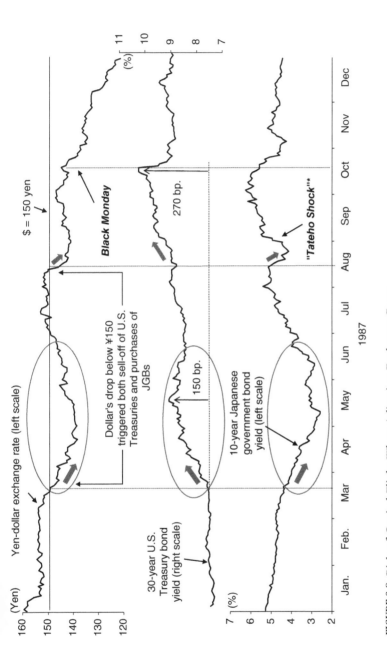

FIGURE 9.8 Risk of Capital Flight When Adjusting Exchange Rates

*Note: Japanese chemical company Tateho incurs massive losses in JGB futures trading, triggering panic in JGB market.

Sources: Federal Reserve Bank of New York, Board of Governors of the Federal Reserve, Japan Bond Trading Company

bond yields, and (3) JGB yields after the dollar slipped below 150 yen, they could confirm for themselves that the dreaded capital flight was happening.

Once U.S. authorities realized that it was the falling dollar that had triggered the fall in bond prices, Volcker announced that the Fed was ready to raise interest rates to defend the dollar. This announcement had an impact because it was the first concrete indication since the Plaza Accord that the United States was willing to defend the dollar, and the U.S. currency returned to 150 yen by early July. The divergence in U.S. and Japanese government bond yields that had begun in March was also reversed, signaling an end to the capital flight.

But policy makers' credibility was shattered when the dollar slipped below 150 yen again just a few days after Alan Greenspan became the next Fed chairman in August. Apparently, the importance of defending the 150 yen/dollar exchange rate was either not conveyed to the new chairman or he chose to ignore the warning. U.S. bond yields renewed their move higher as the dollar resumed its fall, eventually triggering the Black Monday stock market crash in October 1987. On Black Monday, the yield on the 30-year U.S. Treasury bond was a full 270 basis points higher than when the dollar had fallen below 150 yen for the first time six months earlier.

This incident indicates that policy makers must be careful when making exchange rate adjustments if the financial markets are vulnerable to capital flight, as was the case in the United States. This may be one reason why President Trump never talked down the dollar in his four years in office. If U.S. bond yields rose 270 basis points from current levels, not only the U.S. housing market but also the commercial real estate market, with its extremely low capitalization rates, and the stock market, with its extremely high valuations, would likely suffer mightily.

"Paying Back Our Fathers' Debt"

This 1987 incident also begs two questions. First, why did Japanese investors in the late 1980s not dump the dollar earlier as it fell from 240 yen/dollar to 150 yen/dollar? Second, could we expect similar patience from Japanese and other investors today?

Japanese investors refrained from selling the dollar until the end of March 1987 for two reasons. First, they had large unrealized capital gains in their domestic stock portfolios that could be used to absorb losses elsewhere. Those gains had accumulated on their crossholdings of Japanese equities, an arrangement that began in the 1950s. Because the Japanese economy had grown rapidly and share prices had surged in the 30 years to 1987, investors had amassed huge unrealized capital gains by the time the Plaza Accord was implemented.

But having unrealized gains is no reason for Japanese investors to hold on to dollar assets when the U.S. government is openly pushing for a weaker dollar. A very different mindset was at work in the late 1980s—in effect, many Japanese investors told themselves that, by *not* selling dollar assets, they were paying back their fathers' debt to the United States.

"Their fathers' debt" refers to the help the United States extended after the war to rebuild Japan, a former enemy. The author actually heard this phrase many times from Japanese institutional investors during those years. By not selling their dollar assets and absorbing the losses, they were helping the United States bring its exchange rate down nearly 40 percent without a major disruption to its economy and its markets. What should not have been possible was made possible because of the peculiar way Japanese investors viewed the war debt of their fathers.

But when the dollar fell below 150 yen in late March 1987, even those investors found themselves unable to stick to their self-imposed moral obligations any longer. Still, it was extremely fortunate for the United States that this happened at an exchange rate of 150 yen/dollar and not at 180 or 200 yen/dollar.

As for the second question, of whether similar patience can be expected from today's foreign holders of U.S. Treasuries, the Japanese stock market crash that began in 1990 wiped out Japanese investors' unrealized gains. Moreover, mark-to-market accounting is now the norm and crossholdings of shares have been drastically reduced—both, ironically, under pressure from the United States. While Japanese investors had a major presence in the U.S. bond market during the 1980s, today the Chinese and other investors also play important roles, and they are likely to think and act very differently from the Japanese 35 years ago. That means much greater care will be required in bringing the dollar down than in the period from 1985 to 1987.

It should also be noted that not all of the capital flight observed in the late 1980s and 1990s was due to Japanese investors. In

March 1988, about a year after the events described above, it was reported that selling by the Japanese had triggered another plunge in the U.S. Treasury market, sending the dollar lower. Japanese investors—who were *not* selling this time—actually made an official statement to that effect through the Life Insurance Association of Japan.[6] Eventually it was discovered that it was U.S. investors, worried that their Japanese counterparts were about to start selling, who had moved preemptively to unload their U.S. bond holdings.

Today, the potential for investors to move preemptively—correctly or otherwise—is far greater than it was 30 years ago given the prevalence of quick-acting hedge funds and computer-driven program trading. If the U.S. administration wants to adopt a weak-dollar policy, it therefore needs to assume there will be a certain amount of capital flight. In other words, the United States should not have to worry about the trilemma previously noted because it is a deficit country trying to weaken its own currency, but it must be careful to ensure that capital flight out of the dollar—and the rise in domestic interest rates that would result—does not get totally out of control.

Two Types of "Equalizing" Capital Flows and the Quality of Investors

The impact of capital flows on exchange rates also depends on the quality of the investors involved as well as whether those flows are being driven by direct investment or portfolio investment. Although most of the preceding discussion on capital flows assumes that they consist mostly of portfolio flows, direct investment flows from nonfinancial corporations also generate cross-border capital flows. Such flows are becoming increasingly important as businesses in pursued countries seek higher returns on capital by investing in emerging countries.

The distinction between direct and portfolio investment is important because even though both "equalize" returns on capital across national borders, their impact on exchange rates can be quite different. Most investors who are sending money abroad in the form of

---

[6] *Asahi Shimbun* (1988), "Endaka 'Seiho-Hannin-Setsu' ni Kyokai ga Irei no Hanron" ("Accusation that Life Insurers Are Responsible for Strong Yen Is Absurd"), in Japanese, March 30, 1988, p. 9.

direct investment are likely to be nonfinancial operating companies who are building factories after conducting careful studies of the host country, including its trade balance. Careful study is required because they cannot leave easily once they build a factory or set up operations there.

These businesses are investing abroad because of the higher returns on capital available. But returns are higher because of higher growth rates or competitively priced factors of production such as wages, not because of higher interest rates. That means direct investment flows will tend to lift the exchange rates of increasingly competitive pursuing countries while depressing the exchange rates of increasingly uncompetitive pursued countries. Except for direct investments made to avoid tariffs, these investment flows tend to move exchange rates in a direction that equilibrates trade flows.

Portfolio investors, on the other hand, will often buy the financial assets of deficit countries simply because they offer higher interest rates. Such flows often move exchange rates in a way that will enlarge existing trade imbalances, as explained in Figure 9.5.

Another problem facing portfolio investors is that they often have only limited time to study the countries they are investing in, especially when they are competing against global stock market indexes such as those from the MSCI. If a sudden boom in a nation's stock market pushes the MSCI index higher, for example, fund managers who are competing with that index but do not own many of that country's stocks will come under tremendous pressure to include those stocks in their portfolios. Too often they end up rushing to buy without fully understanding all the issues surrounding the country.

When something bad happens to the country, these poorly informed portfolio investors tend to rush to the exits simultaneously in a massive panic that hurts both the market and the country's economy. Although academic economists tend to assume that investors are always rational and know what they are doing, the actual market is littered with examples of ignorance, greed, or worse. The all-too-frequent formation of asset price bubbles proves just how irrational investors can be.

The Latin American debt crisis of 1982 and the Asian currency crisis of 1997 were both precipitated by supposedly sophisticated Western financial institutions lending billions of dollars to poorly managed public-sector borrowers in Latin America and to projects with huge financial mismatches (short-term foreign-currency financing for long-term domestic projects) in Asia. Since the author was involved in both events on the ground, he can attest to the nonsense that was perpetuated by those investors in the runup to the crisis.

In the case of Latin America, the Federal Reserve Bank of New York—the author's employer at the time—was the only agency of the U.S. federal government that had a group dedicated to the evaluation of country risk. And since 1979 that group had been issuing strong warnings that American banks should reduce their exposure to Latin American countries with horrendous inflation rates, out-of-control budget and current account deficits, and poorly managed public-sector borrowers. This warning was conveyed to bankers in periodic meetings the New York Fed had with the banks. Yet, in spite of stern and repeated admonishments, American banks doubled their exposure to Latin America from 1979 to 1982, when the whole mess finally blew up.

In the Asian currency crisis, Nomura's economist in Singapore issued a report only a few months before the crash saying that valuations had gone mad and that investors should get themselves out of the Asian bubble immediately. Nomura received an incredible amount of bashing from some of the top Western investors due to that report, as no one wanted to hear the bad news. One of the top U.S. investors at the time said to the author, "You guys are so pessimistic because Nomura is based in Japan, where everything is in the doldrums. Asia is great!"

Although the Latin American crisis was halted by the actions of Volcker, as is noted in Chapter 8, no one stopped foreign investors from rushing simultaneously to the exits in the Asian crisis, resulting in massive panic and dislocation. These two crises demonstrated that nothing is worse for emerging economies than an influx of cash-rich but ignorant investors from the developed world investing in projects they do not fully understand.

In the wake of the 1997 Asian crisis, for example, many Western investors complained loudly about a wide range of structural problems in Asia, including crony capitalism and the inadequacy of Thai bankruptcy laws. But their very complaints proved that they had done no homework on the countries in which they were investing. After all, it was their duty to investigate those laws *before* investing in the country. In other words, they showed themselves to be totally unqualified to invest in Thailand.

In view of the quality of real-world investors, the authorities might want to consider assigning higher risk weights to institutional investors' holdings of assets denominated in the currencies of current account deficit countries. The purpose of such a measure would be to remind institutions that their investments in such assets may contribute to the widening of global imbalances that could result in large currency losses in the future.

The authorities could also employ risk weights to curb the carry trade, which has undermined monetary policy in many parts of the world. The Russian central bank, for example, has successfully reined in the market for foreign-currency-denominated home mortgages by imposing higher risk weights on banks' holdings of such mortgages.

The point is that, even though both direct and portfolio investment flows serve to equilibrate the return on capital across national borders, the former are based on real competitive factors that tend to move exchange rates in the direction needed to equilibrate trade balances, while the latter are often based on interest rate differentials, which tend to move exchange rates in the opposite direction. It is this latter type of capital flow that is problematic.

Chilean Solution to Deter Uninformed Investors

The authorities in emerging economies on the receiving end of portfolio inflows from advanced countries may also want to consider the Chilean solution. Chile was a victim of the Latin American Debt Crisis in 1982, which is noted in Chapter 8, when U.S. banks that understood little about Latin America lent billions of (petro) dollars to public-sector borrowers there in the belief that governments do not go bankrupt. When Mexico duly went belly up in August 1982, all other borrowers south of the U.S.-Mexico border were caught up in the contagion and suddenly lost access to the market, resulting in devastating recessions that lasted for over a decade.

From this bitter experience, the Chileans correctly concluded that it is dangerous to accept money from foreign investors who have not done their homework. They realized that foreign investors with insufficient knowledge of the country will quickly panic when things go wrong and collectively rush to the exits, causing devastating turmoil in the market and the economy.

To ensure that those bringing money to the country have done their homework, Chile imposed a high tax rate on portfolio inflows that remained in the country only briefly. The tax rate gradually declined with the length of the capital's stay. Although this tax helped enhance the stability of the Chilean economy by forcing outside investors to do their homework, it was later removed, apparently under pressure from U.S. authorities.

The value of the Chilean approach was demonstrated again 15 years later, when Malaysia imposed a similar tax during the devastating Asian currency crisis. The tax succeeded in quickly stabilizing the economy and markets but was harshly condemned by the US Treasury Department. One of Treasury's top officials declared that the Malaysian economy would not recover for the next 10 years given such bad policy choices. In reality, the country was the *first* to recover, emerging from the currency crisis in just 18 months and proving that free portfolio capital flows provided few benefits to Malaysia at its current stage of economic development.

The Malaysian experience also suggests the IMF and the U.S. government should be more careful when asking countries to allow free portfolio capital flows. For Wall Street, more open foreign capital markets mean more playgrounds to play in. But there is no proof that the benefits of foreign portfolio capital flows to the host country outweigh the negatives of heavy fluctuations in asset prices, exchange rates, and economic activity.

At the most fundamental level, emerging economies experiencing a large influx of speculative capital should intervene on the currency market to keep currency appreciation in check and raise reserve requirements applied to banks to prevent asset bubbles from forming. When speculative capital starts to leave the country, authorities should reverse those actions by lowering reserve requirements to curb deflationary pressures while intervening on the foreign exchange market to support the currency.

For this program to be successful, it is critical for the government to have the courage to prevent foreign inflows from pushing up domestic asset prices as well as the courage not to spend the foreign exchange obtained via interventions so it will be available to support the currency when the speculative capital invariably leaves the country. Neither is easy. But Taiwan and China have demonstrated that a disciplined application of this kind of regime will shield the economy from the worst vagaries of international portfolio flows.

Consider Organizing National Teams before Plunging into Protectionism

The COVID-19 pandemic has started a debate on the need to have domestic suppliers of critical public health goods instead of relying on cheaper imports. This push toward industrial policy/protectionism has been reinforced by the fact that the COVID-19 health crisis (1) started in China, which has become the world's factory, and (2) was a pandemic and not just an epidemic.

On the first point, because China has become the key supplier of so many things, the entire world faced shortages of numerous critical items when the nation had to shut down to contain COVID-19. On the second point, the fact that it was a pandemic meant that every country faced the same shortages at the same time, and efforts to diversify foreign suppliers were of little help. Many countries also placed strict limits on exports of many items, including medical supplies and vaccines.

As a result, those who would normally be supporters of free trade had to seriously consider industrial policy combined with protectionism to secure domestic production of critical items. But it is not easy to sustain production of such items at uncompetitive prices.

A remarkable solution to this problem was implemented by Taiwan, a democratic country of 23 million people. Taiwan was also heavily dependent on China for medical masks, the supply of which dried up when the pandemic started in Wuhan, China. But its Ministry of Economy immediately sprang to action by first locating an old mask-making machine collecting dust in a warehouse. It completely disassembled the machine and catalogued all of its thousand or so components. The ministry then sought the help of an industry association to find local companies that could manufacture all of those components as quickly as possible.

The government's goal was to make 10 million masks a day, which manufacturing experts at the time said would take about six months. But the "national mask team," composed of 141 companies and organizations working around the clock to fabricate the necessary parts for the mask-making machines and set up a production line, achieved that goal in only 25 days! That allowed every Taiwanese to have at least two new surgical masks per week by early March 2020. Production of masks surpassed 20 million a day by May. As a result of this and other well-coordinated policies, Taiwan has been able to keep the number of cumulative COVID-19 infections since January 2020 down to 22,463 and the number of total deaths down to just 853 (as of March 27, 2022).

This example shows that even if a particular product is not made in sufficient quantities at home, a government can still safeguard the health and safety of its citizens by organizing a national team of manufacturers to produce that product as quickly as possible. To play such a role, the government must be constantly aware of which companies can be relied upon to produce what, but such effort and preparations will make the economy more resilient at times of crisis.

Not every country in the world has the kind of manufacturing base that Taiwan did when the pandemic hit. It is shocking, however, that the governments of many industrialized countries that *did* have such a base failed to organize national manufacturing teams to provide needed items to their people. With both natural and human-made disasters happening with increased frequency, governments urgently need to put together contingency plans that include the creation of national teams to manufacture necessary items. Industrial policy and protectionism should be invoked only for those items that national teams are unable to supply at short notice.

Time to Rethink Capital Market Liberalization

Financial globalization makes sense if the world is eventually going to become a single nation. The current turmoil and social backlash stems from financial globalization proceeding at a time when *no* country seeks global political integration. Nor has there been any move to create a world government with the authority to redistribute income.

The free-trade component of globalization has not only improved the lives of billions of people on this planet, but has also contributed tremendously to human peace and happiness since 1945 by making war largely obsolete, at least among those nations with free and open societies. The importance of free trade was demonstrated most clearly when the world tried the alternative—protectionism—in the 1930s and experienced a devastating global depression and a horrendous world war as a result. Although measures to help the losers from free trade are needed, the huge benefits countries have obtained from free trade should not be abandoned lightly.

The same cannot be said of the free movement of capital. This component of globalization often enlarges global imbalances and increases cries for protectionism in deficit countries while undermining the effectiveness of monetary policy in all nations. Countries such as Malaysia actually recovered faster when they abandoned the free movement of capital that had been destabilizing their economies. Since it is not at all certain whether free capital movement, especially of the short-term portfolio variety, adds value to the global economy, thorough research on when to allow such flows and when not to allow them should be part of the effort to contain protectionism in all pursued countries. Until conclusive research is available, policy makers facing the choice between free trade and free portfolio capital movements should definitely opt for the former over the latter.

The Most Realistic Solution

With the genie already out of the bottle, that is, capital flowing freely around the world, the most realistic way for governments to stop the loss of manufacturing jobs and contain the backlash against free trade may be to do exactly what former President Trump did—that is, to keep on making loud noises about trade deficits so that portfolio investors around the world will pay greater attention to them. For authorities to remain credible, such talk should be bolstered occasionally by the threat of official intervention on the foreign exchange market to stop the appreciation of deficit-country currencies.

These actions should also be carefully implemented so as not to trigger the kind of capital flight that started in the United States at the end of March 1987. If such "noisy forward guidance" on exchange rates discourages portfolio investors from taking foreign exchange positions that exacerbate trade imbalances, it may be possible to have both free capital movement and free trade, thus benefiting everyone, including investors.

With less-than-perfect investors and less-than-perfect economic and political integration, it is hoped that policy makers will be pragmatic and not beholden to neoliberalism and other unproven ideologies when addressing the problems of capital flows, exchange rates, and trade imbalances. At the very minimum, policy makers must understand that it is free capital flows that are endangering free trade and all the benefits it has brought to humanity.

An incompletely taught theory of free trade, an inappropriate adherence to the I/S balance theory of trade, and the unrealistic assumptions of the policy trilemma have dissuaded policy makers from taking stronger action to rectify trade imbalances. Their inaction, in turn, has increased the number of people who view themselves as losers from free trade. Today this group is large and angry enough to threaten the free trade, which has brought unprecedented peace and prosperity to the world.

Careful examination of those theories in view of what actually happens in the economy and foreign exchange market revealed that policy makers can still do a great deal to rectify trade imbalances and thereby contain the social backlash against free trade. Balancing the trade account does not mean there will be no losers from free trade, but their numbers can be reduced to the point that they will no longer threaten the peace and prosperity made possible by free trade. On the other hand, if no action is taken on capital flows or exchange rates and trade imbalances are allowed to expand unhindered, the resulting social backlash against free trade and the establishment in general might force some governments to opt for protectionism and tribalism, which would be the worst of all possible outcomes.

CHAPTER 10

Rethinking Economics

Rethinking Macroeconomics

Macroeconomics is still a very young science. It began when John Maynard Keynes, who recognized the existence of fallacy-of-composition problems in the macroeconomy, conceived the concept of aggregate demand in the 1930s. Only 90 years old, it is like a toddler when compared with centuries-old disciplines such as physics and chemistry. Nicolaus Copernicus deciphered the workings of the solar system in 1530, and Isaac Newton discovered the universal law of gravity in 1687. These monumental discoveries took place 250 to 400 years before Keynes developed the concept of aggregate demand in 1936. As a young science, economics has been able to explain only a limited range of economic phenomena. Its youth also makes it prone to fads and influences.

The profession's immaturity was amply demonstrated when only a handful of economists saw the post-2008 Great Recession coming, and even fewer predicted how long it would take to recover from it. Most also failed to anticipate that zero interest rates, massive quantitative easing (QE), and inflation targeting would fail to bring about inflation within the forecast time.

These fundamental failures stem from the fact that most macroeconomic theories and models developed during the last 90 years assumed that private-sector agents always seek to maximize profits. For that to be true, it was implicitly assumed that attractive investment opportunities would always be plentiful and that private-sector balance sheets would always be clean. From those two assumptions, it follows that profit-maximizing firms will always be willing to borrow if only the central bank lowers real interest rates far enough. Although these two assumptions are valid throughout most of the golden era, when economies are typically in Case 1 or 2, economists have not realized that most advanced economies today are not only in the pursued phase, but are also experiencing balance sheet recessions, that is, that they are squarely in Cases 3 and 4.

Before realizing that an economy could be in Case 3 or 4, where the private sector may be minimizing debt, economists had to come up with a variety of explanations for phenomena they could not explain with the conventional framework, which assumes a profit-maximizing private sector. Phenomena that eluded explanation included prolonged periods of economic stagnation and unemployment despite record-low interest rates and pump-priming via fiscal stimulus.

The explanations put forward to explain them included allusions to structural problems, deflationary expectations, secular stagnation, the cost of rewriting menus (i.e., the high cost of changing prices), and "external shocks." These are similar to the explanations that astronomers gave for the movements of the planets before Copernicus realized it was the earth that was circling the sun and not the other way around.

Structural or Balance Sheet Problems?

Allusions to structural problems are a common refuge for economists whose conventional macroeconomic policy prescriptions fail to produce the expected results. Too often, they revert to structural explanations without realizing that other factors—such as balance sheet problems or a lack of investment opportunities—can also produce a similar predicament.

Economists started to fall back on structural explanations after Ronald Reagan and Margaret Thatcher made the public aware of the importance of structural or supply-side issues in the 1980s. In contrast, balance sheet problems or shortages of investment opportunities were never discussed in economics departments or business schools until quite recently.

A large number of economists and policy makers therefore jumped onto the structural reform bandwagon in both post-1990 Japan and post-2008 Europe, arguing that there could be no economic recovery without such reforms. But the Reagan and Thatcher era in the United States and United Kingdom could not be more different from the post-bubble period in Japan and Europe.

At the time of Reagan and Thatcher, both the United States and the United Kingdom were facing high inflation and interest rates, incessant labor disputes, and large trade deficits. In present-day Japan and Europe, inflation and interest rates are both extremely low, labor disputes are rare, and trade accounts are deeply in surplus, at least before the pandemic and energy shortage. Moreover, both economies were responding well to conventional macroeconomic policies before 1990 in Japan and before 2008 in Europe. That makes it difficult to argue that the economies suddenly lost steam and are stagnating because of age-old structural issues.

But because of mainstream pundits' near-exclusive focus on structural reforms, Japan has wasted a tremendous amount of time and resources on such policies over the last 30 years, as has Europe for the last 15. In the United States, meanwhile, policy makers understood within the first two years of the global financial crisis (GFC) that the country was suffering from balance sheet problems, not structural issues. As a result, it was the *only* country that did not fall into the structural reform "trap," even though many of its economists had been arrogantly lecturing the Japanese on the need for such reforms only a few years earlier. The United States was doing much better than Japan or Europe because it did not waste any time debating structural reform policies.

Structural Reforms Require a Correct Narrative

The lack of investment opportunities typical of countries in the pursued phase is indeed an argument for structural reform. This is because deregulation and other structural reforms are needed to raise the return on capital at home. What must be made clear, however, is that structural policies are needed to address problems that existed *before* the economy fell into a balance sheet recession. In other words, structural reforms are necessary, even in the United States, but they are not the answer to the sudden deceleration of these economies after the bubble burst in 2008. For these much more urgent balance sheet problems, it is fiscal stimulus and not structural reform that is required.

The policy makers and economists who peddled structural solutions for the post-2008 stagnation lost credibility with the public when their policies failed to produce a recovery within the expected timeframe. Their loss of credibility allowed outsiders and far-right political parties to make substantial political gains, especially in Europe.

In Japan, former Prime Minister Junichiro Koizumi's favorite slogan—"no economic recovery without structural reform"—and his opposition to fiscal stimulus were totally inappropriate for a country that was suffering from massive balance sheet problems. During his five-year tenure from 2001 to 2006, Japan's private sector was saving an average of 9.26 percent of GDP in spite of zero interest rates. Not surprisingly, the economy continued to stagnate during and after his structural reform efforts.

Seventeen years have passed since the end of the Koizumi administration, and Japan's private sector has finally repaired its balance sheet. The remaining challenge for the nation is to fend off pursuers from behind, which is indeed a structural reform issue. The problem is that the public was told two decades ago that structural reforms would lead to economic recovery, but the promised recovery never materialized. Feeling betrayed, people are now rightfully skeptical of any structural reform proposals—including the "third arrow" of Abenomics, which was all about structural reforms. Many are tired of hearing the term itself. Economists may keep their teaching jobs in universities even if their predictions and prescriptions turned out to be wrong, but they have lost credibility, and not just for themselves but for the entire establishment.

What Japan needs now, therefore, is a proper narrative starting with an admission that the earlier emphasis on structural reform was premature and mistaken because at that time, the problem was rooted in balance sheets. The new narrative must indicate that balance sheet problems have been resolved and that structural reforms are now needed to increase the return on capital at home to attract investment and fend off pursuers from behind. It must also explain that, because the private sector is still a huge net saver, fiscal stimulus must continue until private-sector borrowers return.

A similar distinction also needs to be made in Europe, where extreme-right parties have made considerable gains amid economic weakness. It must be emphasized that while structural reforms are necessary to increase the return on capital at home and fend off pursuers from behind, such measures are no substitute for the fiscal stimulus needed to counter the balance sheet recessions engulfing the region since 2008.

Summers's Secular Stagnation Thesis

When Larry Summers first used the term *secular stagnation* in 2013,[1] the United States was in the midst of a balance sheet recession in which the private sector was saving nearly 7 percent of GDP at zero interest rates. He subsequently noted[2] that returns on capital in the West had begun falling in the 1970s, long before the GFC erupted in 2008.

It should be obvious that Western economies have experienced a sudden loss of economic momentum since 2008 because they are suffering from serious balance sheet recessions following the collapse of the housing bubble. Alvin Hansen, who first coined the term *secular stagnation* in 1938, also did so at a time when the United States was in the midst of the greatest balance sheet recession of all, the Great Depression, and the unemployment rate was 19 percent.

At the time of Hansen's speech, however, nobody in Germany was talking about secular stagnation. Speedy, sustained, and substantial fiscal stimulus to fight the balance sheet recession had completely eradicated the German recession and brought the unemployment rate down to just 2 percent in 1938 from a high of 28 percent in 1933. And Hansen's secular stagnation suddenly ended when the U.S. government started the massive military procurement effort to fight World War II. The fact that both Hansen and Summers raised the issue of secular stagnation during balance sheet recessions, and that Germany—which had overcome its own balance sheet recession by 1938—was not suffering from such stagnation, suggests that balance sheet recessions is the main driver of "secular stagnation."

---

[1] See Summers's website for more on secular stagnation: http://larrysummers.com/category/secular-stagnation/.
[2] He noted this, for example, at a private conference held in Paris on June 4, 2015.

The post-1970 decline in the return on capital, however, is likely due to the fact that by then Western economies were all entering the pursued phase, when Japan started chasing them. From that point onward, a growing number of manufacturers in those countries found that the return on capital was higher abroad than at home. Many of them decided to buy from or invest in the pursuing economies themselves. Shrinking capital investment in the advanced countries led to slower growth in productivity and wages.

This pattern—of emerging economies taking away investment opportunities from the developed countries—will continue until all economies have long passed their Lewis Turning Points (LTP) and the return on capital has more or less equalized. Although China has passed the LTP already, India and many other economies have a long way to go. The current transition is therefore likely to continue for many years to come.

This process can be explained using the framework of Figure 3.1 applied in a global context. Most countries can reach their EQ level of wages in Figure 3.1 for ordinary workers in a relatively straightforward fashion if they follow the correct policies for economic growth. But for wages to grow beyond that level, wages in all other countries must also reach their EQ levels so that businesses no longer have the option of using cheaper workers abroad.

This means workers in individual countries can look forward to rising incomes until wages reach their EQ levels, but that then effectively becomes the global ED level of wages in Figure 3.1 applied to global context. These countries must wait until all slack in other labor markets is eliminated for wages to start rising again. Since that could take decades, workers in the pursued countries should start honing their individual skills immediately instead of waiting for the global economy to reach that point.

Beware of Fake "External Shocks"

Economists are also fond of using the term *external shock* to describe what happened after 2008. This implies that the event originated outside the economy and therefore could not have been predicted (hence the "shock"). The author would agree that the recessions triggered by the COVID-19 pandemic, the Russian invasion of Ukraine, and 9/11 were good examples of external shocks. Indeed, the author himself was shocked to find himself, along with many members of the National Association of Business Economists, in the World Trade Center in New York City on the morning of the September 11 attack. But to call the Lehman Brothers bankruptcy and the subsequent GFC an external shock is preposterous.

For years before Lehman's failure, the existence of a housing bubble financed with collateralized debt obligations (CDOs) containing subprime mortgages but carrying outrageously high ratings from corrupt rating agencies was well known. Once the bubble burst, the overwhelming amount of leverage in the system meant that economies *had* to fall into balance sheet recessions. In that sense, what happened after 2008 was largely *endogenous* to the system: it was not caused by unpredictable external factors.

As the crisis unfolded, economists, including former Fed Chairman Alan Greenspan, argued that it was a "once-in-a-hundred-year event" that could not have been predicted. Others called it a "perfect storm" or an "external shock." These terms all imply that economists should not be blamed for failing to predict it.

A young but brilliant Brazilian investor who incurred heavy losses in 2008 decided to leave the field altogether when he heard such statements from prominent economists. He thought that if the financial world contains dangers that even Alan Greenspan ("the Maestro") and other famous economists could not anticipate, he would rather take up a different profession that did not expose him to such unpredictable perils.

After wondering for several months what profession to pursue, it occurred to him that if there was one person on this earth who had seen the crisis coming, then 2008 had not been a perfect storm. It simply meant the big names in economics were working off the wrong models. After conducting the kind of extensive research that he was known for, he did find a few who had seen it coming, and the author was honored to be included in his list. That the list was so short is testimony to the fact that the economics profession has gone badly wrong for too long.

The point here is that the state of the economy prior to the "shock" is absolutely critical in understanding how it will subsequently respond to various policy actions. The nature of the shock itself is also important in predicting what follows.

In the event of a purely external shock, such as 9/11 in the United States or 3/11 in Japan,[3] the economy may need a few years to recover. For a global shock such as the COVID-19 pandemic, it may take a little longer. But an economy suffering from the collapse of a debt-financed bubble will invariably require years, or even decades, to recover. This is because millions of underwater private-sector balance sheets must be repaired, and a fallacy-of-composition problem makes the process even more difficult when everyone tries to repair them at the same time. Although the collapse itself may be triggered by some external event, the long and painful balance sheet recession that follows is no shock at all. Apart from truly unpredictable events such as 9/11 and COVID-19, economists should not use the term *external shock* to brush over their ignorance of the problems that were happening in the economy prior to the shock.

Beware of Fake Allusions to "Expectations"

There is a great deal of economics literature on expectations, and especially inflation expectations. Indeed, those who are pushing for continued monetary stimulus in the face of central banks' repeated failures to reach inflation targets argue that such efforts are still needed to "anchor expectations." But people's expectations are fundamentally based on what they see happening and what they have experienced in the past.

In post-bubble Japan, where commercial real estate prices fell 87 percent nationwide (Figure 2.1), the typical CEO was busy repairing his firm's balance sheet by using cash flow to pay down debt (Figure 2.2). He was also aware that *most other* CEOs in the country were doing the same thing. With no borrowers to take funds out of the financial sector and inject them into the real economy, it was obvious to these executives that no amount of central bank liquidity injections would increase the money circulating in the economy. And with no way to increase the money circulating in the economy, it was clear to them that monetary easing could not boost economic growth or inflation rates.

---

[3] 3/11 refers to the tsunami that devastated northeast Japan on March 11, 2011.

In this environment, the announcement of a 2-percent inflation target by the central bank will have no impact because these CEOs are unable to change their debt-minimizing behavior. The escape from negative equity is a matter of survival for businesses, and CEOs have no choice but to continue deleveraging until their balance sheets are repaired. But if they continue to deleverage, there will be no credit growth and no inflation. Nor are banks allowed to lend money to businesses with underwater balance sheets. The resultant undershooting of inflation targets by the central bank then reinforces CEOs' expectations of no inflation while undermining the credibility of central banks and the economists who pushed for the targets.

In such a world, the announcement that the central bank has raised its inflation target from 2 percent to 4 percent does not lead to expectations of lower real interest rates because the original 2 percent target was not credible to begin with. This is the reality, and it has nothing to do with expectations. Anyone who cared to ask CEOs why they were deleveraging when the central bank had announced a 2-percent inflation target would have received this answer.[4]

This also means that there is a disconnect between central bankers—and their economist friends, along with some of the market participants that are noted in Chapter 2—who are still operating on the assumption that the economy is in Case 1 or 2, and the rest of the population, whose actions are keeping the economy in Case 3 or 4. And it is the CEOs and the general public who have the correct model of the economy in their heads, not the central bankers and economists.

When the economy was in a golden era (in Cases 1 and 2), in contrast, the economy was moving along the upward-sloping labor supply curve KP in Figure 3.1, meaning there was constant upward pressure on wages. Facing ever-rising wages accompanied by ever-increasing demand for their products, most CEOs were busy borrowing funds to carry out additional productivity- and capacity-enhancing investments. Financial institutions were also lending out all available funds, raising the money multiplier to its maximum value. In other words, there was a real macroeconomic foundation

---

[4] Admittedly, the question will have to be asked very carefully and somewhat indirectly because no CEO would admit that his or her company has balance sheet problems.

for inflation expectations in the golden era of the 1960s and 1970s: they did not emerge out of thin air.

In such a world, a central bank could also contain inflation by limiting the supply of reserves because the availability of reserves *was* a constraint on money and credit growth. This is why the three lines in Figures 2.2 to 2.14 and 2.17 moved together before 2008 in the West and before 1990 in Japan. Central banks that succeeded in containing inflation enjoyed high credibility because they were able to deliver on their promises. But that is not the environment central banks in advanced countries find themselves in today.

There are many economists, including some at the Fed, who still fear that the fall in inflationary expectations will lead to the kind of economic stagnation that Japan has experienced. Their view is that if inappropriate inflationary expectations can be eradicated with drastic monetary tightening measures, like those implemented by Paul Volcker in October 1979, then today's inappropriate deflationary expectations can also be eradicated with drastic monetary *easing*.

But the post-1990 Japanese and post-2008 Western economies stagnated not because of deflationary expectations due to inappropriate monetary policies, but because there were *real* reasons for people not to borrow money—namely, private-sector balance sheet problems and inferior returns on capital. These two problems have nothing to do with expectations. But the economy will stagnate if people are still saving money while fewer are borrowing and spending those savings. With the economy moving along the flat global labor supply curve PQ in Figure 3.1 and businesses not borrowing money at home, there are real macroeconomic reasons for people *not* to expect inflation. Without addressing these two real issues with fiscal and structural actions, no amount of monetary easing will improve the economy or the public's expectations of the future. The absence of inflationary expectations in pursued economies does not emerge out of thin air.

Instead of treating "expectations" as some sort of policy objective that a central bank can change, economists should ask why people are behaving the way they are. Japanese CEOs ignored the Bank of Japan (BOJ)'s monetary accommodation not because they had somehow come to expect deflation, but because they knew from their own debt-minimizing actions that *there was no reason why monetary accommodation should work*. If economists only understood these fundamental drivers of behavior, they would make far fewer allusions to expectations.

Where the Analysis Begins Is Important

Some mainstream economists have recently come around in favor of more active fiscal policy given today's low interest rates. Olivier Blanchard, former International Monetary Fund (IMF) chief economist, argued that when interest rates are lower than the economy's growth rate, the government can administer more fiscal stimulus without causing a deterioration of debt-to-GDP ratios. That is arithmetically true, of course, and the author welcomes the fact that some economists have finally found a reason to make greater use of fiscal policy.

The problem is that their analysis starts from the premise of low interest rates without bothering to explain *why* they are so low. Blanchard, for example, uses just five words to elucidate the causes of today's low interest rates: "savings, investment, risk aversion, and liquidity." This is no different from the economists who pushed for more monetary accommodation to fight deflation without explaining why economies were suffering from deflation in the first place. Paul Krugman, a Nobel laureate, even argued that how a country fell into deflation was not important as long as it implemented sufficient monetary easing to overcome it.

But without a full understanding of the drivers of observed phenomena, policies implemented to address them will be thrown off course by even slight changes in those phenomena. If fiscal stimulus is premised on low interest rates, for example, it will have to be abandoned when interest rates shoot up, as happened during the taper tantrum of 2013.

But if fiscal stimulus is implemented based on the understanding that it is needed to fight a recession caused by the private sector's minimization of debt to repair damaged balance sheets, it will not be discontinued until private-sector is back borrowing money again. If policy makers are also aware that private-sector deleveraging is the fundamental driver of low interest rates, they will not be concerned about occasional bouts of interest rate volatility until the deleveraging process itself comes to an end.

The same problem appeared when monetary easing was used to fight deflation. Despite astronomical amounts of QE and zero or negative interest rates, central banks failed to reach their inflation targets because the deflation was driven by private-sector balance sheet problems and inferior returns on capital. Neither of those problems responds well to monetary policy easing. The point is that policy makers should be wary of economists peddling quick fixes to a problem without being able to explain how the problem started.

Conventional Models Have Trouble Dealing with Abrupt Reversals

Economists also assumed, mostly unconsciously, that the responses of economic agents to changes in prices and other external factors are always continuous and in the same direction. As Brendan Markey-Towler of the University of Queensland pointed out, traditional economics is based on the implied principle of universal substitutability, which means a change in relative prices will always prompt a reaction in the economy.[5] For example, if the price of good A rises relative to the price of substitute good B, a certain number of consumers will stop buying A and start buying B. From this perspective, which assumes that changes in prices—including interest rates and exchange rates—always lead to corresponding changes in the economy, it is natural to assume that a decline in real interest rates, if large enough, will always encourage willing borrowers to step forward.

It was this kind of thinking that led economist Krugman to argue that the monetary authorities should opt for a 4-percent inflation target if a 2-percent target was not working. Similar thinking also led some central bankers to conclude that if zero interest rates were not adequate, rates should be taken into negative territory. The assumption here, of course, is that in a world of universal substitutability there should be at least *some* response to their policy actions.

---

[5] Markey-Towler, Brendan (2017a), *Foundations for Economic Analysis: The Architecture of Socioeconomic Complexity,* PhD thesis, School of Economics, University of Queensland.

But when businesses and households face the threat of insolvency, their responses are highly discontinuous as they shift abruptly from profit maximization to debt minimization. Debt minimization is also an urgent matter because a technically insolvent business faces extinction unless it can quickly emerge from that state of negative equity. If the true state of the company's finances becomes known, no supplier will do business with it unless it pays in cash given the imminent possibility that it will seek bankruptcy protection. Banks are also prevented by law from lending money or rolling over loans to insolvent borrowers in order to protect depositors. And the best employees of such a firm might also seek employment elsewhere.

This means the principle of universal substitutability does not apply when individuals and businesses face insolvency because they not only abruptly stop borrowing but also start paying down debt, which is the opposite of borrowing. And this abrupt reversal happens regardless of how low the central bank takes interest rates.

The problem is that economists who were trained under the assumption of universal substitutability are unable to comprehend such disconnects and abrupt reversals in human behavior. As a result, their theories and models are often incapable of incorporating sudden shifts and reversals in private-sector behavior, rendering them useless when such reversals happen.

Obsession with Mathematics Is Killing Macroeconomics' Credibility

Although noneconomist readers may find the preceding discussion hard to believe, the reliance on universal substitutability became essential when mathematical modeling became an obsession for mainstream economists. Today, many in the profession would not consider anything that is not expressed in mathematical terms (such as this book) to be serious economics. But for mathematical equations to be useful (i.e., continuously differentiable), models must assume that the behavioral changes of economic agents are smooth, continuous, and always in the same direction. That, in turn, makes these models useless when households and businesses are forced to make abrupt changes or even reverse their behavior. That was why they failed to predict the post-2008 Great Recession.

Economists such as Gauti Eggertsson and Krugman (2012)[6] have argued that their models still indicate that monetary easing is effective even in a "Fisher-Minsky-Koo" environment, and that inflation targeting and QE should work. The fact that Krugman himself admitted three years later that these policies have failed to be a "game changer"[7] in the real world suggests that their models and equations did not fully incorporate the possibility of abrupt reversals following a bubble collapse.

The inability of most mathematical models to handle abrupt reversals is a sad betrayal of the very spirit of macroeconomics. After all, the discipline was born in the midst of the Great Depression, the most abrupt shift to debt minimization in history. The fact that only a few economists were able to predict the Great Recession and its long and unpleasant aftermath says a lot about the usefulness of mathematical tools in understanding the economy.

The advanced mathematics used in astrophysics succeeded in landing a man on the moon. The advanced mathematics used in economics (and the professors who ply the trade) failed to predict not only the biggest macroeconomic event since the Great Depression but also the substantial changes to the effectiveness of monetary and fiscal policy that occurred after 2008.

Astrophysicists could send a person to the moon because the moon does not change direction abruptly. Physicists won the respect of others by finding a mathematical formula that accurately predicted where the moon would be or when the next high tide would come, matters that affect our daily lives. In addition to mathematical tools, these predictions required long years of observation and hard work to find the correct mathematical equations to fit the data.

Economists failed to predict the Great Recession because people react to events and change direction *all the time*. Economists failed precisely because their mathematical models did not allow

---

[6]Eggertsson, Gauti B. and Krugman, Paul (2012), "Debt, Deleveraging, and the Liquidity Trap: A Fisher-Minsky-Koo Approach," *The Quarterly Journal of Economics*, Volume 127, Issue 3, pp. 1469–1513.

[7]International Monetary Fund (2015), "IMF Survey: Top Researchers Debate Unconventional Monetary Policies," Maurice Obstfeld and Gustavo Adler, *IMF News* on November 20, 2015. http://www.imf.org/en/news/articles/2015/09/28/04/53/sores111915a.

households and businesses to change their behavior. By relying on mathematics as their primary tool, economists treat human beings as they would treat planetary objects like the moon or Mars, and not as thinking and reacting individuals.

Economists may have latched on to mathematics because of what George Soros called "physics envy."[8] Indeed, Soros has been arguing for decades with his theory of reflexivity that economists need to regard businesses and households as thinking and reacting entities.

Power of Plain Language in Economics

The ultimate goal of any scientific discipline, including economics and physics, is to find the truth. On that score, economists have one huge advantage over physicists: they are analyzing the behavior of people just like themselves. As Alfred Marshall said, economics is the science of everyday life.[9] Economists are themselves workers, consumers, savers, and investors. Economists even have the luxury of directly asking households and businesses why they are doing what they are doing. They could, for example, have asked Japanese CEOs why they were deleveraging at a time of zero interest rates. Unfortunately, few did.

Economists could have examined what businesses were doing with their financial assets and liabilities by looking at the statistics shown in Figures 2.2 and 4.2. If they had, they would have noticed that businesses were minimizing debt. Again, not many did. But that is like an astrophysicist trying to predict the motion of a planet without looking at the data.

Because economic phenomena are the result of human beings interacting with each other, nothing in economics is outside human cognitive experience. That means that everything in economics, including the behavior of households and businesses, must be

---

[8] Soros, George (2009), "Soros: General Theory of Reflexivity," *Financial Times,* October 27, 2009, p. 11. https://www.ft.com/content/0ca06172-bfe9-11de-aed2-00144feab49a.

[9] Markey-Towler, Brendan (2017b), "Poetry and Economics: Maintaining Our Link to Humanity," from Brendan Markey-Towler's blog, July 24, 2017. https://medium.com/@brendanmarkeytowler/poetry-and-economics-maintaining-our-link-to-humanity-532785047f0e.

explainable in *plain* language. This is the opposite of physics, which cannot describe the movement of comets or electrons without using mathematical tools. Physicists also get nowhere by asking a comet or an electron why it does what it does.

It should be possible, therefore, to spell out in plain language the assumed or expected behavior of individual consumers or businesses in any economic theory or model, mathematical, or otherwise. That exercise should help determine whether the model is treating people as planetary objects or as thinking and reacting beings. The problem is that once the elegant mathematical models have been deciphered and translated into plain language, it will be found that many of them do indeed treat human beings as planets and comets.

When the author took part in a debate on trade frictions in Japan with a professor known for his elegant mathematical models, the professor inadvertently spelled out in plain language what was happening in his model. He revealed that a worker in his model who had lost his job due to imports would immediately find another equally well-paying job. But if that were the case, there would be no trade frictions to start with.

Trade frictions exist because people in importing countries are losing jobs and income. In real life, a worker who loses his job to imports will have to go through years of often painful retraining to regain the income he enjoyed earlier. In many cases, his income may never recover fully. It is this loss of income that causes trade frictions. The professor's model, however, was saying there should be no trade frictions because there are no income losses. This "discovery" effectively ended the debate.

Practitioners of economics should constantly check to see what their models expect households and businesses to do. Students of economics should always ask professors to explain in plain language what is happening to households and businesses in their mathematical models. Only then can they judge for themselves whether the model makes any sense.

Because of the discipline's half-century-long infatuation with mathematics and the belief that mathematically formulated economics is the only "legitimate" form of economics, important phenomena falling outside its assumptions—such as balance sheet recessions and a shortfall of domestic investment opportunities—have been completely overlooked. The economics taught at universities therefore applies only to nonbubble, largely closed economies in a golden era where balance sheet problems and a shortage of investment opportunities do not exist.

But under those conditions, who needs economists? Economists are needed when an economy is in Case 3 or 4, that is, when it is plagued by the counterintuitive fallacy-of-composition problems that are noted in Chapter 1 that only trained economists can see through and analyze. These are also the times when the economy is suffering from slow growth or worse. Unfortunately, most economists today are only trained to look at economies in Cases 1 and 2 (or their models only work in those cases). Hence, the public's ongoing disappointment with economists and their friends in the establishment.

Economists Should Learn from Medical Science, Not Physics

If economists are to an economy what medical doctors are to the human body, then the former have much to learn from the latter. Even though medical science has made great strides in improving human health, no medical scientist in his right mind would try to come up with a mathematical model of the human body before finding a cure for an ailment. This is not only because building a mathematical model of the human body is a ridiculously roundabout way of getting to the solution, but also because it should be possible with careful observation and deductive reasoning to isolate the cause of an ailment in specific viruses, bacteria, genes, or chemical compounds. Once the cause of the ailment is identified, a remedy can be developed to help patients fight the disease.

The same is true in economics. With millions of thinking and reacting households and businesses who are changing their minds all the time, building a mathematical model to find a solution to an economic ailment is terribly inefficient. On the other hand, just as in medical science, careful observation and deductive reasoning can go a long way to helping the economy recover.

When Japan was suffering from economic stagnation and banking problems in the mid-1990s, many economists, especially those in the West, argued that the government must tackle the banking crisis first because it was the cause of the economy's poor performance. But if that were true, a number of other phenomena should also have been observed. For example, foreign banks that were not affected by the bursting of Japan's bubble in 1990 should have been increasing their market share in the country. Similarly, the corporate bond market, which is a good proxy for bank lending to large companies, should have been booming. The spread between the lending rate and banks' funding rate should also have been widening if there were plenty of borrowers but a lack of capital kept bankers from lending.

None of these three phenomena typically observed in a banking crisis were reported in Japan. Instead, foreign banks were leaving the country, the corporate bond market was shrinking, and the interest rate spread was narrowing. This suggests that even though there was a banking crisis, it was not the main reason for Japan's economic stagnation.

The deductive reasoning from the preceding observations suggests that the primary reason for the slump was that borrowers, whose balance sheets were badly damaged after the bubble burst, disappeared faster than lenders. And this can be confirmed by comparing the BOJ's Tankan survey of borrowers with their actual borrowings, as shown in Figure 8.6. Although borrowers in the survey indicated that banks were willing lenders, they were not borrowing. The correct treatment for economic stagnation driven by a lack of borrowers, therefore, is for the government to act as borrower of last resort. The banking crisis must be addressed, but its resolution will not lead to economic recovery until the absence of borrowers is addressed.

Similarly, when the private sector abruptly shifts to deleveraging after a bubble bursts—in spite of zero or negative interest rates—as happened in the West after 2008, economists should suspect that its balance sheet is in trouble instead of assuming that it suffers from "deflationary expectations" or "structural problems." This is because both of those issues take years to manifest themselves and cannot explain an abrupt slowdown in the economy.

Medical science is not as precise as physics because of the complexity of the human body, which consists of billions of live and interacting cells. But medical scientists still command great respect because they have been able to improve human health in so many ways. Economists should put aside their physics envy and embrace the methods of medical science so that they can contribute to human welfare in the same way that medical scientists have contributed to human health.

Economics Has No Meaningful Theory of Growth

By presuming that there are always willing borrowers, economists have also unwittingly assumed away the two most critical challenges to economic growth: the availability of domestic investment opportunities worth borrowing for and the presence of businesses with clean balance sheets. While the public is desperately waiting for economists to come up with policy recommendations to get the economy growing again, that is, to pull it out of Cases 3 and 4 and push it back into Cases 1 and 2, economists themselves have largely assumed away the problem of growth because their models take it for granted that the economy is already in Case 1 or 2.

Moreover, most economists simply *assume* a rate of long-term "potential" growth that is based on trend growth in capital, labor, and productivity. They then argue that policy makers should strive to bring the economy back to that trajectory. But such "potential growth rates" mean absolutely nothing when businesspeople are either unable (because of balance sheet concerns) or unwilling (because of a lack of investment opportunities) to borrow money and invest it at home. Indeed, extrapolating trends observed during the golden era into the pursued era makes no sense whatsoever. This means conventional economics has no meaningful theory of economic growth because economists have assumed away all the relevant questions on growth that the public expects them to answer.

An Existential Issue for Economics Profession

The biggest concern for the economics profession at this juncture should be that the parents, students, and taxpayers who pay for or subsidize college tuition may eventually realize that what passes as "economics" in universities has little to do with reality. Of all the social sciences, economics would probably win the prize for straying the farthest from reality. When the public realizes that the vast majority of economics professors had no clue about the Great Recession, which lasted nearly 10 years in many countries and cost eight million jobs on both sides of the Atlantic, it may understandably want to cut the funding for university economics departments.

New groups such as the World Economic Association and the Institute of New Economic Thinking are keenly aware of this deficiency in the profession and are working hard to make the discipline relevant for society again. Professor Takamitsu Sawa[10] of Kyoto University has also issued warnings that the funding for university economics departments might be cut by the Japanese Ministry of Education[11] if the profession's unrealistic obsession with mathematics is not rectified.

Unfortunately, many if not most economics professors continue to teach the same old material, as if 2008 had never happened and another golden era is just around the corner. This means the profession as a whole needs to reinvent itself before the public realizes what is actually happening.

Economics: A History of Changing Fads

Young disciplines, like young people, are easily influenced by fads. When macroeconomics was in its formative years in the 1940s and 1950s, most Western economies had passed the LTP and were in their golden eras with no one chasing them. New products were continually being invented, and people were optimistic about the future. Balance sheets were also strong thanks to massive government spending during the war, which had repaired the balance sheet damage wrought by the Great Crash of 1929. With strong demand for borrowings from the corporate sector, the economy was squarely in Case 1 or 2.

At the same time, the extraordinary effectiveness of fiscal policy in lifting economies out of the Great Depression during World War II was obvious for everyone to see. The tragedy was that Keynes, who had argued for such policies, never realized that fiscal stimulus should be used *only* when the private sector is minimizing debt, that is, when the economy is in Case 3 or 4. Because of this monumental omission on his and his followers' part, the postwar fad among economists was to believe that fiscal policy could solve most problems.

---

[10] Sawa, Takamitsu (2016), *Keizaigaku no Susume: Jimbun-chi to Hihan-seishin no Fukken* (*Introduction to True Economics: Reintegration of Humanities and Critical Thinking*), Tokyo: Iwanami Shinsho, p. 52.
[11] Its full name is the Ministry of Education, Culture, Sports, Science and Technology.

Since private-sector balance sheets had already been repaired, the government's attempt to fine-tune the economy with fiscal policy in the 1950s and 1960s only resulted in more inflation, higher interest rates, and a general misallocation of resources. These were the undesirable results of an overreliance on fiscal policy when the economy is in Case 1 or 2. These outcomes lie at the opposite end of the spectrum from the pernicious cycle of bubbles and balance sheet recessions that results from an overreliance on *monetary* policy when the economy is in Case 3 or 4, as is discussed in Chapter 4.

Even though the postwar economy had already returned to Case 1, it still took Americans another 14 years after 1945 to overcome their debt trauma (long- and short-term U.S. interest rates did not return to the average levels of the 1920s until 1959, as shown in Figure 2.22). But with the advanced economies in their golden era, inflation was becoming an ever-larger problem. By the early 1970s, inflation had caused a significant loss of credibility for Keynesian economics and its emphasis on fiscal policy.

When inflation reached double-digit levels and became a national concern in the late 1970s, the pendulum shifted to the opposite extreme, with neoliberals led by Milton Friedman arguing that monetary policy and smaller government were the answer to most problems. They claimed that central banks should be able to control inflation by controlling the money supply, and the Fed actually adopted a policy of targeting the money supply in October 1979. Although that policy did not work as smoothly as expected, the enthusiasm for monetary policy among academic economists was such that some even tried to rewrite history, arguing that the Great Depression could have been avoided with better use of monetary policy by the Fed.[12]

The tragedy was that Friedman, who had argued for such policies, never realized that monetary stimulus should be used *only* when the private sector is maximizing profits, that is, when the economy is in Case 1 or 2. Because of this monumental omission on his and his followers' part, the fad among economists was to believe that monetary policy could solve most problems—including what would later become known as balance sheet recessions.

---

[12] See Koo, Richard C. (2008), *The Holy Grail of Macroeconomics: Lessons from Japan's Great Recession*, John Wiley & Sons (Asia), Singapore, Chapter 3.

When the private sector subsequently lost its head in a bubble and sustained massive balance sheet damage, first in Japan in 1990 and then in the West in 2008, the advanced economies were already in the pursued phase, with falling demand for borrowings from businesses. The economics profession, however, was still beholden to the golden era neoliberal mindset centered on small government and monetary policy. Although nearly all advanced economies were squarely in Case 3 or 4 by 2008, many economists argued for ever more radical monetary accommodation—even though fiscal policy is the only tool that can address a recession caused by a disappearance of borrowers.

Fiscal policy was mobilized soon after Lehman's failure at an emergency G20 meeting held in Washington, D.C., in November 2008. Although that fiscal package succeeded in preventing an immediate meltdown of the global economy, the golden-era orthodoxy had regained its grip on power by 2010. At the G20 summit held in Toronto that year, participating countries pledged to halve their fiscal deficits by 2013,[13] even though the private sectors in nearly all of these countries were still engaged in massive deleveraging to repair their badly damaged balance sheets. That summit effectively threw the global economy into reverse.

Policy makers who realized soon afterward that the Toronto agreement had been a mistake, including former Fed Chairs Ben Bernanke and Janet Yellen, issued stern warnings about the "fiscal cliff" to encourage the U.S. government to continue serving as borrower of last resort, which helped keep the U.S. economy from contracting. Japanese Finance Minister Taro Aso also recognized this danger and incorporated fiscal stimulus as the second "arrow" of Abenomics, which was unveiled late in 2012. Their actions provided essential support for the U.S. and Japanese economies.

In the Eurozone, however, no such understanding emerged in policy circles. As a result, millions have suffered from unemployment and deprivation because the Stability and Growth Pact (SGP), which never considered Cases 3 and 4, requires member governments to do the opposite of what is needed to fight a balance sheet recession.

---

[13] 2010 G20 Toronto communique. https://www.treasury.gov/resource-center/international/Documents/The%20G-20%20Toronto%20Summit%20Declaration.pdf.

It is deeply ironic that the Germans are imposing this fiscal strait-jacket on all the countries in the Eurozone. After all, it was they who suffered the most from the fiscal straitjacket imposed on the country by the Allied powers prior to 1933, and it was they who were the first to discover the effectiveness of fiscal policy in fighting balance sheet recessions after 1933. If anyone should understand the horrible economic and political risks of not administering fiscal stimulus when it is needed, it should be the Germans. This was famously noted by Joan Robinson, a British economist and contemporary of Keynes, when she said, "I do not regard the Keynesian revolution as a great intellectual triumph. On the contrary, it was a tragedy because it came so late. Hitler had already found how to cure unemployment before Keynes had finished explaining why it occurred."[14]

Keynes was definitely trying to understand the economy in Cases 3 and 4 when he wrote the *General Theory* in the midst of the Depression in 1936. But he could not free himself from the established notion in economics that the private sector always seeks to maximize profits. As a result, he and his followers had to come up with highly convoluted explanations for why the Great Depression was so severe.

It took the post-1990 Japanese experience 60 years later for people to realize that the private sector can shift its priority from profit maximization to debt minimization when faced with daunting balance sheet challenges. That shift, in turn, can trigger the \$1,000–\$900–\$810–\$730 deflationary spiral that leads to depression if left unattended.

Recently, the faddish pendulum of economics seems to have swung to the opposite extreme again. Even though the author was the first to bring up the importance of debt and deleveraging in economics with the concept of balance sheet recessions in the late 1990s, many in the profession are now running about issuing warnings about excessive debt in the system, citing ever-increasing debt numbers. In so doing, they are forgetting the two fundamental laws of macroeconomics mentioned in Chapter 1—namely, for debt to grow, someone must be saving, and if someone is saving, someone else must borrow and spend those savings to keep the economy going.

---

[14] Robinson, Joan (1972), "The Second Crisis of Economic Theory," *American Economic Review* 62(1/2), pp. 1–10.

If both the public and private sectors borrow less and save more, as urged by these economists, the economy will fall into the $1,000–$900–$810–$730 deflationary spiral in a race toward depression.

A mere emphasis on the size of the debt is also absolutely meaningless without looking at what is on the other side of it. If the debt was incurred to finance investments expected to yield a return in excess of debt servicing costs, there is absolutely no problem with it, no matter how large. And most private-sector debt meets this condition (except during bubbles, when businesses and households lose their heads). Moreover, borrowing allows businesses and households to over-stretch, which is essential for economic growth.

The fact that the private sectors of most advanced countries are running a financial surplus despite record low interest rates suggests there is actually too *little* borrowing relative to savings. Indeed, interest rates are so low precisely because there are too few borrowers in the real economy.

The fact that economists can get away with statements like "everyone should borrow less and save more" shows how little they understand the interactive nature of the macroeconomy. They have forgotten that macroeconomics is a science of feedback loops. It also shows how easily the young profession can be corrupted by fads.

Better Data Are Needed

Medical science received a huge boost from advances in scanning technology, such as magnetic resonance imaging (MRIs), that allowed doctors to visualize problems with ever-greater clarity and precision. Economic science could also use better data to help reveal the core of the problems it faces.

In particular, the economics profession should demand that central banks in all countries gather data from *borrowers* similar to those collected by the BOJ in its quarterly Tankan survey (top of Figure 8.6). Many central banks collect data from lenders, one example being the Fed's Senior Loan Officer Survey, but not enough collect data from borrowers. Information about how borrowers view lenders makes it possible to visualize whether the constraint to economic growth is on the borrowers' or the lenders' side. If such surveys indicate that lenders are willing to lend but borrowers are not borrowing, then it can be inferred that the problem rests with the latter.

By supplementing such surveys with interest rate and flow-of-funds data like those shown in Figures 2.5 to 2.7 as well as Figures 7.1 to 7.8, economists can see what borrowers are doing with their financial assets and liabilities. Indeed flow of funds data *is* the MRI of macroeconomics as it allows the public to visualize not only balance sheet recessions (charts previously mentioned) but also banking problems (Figures 8.7 to 8.11).

If borrowers are not borrowing or are actually paying down debt despite low lending rates, they are likely to be suffering from balance sheet problems, and the economy is probably in Case 3. In such cases, the government must act as borrower of last resort to overcome the constraint on growth.

If the borrower survey indicates that lenders are unwilling to lend, it can be concluded that the problem lies with the lenders. By supplementing this information with data on interest rate spreads and flow-of-funds data for the financial sector, as shown in Figures 8.7 to 8.11, economists can determine whether banks are trying to expand lending or economize on capital. If lending rates are high (even if policy rates are low) but lending is still growing slowly or contracting, the problem probably rests with the lenders. In that case, monetary easing and capital injections or other bank rescue policies should be implemented to remove the constraint to growth.

The economics profession should also demand that governments and central banks improve the accuracy and timeliness of their flow-of-funds data. In some countries, such as China, the Netherlands, and Austria, these data are only released once a year. In other countries, such as Taiwan, the data come out too late to be of any use. And in the United States and Germany, they are subject to huge revisions.

As explained in the author's previous book,[15] compiling flow-of-funds data is a massive and costly undertaking with much room for improvement. In spite of all the resources governments have invested in compiling these data, most economists still appear unable or unwilling to use them. And that is probably because they never anticipated borrower-side problems—after all, economics has traditionally assumed that economies were always in Case 1 or 2. Now

---

[15] Koo, Richard C. (2015), *The Escape from Balance Sheet Recession and the QE Trap*, Singapore: John Wiley & Sons, pp. 143–148.

that the existence of borrower-side problems has been recognized, economists will have a better appreciation of the role of these data in identifying whether growth is being held back by lenders or by borrowers.

Last but not least, it is essential to have data indicating the amount of borrowing that is earmarked for real investment—and therefore adds to GDP—as distinct from money borrowed to finance purchases of existing assets. To use the leasing industry terminology that is suggested in Chapter 6, the two types of borrowing may be referred to as "operating loans" and "financing loans," respectively. Data on operating loans will be a good indicator of economic activity going forward because it can indicate over-stretching by businesses, which is essential for economic growth. Data on financing loans, meanwhile, may be a useful indicator of asset prices going forward.

Typical lenders do not care whether the borrowed money is used to build new factories or to buy back shares, as long as the borrower appears willing and able to pay back the debt. But for economists, the distinction is critically important. The government should collect these data not only from banks but also from the capital markets.

The share of financing loans appears to increase relative to the share of operating loans as the economy moves from the golden era to the pursued era. And that is because there is less demand for operating loans in pursued economies.

Political Implications of Dysfunctional Economics

The economic profession's overreliance on monetary policy when advanced economies have already entered the pursued era has not only created pernicious cycles of bubbles and balance sheet recessions, but has also worsened inequality between the haves and the have-nots by pushing asset prices higher. That, in turn, exacerbated political divisions. This is because monetary easing in Case 3 works mostly through the mechanism of rising asset prices in a process known as the portfolio rebalancing effect.

Specifically, bond prices rise when the central bank buys government bonds under the policy of QE. The higher bond prices then push investors into other asset classes, such as equities, that are still cheap relative to bonds. The resultant overall increase in asset prices is then expected to boost consumption by the holders of those assets, who are feeling richer than before. Although there is reason to believe that such a policy may have some positive impact on consumption, it definitely and directly benefits the rich who hold the assets.

Today, economic inequality in the United States has reached the point where 50 percent of people under the age of 38 say they would prefer to live in a socialist system. To the extent that asset price gains over the past three decades have been driven by an overreliance on monetary policy, often called the "central bank put," central banks should be especially careful when using monetary easing going forward.

These social and political problems have been aggravated by the years of inaction on trade imbalances perpetuated by economists' incomplete understanding of free trade and free flows of capital. In particular, economists have overlooked the possibility that those who consider themselves losers from free trade might eventually outnumber the winners if large trade deficits are allowed to continue for too long. By November 2016, the losers from free trade, together with other disgruntled groups, amassed enough votes to elect an openly protectionist Donald Trump as president. In the process, traditional center-right Republicans who had championed free trade and globalization were squeezed out as the Trump faction hijacked their party.

To be sure, many of Trump's economic policies, including tax cuts and deregulation, were the correct responses for a pursued economy in Case 3, and the U.S. unemployment rate fell to a 50-year low of 3.5 percent just before the onset of the pandemic. That allowed people at the bottom of U.S. society to obtain good jobs for the first time in decades. Unfortunately, Trump's utter failure to understand the social and educational challenges facing the pursued U.S. economy, together with his botched and unscientific response to the COVID-19 pandemic, left the country in a dangerous state of disarray.

President Joe Biden is pushing for infrastructure spending, which is also the right thing to do in a Case 3 economy where the private sector is still saving 7 percent of GDP despite very low interest rates (Figure 1.1). Given the truly sorry state of infrastructure in the country, it should also be easy to find public works projects that have social rates of return in excess of low U.S. government bond yields. The same is true in Europe, including Germany, where additional spending can go a long way in reviving its aging infrastructure. It is hoped that the Europeans and Japanese will also come to appreciate the importance of fiscal policy when the economy is in Case 3.

President Biden's push for more union jobs and higher taxes, on the other hand, is *not* appropriate for pursued economies. Such policies may actually sap the economy's forward momentum by reducing the return on capital at home in manufacturing. Instead, he should strengthen the social safety net and improve education and retraining opportunities for workers so that the labor market itself will remain flexible.

In Europe, far-right political parties have gained ground because the economists who created the SGP never considered Cases 3 and 4 and prevented member governments from using fiscal policy to help those who have been hurt by the post-2008 balance sheet recessions. The pact has effectively put many Eurozone countries in the same position the Germans found themselves in back in 1930, when the center-left and center-right establishment parties were both beholden to the Treaty of Versailles and were unable to rescue the economy. Against this dire political background, the European Union (EU)'s decision in 2020 to issue its own bonds to help economies pummeled by the pandemic was a step in the right direction.

A few percent of the people in any country may hold xenophobic, far-right, anti-immigration views. But when economic hardships continue, those who have lost jobs or businesses will become increasingly desperate. Some may even backtrack on progress made on civil rights if they feel a Nazi-like government is the only way to break through a policy orthodoxy that is destroying their lives. The ability of politicians espousing such views to garner significant support from voters in the United States, the United Kingdom, and France—countries that have traditionally been champions of democracy and human rights—underscores voters' unhappiness with orthodox thinking. With the credibility of established center-right and center-left parties eroding, it is urgent that the public be made aware that their economies are in Case 3, the pursued phase, which requires appropriate fiscal, structural, and educational policies. And that has to happen before the next Hitler makes his appearance.

Difficulty of Maintaining Fiscal Stimulus in Peacetime Democracies

Until universities start explicitly teaching students about economies in Case 3, central banks and their financial market counterparts must inform policy makers that there is indeed a dearth of borrowers for real investments even with interest rates near zero, and that the economy is not in Case 1 as assumed by most economists. As Ben Bernanke and Janet Yellen did with the expression "fiscal cliff," they must tell the public that the government needs to borrow and spend to stabilize the economy when the private sector is a net saver despite very low interest rates.

The central bank needs to point this out because it will be difficult for elected leaders to convince the public that the economy is actually in the other half and that the government must act as borrower of last resort to keep it going. It is difficult because the economics taught to the public is based on golden era economies that disparaged fiscal stimulus. As a result, most elected officials will not even try to convince the public because the risk of being labeled a pork-barrel politician is too great. History also shows that administering speedy, sustained, and sufficient fiscal stimulus is extremely difficult in a democracy—except during wartime, when the nation is under military threat.

During peacetime, even leaders who understand the need for speedy, substantial, and sustained fiscal stimulus will only propose it when the economy is in desperate shape. Most will simply choose the path of least resistance, which means going along with the usual anti-deficit chorus until the economy's pain threshold is reached. But by then the medical cost of restoring economic health will be many times higher than if the disease had been treated when it first appeared.

Another political pitfall is that, because government spending, unlike monetary easing, always adds to gross domestic product (GDP), the economy will react quickly and positively to such expenditures even if the private sector is still deleveraging. Those initial positive signs, however, will trigger a pushback from the anti-fiscal-policy chorus. Since the economy is already recovering, they will argue, it is time for fiscal consolidation. But if the private sector is still deleveraging, a withdrawal of fiscal stimulus will tip the economy back into a balance sheet recession. That may prompt another round of fiscal stimulus, only to be aborted again when the economy shows fresh signs of life.

Japan lost more than two decades after 1990 because of this sort of stop-and-go fiscal stimulus that was nowhere near sufficient to pull the economy out of the balance sheet recession. And because the economy remained stagnant, many argued that not only monetary but also fiscal policy did not work. But one or two years of pump-priming fiscal stimulus was far from sufficient to repair the hole in private sector balance sheets brought about by an 87 percent decline in commercial real estate prices.

Fortunately, there were enough pork-barrel politicians in Japan to sustain the minimum level of government spending needed to prevent GDP from falling below the bubble peak. That was quite an achievement for fiscal policy in the country that lost wealth equivalent to three years' worth of GDP. Many in Europe and elsewhere were not so lucky. Their misfortune lengthened the recession and led to a loss of public confidence in established political parties and economists.

To prevent such an outcome, central bankers and financial market participants who face a lack of borrowers for real investment on a daily basis must speak out. They need to do so because most academic economists remain totally unaware that there is a shortage of borrowers even at zero interest rates. It is also hoped that universities will begin teaching students about the possibility of economies in Case 3 so that democratically elected leaders can apply fiscal stimulus as soon as it is needed.

Krugman, who fully understood the need for fiscal stimulus from the outset in the post-2008 West, correctly realized early on that there was no political appetite in Washington, D.C., for additional fiscal stimulus beyond the initial $787 billion package unveiled in early 2009. He then went on to argue for more monetary stimulus as a second-best solution.

A lack of political appetite for fiscal stimulus was also apparent in Japan in 1997. At that time, the whole country was obsessed with the need for fiscal consolidation when its public debt as a percentage of GDP passed that of Italy and became the highest among the G7 nations. Both the IMF and the Organisation for Economic Co-operation and Development (OECD) also put strong pressure on Japan to cut its fiscal deficit.

When the author and his assistant, Shigeru Fujita, became the only two economists in Japan[16] to warn publicly that fiscal consolidation would destroy the economic recovery, it was an extremely unpopular and politically untenable stance to take (the only other person who openly opposed fiscal consolidation in Japan was U.S. Treasury Secretary Larry Summers). But when our prediction came true and the economy collapsed, policy makers were able to change direction quickly because an alternative road map had already been provided by the author and Mr. Fujita. The point is that economists must continue telling the public what is needed even if there is no political appetite for it. If their predictions come true, the public will change its mind, and that is the best an economist can hope for.

Krugman also expressed his disbelief at the author's adamant opposition to additional monetary stimulus when there was no obvious harm to such policy. But the author was flabbergasted by the fact that 80 to 90 percent of the policy debate after 2009 was focused on monetary easing, when 80 to 90 percent of the problem originated from a lack of borrowers, which monetary easing is ill-equipped to handle. The author was worried that not only would precious time be lost debating ineffective policies, but the credibility of the government and the central bank could also be undermined when monetary accommodation failed to produce the expected results.

Danger Posed by the Half-Educated

Chinese philosopher and educator Ku Hung-Ming once said it is not the educated or uneducated who cause problems, but rather the presence of a large number of "half-educated" people.[17] By half-educated, he meant people who *think* they know something but, in fact, do not. Naturally, not everyone can be educated on all issues at all times. The problem arises when a policy maker turns out to be only half-educated in his or her area of responsibility.

---

[16] Koo, Richard and Fujita, Shigeru (1997), "Zaisei-saiken no Jiki wa Shijo ni Kike: Zaisei-saiken ka Keiki-kaifuku ka" ("Listen to the Bond Market for the Timing of Fiscal Reform"), *Shukan Toyo Keizai*, February 8, 1997, pp. 52–59.
[17] Ku, Hung-Ming (1915), *The Spirit of the Chinese People*, Beijing, 1915, reprinted in Taipei, 1956, p. 106.

The author was a panelist at a 2017 conference held in Europe when a central bank governor said, "If Mr. Koo's argument is correct, then Italy and France should be the champions of economic growth because they both have large public sectors." He knew about the author's recommendation for fiscal stimulus but missed the central point of the author's argument—that such a policy should be used *only* when the economy is in Case 3 or 4, that is, when the private sector is minimizing debt.

The size of the public sector or public debt *before* the economy fell into a balance sheet recession is therefore irrelevant to the discussion of post-2008 economies. The high level of government spending and debt in France and Italy was probably harmful to those economies before 2008, when they were in Cases 1 and 2. But it was a mistake for France and Italy to reduce their deficits to satisfy SGP criteria *after* 2008, when their private sectors had shifted from profit maximization to debt minimization despite near-zero interest rates. From this encounter, the author received the impression that the central bank governor was only half-educated on the subject of balance sheet recessions.

Summary of Appropriate Policy Mix in Different Stages of Economic Development

The stages of economic development, which can be divided into the pre-LTP urbanizing era, the post-LTP golden era, and the pursued era, have huge influences on the behavior of economic agents and on inflation, growth, and the effectiveness of monetary or fiscal policy. Economies in the golden era are fundamentally inflationary because wages are increasing along the upward-sloping labor supply curve of Figure 3.1, resulting in increased consumption and increased corporate borrowing for productivity- and capacity-enhancing investments. This means that economies are in Case 1 or 2 and that central banks must be vigilant against inflation to ensure price stability and maximum sustainable growth.

In the pursued era, however, economies are fundamentally noninflationary because wages are stagnant, consumers are fastidious, inexpensive imports are flooding the market, and businesses are cutting back on productivity- and capacity-enhancing investments at home. With households saving but businesses not borrowing to finance real investments, the economy is likely to be in, or close to, Case 3. If private-sector demand for borrowings falls below the level of savings even at very low interest rates, the government must mobilize fiscal policy and act as borrower of last resort to keep the economy away from a deflationary spiral.

The economy can also move from Case 1 to Case 3 or 4 very quickly after a bubble bursts. Even though the government and central bank have the tools needed to nudge the economy from Case 4 to Case 3 (or from Case 2 to Case 1) in a year or two, it may take years, if not decades, for an economy in Case 3 to return to Case 1. Only fiscal policy can support an economy in Case 3 or 4, and it must be kept in place until the private sector is ready to borrow again.

Although the public debt is already large in most advanced countries, government bond yields fall to extremely low levels when an economy is in Case 3 because the private sector is a net saver and government is the only borrower remaining. Those low yields are the market's way of telling the government that if any public works projects are needed for the nation's future, the time to implement them is now. Many public works projects also become self-financing at such low bond yields.

Indeed, the most important task for policy makers in Case 3 and 4 economies is to (1) inform the public that there is an excess savings problem in the private sector even with zero interest rates, and (2) assign their best and brightest to an independent commission to identify and implement public works projects capable of earning a social rate of return in excess of these extremely low government bond yields. Such projects will increase the national debt, but they will not increase the burden on future taxpayers because they are self-financing. This policy option is not available when the economy is in Cases 1 and 2, when interest rates are high and self-financing public works projects are more difficult to find.

This commission will have to continue identifying self-financing projects until private-sector borrowers return. Instead of the independent central bank, which played a key role in stabilizing the economy during the golden era, it is the as-yet-to-be-created independent fiscal commission that will be critical in stabilizing the economy during the pursued era.

In terms of monetary policy, the authorities should recognize that monetary policy in the pursued phase is not as effective as it was during the golden era, but the economy itself is also fundamentally non-inflationary. In this environment, central banks' all-out efforts to meet golden-era-inspired inflation targets using such tools as QE and negative interest rates have not only failed to achieve their targets, but have also increased inequality and pushed these economies into unproductive cycles of bubbles and balance sheet recessions. The QE policies that have been implemented since 2008 to attain those targets have also left the authorities with the daunting task of draining excess liquidity when the inflation returned with energy shortages and supply chain disruptions. Because trying to rekindle inflation in a fundamentally non-inflationary environment does more harm than good, central banks should distance themselves from inflation targets and other legacies of the golden era.

The increased destruction brought about by climate change is forcing the whole world to move away from its reliance on fossil fuels and embrace renewable sources of energy. But all the new investment required for this endeavor, together with higher energy prices, could create strong inflationary pressures for years. Central banks should therefore finish normalizing monetary policy as soon as practical in order to prepare for this new energy-driven era. It is even possible that the sheer volume of new investment required will push economies back into Case 1, in which case the central bank will really have to worry about demand-driven inflation.

For all advanced countries facing an absence of borrowers due to a lack of worthwhile investment opportunities at home, the government must not only implement (self-financing) fiscal stimulus to stabilize the economy, but also carry out supply-side reforms in the tax and regulatory regimes to maximize domestic investment opportunities. It must enhance labor market flexibility so that businesses can take evasive action when being pursued. It must also revamp the educational system to meet much larger human capital requirements of the pursued era compared with the golden era.

Supply-side policies are needed because for an economy to grow, someone must over-stretch, either by borrowing money or withdrawing savings. For businesses to over-stretch, profitable investment opportunities that can more than pay for themselves are needed. Investment opportunities at home must also offer an expected (country-risk-adjusted) return on capital that is higher than that available abroad. In addition, businesses must have presentable balance sheets to even contemplate over-stretching.

Most of the conditions previously noted were met during the golden era, which ended for the West in the 1980s and for Japan in the 1990s. In the pursued phase that followed, however, the return on capital was often higher in emerging economies than at home. Private-sector balance sheets were also badly damaged after the bubble burst in Japan in 1990 and in the West in 2008.

In this new and challenging environment, policy makers must recognize that tax and regulatory regimes that were not a noticeable economic drag in the golden era, when there was a surfeit of domestic investment opportunities, may weigh heavily on growth when those opportunities have been exhausted and the country must come up with new products and services to stay ahead of its pursuers. That means they should review every tax and regulation and ask whether it is serving to maximize the nation's creative and innovative potential. This includes minimizing the time people waste on crafting tax avoidance schemes that distort resource allocation in the economy.

Policy makers should also ensure that the educational system is encouraging students to think critically and independently so they can support businesses pursuing Strategy A with new ideas and products. Investment in education is also far more important in the pursued era where most good jobs are in knowledge-based areas. The fact that workers are on their own in the pursued phase also means they must have continued access to education if they want to improve their living standards. Education is also one of the few areas where policy makers can address pursued economies' inherent tendency to worsen inequality.

Conclusions

During the golden era, when private-sector investment opportunities were plentiful and interest rates were high, economists rightfully focused on strengthening monetary policy's ability to curb inflation while disparaging profligate fiscal policy. But that era ended in the 1980s for the West and in the 1990s for Japan.

The effectiveness of monetary and fiscal policy is reversed once an economy is in the pursued phase and the private sector often becomes a net saver in spite of very low interest rates. In particular, once the government becomes the last borrower standing, the effectiveness of monetary policy comes to depend on the size of government borrowing, because government is the only entity able and willing to borrow money and inject it into the real economy. Policy makers must therefore shift their focus from easing monetary policy to building an independent commission to seek out self-financing infrastructure projects so that the government can, in good conscience, continue to serve as borrower of last resort.

Policy makers should also recognize that multipliers and elasticities estimated in an earlier stage of economic development may be useless during the pursued phase. These parameters can even change—sometimes drastically—within the same phase depending on whether the economy is in Cases 1 and 2 or in Cases 3 and 4. For example, while an economy might fundamentally be in a golden era, the collapse of an asset price bubble could push it into Case 3 or 4 as private-sector borrowers disappear. That is basically what happened to the United States during the Great Depression and to Asian countries during the currency crisis of 1997.

At the global level, it must be recognized that the number of Americans who view themselves as losers from "free trade," with some help from other groups, had grown large enough in 2016 to put the openly protectionist Trump into the White House. That means the 70-year postwar era, in which the United States led the global free-trade system, and the 40-year post-1980 era, during which it continued to take in so many imports despite running large trade deficits, are becoming unsustainable. Since it was this U.S.-led free trade regime that rendered wars obsolete and made global prosperity possible, everyone—and especially the countries that benefited from the U.S.-led framework—must now think about what must be done to maintain a system that has brought so much peace and prosperity to humanity.

A careful observer will note that free trade is under threat not because of internal contradictions within the regime, but rather because of the free flows of *capital* that have distorted both exchange rates and trade flows. And free flows of capital have done this because market forces adjust exchange rates and interest rates in individual countries so as to equalize the return on capital across countries, as though they were coming together to form a single nation. The problem is that none of the countries involved has any intention of joining with others to form a single political entity.

In other words, there is a fundamental conflict between free capital flows, which try to equalize the return on capital across countries, and the efforts of individual countries to equalize, or balance, their trade and current accounts under a free-trade framework. And it was free trade that brought about the greatest peace and prosperity in human history. This means it must be defended against unfettered capital flows, which are exacerbating trade imbalances, spawning protectionist pressures, and undermining the effectiveness of monetary policy.

This means policy makers cannot be indifferent to trade imbalances and exchange rates. They should not let market-determined exchange rates, which are often determined by capital flows, diverge too far from trade-equilibrating exchange rates. And Trump has proven that this *can* be achieved if the authorities constantly harp on about the need to reduce trade imbalances, thereby dissuading portfolio investors from betting on a movement of exchange rates that would exacerbate trade imbalances. Occasional threats of official intervention in the foreign exchange market may also be helpful in this regard.

Balancing every bilateral trade account is neither possible nor desirable in a world of more than 200 countries. But allowing trade imbalances to grow without limit is also an unsustainable policy when those who consider themselves losers from free trade will soon outnumber the winners. Governments must therefore keep trade imbalances within manageable limits.

For emerging countries seeking export-led growth with Strategy B, the already substantial social backlash against free trade in the pursued countries also means the easy days are over. Emerging countries that have relied on the export-led growth model must open their own markets to imports from pursued countries faster or accept higher exchange rates if they want to maintain access to the markets of the latter.

If there is a choice between accepting a higher exchange rate or opening up the domestic market, they should opt for the latter because it is always better for themselves and the world to reduce trade imbalances by having surplus countries increase their imports instead of reducing their exports. They should not make the mistake that Japan made in the early 1990s, when it resisted market-opening pressures from abroad and ended up with a strong yen that forced many of its best manufacturers to leave the country.

Russia's invasion of Ukraine has reminded the world that the threat to world peace from autocrats is still present. When the United States confronted a similar threat during World War II and the Cold War, the country was in its golden era and Americans were confident that they were in possession of a superior system offering a brighter future. In the Soviet Union, which had outlawed the market mechanism and profit motive, no one except the government's central planners could decide on over-stretching to maintain economic growth, and the resultant accumulation of inefficiencies and unviable enterprises led to its eventual demise.

Today, it is China that is in the golden era. The United States is in the pursued era and is facing a wide range of challenges. With a polarized polity, the Americans are also far less confident of themselves, especially in relation to rapidly growing China. Some Wall Street types are even increasing investments in China as a "protest vote" to the hopelessly divided and dysfunctional Washington, D.C.

But the pursued era need not entail national decline once the source of the problem is identified and correct policies are implemented. And the United States, having enacted at least two of the three key structural policies that are required for this era, is enjoying faster economic growth than other pursued countries such as Japan and Europe. Perhaps U.S. President Joe Biden's "Build Back Better" program should be specifically directed at the unaddressed issue of education and social welfare to rectify the remaining problems. If these structural policies are combined with reoriented fiscal, monetary, and trade policies that are appropriate for the pursued era, the United States and other pursued economies should be doing much better than they are doing now. And that should give self-confidence to the peoples of these countries that is essential in their efforts to compete with China.

At the most fundamental level, everyone must realize that, apart from the post-LTP golden era of industrialization, which is characterized by a surfeit of low-hanging investment opportunities, shortages of borrowers have always been a bigger problem for growth than shortages of lenders. The poor economic performance of the advanced countries today stems from the fact that households continue to save for an uncertain future, but businesses are unable to find enough attractive domestic investment opportunities to absorb those savings.

Instead of making facile assumptions about trend growth rates and assuming that there are always willing borrowers, policy makers and economists need to forcefully confront this problem of inferior domestic returns on capital. The availability of investment opportunities and willing borrowers should never be taken for granted. This is particularly true in countries that are in balance sheet recessions or are being pursued, a group that includes nearly every advanced economy in the world today.

References and Bibliography

Afonso, Gara, Cipriani, Marco, Copeland, Adam, Kovner, Anna, La Spada, Gabriele and Martin, Antoine, "The Market Events of Mid-September 2019," *Federal Reserve Bank of New York Staff Reports* No. 918, March 2020. https://www.newyorkfed.org/medialibrary/media/research/staff_reports/sr918.pdf.

Asahi Shimbun (1988), "Endaka 'Seiho-Hannin-Setsu' ni Kyokai ga Irei no Hanron" ("Accusation That Life Insurers Are Responsible for Strong Yen Is Absurd"), in Japanese, March 30, 1988, p. 9.

Australian Bureau of Statistics. *Australian National Accounts.*

Banco de España. *Financial Accounts of the Spanish Economy.*

Banco de Portugal. *National Financial Accounts.*

_____. *Residential Property Prices: Detailed Series (Nominal).*

_____. *Residential Property Prices: Selected Series (Nominal and Real).*

Banca d'Italia. *Financial Accounts.*

Bank of England. *M4 and M4 Lending Excluding Intermediate OFCs.*

_____. *Notes and Coin and Reserves Balances.*

Bank of Greece. *Financial Accounts.*

Bank of Japan. *Assets and Liabilities of Domestically Licensed Banks (Banking Accounts).*

_____. *Flow of Funds.*

_____. *Monetary Base.*

_____. *Money Stock.*

_____. *Reserves.*

_____. *Tankan.*

Bernanke, Ben S. (1995), "The Macroeconomics of the Great Depression: A Comparative Approach," *Journal of Money, Credit, and Banking*, 27(1).

_____. (2005), "The Global Saving Glut and the U.S. Current Account Deficit," at the Sandridge Lecture, Virginia Association of Economists, Richmond, Virginia, March 10, 2005. https://www.federalreserve.gov/boarddocs/speeches/2005/200503102/.

_____. (2010), "What the Fed Did and Why: Supporting the Recovery and Sustaining Price Stability," *Washington Post*, November 4, 2010. http://www.washingtonpost.com/wp-dyn/content/article/2010/11/03/AR2010110307372.html.

_____. (2017), "Shrinking the Fed's Balance Sheet," from his blog at Brookings Institution, January 26, 2017. https://www.brookings.edu/blog/ben-bernanke/2017/01/26/shrinking-the-feds-balance-sheet/.

Board of Governors of the Federal Reserve System (1976), *Banking & Monetary Statistics, 1914–1970*. 2 vols. Washington D.C.

_____. (2009), "Prudent Commercial Real Estate Loan Workouts," *Supervision and Regulation Letters*, SR 09-7, on October 30, 2009. https://www.federalreserve.gov/boarddocs/srletters/2009/SR0907.htm.

_____. (2012), "Transcript of Chairman Bernanke's Press Conference," Washington, D.C., April 25, 2012. https://www.federalreserve.gov/mediacenter/files/FOMCpresconf20120425.pdf.

_____. (2015), "Transcript of Chair Yellen's Press Conference, December 16, 2015." https://www.federalreserve.gov/mediacenter/files/FOMCpresconf20151216.pdf.

_____. (2016), Monetary Policy Report, submitted on June 21. https://www.federalreserve.gov/monetarypolicy/files/20160621_mprfullreport.pdf.

_____. (2017), "Transcript of Chair Yellen's Press Conference, June 14, 2017," pp. 16–17. https://www.federalreserve.gov/mediacenter/files/FOMCpresconf20170614.pdf.

_____. (2021a) "The Beige Book: August 2021," released September 8, 2021. https://www.federalreserve.gov/monetarypolicy/files/BeigeBook_20210908.pdf

_____. (2021b) "The Beige Book: November 2021," released December 1, 2021.

_____. *Assets and Liabilities of Commercial Banks in the United States.*

_____. *Financial Accounts of the Unites States.*

_____. *Foreign Exchange Rates.*

_____. *Money Stock Measures.*

_____. *Selected Interest Rates.*

Brainard, Lael (2021), "Remaining Steady as the Economy Reopens," at The Economic Club of New York, New York, NY (via webcast), June 1, 2021. https://www.federalreserve.gov/newsevents/speech/brainard20210601a.htm.

Cabinet Office, Japan. *Annual Report on National Accounts.*

_____. *Quarterly Estimates of GDP.*

Central Bank of Ireland. *Quarterly Financial Accounts.*

Central Statistics Office, Ireland. *Quarterly National Accounts.*

CNBC (2016), "Fed's Fischer: Markets Missing Mark on Future Rates," January 6, 2016. http://www.cnbc.com/2016/01/06/feds-fischer-uncertainty-has-risen-in-markets-unsure-of-n-korea-news-impact.html.

Cooper, Richard N. (1997), "Should Capital-Account Convertibility Be a World Objective?" in Peter B. Karen et al. (ad.), "Should the IMF Pursue Capital-Account Convertibility?" *Essays in International Finance* 207, Princeton NJ: Princeton University International Finance Section, May 1998, pp. 11–19.

Deutsche Bundesbank. *Financial Accounts.*

Directorate General of Budget, Accounting and Statistics (DGBAS), the Executive Yuan, Taiwan. *Consumer Price Indices.*

_____. *Monthly Average Earnings.*

Draghi, Mario (2015), "Introductory Statement to the Press Conference (with Q&A)," ECB press conference in Frankfurt am Main, January 22, 2015. https://www.ecb.europa.eu/press/pressconf/2015/html/is150122.en.html.

Duncan, Richard (2022), *The Money Revolution: How to Finance the Next American Century.* John Wiley & Sons (U.K.) pp. 392.

Eggertsson, Gauti B. and Krugman, Paul (2012), "Debt, Deleveraging, and the Liquidity Trap: A Fisher-Minsky-Koo Approach," *The Quarterly Journal of Economics*, Volume 127, Issue 3, pp. 1469–1513.

European Central Bank (2021), "An Overview of the ECB's Monetary Policy Strategy," *Strategy Review*, July 2021. https://www.ecb.europa.eu/home/search/review/html/ecb.strategyreview_monpol_strategy_overview.en.html.

_____. Balance Sheet Items.

_____. *Internal Liquidity Management.*

_____. *Long-Term Interest Rate Statistics for EU Member States.*

European Central Bank and Eurostat. *Quarterly Sector Accounts.*

Eurostat. *Harmonised Index of Consumer Prices (HICP).*

_____. *Quarterly National Accounts.*

Federal Reserve Bank of Chicago. *National Financial Conditions Index (NFCI).*

Federal Reserve Bank of St. Louis. *FRED (Federal Reserve Economic Data).*

Federal Statistical Office (Destatis), Germany. Gross Domestic Product.

Financial Services Agency, Japan. *Status of Non-Performing Loans.*

Fischer, Stanley (2016), "Reflections on Macroeconomics Then and Now," remarks at Policy Challenges in an Interconnected World, 32nd Annual National Association for Business Economics Economic Policy Conference, Washington, D.C., March 7, 2016. https://www .federalreserve.gov/newsevents/speech/fischer20160307a.htm.

Flora, Peter, Kraus, Franz and Pfenning, Winfried ed. (1987), *State, Economy and Society in Western Europe 1815–1975. Volume II. The Growth of Industrial Societies and Capitalist Economies.* Campus Verlag: Frankfurt am Main.

Forbes, "The Forbes 400: The Definitive Ranking of the Wealthiest Americans in 2021," edited by Kerry A. Dolan.

French National Institute of Statistics and Economic Studies (INSEE). *Annual Wages.*

Frydl, Edward J. (1992), "Overhangs and Hangovers: Coping with the Imbalances of the 1980s," *Federal Reserve Bank of New York Seventy-Seventh Annual Report for the Year Ended December 31, 1991.*

Greenwood, John (2016), "Successful Central Banks Focus on Greater Purchasing," *Financial Times*, May 31, 2016. https://next.ft.com/content/f7a98fb2-241f-11e6-9d4d-c11776a5124.

G20 Toronto communique (2010). https://www.treasury.gov/resource-center/international/Documents/The%20G-20%20Toronto%20Summit%20Declaration.pdf.

Guha, Krishna (2009), "Bernanke Warns on Deficits," *Financial Times* Asian edition, June 4, 2009.

Harvard Business School "Trade Union Membership: Percentage of Working Force as Member of a Trade Union 1880–2010." https://www.hbs.edu/businesshistory/courses/resources/historical-data-visualization/Pages/details.aspx?data_id=37.

Hellenic Statistical Authority, Greece. *Gross Domestic Product.*

Institute of International Finance (2017), Capital Market Monitor, March 2017, Chart 6.

International Monetary Fund (2010), "Press Release: IMF Executive Board Approves €30 Billion Stand-By Arrangement for Greece," on May 2010. https://www.imf.org/en/News/Articles/ 2015/09/14/01/49/pr10187.

_____ (2015), "IMF Survey: Top Researchers Debate Unconventional Monetary Policies," by Maurice Obstfeld and Gustavo Adler, *IMF News* on November 20, 2015. http://www.imf.org/en/ news/articles/2015/09/28/04/53/sores111915a.

_____ (2021), *World Economic Outlook October 2021*. https:// www.imf.org/en/Publications/WEO/Issues/2021/10/12/world-economic-outlook-october-2021.

_____. *International Financial Statistics.*

Italian National Institute of Statistics. *Quarterly National Accounts.*

Iwata, Kikuo (2001), *Defure no Keizaigaku (The Economics of Deflation)*, Tokyo: Toyo Keizai.

Jakab, Zoltan and Kumhof, Michael (2015), "Banks Are Not Intermediaries of Loanable Funds—And Why This Matters," *Bank of England Working Paper*, No. 529. https://www.bankofengland. co.uk/-/media/boe/files/working-paper/2015/banks-are-not-intermediaries-of-loanable-funds-and-why-this-matters.pdf.

Japan Bond Trading Company. *Long-Term (10y) JGB Yield.*

Japan Real Estate Institute. *Urban Land Price Index.*

Japanese Bankers Association. *Financial Statements of All Banks.*

Koo, Richard C. (1994), *Good Strong Yen and Bad Strong Yen (Yoi Endaka, Warui Endaka)*, Tokyo: Toyo Keizai.

_____ (2001), "The Japanese Economy in Balance Sheet Recession." *Business Economics,* National Association of Business Economists, Washington, D.C., April 2001.

_____ (2003), *Balance Sheet Recession: Japan's Struggle with Uncharted Economics and its Global Implications*, Singapore: John Wiley & Sons (Asia).

_____ (2008), *The Holy Grail of Macroeconomics: Lessons from Japan's Great Recession*, Singapore: John Wiley & Sons (Asia).

_____ (2015a), *The Escape from Balance Sheet Recession and the QE Trap*, Singapore: John Wiley & Sons.

_____ (2015b), "China and the US-led International Order" in *How Do Asians See Their Future?* edited by François Godement,

European Council on Foreign Relations. http://www.ecfr.eu/page/-/ECFR130_CHINA_ASIA_REPORT_pdf.pdf.

_____ and Fujita, Shigeru (1997), "Zaisei-saiken no Jiki wa Shijo ni Kike: Zaisei-saiken ka Keiki-kaifuku ka" ("Listen to the Bond Market for the Timing of Fiscal Reform')," *Shukan Toyo Keizai*, February 8, 1997. pp. 52–59.

_____ and Krugman, Paul (1999), "Gekitotsu Taidan: Nihon Keizai Endaka wa Akuka" ("Big Debate on Japan's Economy: Is Strong Yen a Bad Thing?"), *Bungeishunju*, November 1999, edited by Yasuhara Ishizawa, pp. 130–143.

_____ (2018), *The Other Half of Macroeconomics and the Fate of Globalization*, John Wiley & Sons (U.K.).

Krugman, Paul (2011), "Credibility and Monetary Policy in a Liquidity Trap (Wonkish)," *New York Times*, March 18, 2011.

Ku, Hung-Ming (1915), *The Spirit of the Chinese People*, Beijing, reprinted in Taipei in 1956.

Kuroda, Haruhiko (2013), "Quantitative and Qualitative Monetary Easing," speech at a meeting held by Yomiuri International Economic Society in Tokyo, April 12, 2013. http://www.boj.or.jp/en/announcements/press/koen_2013/ko130412a.htm/.

Lagarde, Christine (2021), "Interview with Financial Times," Interview with Christine Lagarde, President of the ECB, conducted by Martin Arnold on 11 July 2021, July 13, 2021. https://www.ecb.europa.eu/press/inter/date/2021/html/ecb.in210713~ff13aa537f.en.html.

Lawrence H. Summers's webpage on secular stagnation. http://larrysummers.com/category/secular-stagnation/.

Maddison, Angus (2006), *The World Economy: A Millennial Perspective (Vol. 1), Historical Statistics (Vol. 2)*. Paris: OECD.

_____. "Historical Statistics of the World Economy: 1-2008 AD." http://www.ggdc.net/maddison/Historical_Statistics/vertical-file_02-2010.xls.

Markey-Towler, Brendan (2017a), *Foundations for Economic Analysis: The Architecture of Socioeconomic Complexity*, PhD thesis, School of Economics, University of Queensland.

_____ (2017b), "Poetry and Economics: Maintaining our link to humanity," from Brendan Markey-Towler's blog, July 24, 2017. https://medium.com/@brendanmarkeytowler/poetry-and-economics-maintaining-our-link-to-humanity-532785047f0e.

McLeay, Michael, Radia, Amar and Thomas, Ryland (2014), "Money Creation in the Modern Economy," *Bank of England Quarterly Bulletin* 2014 Q1, pp. 14–27. https://www.bankofengland.co.uk/-/media/boe/files/quarterly-bulletin/2014/money-creation-in-the-modern-economy.pdf.

Ministry of Commerce, People's Republic of China (2018), "Regular Press Conference of the Chinese Ministry of Commerce," July 5, 2018. http://english.mofcom.gov.cn/article/newsrelease/press/201807/20180702766291.shtml.

Ministry of Employment and Labor, Korea. *Strikes Statistics.*

Ministry of Finance, Japan. *Budget Statistics.*

_____. *Interest Rate.*

Ministry of Finance, Republic of China, Taiwan. *Finance Statistics,* in traditional Chinese.

Ministry of Health, Labour and Welfare, Japan. *Monthly Labour Survey.*

_____. *Survey on Labour Disputes.*

National Statistics Institute, Spain. *Quarterly Spanish National Accounts.*

Nikkei. *Tai Kokyaku Denshin Baibai Soba (Telegraphic Transfer Buying and Selling rate).*

Nikkei Business (2015), "Tokushu: Nisen Mannin-no Hinkon (20 Million Japanese in Poverty)," in Japanese, Tokyo: Nikkei BP, March 23, 2016, pp. 24–43.

Oakley, David (2009), "A Bold Bid to Revive Lending," *Financial Times*, March 7, 2009. https://next.ft.com/content/9b3fd930-0a90-11de-95ed-0000779fd2ac.

Office for National Statistics, U.K. (2021), "UK Balance of Payments, The Pink Book: 2021," October 29, 2021. https://www.ons.gov.uk/economy/nationalaccounts/balanceofpayments/bulletins/unitedkingdombalanceofpaymentsthepinkbook/2021#trade.

_____. *Average Weekly Earnings Time Series.*

_____. *Consumer Price Inflation.*

_____. *Retail Prices Index: Long Run Series.*

_____. *UK Economic Accounts.*

Organisation for Economic Co-operation and Development (OECD) (2017), *PISA 2015 Results (Volume III): Students' Well-Being*, Paris: OECD Publishing.

_____ (2021), *Unit Labor Costs and Labor Productivity.*

Overholt, William (2020), "Myths and Realities in Sino-American Relations," lecture given for Harvard's Fairbank Center for Chinese Studies on November 12, 2020.

Piketty, Thomas (2014), *Capital in the Twenty-First Century*, translated by Arthur Goldhammer, Cambridge, MA: Belknap Press of Harvard University Press.

Real Capital Analytics. *RCA CPPI (Commercial Property Price Indices)*.

Robinson, Joan (1972), "The Second Crisis of Economic Theory," *American Economic Review* 62(1/2), pp. 1–10.

Rogoff, Kenneth S. (2016), *The Curse of Cash*, Princeton, NJ: Princeton University Press.

Sawa, Takamitsu (2016), *Keizaigaku no Susume: Jimbun-chi to Hihan-seishin no Fukken (Introduction to True Economics: Re-integration of Humanities and Critical Thinking)*, Iwanami Shinsho, Tokyo.

Soros, George (2009), "Soros: General Theory of Reflexivity," *Financial Times*, October 27, 2009, p. 11. https://www.ft.com/content/0ca06172-bfe9-11de-aed2-00144feab49a.

Standard and Poor's (S&P) Dow Jones Indices. *S&P CoreLogic Case-Shiller Home Price Indices*.

_____. *S&P Eurozone Investment Grade Corporate Bond Index*.

_____. *S&P Japan Investment Grade Corporate Bond Index*.

_____. *S&P 500® Investment Grade Corporate Bond Index*.

Statistics Bureau, Ministry of Internal Affairs and Communications, Japan. *Consumer Price Index*.

_____. *Report on Internal Migration in Japan*.

Statistics Canada. *Financial Flow Accounts*.

_____. *Gross Domestic Product, Expenditure-Based*.

Statistics Korea. *Flow of Funds*.

_____. *Internal Migration Statistics*.

_____. *Korea Statistical Year Book*.

_____. *National Accounts*.

Statistics Portugal. *Portuguese National Accounts*.

Stevens, Glenn (2003), "Inflation Targeting: A Decade of Australian Experience," address to South Australian Centre for Economic Studies April 2003 Economic Briefing, April 10, 2003. http://www.rba.gov.au/speeches/2003/sp-dg-100403.html.

Summers, Lawrence H. (2009), "Rescuing and Rebuilding the U.S. Economy: A Progress Report," remarks at the Peterson Institute for International Economics on July 17, 2009. https://piie.com/commentary/speeches-papers/rescuing-and-rebuilding-us-economy-progress-report.

Swiss Federal Statistical Office. *Consumer Prices Index.*

_____. *Swiss Wage Index.*

Swiss National Bank. *Minimum Reserves for Selected Bank Categories.*

Temin, Peter (2017), *The Vanishing Middle Class: Prejudice and Power in a Dual Society*, Cambridge, MA: MIT Press.

The Economist. The Big Mac Index.

Toyotimes "JAMA Chairman Akio Toyoda Talks Earnestly about Carbon Neutrality in Japan," Toyota Motor Corporation's website, January 8, 2021. https://toyotatimes.jp/en/toyota_news/111.html.

Uchihashi, Katsuto (2009), "Shinpan Akumu-no Saikuru: Neoriberarizumu Junkan" ("Cycle of Nightmares: The Recurrence of Neoliberalism"), updated version, in Japanese, *Bunshun Bunko*, Japan, pp. 88–89.

Ukueberuwa, Mene (2020), "Boomer Socialism Led to Bernie Sanders," *Wall Street Journal*, January 17, 2020. https://www.wsj.com/articles/boomer-socialism-led-to-bernie-sanders-11579304307.

United Nations, Department of Economic and Social Affairs, Population Division (2018), *World Urbanization Prospects: The 2018 Revision.*

_____ (2019), *World Population Prospects 2019, Online Edition.*

U.S. Bureau of Economic Analysis, "U.S. International Transactions, Third Quarter 2021," December 21, 2021. https://www.bea.gov/sites/default/files/2021-12/trans321.pdf.

U.S. Bureau of Labor Statistics, "Union Members—2020," *U.S. Bureau of Labor Statistics Economic News Release*, January 22, 2021. https://www.bls.gov/news.release/archives/union2_01222021.htm.

U.S. Congressional Budget Office, *Historical Budget Data.*

U.S. Department of Commerce, Bureau of Economic Analysis (2021), "U.S. International Transactions, Third Quarter 2021," December 21, 2021. https://www.bea.gov/sites/default/files/2021-12/trans321.pdf

_____. *Gross Domestic Product (GDP).*

_____. *Price Indexes for Personal Consumption Expenditures by Major Type of Product.*

_____. *U.S. International Transactions.*

U.S. Department of Commerce, Census Bureau (2012), *2010 Census.*
_____. *Current Population Survey, 1948 to 2021 Annual Social and Economic Supplements (CPS ASEC).*
_____. *U.S. Trade in Goods by Country.*

Volcker, Paul A. (2001), "Jinsoku na Furyo-saiken Shori ga Hitsuyo daga Shori no Seigensokudo wa Daiji" ("Prompt Disposal of NPLs Is Needed, But So Is Setting a Speed Limit"), *Shukan Toyo Keizai*, June 23, 2001, p. 58.

Wakakura, Masato (2006), "Kokusai Hikaku: Nihon-no Iryo-hi ha Yasusugiru" ("International Comparison: Japan's Medical Costs Are Too Inexpensive")," Voice, June 2006, Tokyo, PHP Institute, p. 159.

Wakatabe, Masazumi (2016), "Herikoputa Mane to wa Nanika (3)" ("What Is Helicopter Money?"), *Nikkei*, June 20, 2016.

Werner, Richard A. (2016), "A Lost Century in Economics: Three Theories of Banking and the Conclusive Evidence," *International Review of Financial Analysis*, 46: pp. 361–379.

Williams, John C. (2016), "The Right Profile: Economic Drivers and the Outlook," a presentation to Town Hall Los Angeles, February 18, 2016. http://www.frbsf.org/our-district/files/Williams-Speech-The-Right-Profile_Economic-Drivers-and-the-Outlook.pdf.

Wolf, Martin (2015), "A Handy Tool—But Not the Only One in the Box," *Financial Times*, January 4, 2015. https://www.ft.com/content/0d3f41dc-86bf-11e4-8a51-00144feabdc0.

Afterword

I take economics, the science of everyday life, very seriously because I believe many human tragedies could have been averted if economists had correctly understood what was happening around them and recommended appropriate policies. Indeed, people's well-being often depends on how economic policy makers at the time perceive the world around them.

If economists are to an economy what medical doctors are to the human body, they bear a huge responsibility. But unlike medical science, which has made huge strides over the years, economics, a very young science, continues to grapple with silly notions and fads that are not only outdated and useless, but often detrimental to understanding and managing the economy.

Whenever I confronted such notions that I felt were detrimental in understanding the economy, I felt it was my duty as an economist to write papers and books to share my concerns with the public. That was made possible largely because I had the good fortune to work for Nomura Research Institute (NRI),[1] a think-tank that started out as the research department of Nomura Securities, the largest investment bank in Japan. It is a unique institution where researchers are fully exposed to the discipline of the market because they must present their views to investors and fund managers around the world, just like economists and analysts at Wall Street investment banks. But at the same time, they are expected to think independently of any positions that Nomura Securities may have taken. By maintaining this "correct" distance from the market, NRI researchers are often able to develop a broad-based view of markets, industries, and the economy.

Indeed, I was surprised to find that the nature of my work did not change at all when I moved from the research department of the

---

[1] As a legal entity, Nomura Research Institute has been independent of Nomura Securities since 2001.

Federal Reserve Bank of New York to the NRI because the former job also faced market discipline because the NY Fed was in the market, but also required thinking about broader and longer term issues. There was one difference, however. Whereas staff at the central bank are supposed to avoid contact with the media, those at NRI are all expected to think independently, speak out publicly, and win the public's confidence.

This unique role kept me from going off on tangents because investors managing billions of dollars do not want to waste time. But the role also allowed me to think long and hard about where the world is going instead of just reacting to day-to-day fluctuations in the market. Although I was in the market for perhaps 60 percent of the time, I was allowed to think outside the market box for the remaining 40 percent.

The COVID-19 pandemic, which forced the cancellation of all business trips, changed the ratio to something closer to 50–50. And the result was this book.

Writing a book takes an enormous amount of time, and that is time I could not spend with my family. So I am eternally grateful to my wife, Chyen-Mei, who allows me to spend so much time writing books like this one. I am also indebted to my daughter, Jacqueline, and my son, Richard, both in the United States, who kept up the family conversation via LINE so my wife would not feel too lonely.

This book would have been impossible without the help of my two able assistants. Mr. Masaya Sasaki, who prepared all the charts and checked the numbers, has long been the resident expert on flow-of-funds data, among many other things. Ms. Yuko Terado, who often works harder than I do, managed my schedule to ensure my health was not compromised despite demanding professional circumstances, both at home and abroad. I can never thank them enough for their hard work and dedication.

I am also extremely grateful to Mr. Chris Green, who edited the manuscript. This is our fourth book together, and I am fortunate to have an editor who understands my thinking. I would also like to thank Mr. Edward Fullbrook of the World Economic Association, who offered his support and encouraged me to complete this book. The assistance, encouragement, and constructive criticism I received from Nomura staff and clients over the last 38 years have also been invaluable in keeping me focused on the issues that matter, and I am forever grateful for their continuing support.

Richard C. Koo
March 2022, Tokyo

Index